Zippy Ziggy

1

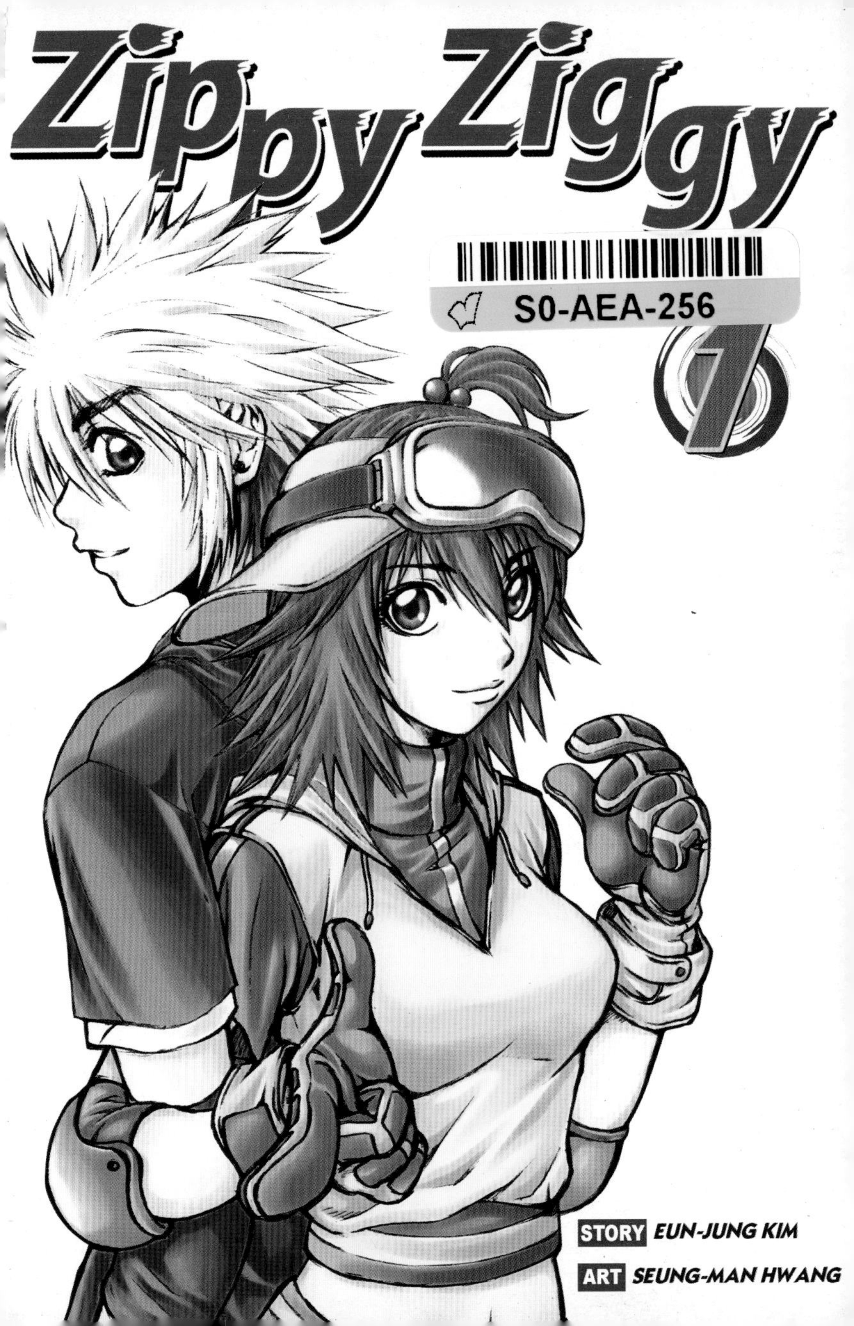

STORY *EUN-JUNG KIM*

ART *SEUNG-MAN HWANG*

Zippy Ziggy

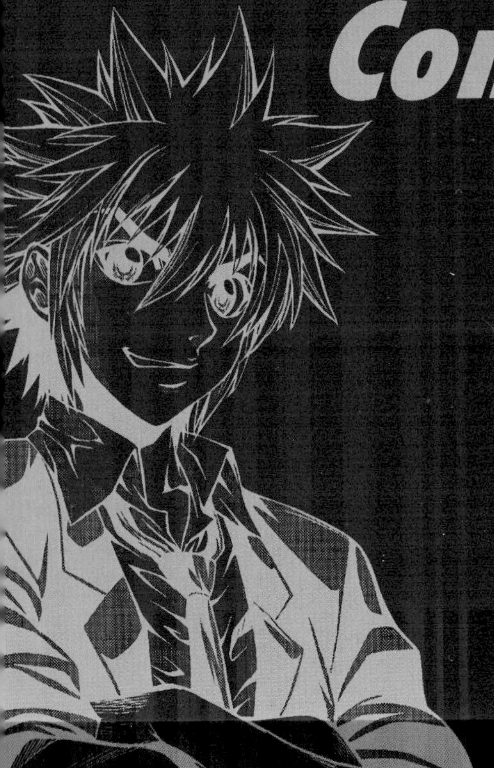

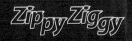

Contents

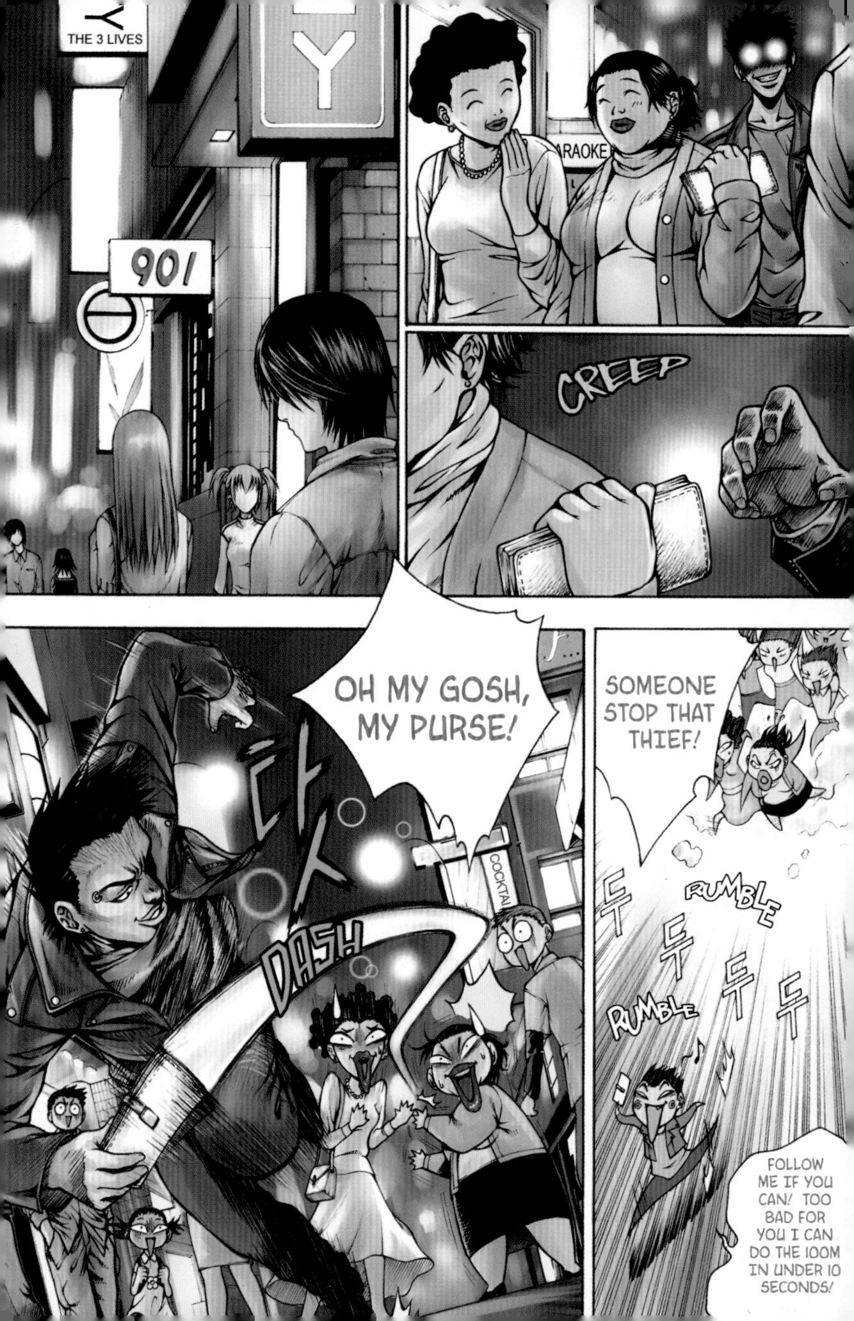
901
ARAOKE
CREEP
OH MY GOSH, MY PURSE!
DASH
COCKTAI
SOMEONE STOP THAT THIEF!
RUMBLE
RUMBLE
FOLLOW ME IF YOU CAN! TOO BAD FOR YOU I CAN DO THE 100M IN UNDER 10 SECONDS!

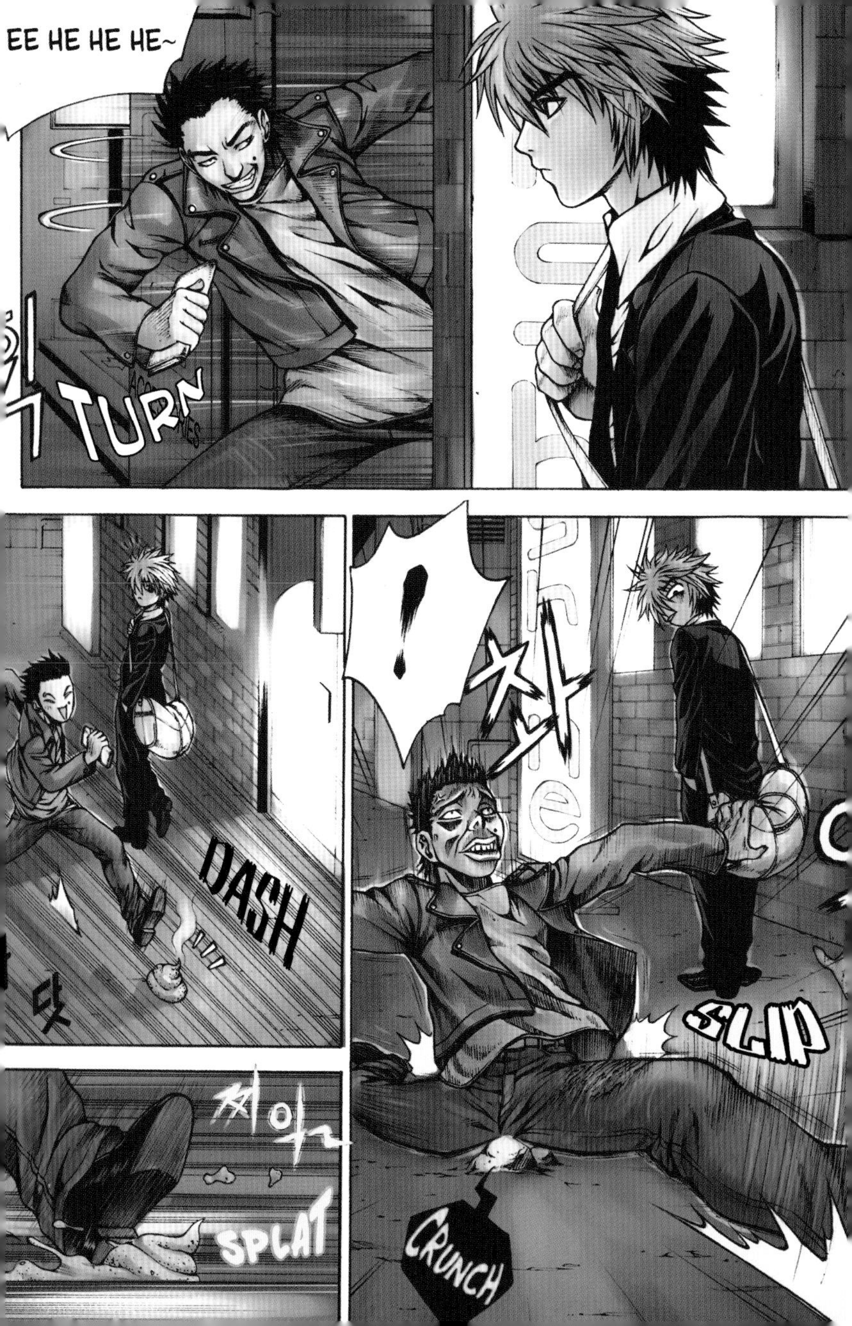
EE HE HE HE~
TURN
DASH
SPLAT
!
SLIP
CRUNCH

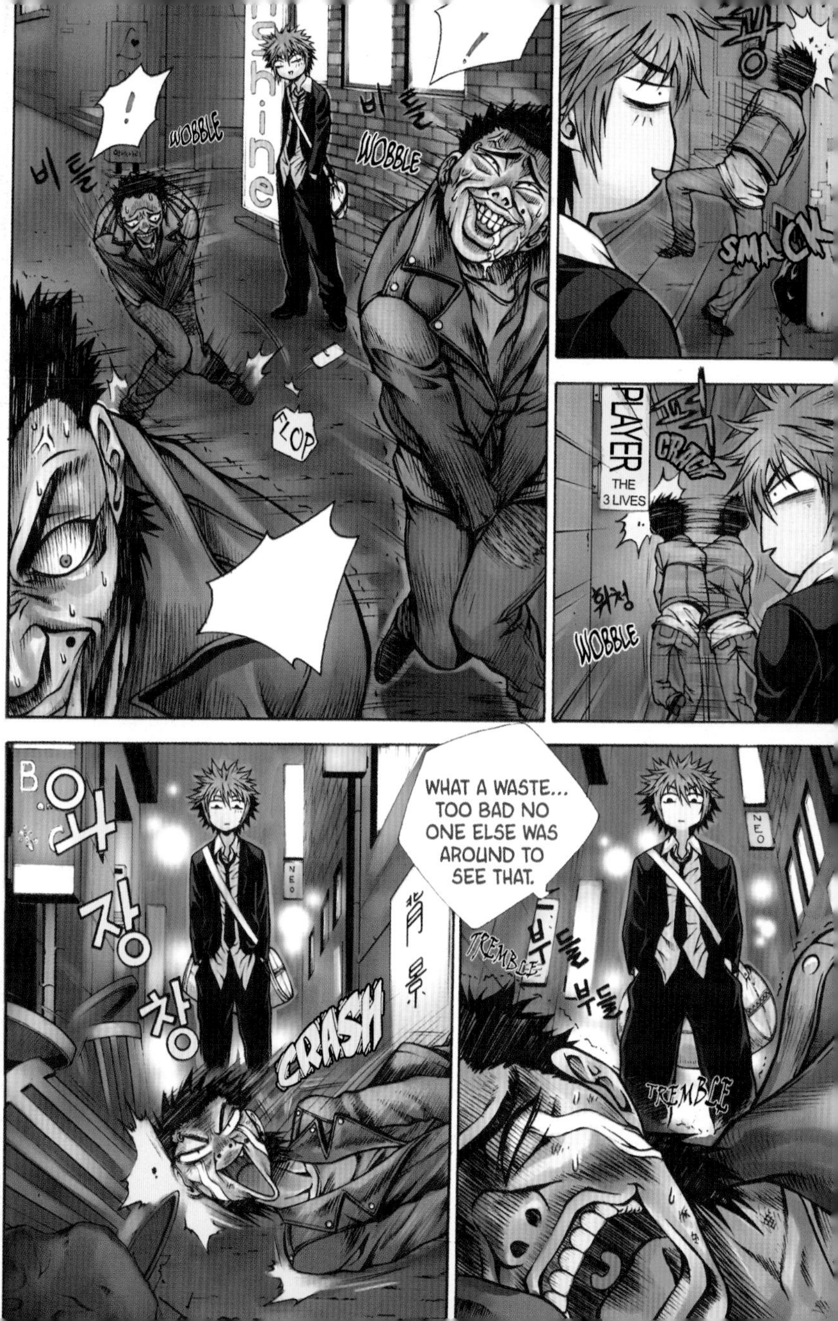
!
비틀
WOBBLE
!
비틀
WOBBLE
FLOP
꽝
SMACK
PLAYER
THE
3 LIVES
CRACK
휘청
WOBBLE
와장창
CRASH
NEO
WHAT A WASTE... TOO BAD NO ONE ELSE WAS AROUND TO SEE THAT.
NEO
TREMBLE
부들부들
TREMBLE

Chapter 1 : The Way the Young Man Lives

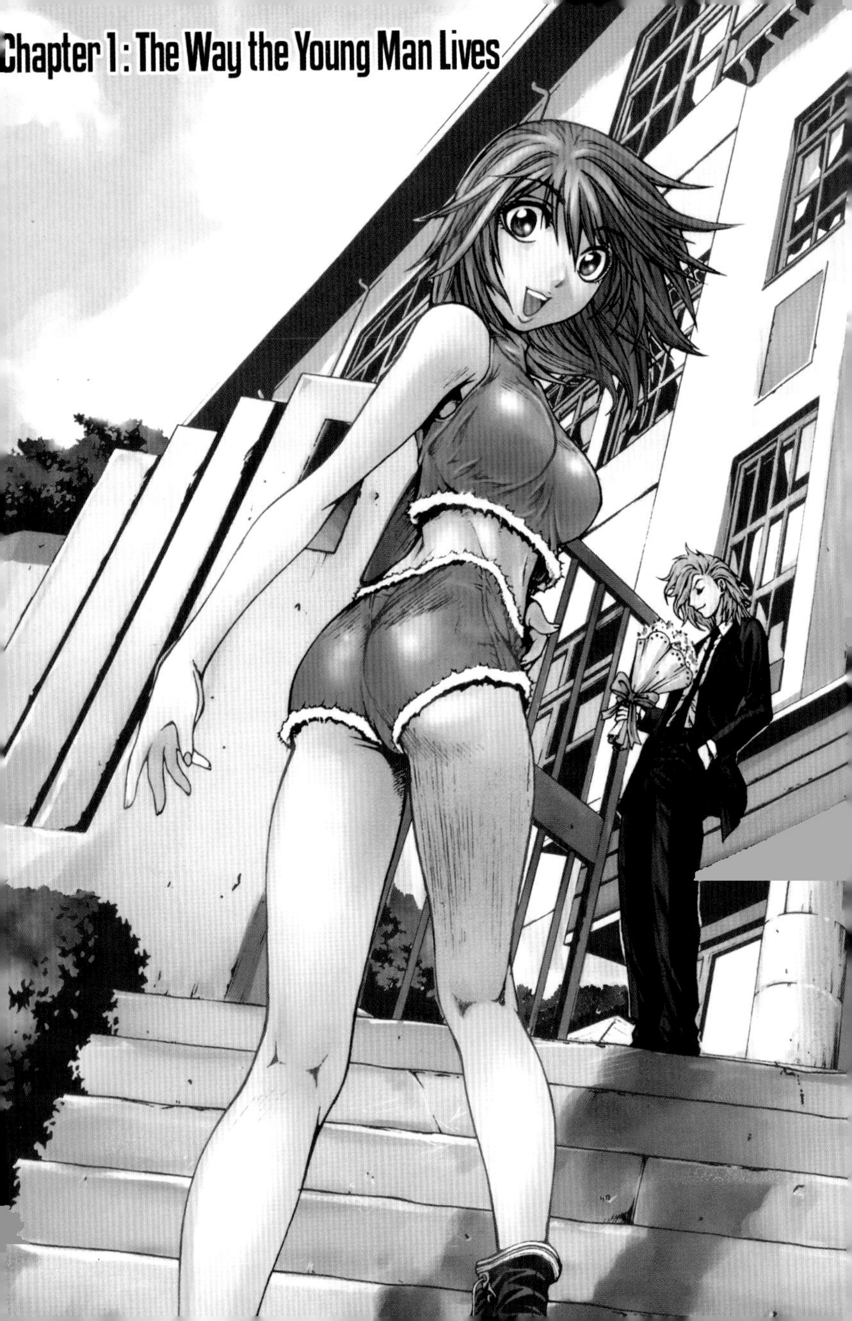

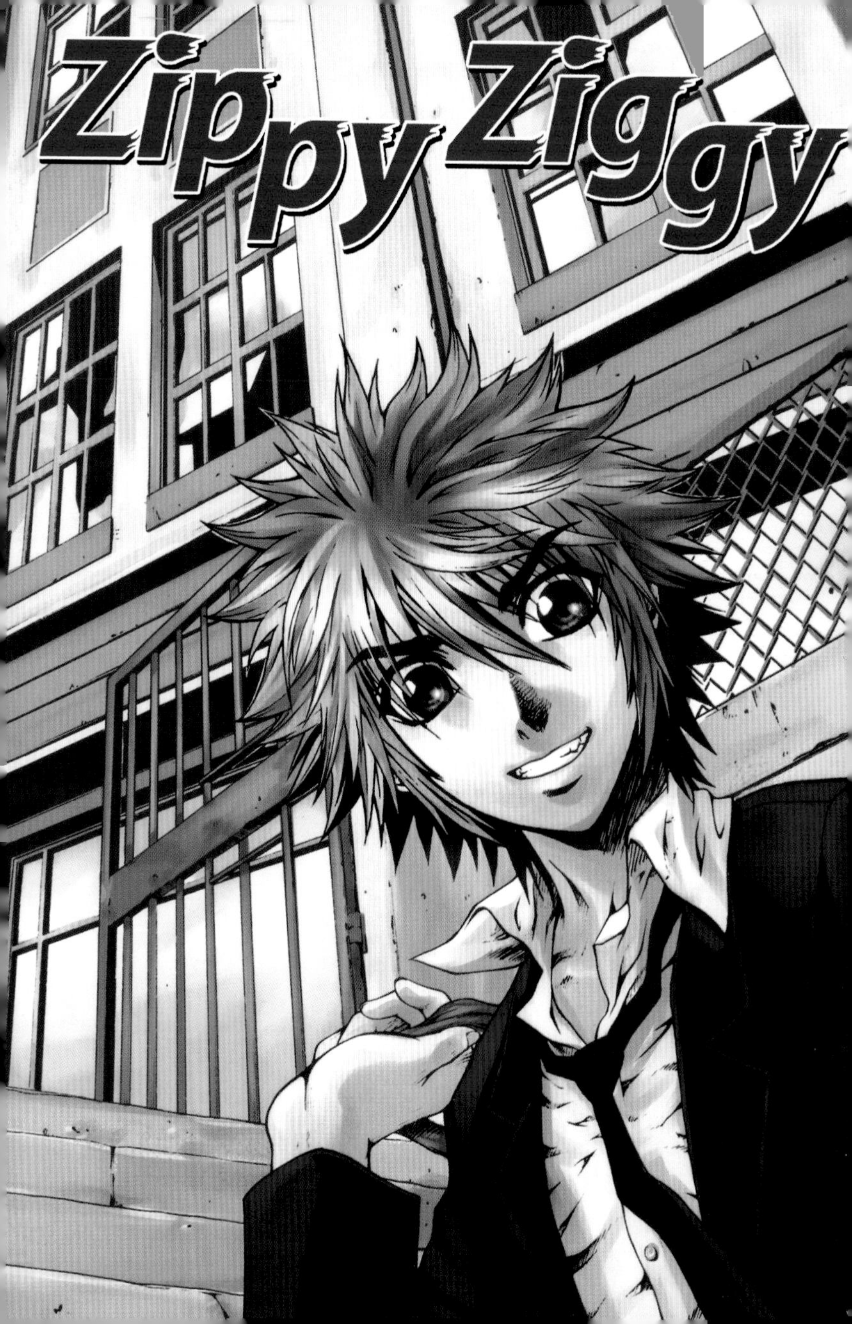
Zippy Ziggy

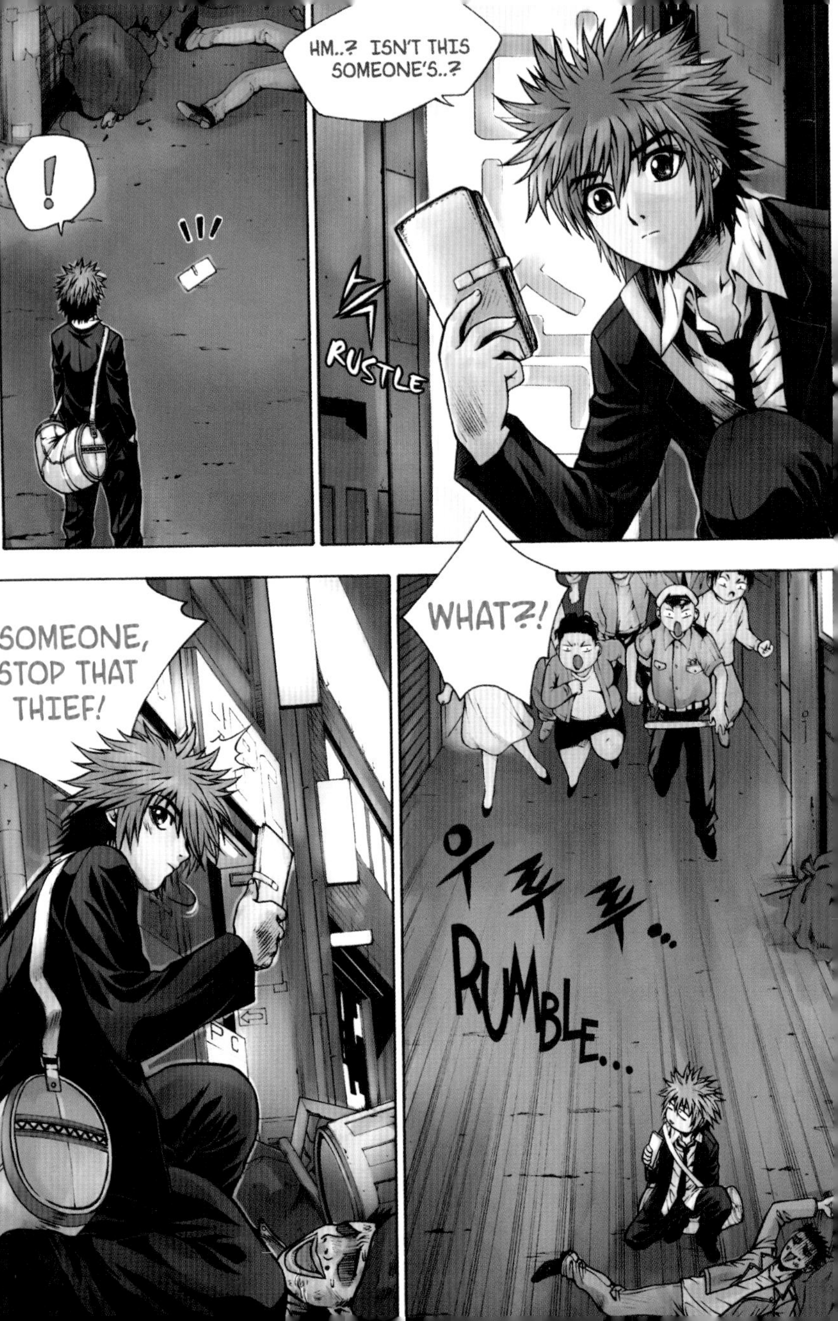
!
HM..? ISN'T THIS SOMEONE'S..?
RUSTLE
SOMEONE, STOP THAT THIEF!
WHAT?!
우루루...
RUMBLE...

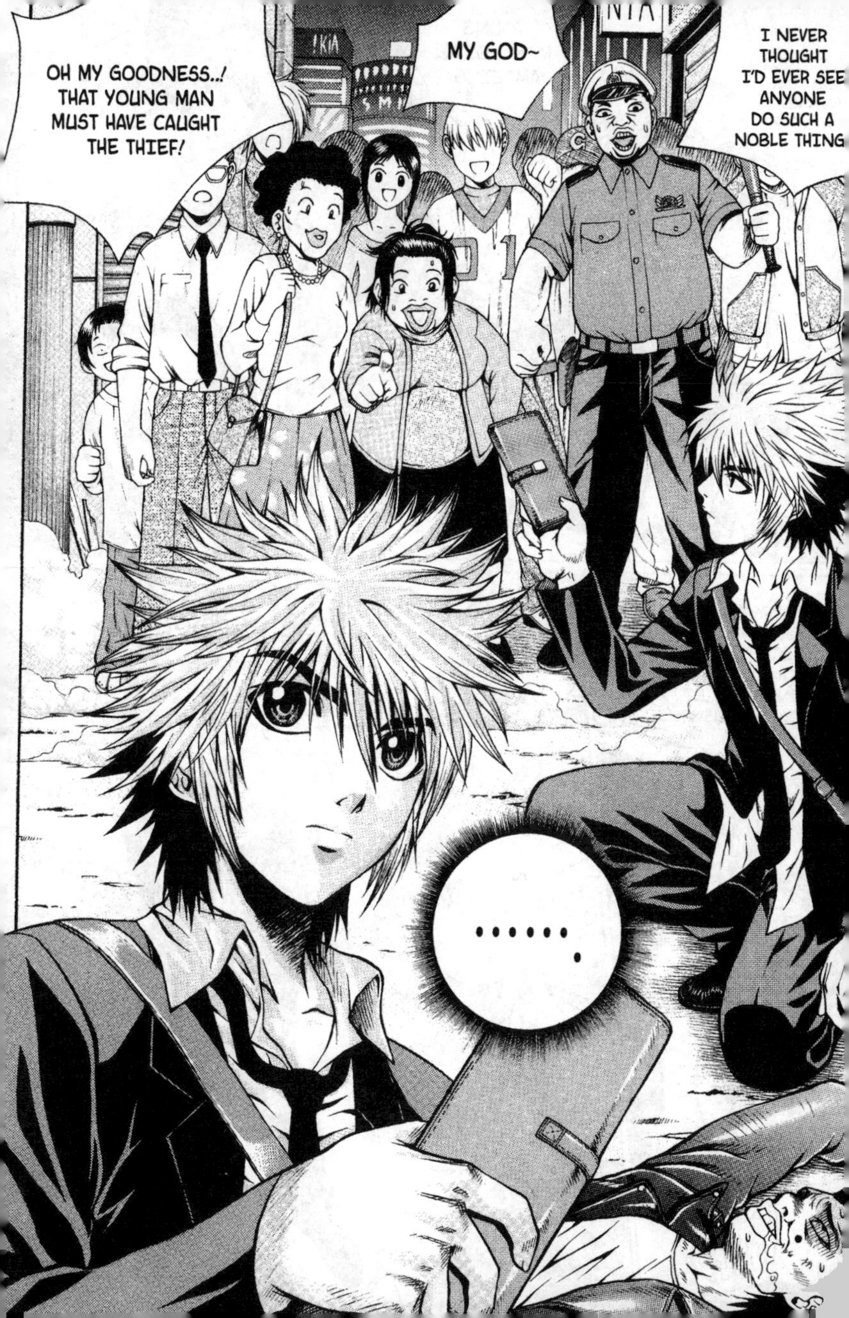
OH MY GOODNESS..! THAT YOUNG MAN MUST HAVE CAUGHT THE THIEF!
MY GOD~
I NEVER THOUGHT I'D EVER SEE ANYONE DO SUCH A NOBLE THING
......

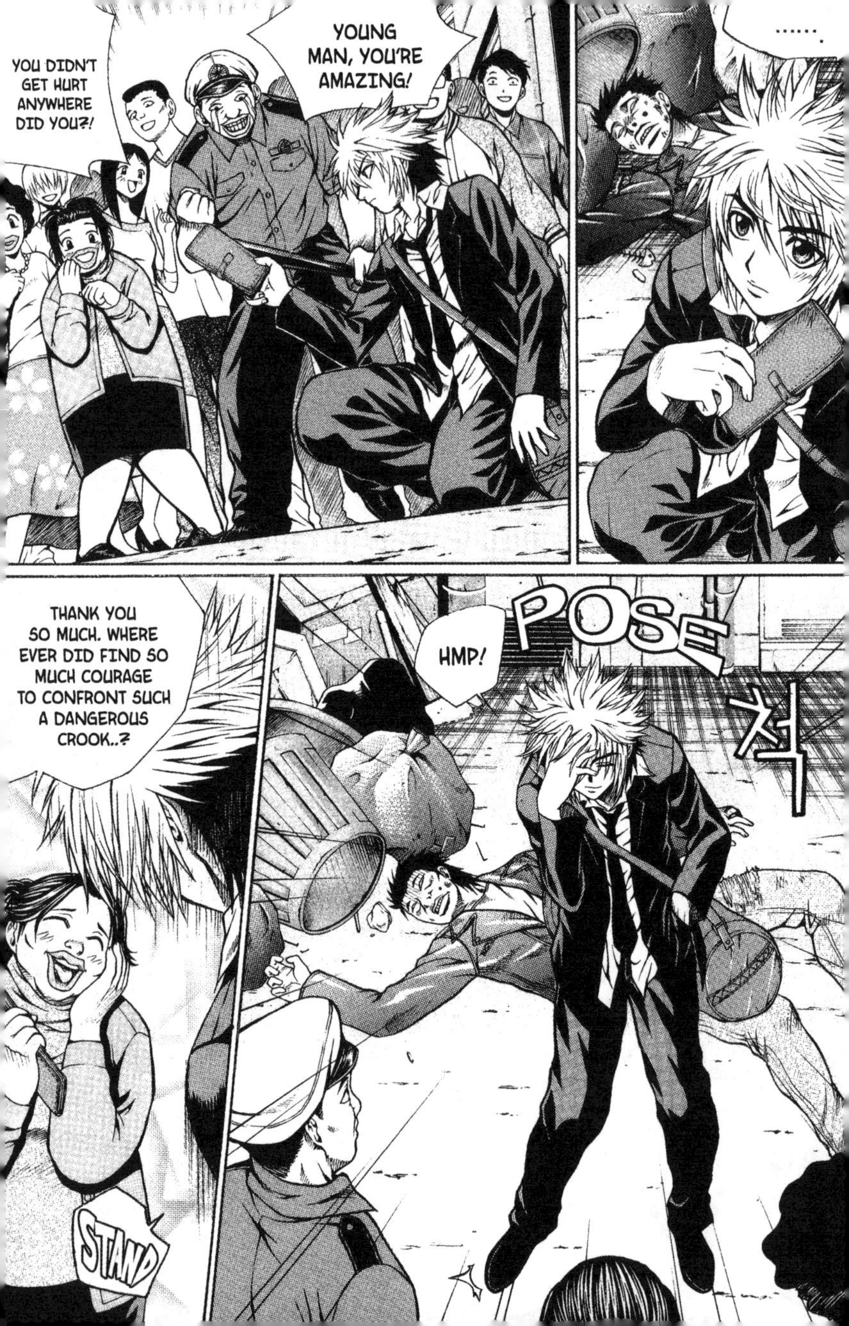
YOU DIDN'T GET HURT ANYWHERE DID YOU?!
YOUNG MAN, YOU'RE AMAZING!
....
THANK YOU SO MUCH. WHERE EVER DID FIND SO MUCH COURAGE TO CONFRONT SUCH A DANGEROUS CROOK..?
STAND
HMP!
POSE
척

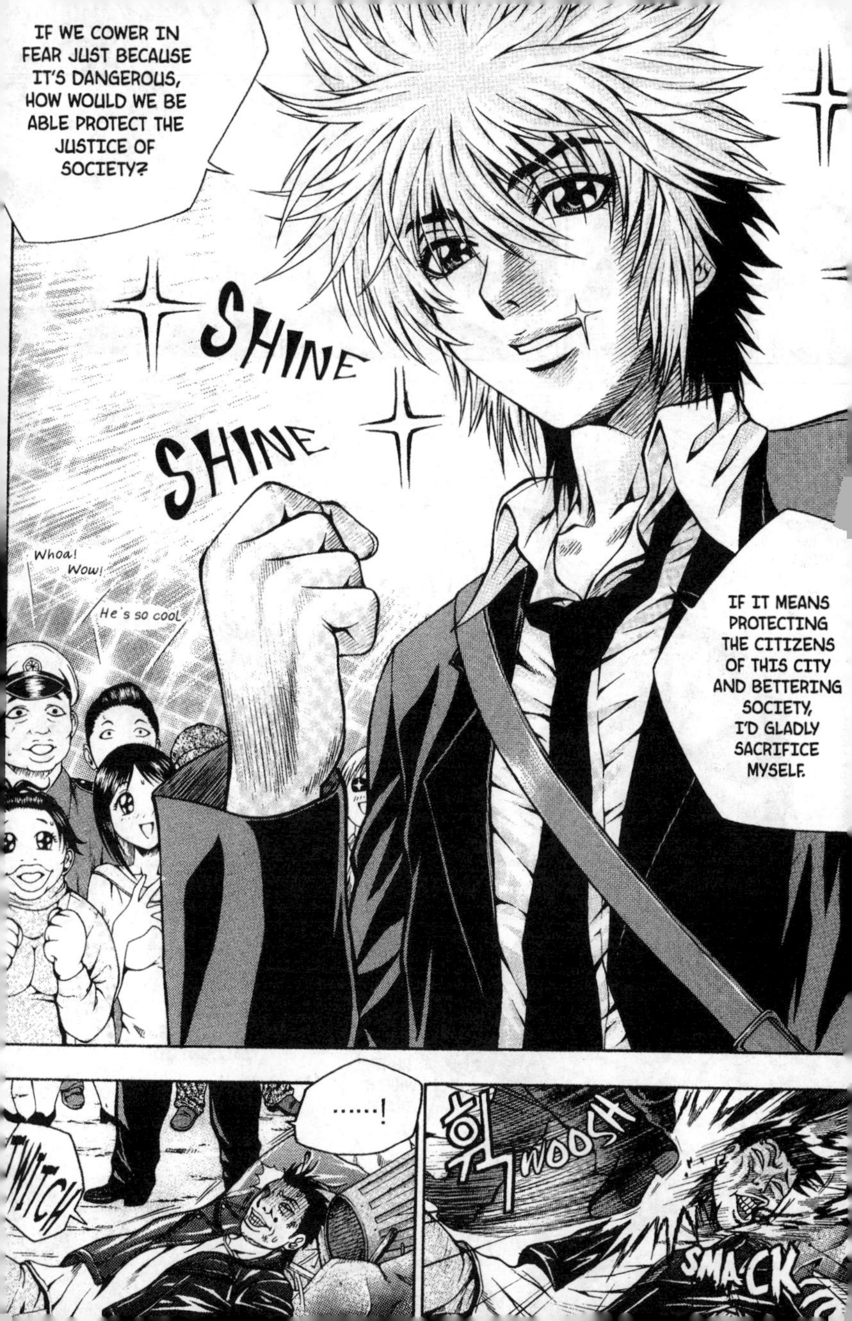
IF WE COWER IN FEAR JUST BECAUSE IT'S DANGEROUS, HOW WOULD WE BE ABLE PROTECT THE JUSTICE OF SOCIETY?
SHINE
SHINE
Whoa!
Wow!
He's so cool
IF IT MEANS PROTECTING THE CITIZENS OF THIS CITY AND BETTERING SOCIETY, I'D GLADLY SACRIFICE MYSELF.
TWITCH
......!
휙
WOOSH
SMACK

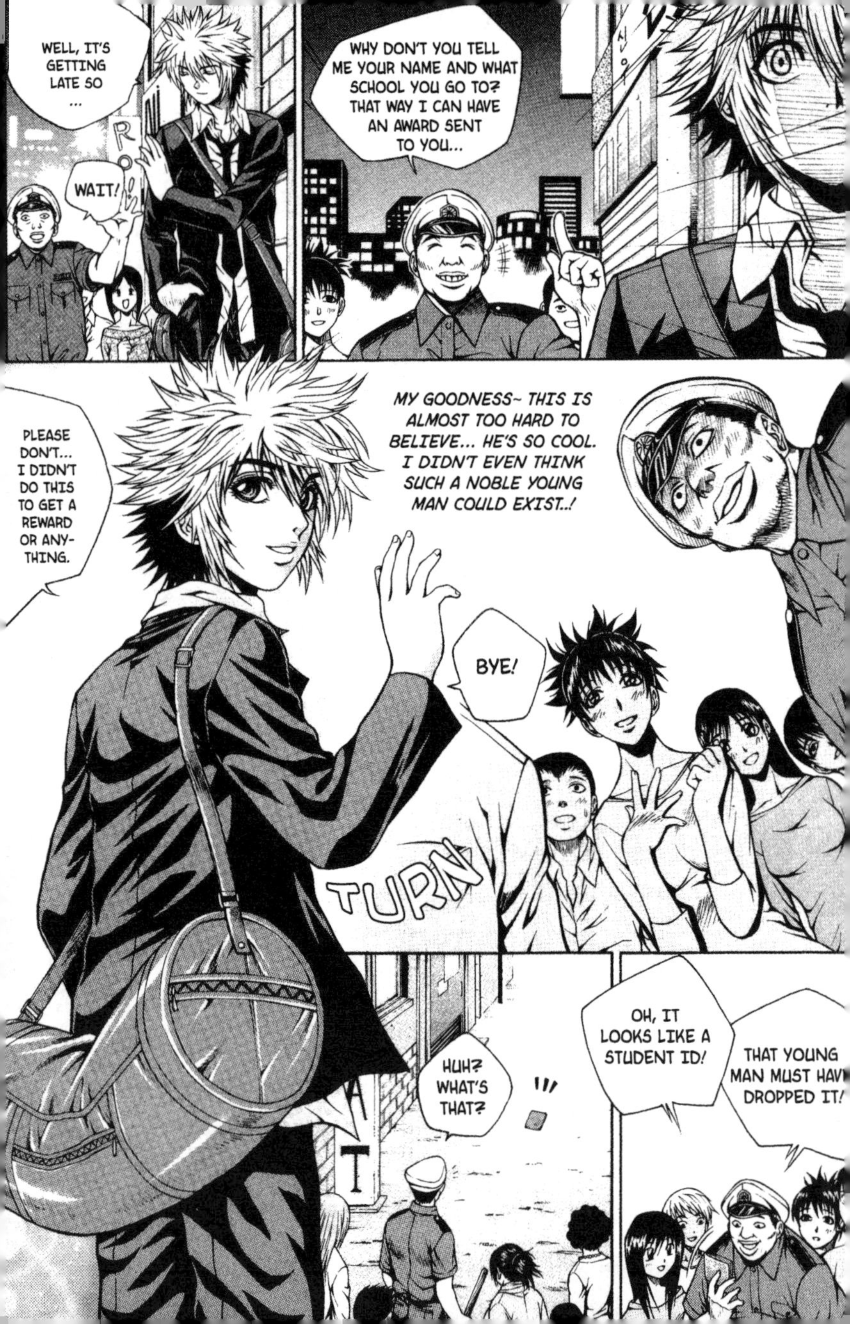
WELL, IT'S GETTING LATE SO ...
WAIT!
WHY DON'T YOU TELL ME YOUR NAME AND WHAT SCHOOL YOU GO TO? THAT WAY I CAN HAVE AN AWARD SENT TO YOU...
PLEASE DON'T... I DIDN'T DO THIS TO GET A REWARD OR ANY-THING.
MY GOODNESS~ THIS IS ALMOST TOO HARD TO BELIEVE... HE'S SO COOL. I DIDN'T EVEN THINK SUCH A NOBLE YOUNG MAN COULD EXIST..!
BYE!
TURN
HUH? WHAT'S THAT?
OH, IT LOOKS LIKE A STUDENT ID!
THAT YOUNG MAN MUST HAV DROPPED IT!

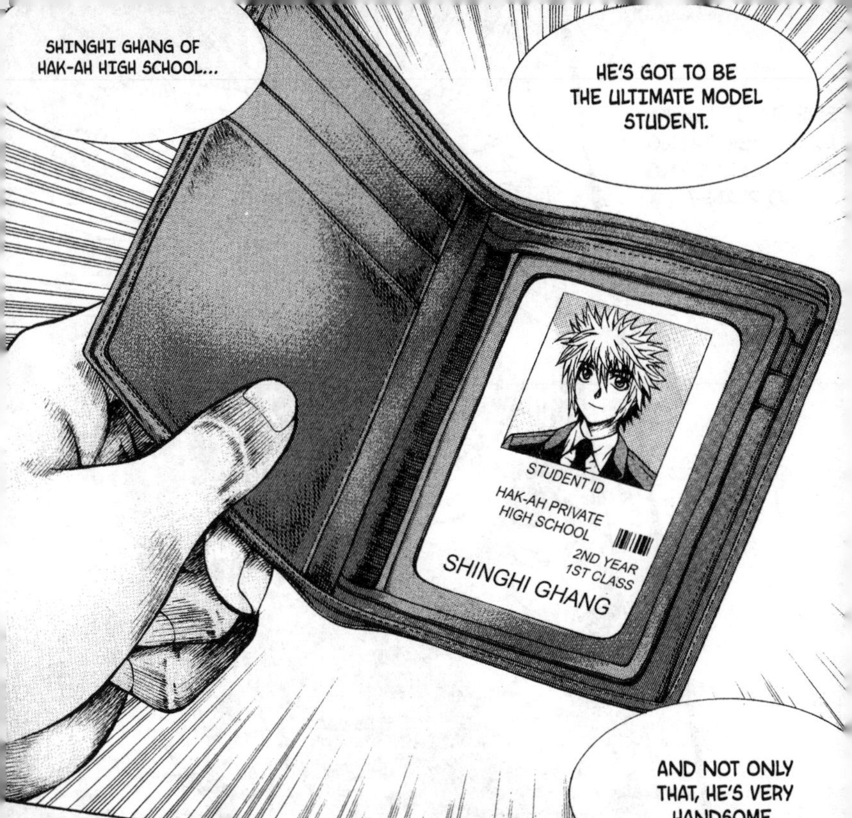
SHINGHI GHANG OF HAK-AH HIGH SCHOOL...
HE'S GOT TO BE THE ULTIMATE MODEL STUDENT.
STUDENT ID
HAK-AH PRIVATE HIGH SCHOOL
2ND YEAR 1ST CLASS
SHINGHI GHANG
AND NOT ONLY THAT, HE'S VERY HANDSOME...

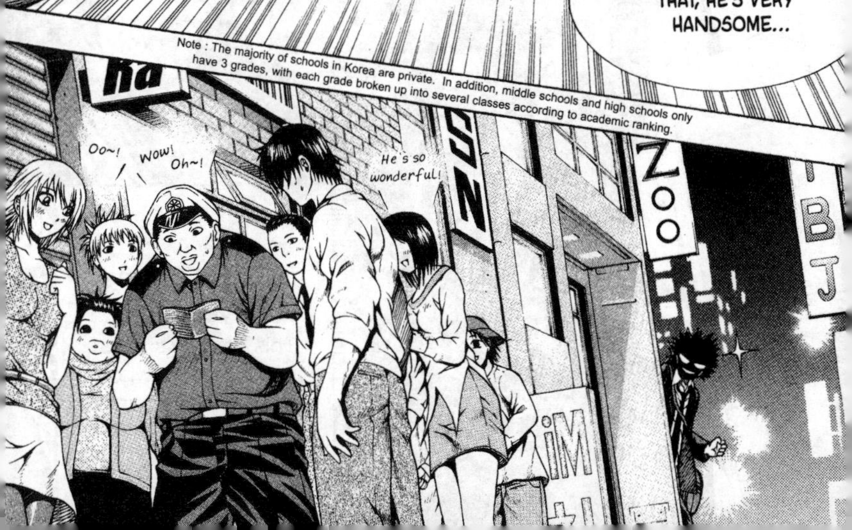
Note : The majority of schools in Korea are private. In addition, middle schools and high schools only have 3 grades, with each grade broken up into several classes according to academic ranking.
Oo~!
Wow!
Oh~!
He's so wonderful!
ZOO

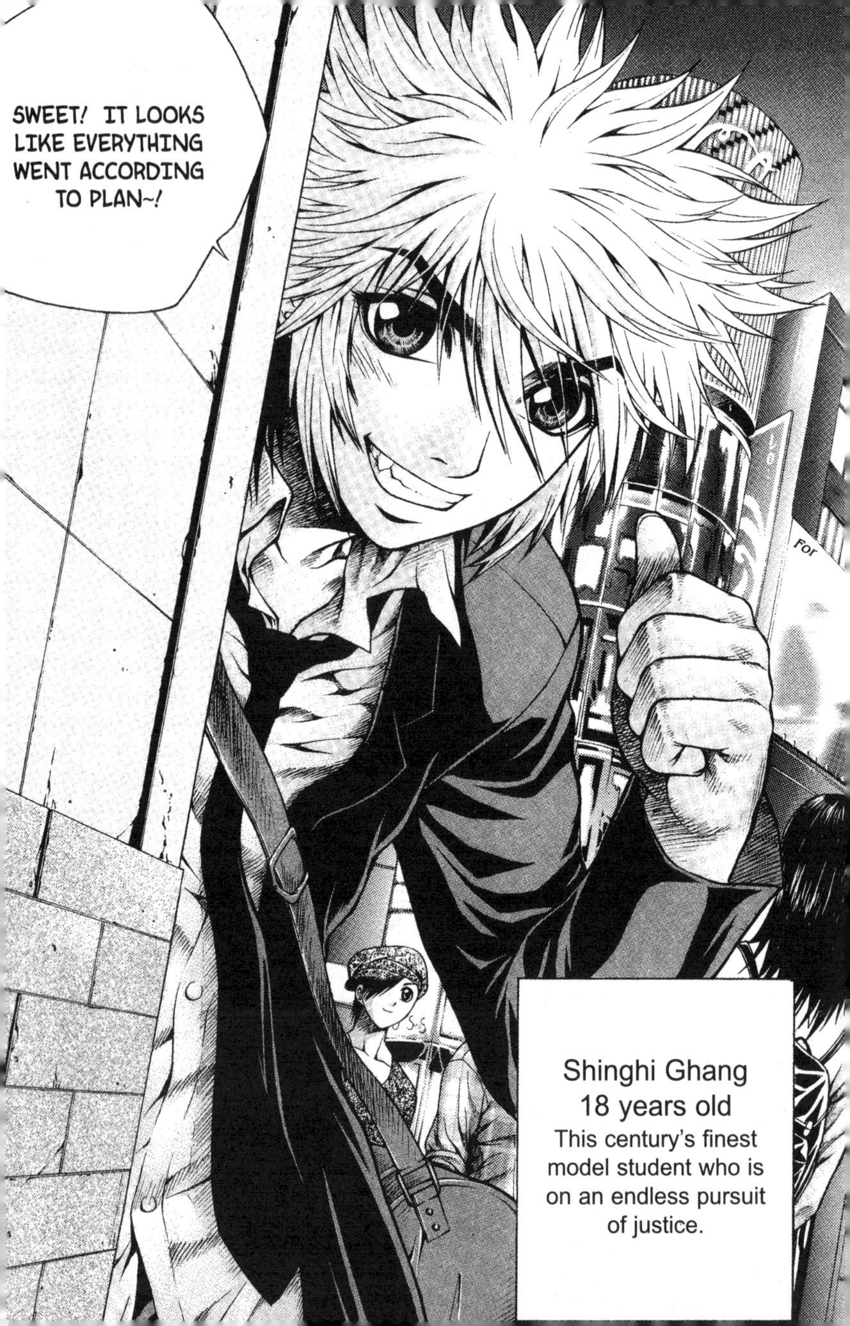
SWEET! IT LOOKS LIKE EVERYTHING WENT ACCORDING TO PLAN~!
For
Shinghi Ghang
18 years old
This century's finest model student who is on an endless pursuit of justice.

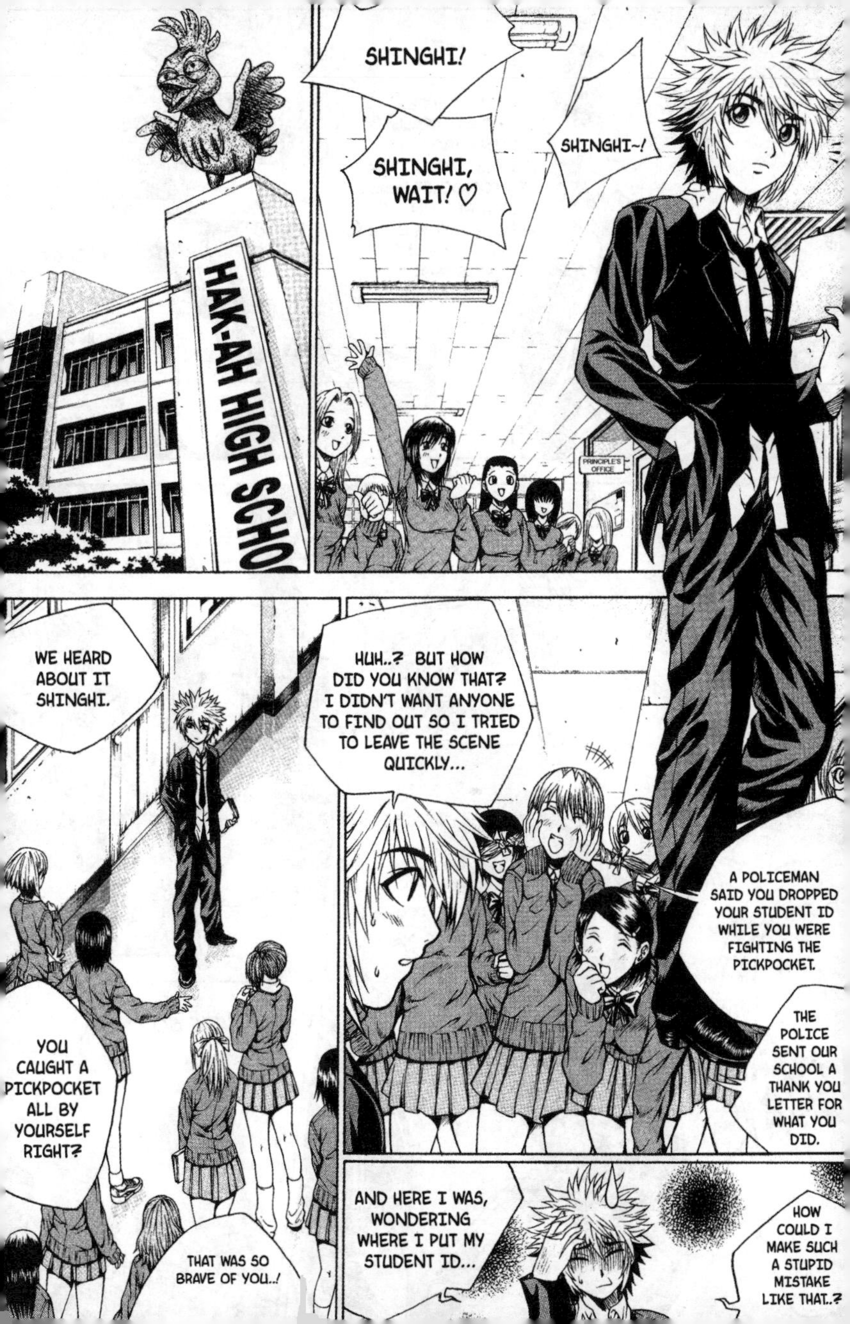

HAK-AH HIGH SCHO
SHINGHI!
SHINGHI, WAIT! ♡
SHINGHI~!
PRINCIPLE'S OFFICE
WE HEARD ABOUT IT SHINGHI.
YOU CAUGHT A PICKPOCKET ALL BY YOURSELF RIGHT?
THAT WAS SO BRAVE OF YOU..!
HUH..? BUT HOW DID YOU KNOW THAT? I DIDN'T WANT ANYONE TO FIND OUT SO I TRIED TO LEAVE THE SCENE QUICKLY...
A POLICEMAN SAID YOU DROPPED YOUR STUDENT ID WHILE YOU WERE FIGHTING THE PICKPOCKET.
THE POLICE SENT OUR SCHOOL A THANK YOU LETTER FOR WHAT YOU DID.
AND HERE I WAS, WONDERING WHERE I PUT MY STUDENT ID...
HOW COULD I MAKE SUCH A STUPID MISTAKE LIKE THAT..?

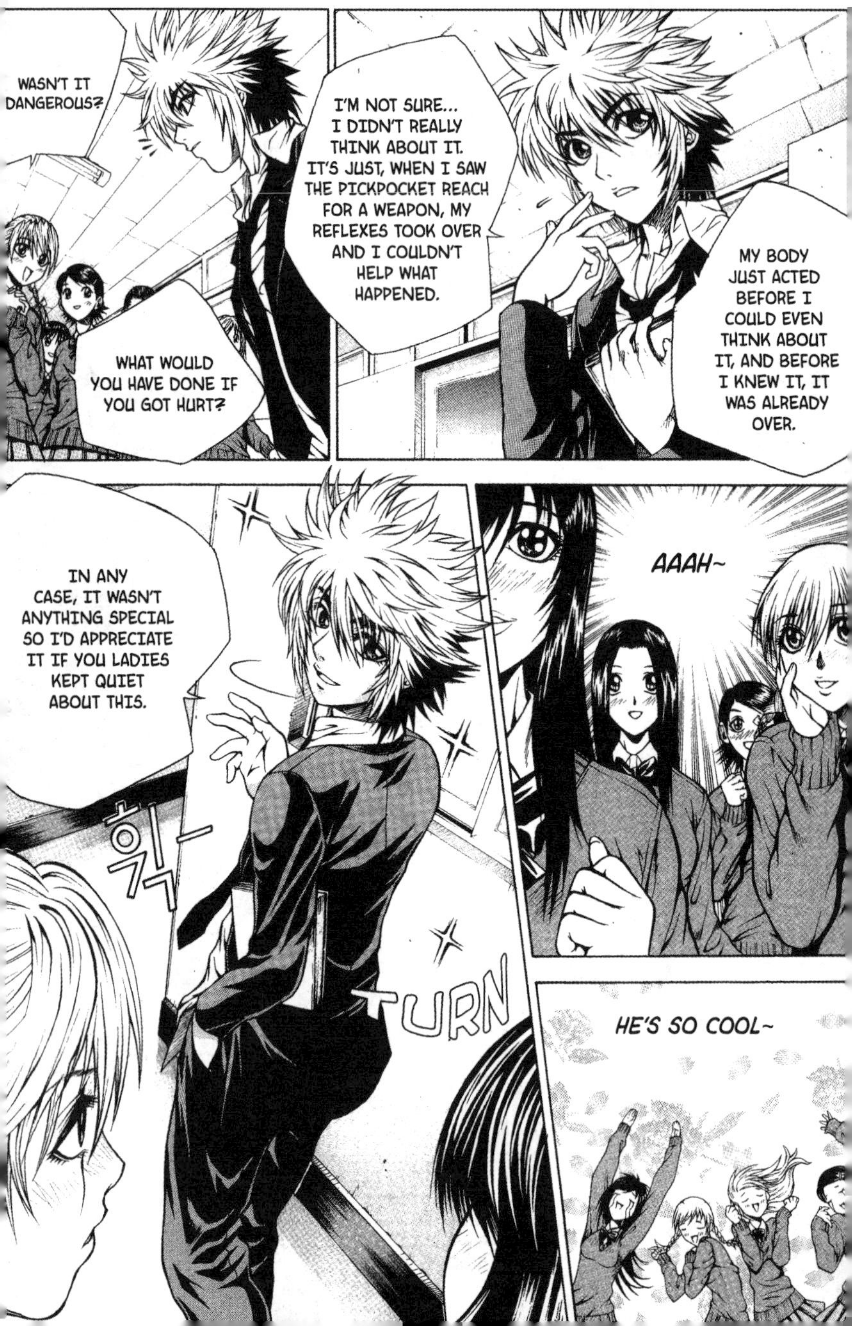
WASN'T IT DANGEROUS?
WHAT WOULD YOU HAVE DONE IF YOU GOT HURT?
I'M NOT SURE... I DIDN'T REALLY THINK ABOUT IT. IT'S JUST, WHEN I SAW THE PICKPOCKET REACH FOR A WEAPON, MY REFLEXES TOOK OVER AND I COULDN'T HELP WHAT HAPPENED.
MY BODY JUST ACTED BEFORE I COULD EVEN THINK ABOUT IT, AND BEFORE I KNEW IT, IT WAS ALREADY OVER.
IN ANY CASE, IT WASN'T ANYTHING SPECIAL SO I'D APPRECIATE IT IF YOU LADIES KEPT QUIET ABOUT THIS.
TURN
AAAH~
HE'S SO COOL~

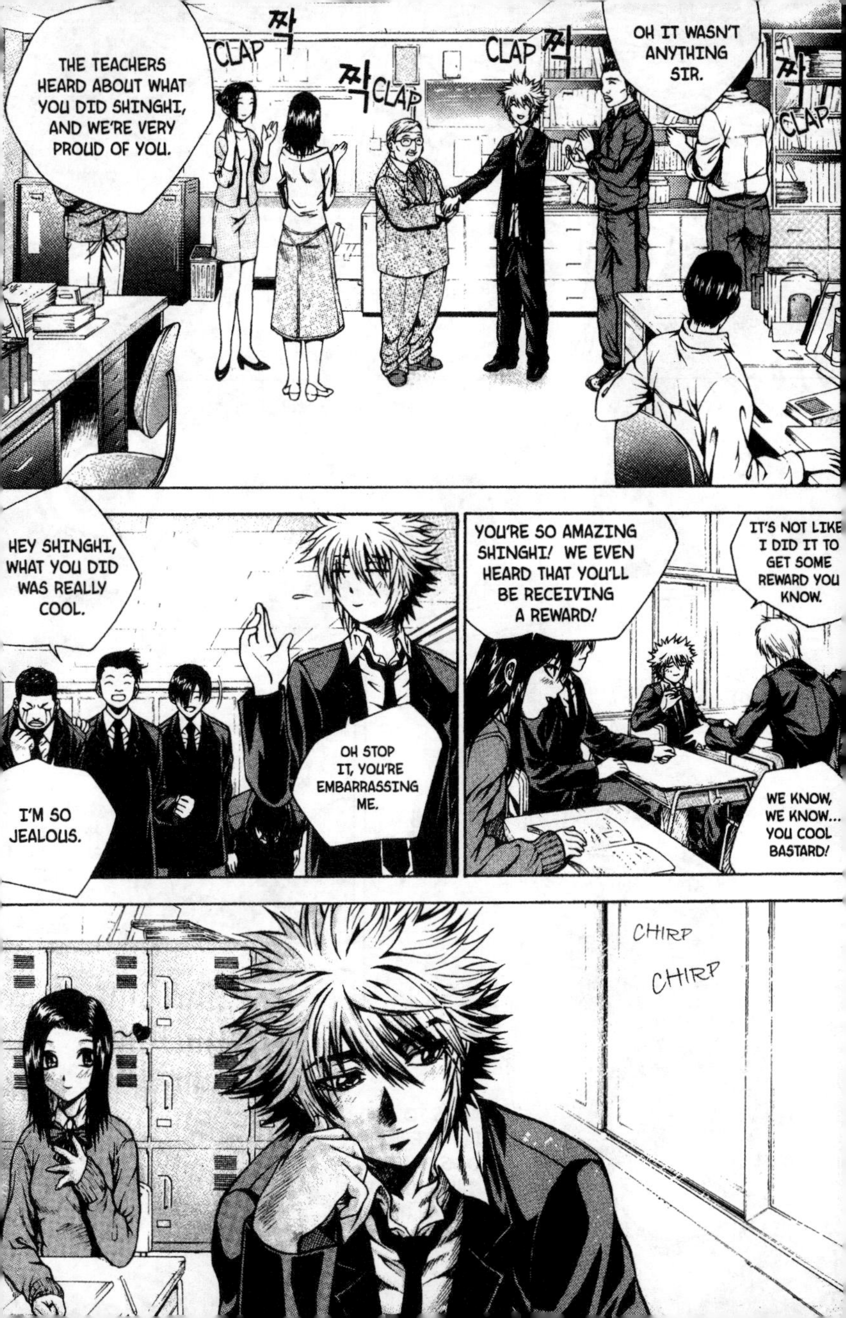
THE TEACHERS HEARD ABOUT WHAT YOU DID SHINGHI, AND WE'RE VERY PROUD OF YOU.
CLAP 짝
짝 CLAP
CLAP 짝
OH IT WASN'T ANYTHING SIR.
짝 CLAP
HEY SHINGHI, WHAT YOU DID WAS REALLY COOL.
I'M SO JEALOUS.
OH STOP IT, YOU'RE EMBARRASSING ME.
YOU'RE SO AMAZING SHINGHI! WE EVEN HEARD THAT YOU'LL BE RECEIVING A REWARD!
IT'S NOT LIKE I DID IT TO GET SOME REWARD YOU KNOW.
WE KNOW, WE KNOW... YOU COOL BASTARD!
CHIRP
CHIRP

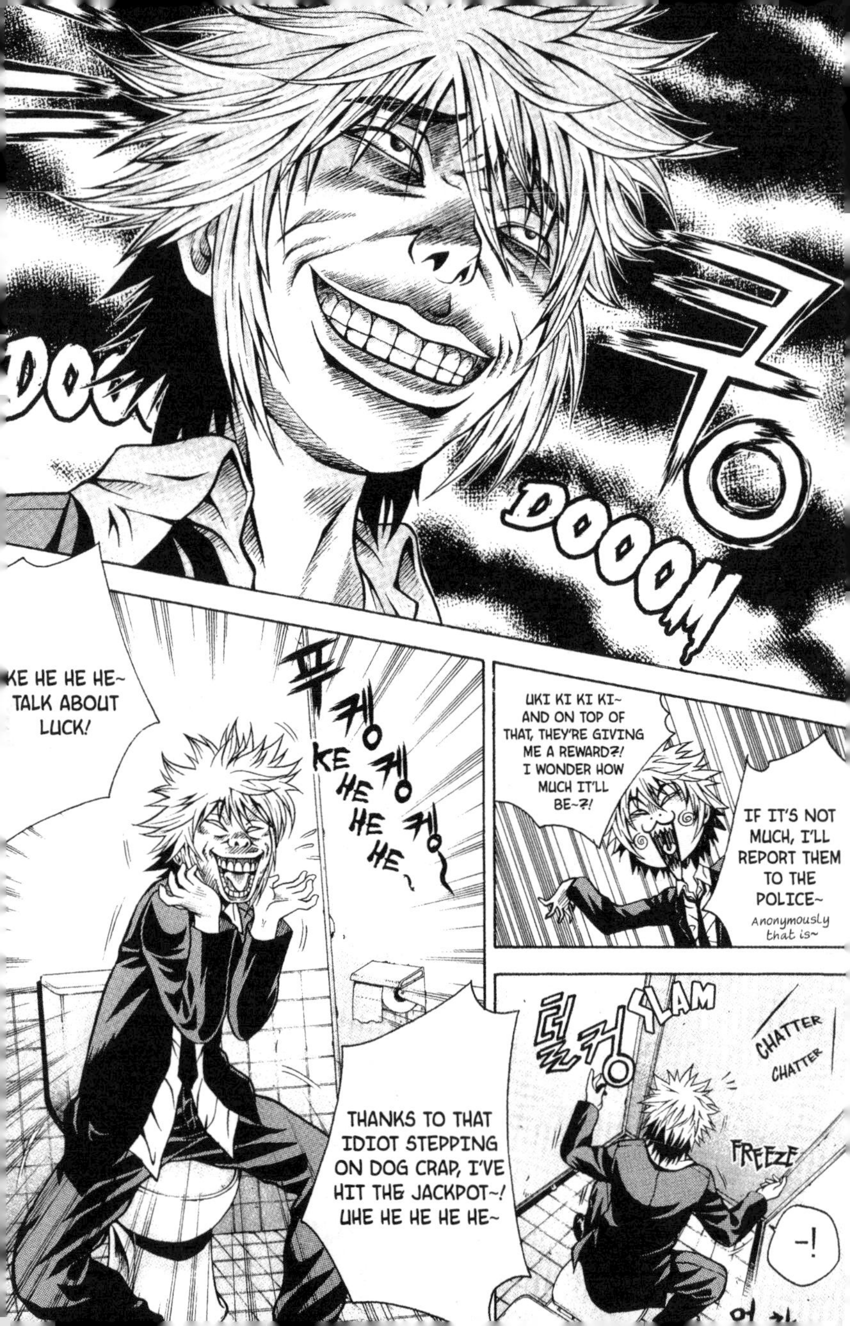
DOO
쿵
DOOOOM
KE HE HE HE~ TALK ABOUT LUCK!
KE HE HE HE~
THANKS TO THAT IDIOT STEPPING ON DOG CRAP, I'VE HIT THE JACKPOT~! UHE HE HE HE HE~
UKI KI KI KI~ AND ON TOP OF THAT, THEY'RE GIVING ME A REWARD?! I WONDER HOW MUCH IT'LL BE~?!
IF IT'S NOT MUCH, I'LL REPORT THEM TO THE POLICE~
Anonymously that is~
덜컹
SLAM
CHATTER
CHATTER
FREEZE
–!

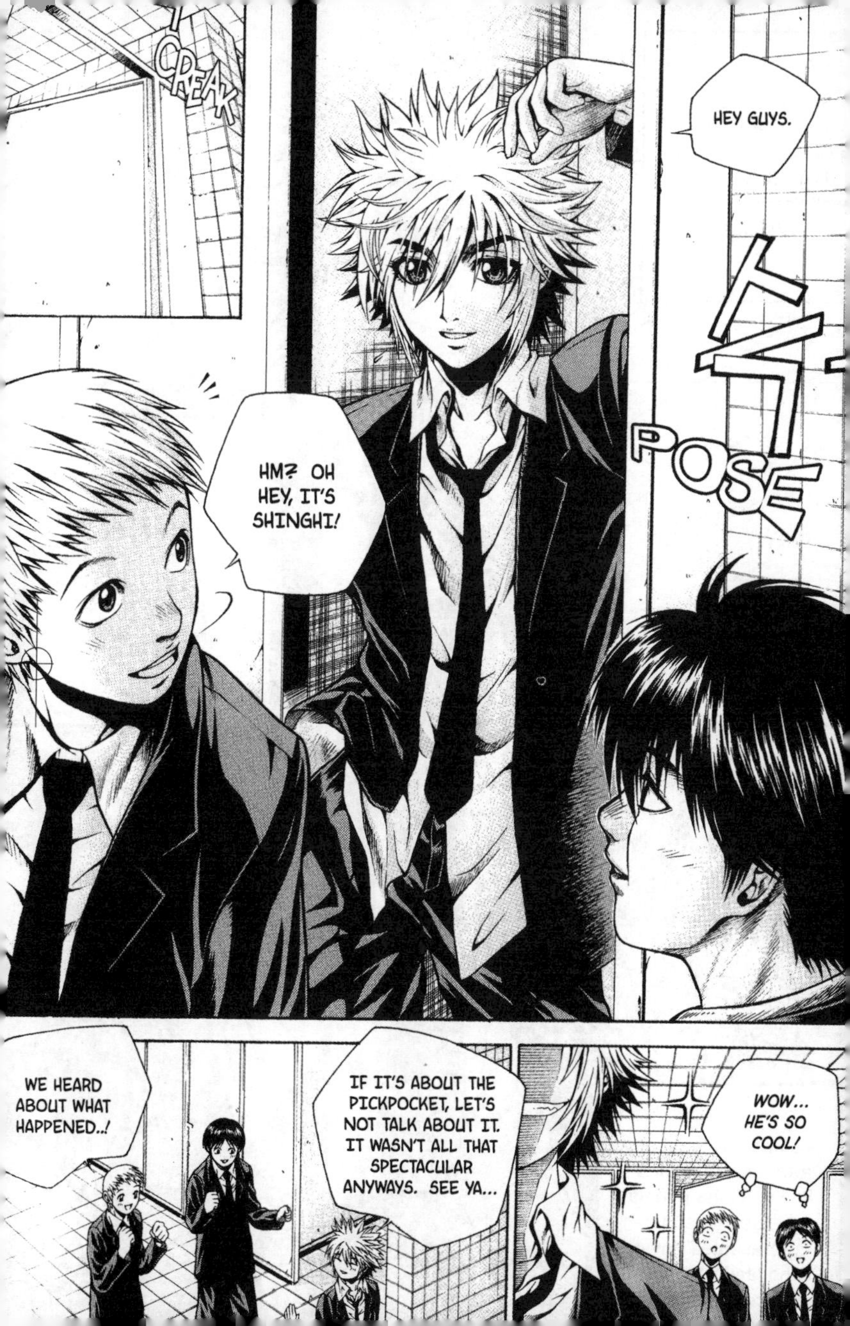
CREAK
HEY GUYS.
POSE
HM? OH HEY, IT'S SHINGHI!
WE HEARD ABOUT WHAT HAPPENED..!
IF IT'S ABOUT THE PICKPOCKET, LET'S NOT TALK ABOUT IT. IT WASN'T ALL THAT SPECTACULAR ANYWAYS. SEE YA...
WOW... HE'S SO COOL!

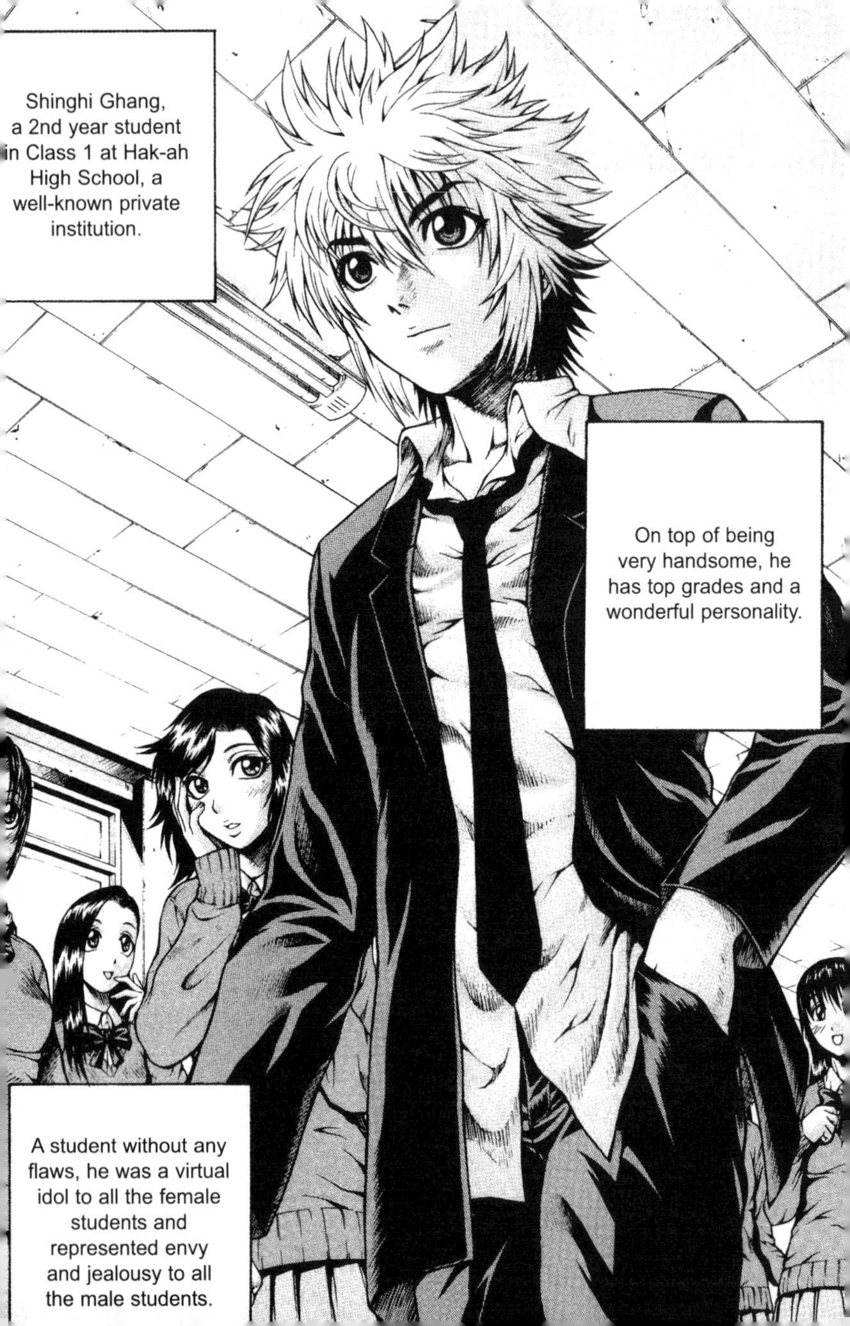

Shinghi Ghang, a 2nd year student in Class 1 at Hak-ah High School, a well-known private institution.
On top of being very handsome, he has top grades and a wonderful personality.
A student without any flaws, he was a virtual idol to all the female students and represented envy and jealousy to all the male students.

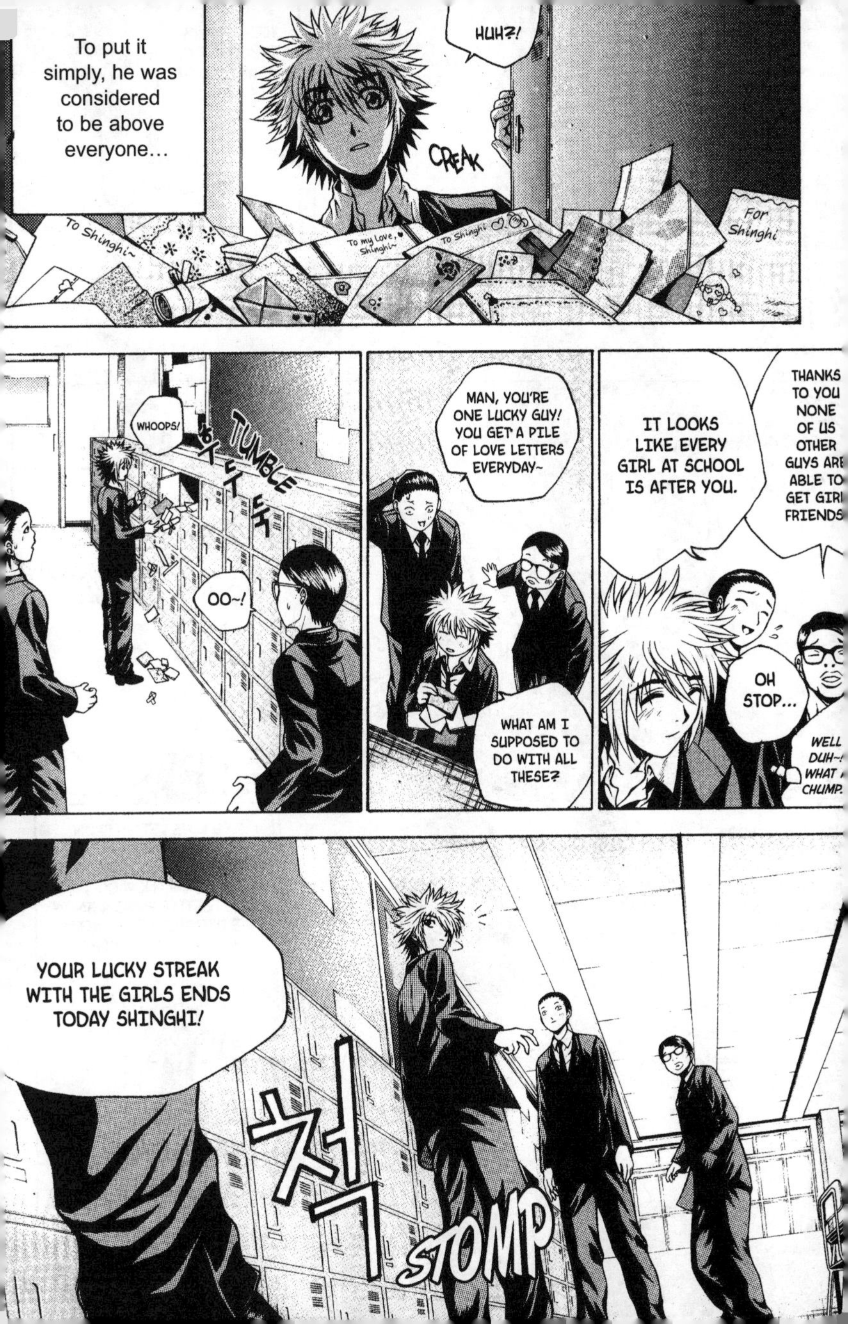
To put it simply, he was considered to be above everyone…
HUH?!
CREAK
To Shinghi~
To my love, Shinghi~
To Shinghi
For Shinghi
WHOOPS!
TUMBLE
OO~!
MAN, YOU'RE ONE LUCKY GUY! YOU GET A PILE OF LOVE LETTERS EVERYDAY~
WHAT AM I SUPPOSED TO DO WITH ALL THESE?
IT LOOKS LIKE EVERY GIRL AT SCHOOL IS AFTER YOU.
THANKS TO YOU NONE OF US OTHER GUYS AR ABLE TO GET GIR FRIENDS
OH STOP...
WELL DUH~! WHAT CHUMP.
YOUR LUCKY STREAK WITH THE GIRLS ENDS TODAY SHINGHI!
STOMP

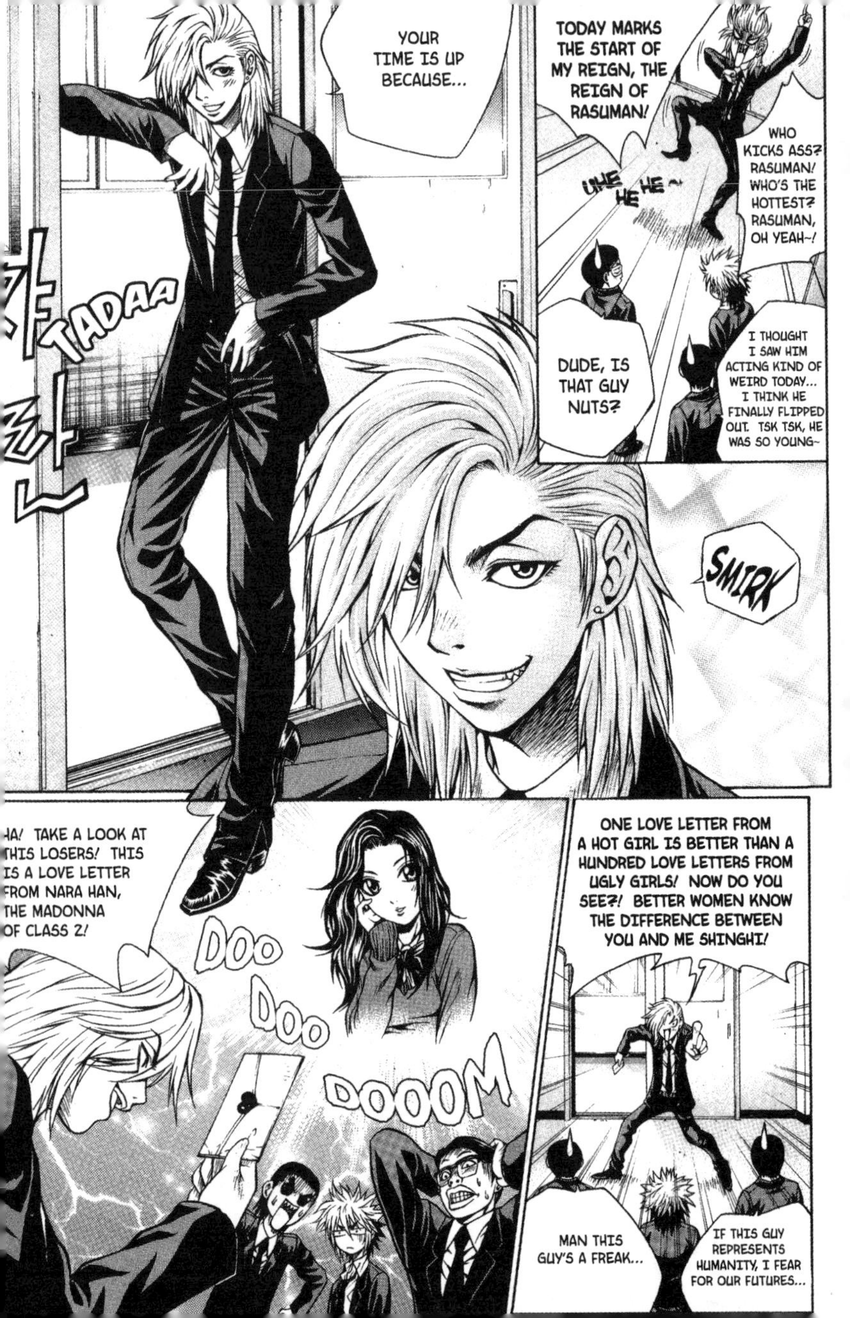
YOUR TIME IS UP BECAUSE...
TADAA
TODAY MARKS THE START OF MY REIGN, THE REIGN OF RASUMAN!
UHE HE HE~
WHO KICKS ASS? RASUMAN! WHO'S THE HOTTEST? RASUMAN, OH YEAH~!
DUDE, IS THAT GUY NUTS?
I THOUGHT I SAW HIM ACTING KIND OF WEIRD TODAY... I THINK HE FINALLY FLIPPED OUT. TSK TSK, HE WAS SO YOUNG~
SMIRK
HA! TAKE A LOOK AT THIS LOSERS! THIS IS A LOVE LETTER FROM NARA HAN, THE MADONNA OF CLASS 2!
DOO
DOO
DOOOM
ONE LOVE LETTER FROM A HOT GIRL IS BETTER THAN A HUNDRED LOVE LETTERS FROM UGLY GIRLS! NOW DO YOU SEE?! BETTER WOMEN KNOW THE DIFFERENCE BETWEEN YOU AND ME SHINGHI!
MAN THIS GUY'S A FREAK...
IF THIS GUY REPRESENTS HUMANITY, I FEAR FOR OUR FUTURES...

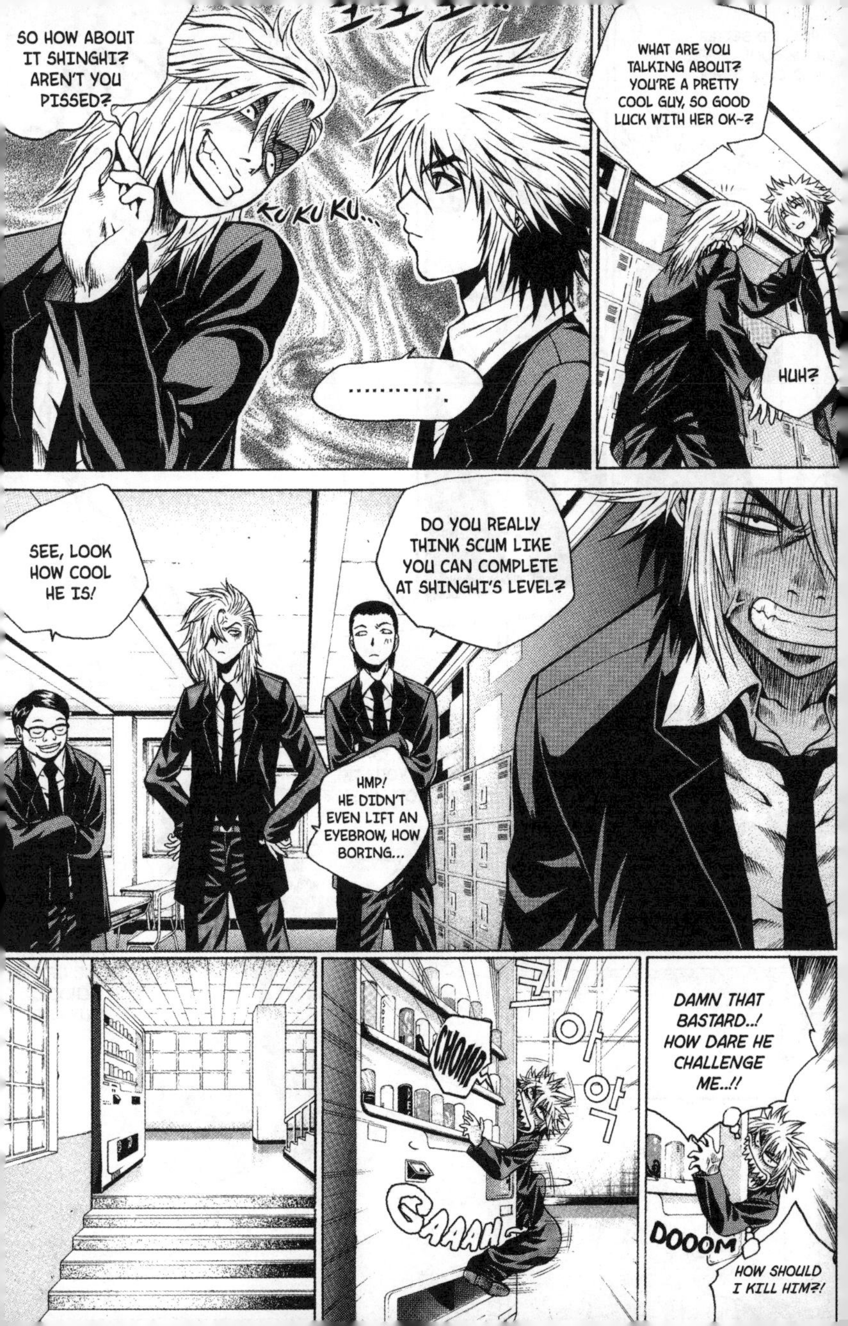
SO HOW ABOUT IT SHINGHI? AREN'T YOU PISSED?
KU KU KU...
....
WHAT ARE YOU TALKING ABOUT? YOU'RE A PRETTY COOL GUY, SO GOOD LUCK WITH HER OK~?
HUH?
SEE, LOOK HOW COOL HE IS!
DO YOU REALLY THINK SCUM LIKE YOU CAN COMPLETE AT SHINGHI'S LEVEL?
HMP! HE DIDN'T EVEN LIFT AN EYEBROW, HOW BORING...
CHOMP
GAAAH
DAMN THAT BASTARD..! HOW DARE HE CHALLENGE ME..!!
DOOOM
HOW SHOULD I KILL HIM?!

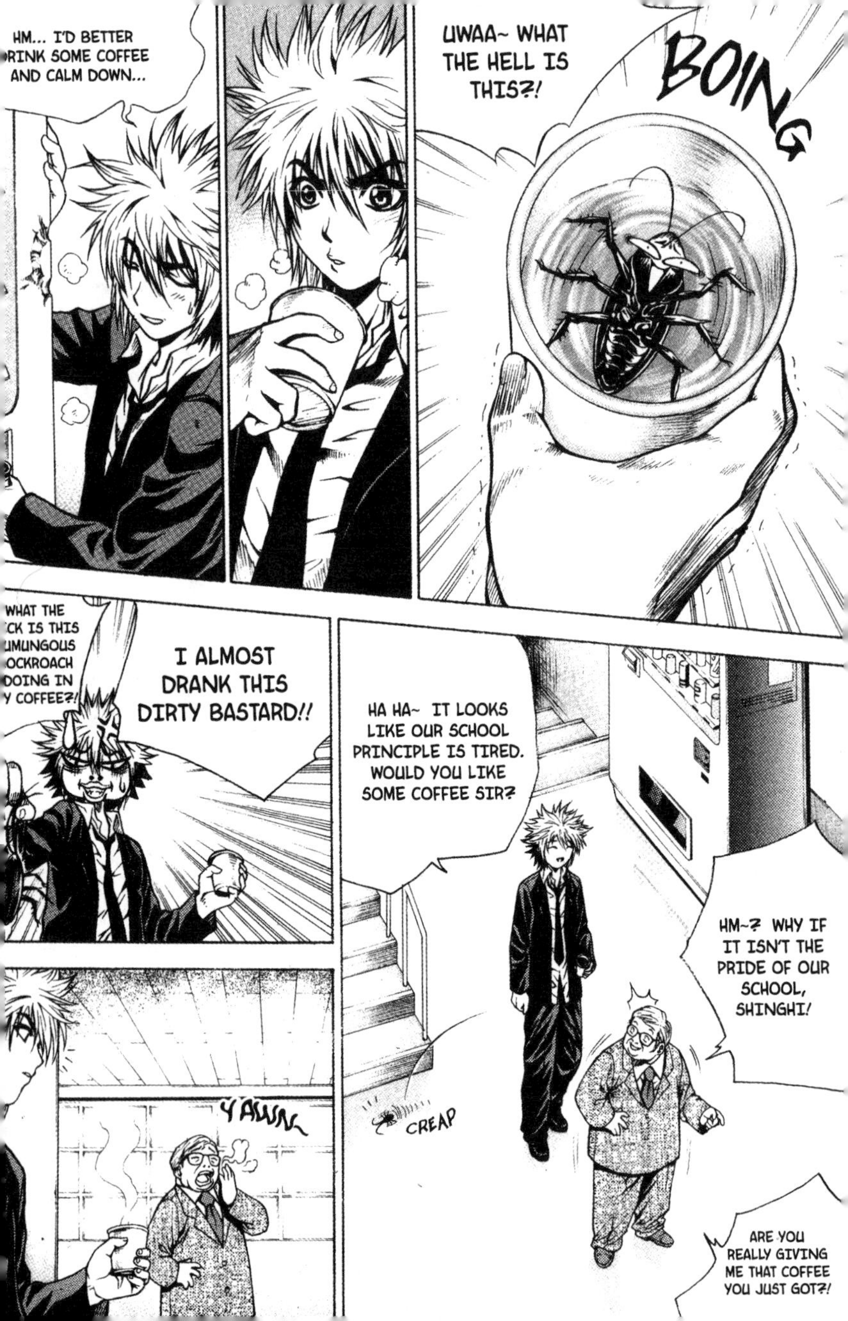
HM... I'D BETTER RINK SOME COFFEE AND CALM DOWN...
UWAA~ WHAT THE HELL IS THIS?!
BOING
WHAT THE CK IS THIS UMUNGOUS OCKROACH DOING IN Y COFFEE?!
I ALMOST DRANK THIS DIRTY BASTARD!!
YAWN
HA HA~ IT LOOKS LIKE OUR SCHOOL PRINCIPLE IS TIRED. WOULD YOU LIKE SOME COFFEE SIR?
HM~? WHY IF IT ISN'T THE PRIDE OF OUR SCHOOL, SHINGHI!
CREAP
ARE YOU REALLY GIVING ME THAT COFFEE YOU JUST GOT?!

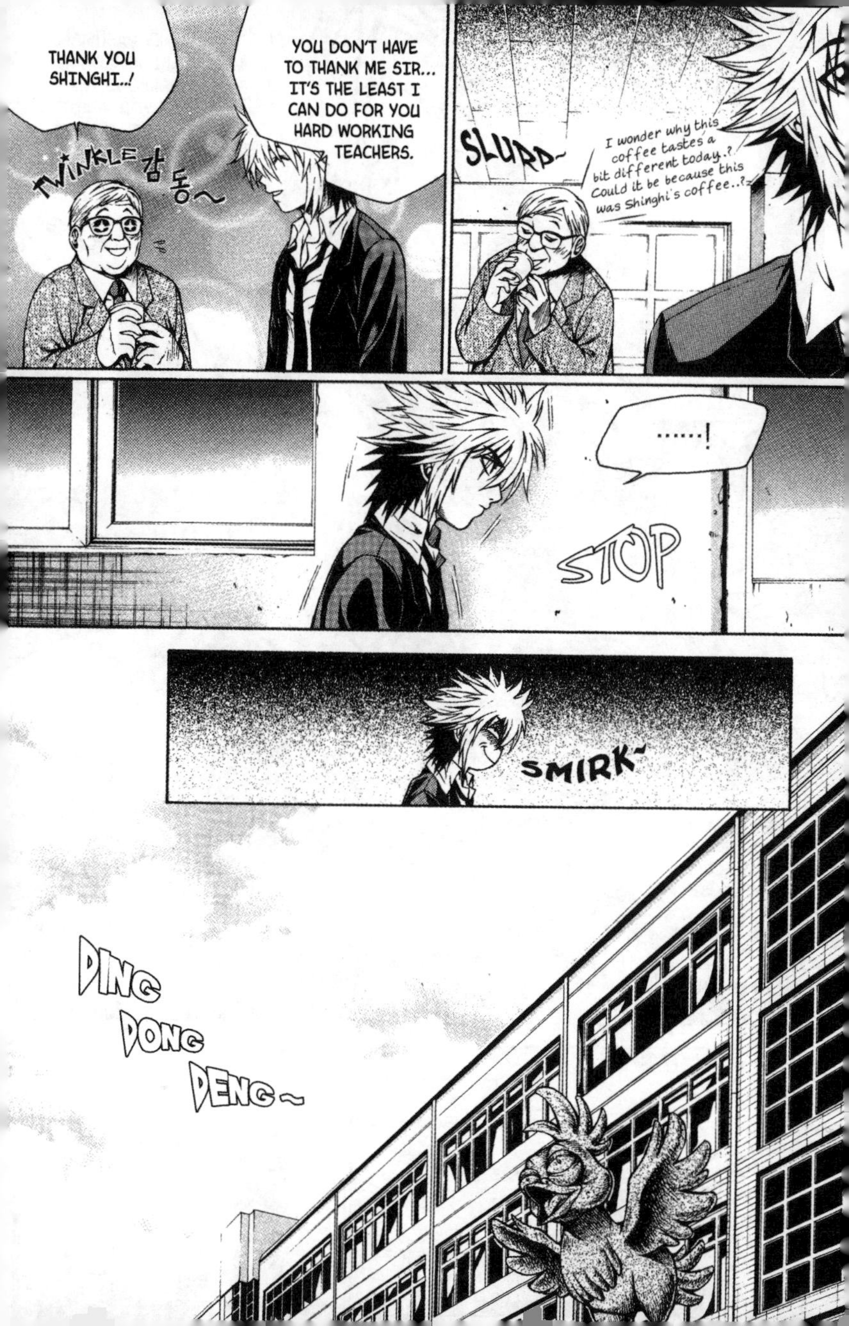
THANK YOU SHINGHI..!
TWINKLE 감동~
YOU DON'T HAVE TO THANK ME SIR... IT'S THE LEAST I CAN DO FOR YOU HARD WORKING TEACHERS.
SLURP~
I wonder why this coffee tastes a bit different today..? Could it be because this was Shinghi's coffee..?
......!
STOP
SMIRK~
DING DONG DENG~

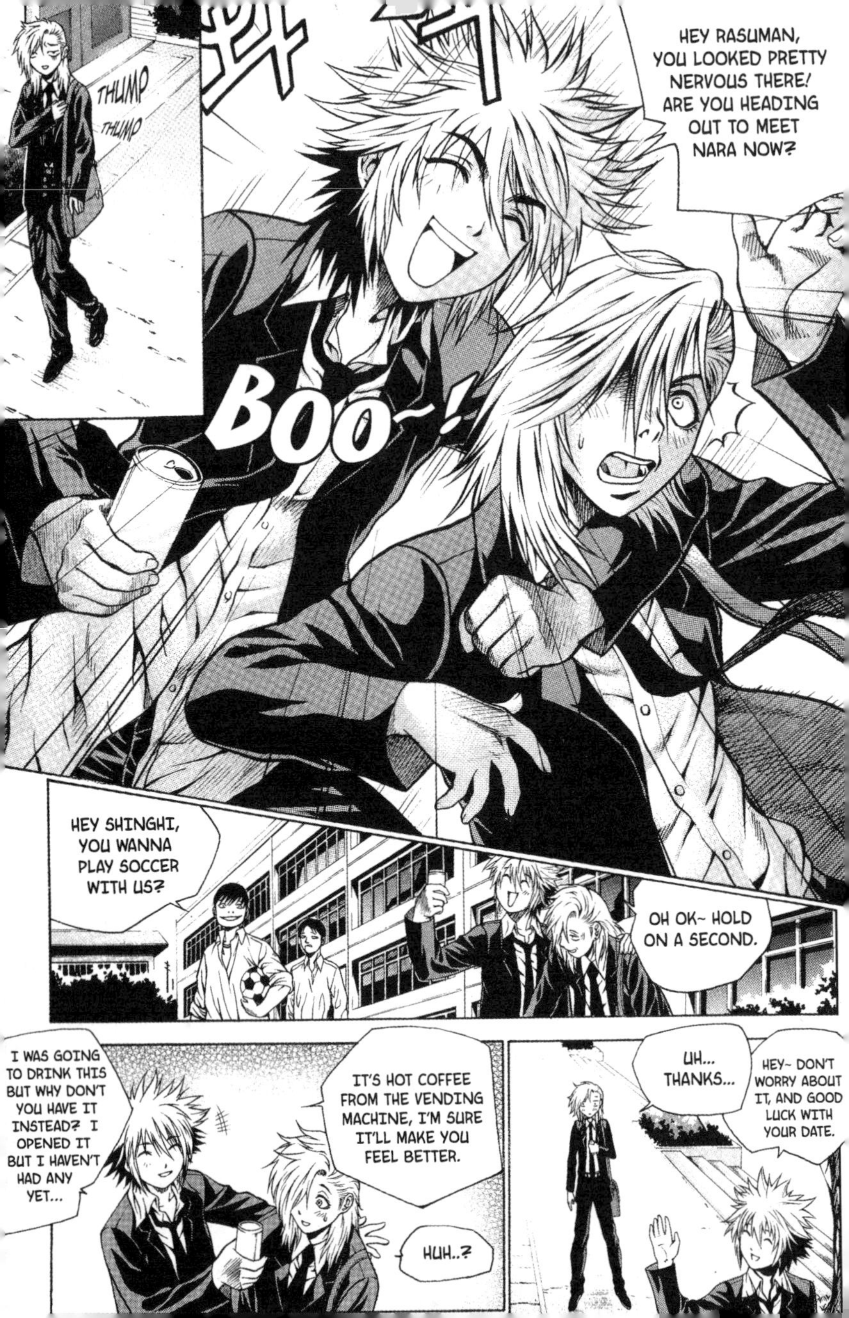
THUMP
THUMP
HEY RASUMAN, YOU LOOKED PRETTY NERVOUS THERE! ARE YOU HEADING OUT TO MEET NARA NOW?
BOO~!
HEY SHINGHI, YOU WANNA PLAY SOCCER WITH US?
OH OK~ HOLD ON A SECOND.
I WAS GOING TO DRINK THIS BUT WHY DON'T YOU HAVE IT INSTEAD? I OPENED IT BUT I HAVEN'T HAD ANY YET...
IT'S HOT COFFEE FROM THE VENDING MACHINE, I'M SURE IT'LL MAKE YOU FEEL BETTER.
HUH..?
UH... THANKS...
HEY~ DON'T WORRY ABOUT IT, AND GOOD LUCK WITH YOUR DATE.

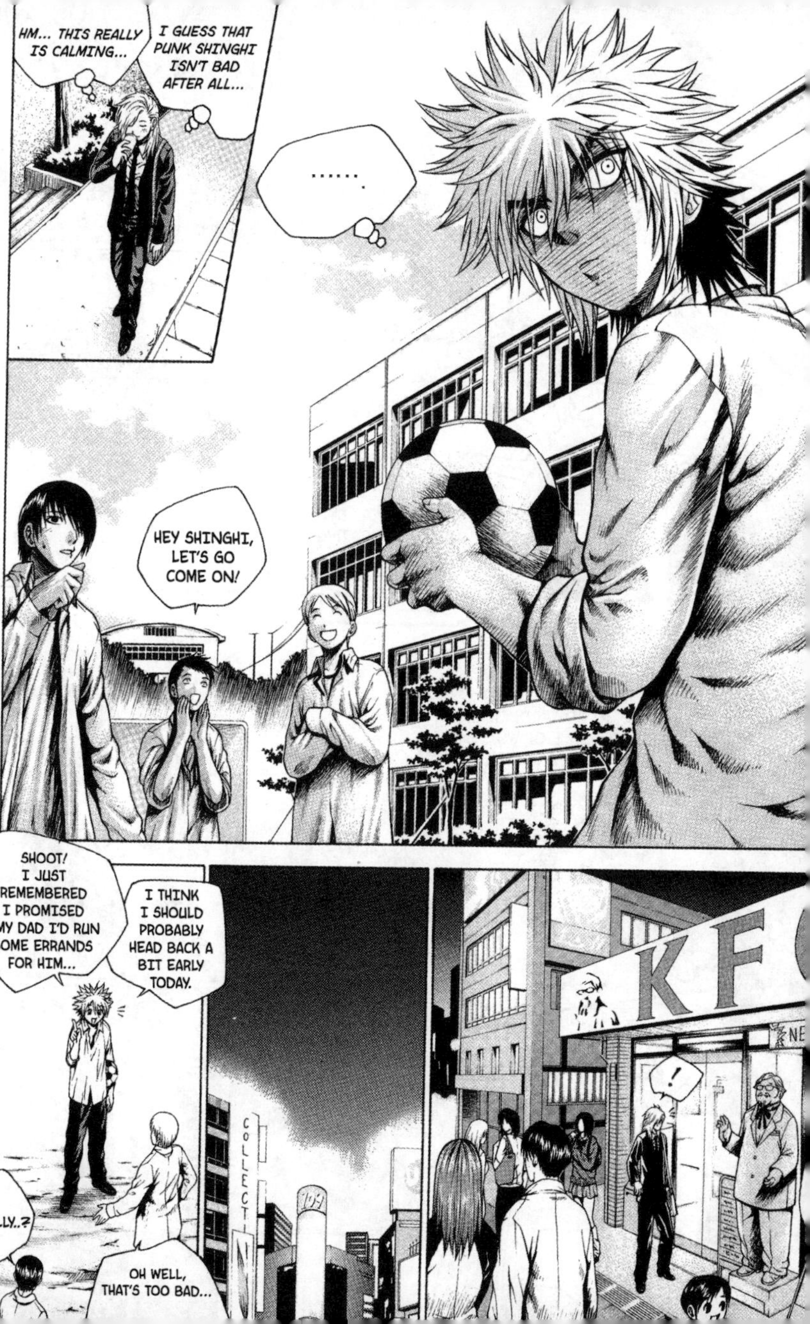

HM... THIS REALLY IS CALMING...
I GUESS THAT PUNK SHINGHI ISN'T BAD AFTER ALL...
....
HEY SHINGHI, LET'S GO COME ON!
SHOOT! I JUST REMEMBERED I PROMISED MY DAD I'D RUN SOME ERRANDS FOR HIM...
I THINK I SHOULD PROBABLY HEAD BACK A BIT EARLY TODAY.
REALLY..?
OH WELL, THAT'S TOO BAD...
!

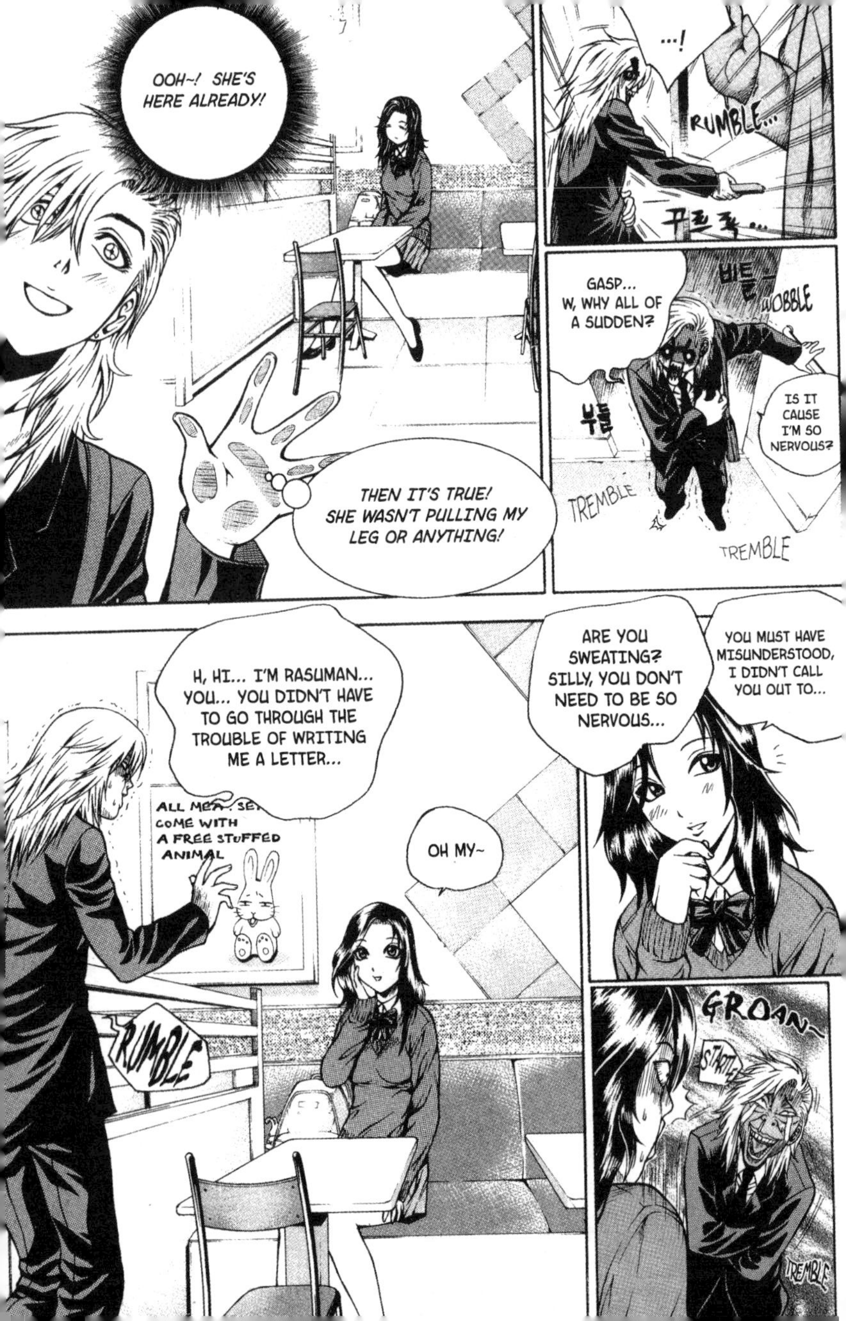
OOH~! SHE'S HERE ALREADY!
THEN IT'S TRUE! SHE WASN'T PULLING MY LEG OR ANYTHING!
...!
RUMBLE...
꾸르륵...
GASP... W, WHY ALL OF A SUDDEN?
비틀
WOBBLE
부들
IS IT CAUSE I'M SO NERVOUS?
TREMBLE
TREMBLE
H, HI... I'M RASUMAN... YOU... YOU DIDN'T HAVE TO GO THROUGH THE TROUBLE OF WRITING ME A LETTER...
COME WITH
A FREE STUFFED
ANIMAL
OH MY~
RUMBLE
ARE YOU SWEATING? SILLY, YOU DON'T NEED TO BE SO NERVOUS...
YOU MUST HAVE MISUNDERSTOOD, I DIDN'T CALL YOU OUT TO...
GROAN~
STARTLE
TREMBLE

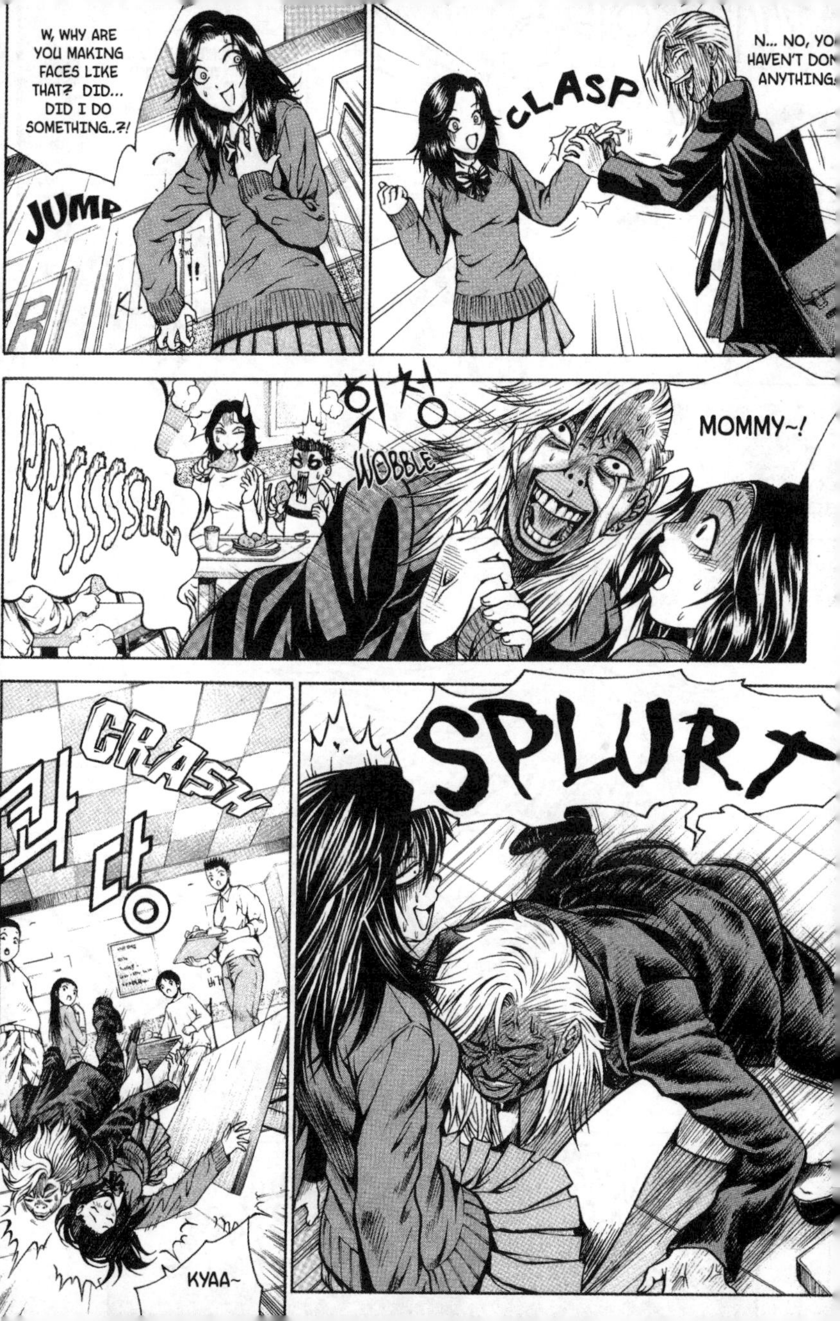

W, WHY ARE YOU MAKING FACES LIKE THAT? DID... DID I DO SOMETHING..?!
JUMP
!!
CLASP
N... NO, YO HAVEN'T DON ANYTHING.
PPSSSSSHH
휘청
WOBBLE
MOMMY~!
CRASH
콰당
KYAA~
SPLURT

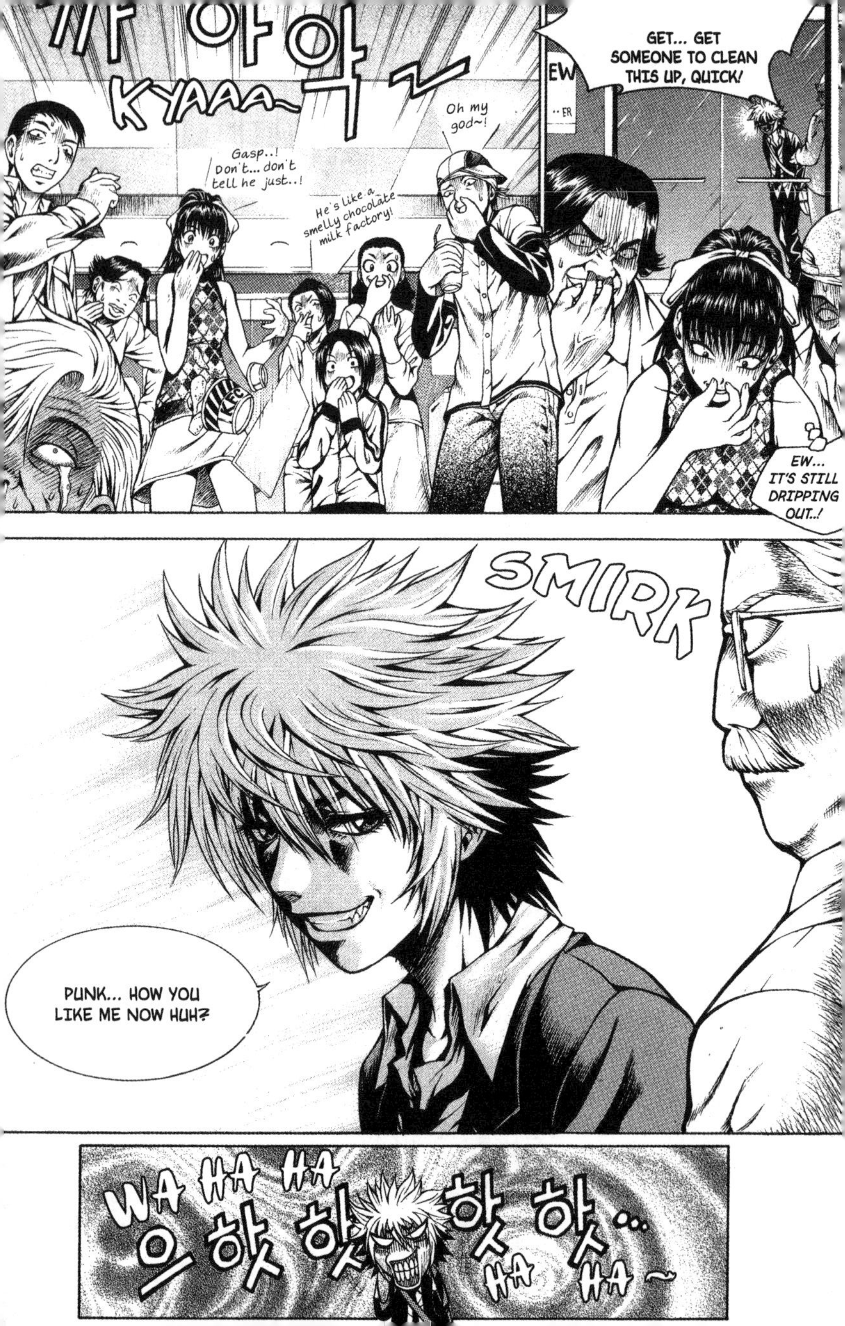
KYAAA~
Gasp..! Don't... don't tell he just..!
He's like a smelly chocolate milk factory!
KFC
Oh my god~!
GET... GET SOMEONE TO CLEAN THIS UP, QUICK!
EW... IT'S STILL DRIPPING OUT..!
SMIRK
PUNK... HOW YOU LIKE ME NOW HUH?
WA HA HA
으핫핫핫핫..
HA HA~

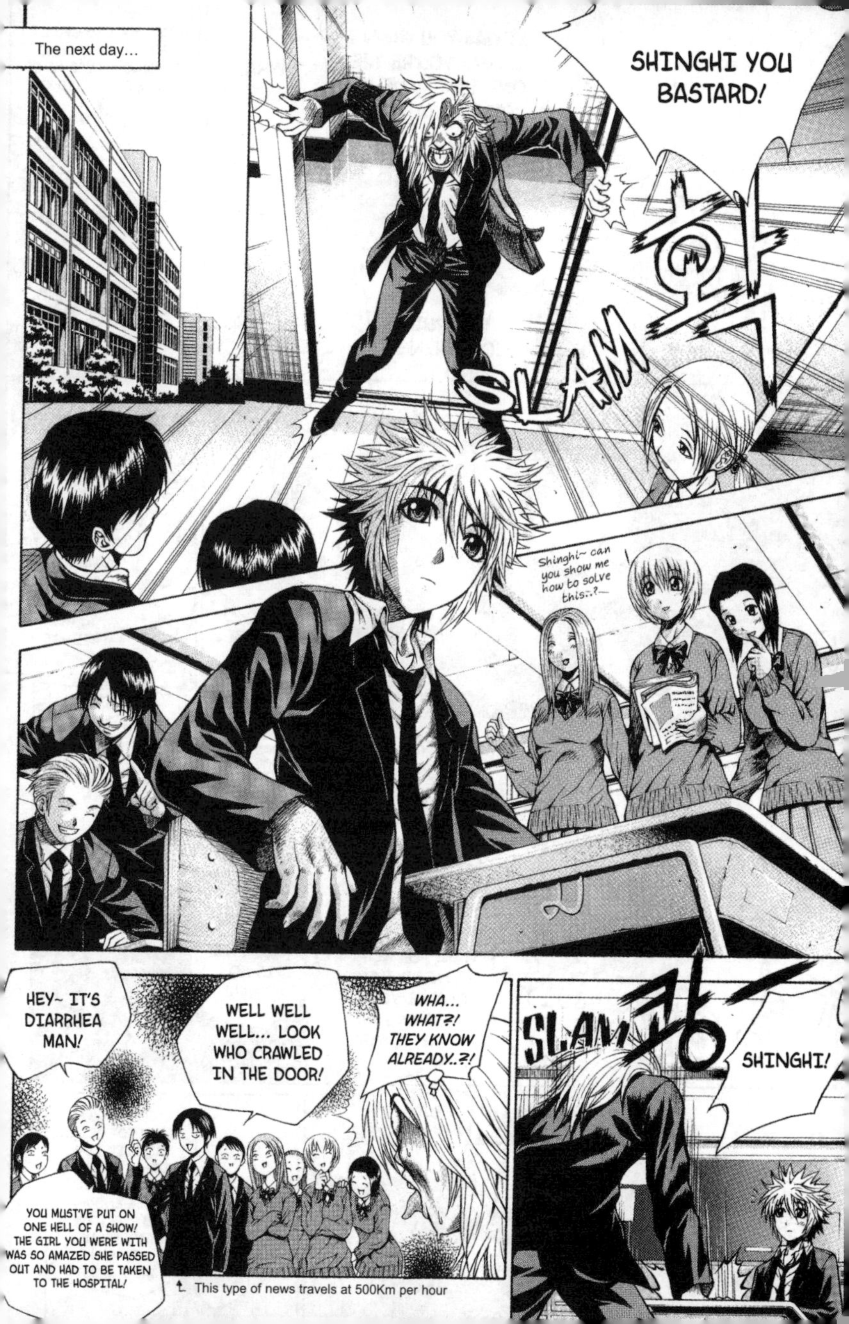
The next day...
SHINGHI YOU BASTARD!
SLAM
Shinghi~ can you show me how to solve this..?
HEY~ IT'S DIARRHEA MAN!
WELL WELL WELL... LOOK WHO CRAWLED IN THE DOOR!
WHA... WHAT?! THEY KNOW ALREADY..?!
YOU MUST'VE PUT ON ONE HELL OF A SHOW! THE GIRL YOU WERE WITH WAS SO AMAZED SHE PASSED OUT AND HAD TO BE TAKEN TO THE HOSPITAL!
This type of news travels at 500Km per hour
SLAM
SHINGHI!

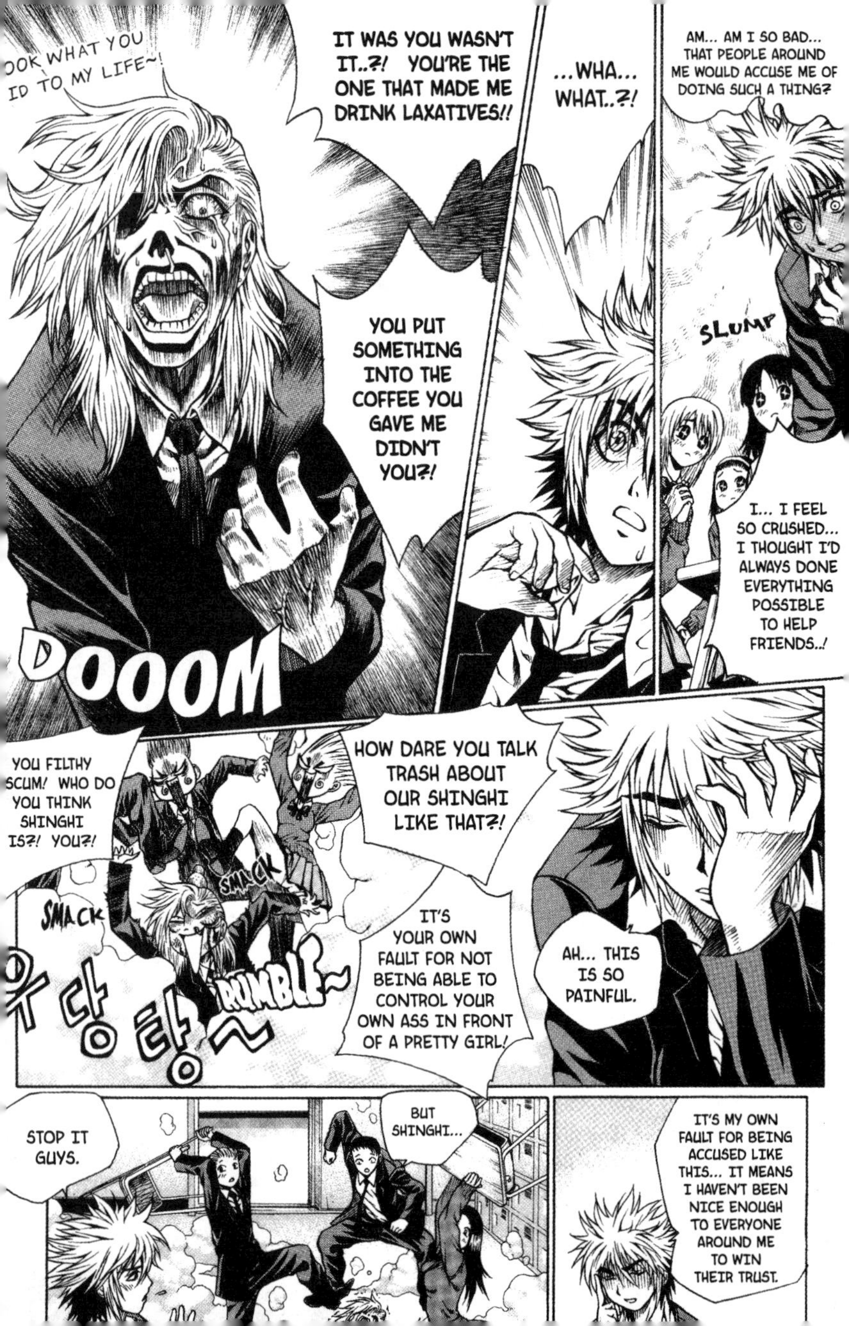
OOK WHAT YOU
ID TO MY LIFE~!
IT WAS YOU WASN'T IT..?! YOU'RE THE ONE THAT MADE ME DRINK LAXATIVES!!
YOU PUT SOMETHING INTO THE COFFEE YOU GAVE ME DIDN'T YOU?!
DOOOM
...WHA... WHAT..?!
AM... AM I SO BAD... THAT PEOPLE AROUND ME WOULD ACCUSE ME OF DOING SUCH A THING?
SLUMP
I... I FEEL SO CRUSHED... I THOUGHT I'D ALWAYS DONE EVERYTHING POSSIBLE TO HELP FRIENDS..!
YOU FILTHY SCUM! WHO DO YOU THINK SHINGHI IS?! YOU?!
HOW DARE YOU TALK TRASH ABOUT OUR SHINGHI LIKE THAT?!
SMACK
SMACK
와당탕~
RUMBLE~
IT'S YOUR OWN FAULT FOR NOT BEING ABLE TO CONTROL YOUR OWN ASS IN FRONT OF A PRETTY GIRL!
AH... THIS IS SO PAINFUL.
STOP IT GUYS.
BUT SHINGHI...
IT'S MY OWN FAULT FOR BEING ACCUSED LIKE THIS... IT MEANS I HAVEN'T BEEN NICE ENOUGH TO EVERYONE AROUND ME TO WIN THEIR TRUST.

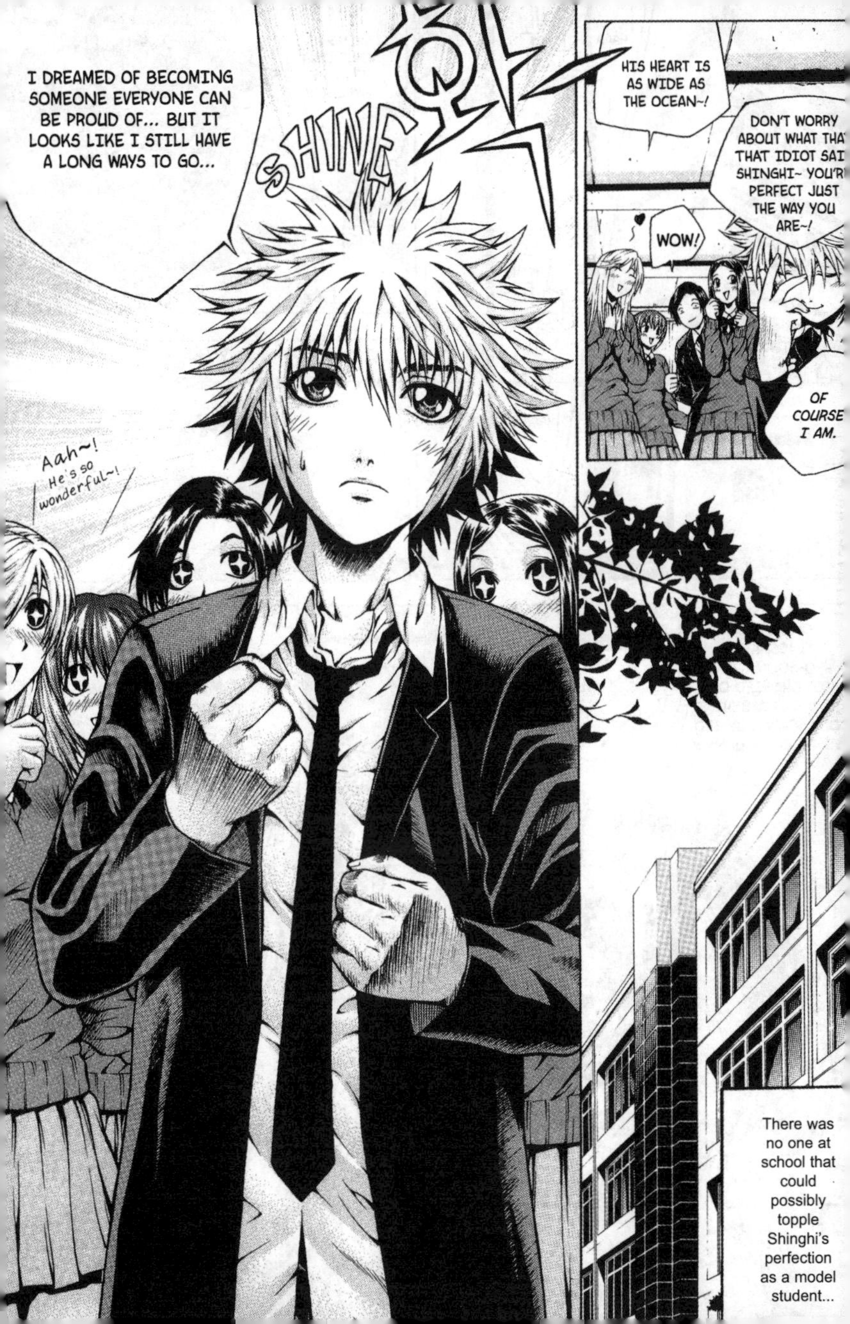
I DREAMED OF BECOMING SOMEONE EVERYONE CAN BE PROUD OF... BUT IT LOOKS LIKE I STILL HAVE A LONG WAYS TO GO...
SHINE
Aah~! He's so wonderful~!
HIS HEART IS AS WIDE AS THE OCEAN~!
DON'T WORRY ABOUT WHAT THAT THAT IDIOT SAI SHINGHI~ YOU'R PERFECT JUST THE WAY YOU ARE~!
WOW!
OF COURSE I AM.
There was no one at school that could possibly topple Shinghi's perfection as a model student...

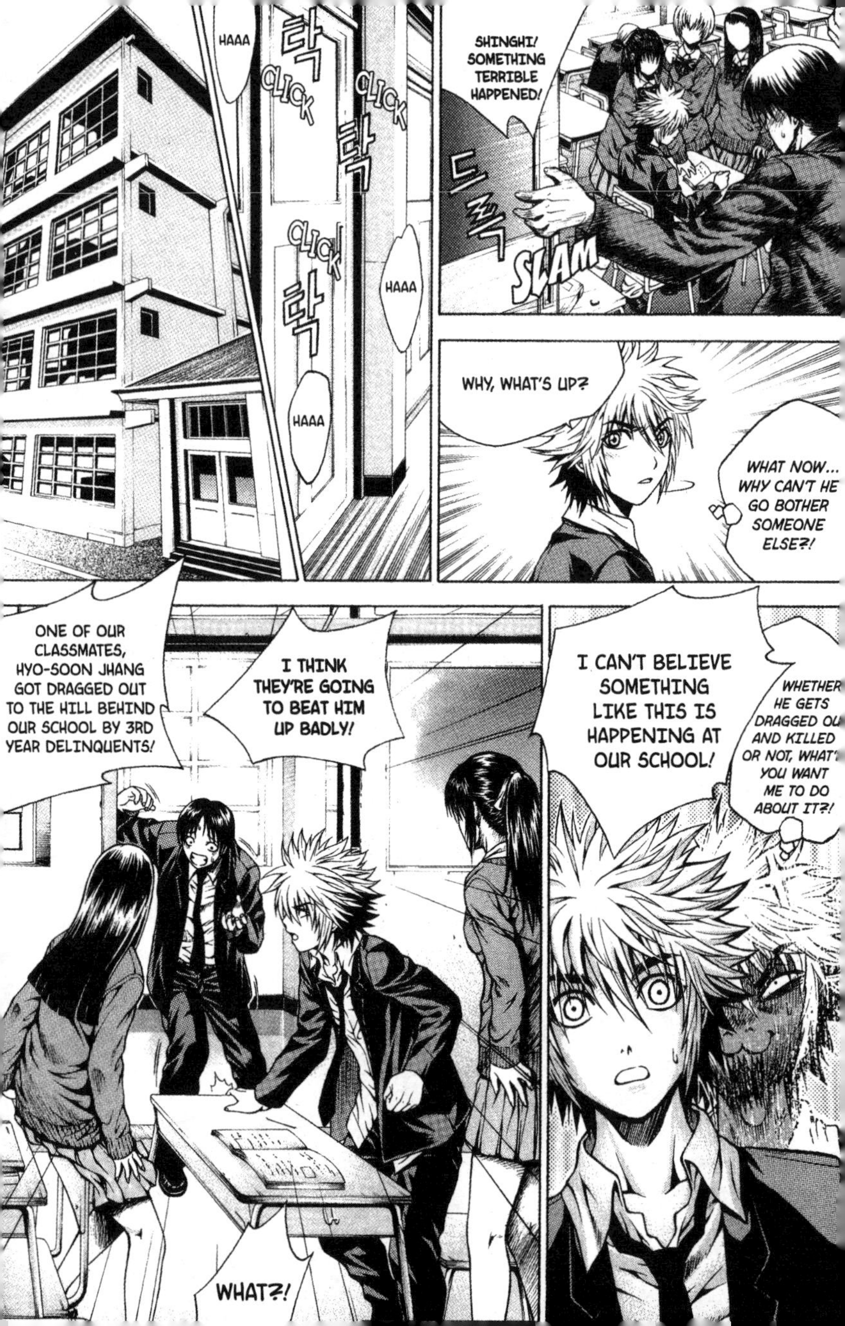
HAAA
CLICK
탁
CLICK
탁
CLICK
탁
HAAA
HAAA
SHINGHI! SOMETHING TERRIBLE HAPPENED!
SLAM
WHY, WHAT'S UP?
WHAT NOW... WHY CAN'T HE GO BOTHER SOMEONE ELSE?!
ONE OF OUR CLASSMATES, HYO-SOON JHANG GOT DRAGGED OUT TO THE HILL BEHIND OUR SCHOOL BY 3RD YEAR DELINQUENTS!
I THINK THEY'RE GOING TO BEAT HIM UP BADLY!
WHAT?!
I CAN'T BELIEVE SOMETHING LIKE THIS IS HAPPENING AT OUR SCHOOL!
WHETHER HE GETS DRAGGED OU AND KILLED OR NOT, WHAT' YOU WANT ME TO DO ABOUT IT?!

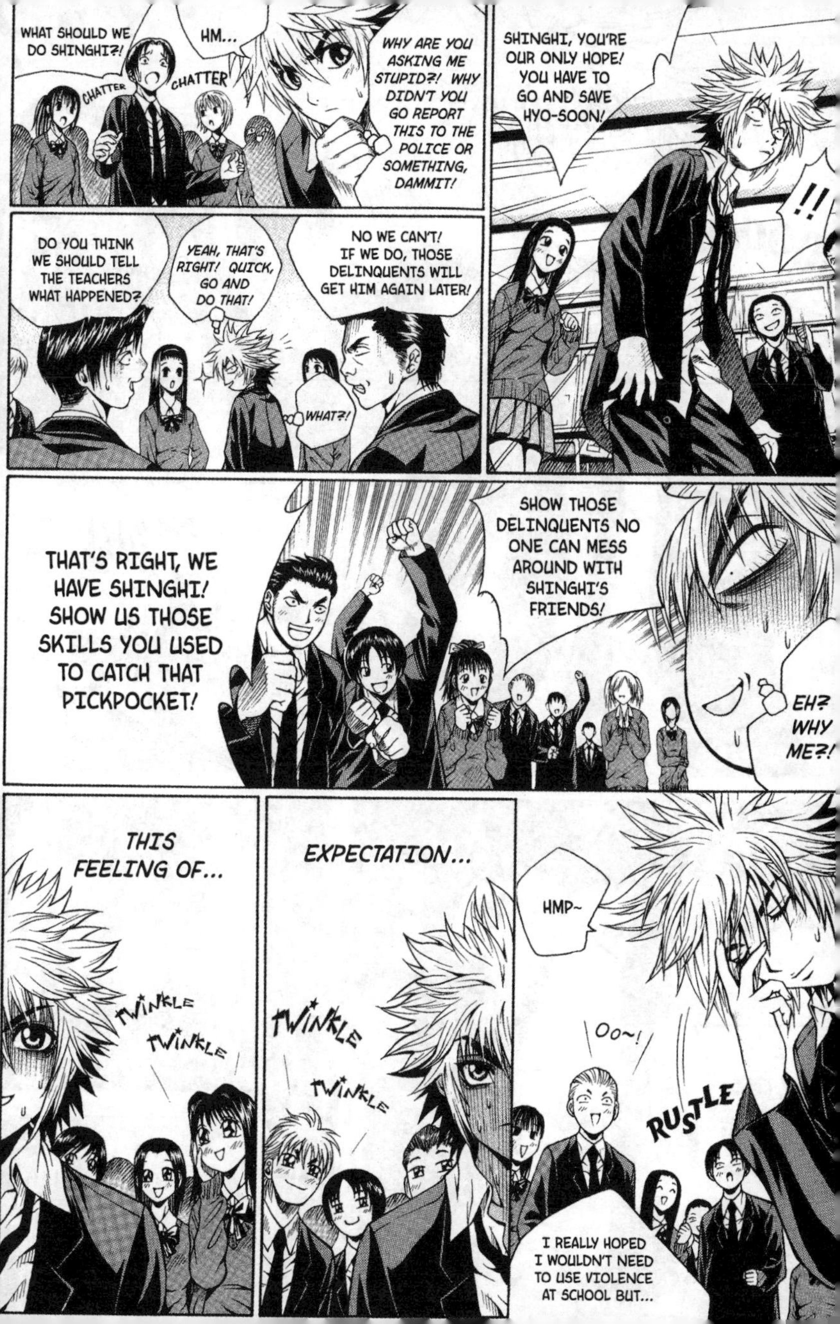
WHAT SHOULD WE DO SHINGHI?!
CHATTER
CHATTER
HM...
WHY ARE YOU ASKING ME STUPID?! WHY DIDN'T YOU GO REPORT THIS TO THE POLICE OR SOMETHING, DAMMIT!
SHINGHI, YOU'RE OUR ONLY HOPE! YOU HAVE TO GO AND SAVE HYO-SOON!
!!
DO YOU THINK WE SHOULD TELL THE TEACHERS WHAT HAPPENED?
YEAH, THAT'S RIGHT! QUICK, GO AND DO THAT!
NO WE CAN'T! IF WE DO, THOSE DELINQUENTS WILL GET HIM AGAIN LATER!
WHAT?!
THAT'S RIGHT, WE HAVE SHINGHI! SHOW US THOSE SKILLS YOU USED TO CATCH THAT PICKPOCKET!
SHOW THOSE DELINQUENTS NO ONE CAN MESS AROUND WITH SHINGHI'S FRIENDS!
EH? WHY ME?!
THIS FEELING OF...
TWINKLE
TWINKLE
EXPECTATION...
TWINKLE
TWINKLE
HMP~
OO~!
RUSTLE
I REALLY HOPED I WOULDN'T NEED TO USE VIOLENCE AT SCHOOL BUT...

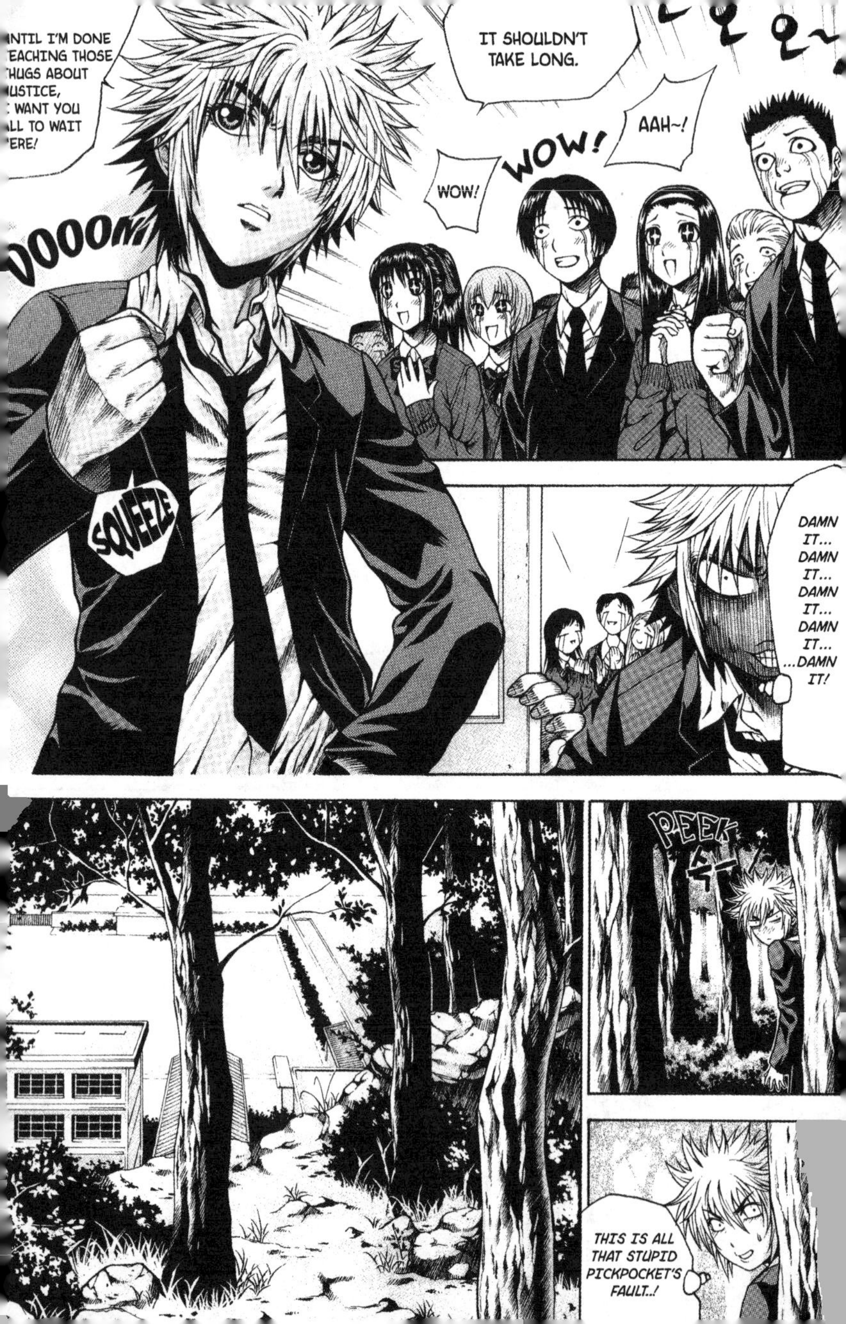
NTIL I'M DONE
EACHING THOSE
HUGS ABOUT
USTICE,
WANT YOU
LL TO WAIT
ERE!
VOOOM
SQUEEZE
IT SHOULDN'T TAKE LONG.
WOW!
WOW!
AAH~!
DAMN IT... DAMN IT... DAMN IT... DAMN IT... ...DAMN IT!
PEEK
THIS IS ALL THAT STUPID PICKPOCKET'S FAULT..!

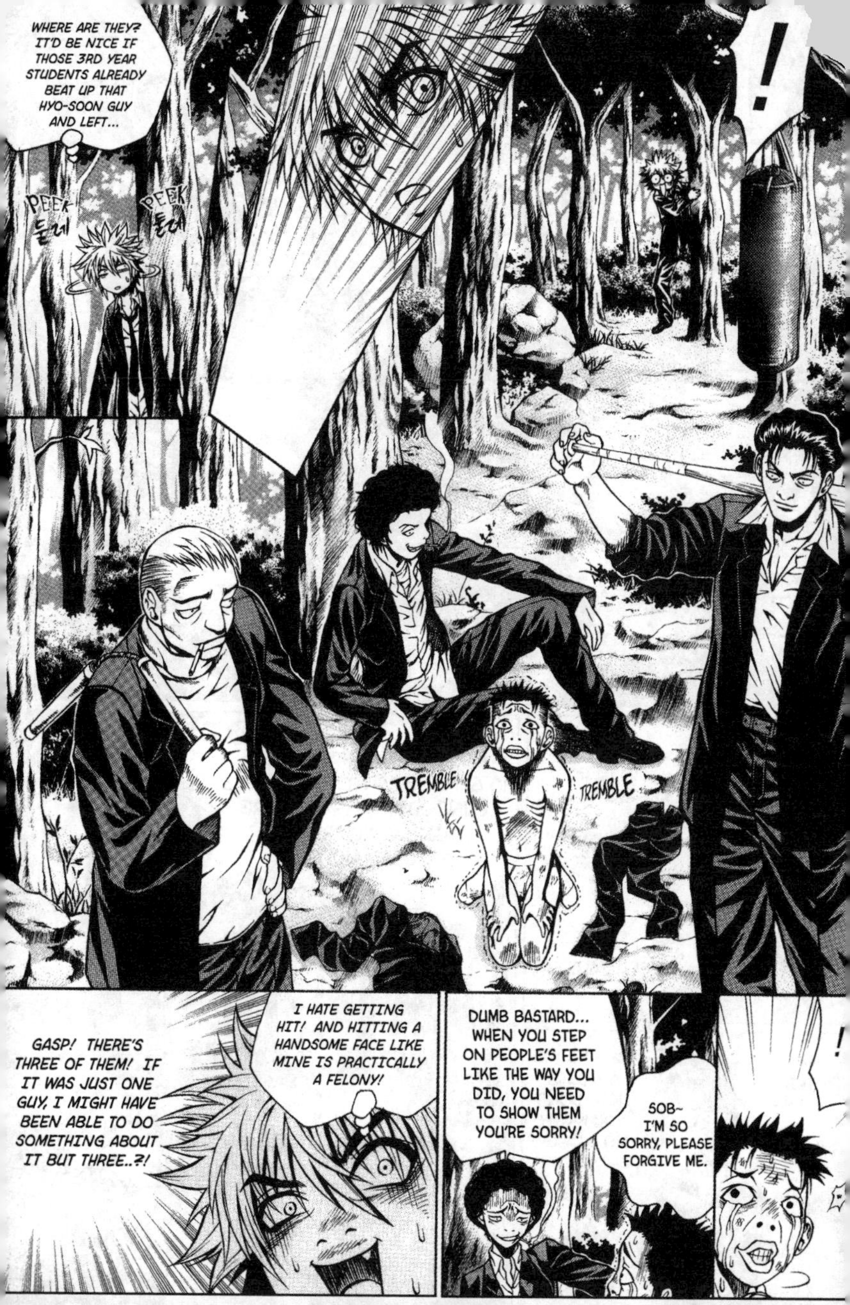

WHERE ARE THEY? IT'D BE NICE IF THOSE 3RD YEAR STUDENTS ALREADY BEAT UP THAT HYO-SOON GUY AND LEFT...
PEEK 둘레
PEEK 둘레
!
TREMBLE
TREMBLE
GASP! THERE'S THREE OF THEM! IF IT WAS JUST ONE GUY, I MIGHT HAVE BEEN ABLE TO DO SOMETHING ABOUT IT BUT THREE..?!
I HATE GETTING HIT! AND HITTING A HANDSOME FACE LIKE MINE IS PRACTICALLY A FELONY!
DUMB BASTARD... WHEN YOU STEP ON PEOPLE'S FEET LIKE THE WAY YOU DID, YOU NEED TO SHOW THEM YOU'RE SORRY!
SOB~ I'M SO SORRY, PLEASE FORGIVE ME.
!

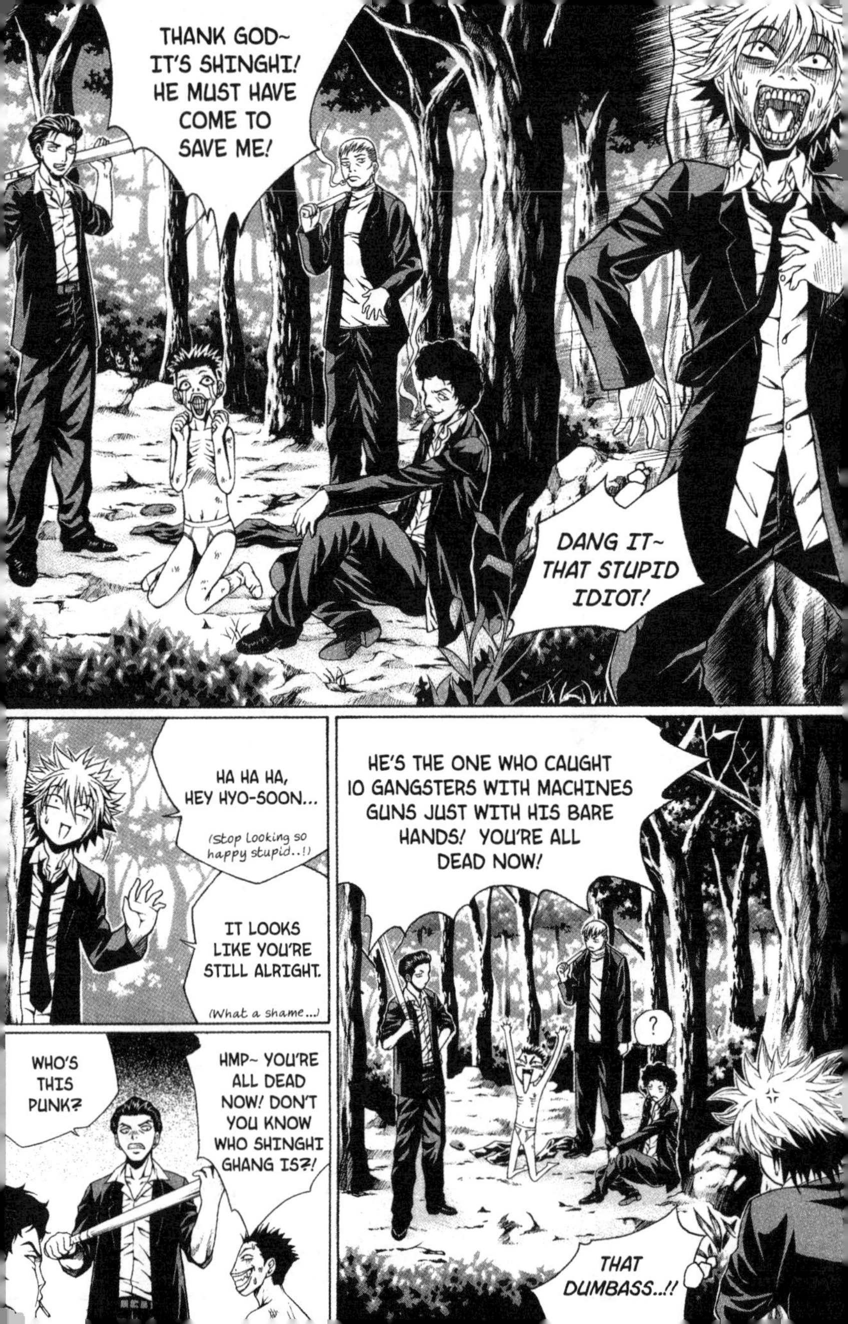
THANK GOD~ IT'S SHINGHI! HE MUST HAVE COME TO SAVE ME!
DANG IT~ THAT STUPID IDIOT!
HA HA HA, HEY HYO-SOON...
(Stop Looking so happy stupid..!)
IT LOOKS LIKE YOU'RE STILL ALRIGHT.
(What a shame...)
WHO'S THIS PUNK?
HMP~ YOU'RE ALL DEAD NOW! DON'T YOU KNOW WHO SHINGHI GHANG IS?!
HE'S THE ONE WHO CAUGHT 10 GANGSTERS WITH MACHINES GUNS JUST WITH HIS BARE HANDS! YOU'RE ALL DEAD NOW!
?
THAT DUMBASS..!!

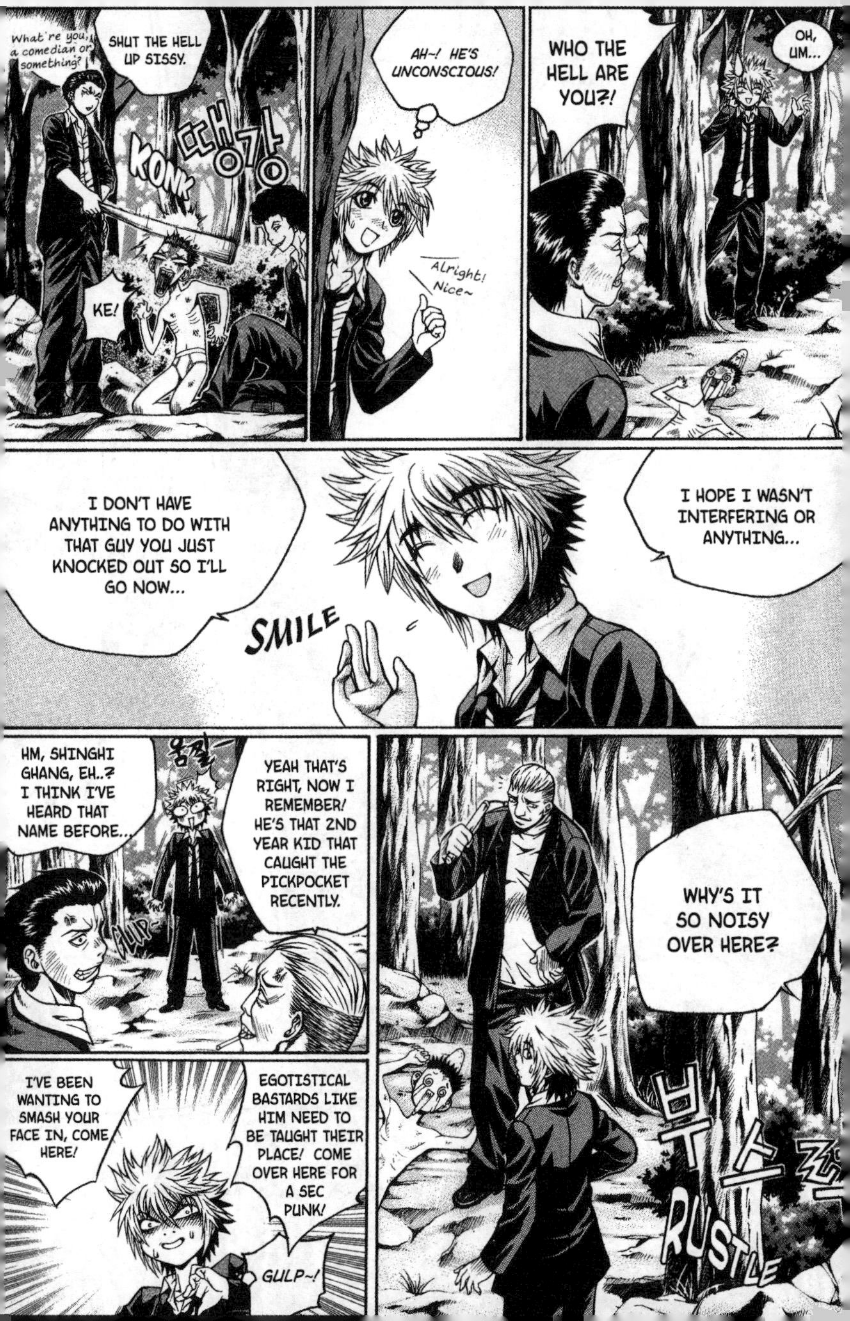
What're you, a comedian or something?
SHUT THE HELL UP SISSY.
KONK
KE!
AH~! HE'S UNCONSCIOUS!
Alright! Nice~
WHO THE HELL ARE YOU?!
OH, UM...
I DON'T HAVE ANYTHING TO DO WITH THAT GUY YOU JUST KNOCKED OUT SO I'LL GO NOW...
SMILE
I HOPE I WASN'T INTERFERING OR ANYTHING...
HM, SHINGHI GHANG, EH..? I THINK I'VE HEARD THAT NAME BEFORE...
움찔
GLUP-
YEAH THAT'S RIGHT, NOW I REMEMBER! HE'S THAT 2ND YEAR KID THAT CAUGHT THE PICKPOCKET RECENTLY.
I'VE BEEN WANTING TO SMASH YOUR FACE IN, COME HERE!
EGOTISTICAL BASTARDS LIKE HIM NEED TO BE TAUGHT THEIR PLACE! COME OVER HERE FOR A SEC PUNK!
GULP~!
WHY'S IT SO NOISY OVER HERE?
RUSTLE

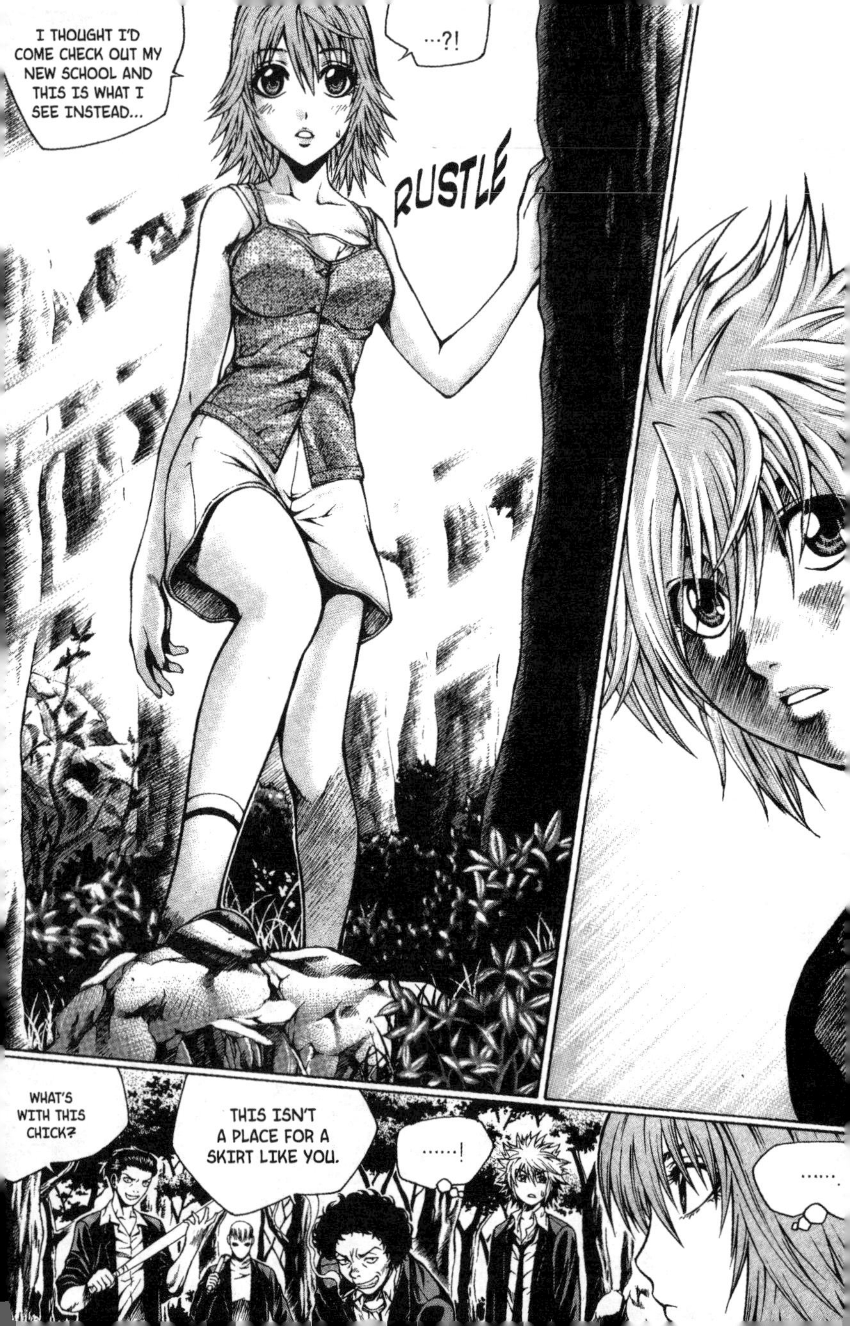
I THOUGHT I'D COME CHECK OUT MY NEW SCHOOL AND THIS IS WHAT I SEE INSTEAD...
...?!
RUSTLE
WHAT'S WITH THIS CHICK?
THIS ISN'T A PLACE FOR A SKIRT LIKE YOU.
......!
......

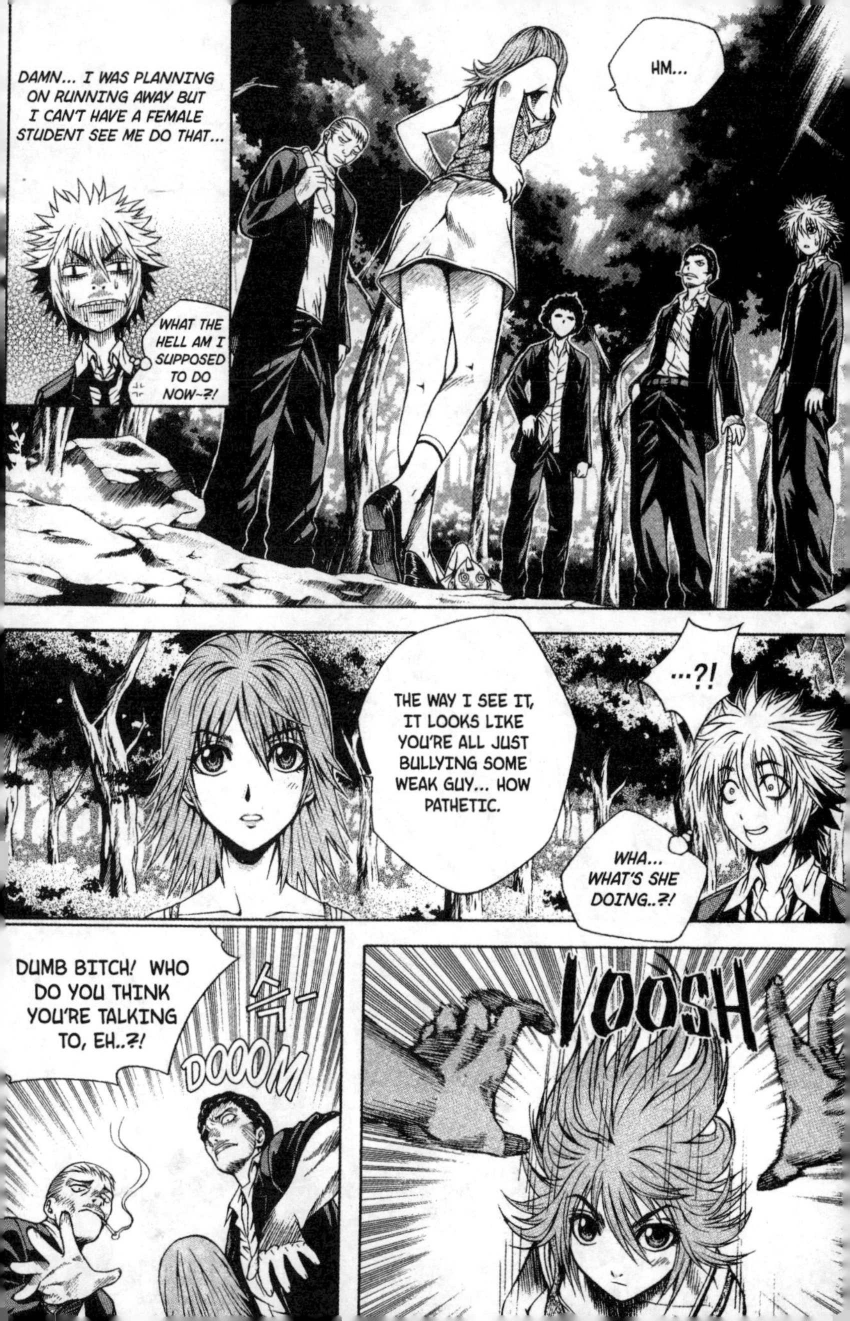
DAMN... I WAS PLANNING ON RUNNING AWAY BUT I CAN'T HAVE A FEMALE STUDENT SEE ME DO THAT...
WHAT THE HELL AM I SUPPOSED TO DO NOW~?!
HM...
THE WAY I SEE IT, IT LOOKS LIKE YOU'RE ALL JUST BULLYING SOME WEAK GUY... HOW PATHETIC.
...?!
WHA... WHAT'S SHE DOING..?!
DUMB BITCH! WHO DO YOU THINK YOU'RE TALKING TO, EH..?!
DOOOM
VOOSH

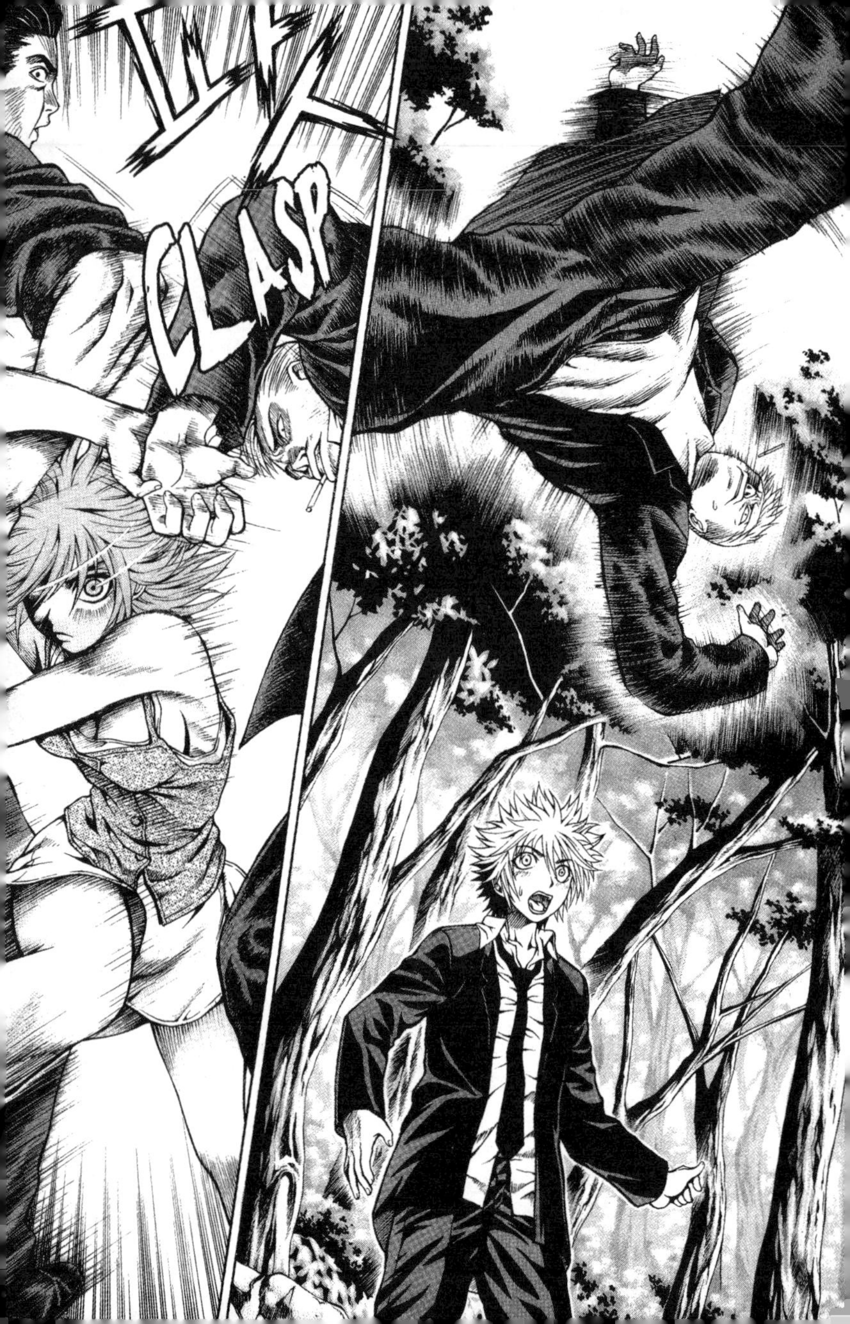
CLASP

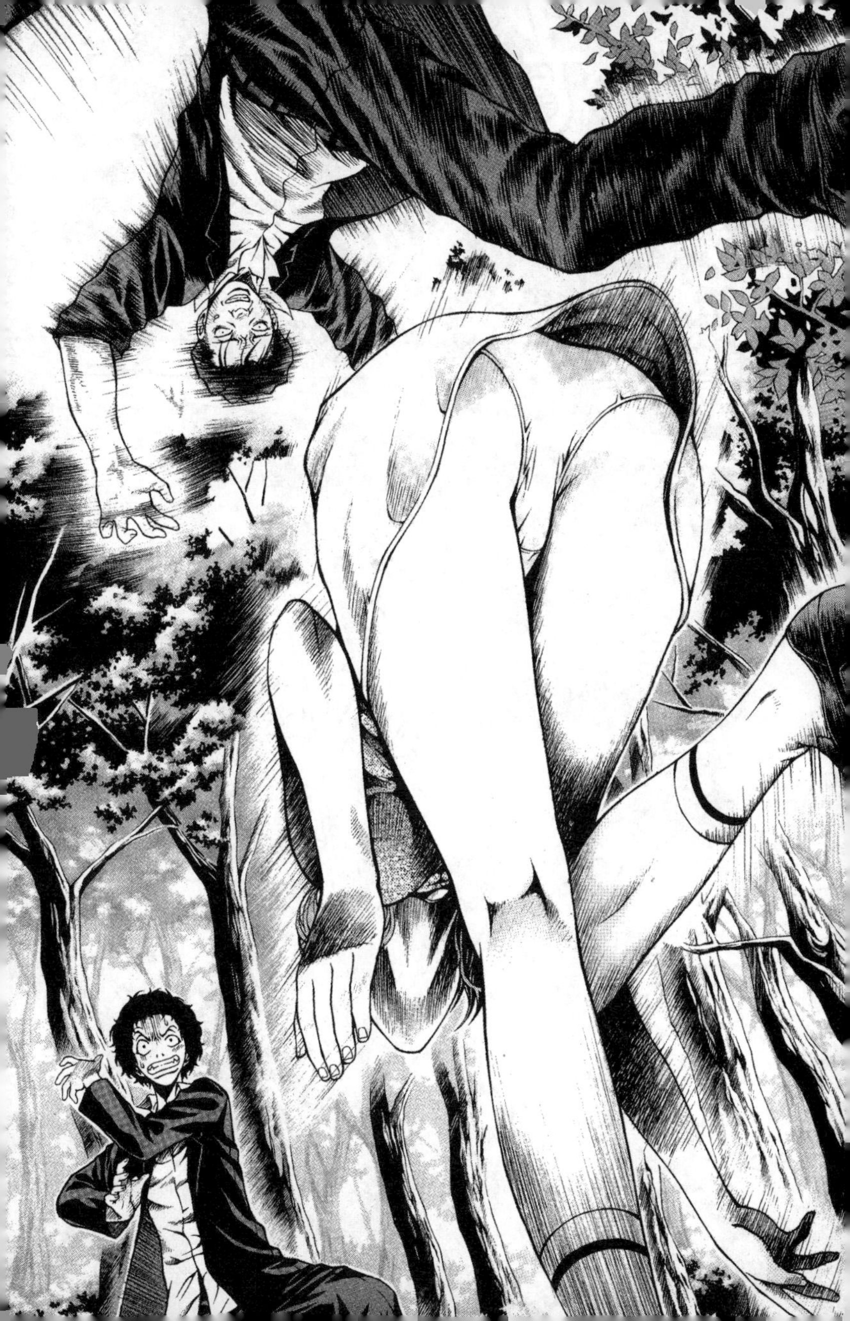

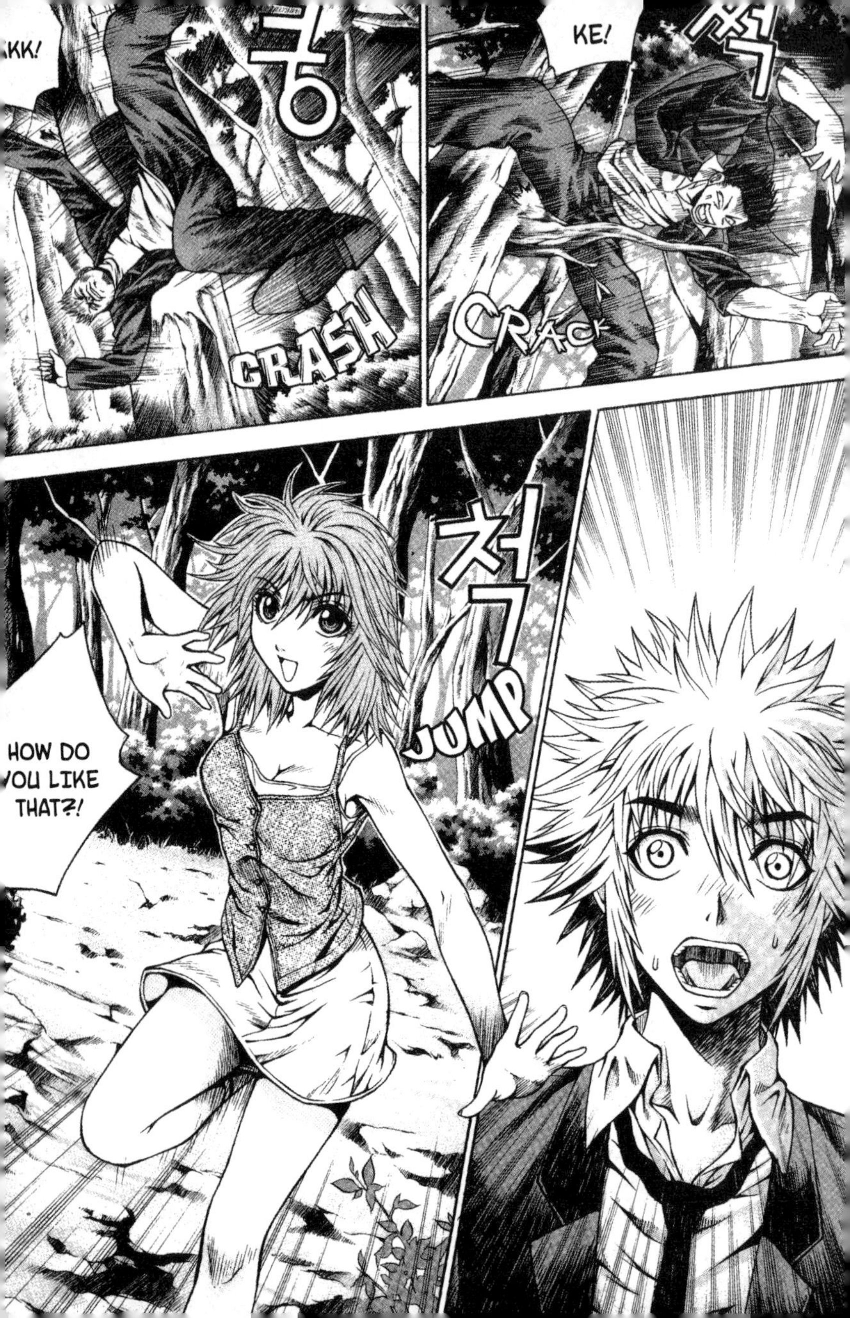
AKK!
CRASH
KE!
CRACK
HOW DO YOU LIKE THAT?!
JUMP

Chapter 2: The Young Man Meets the Young Woman

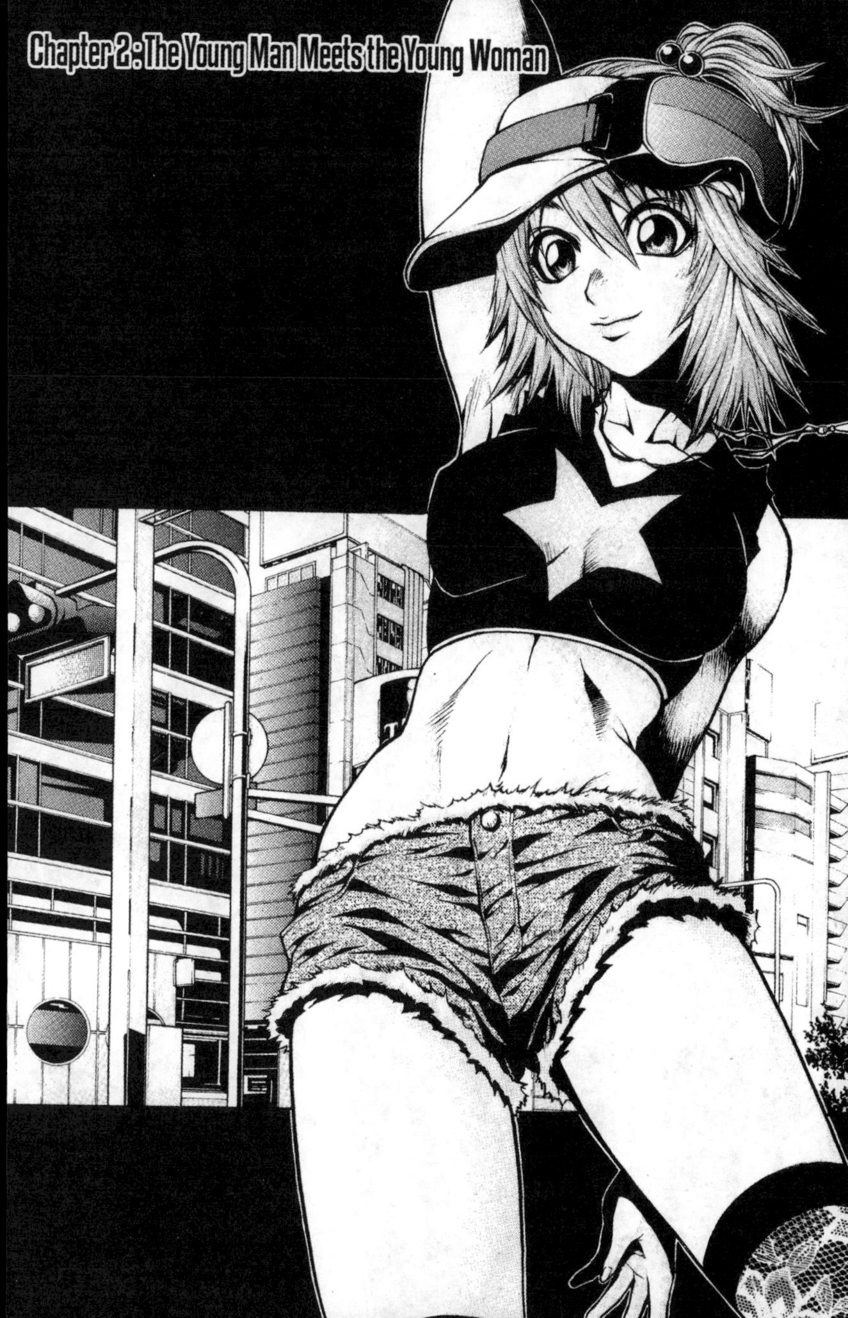

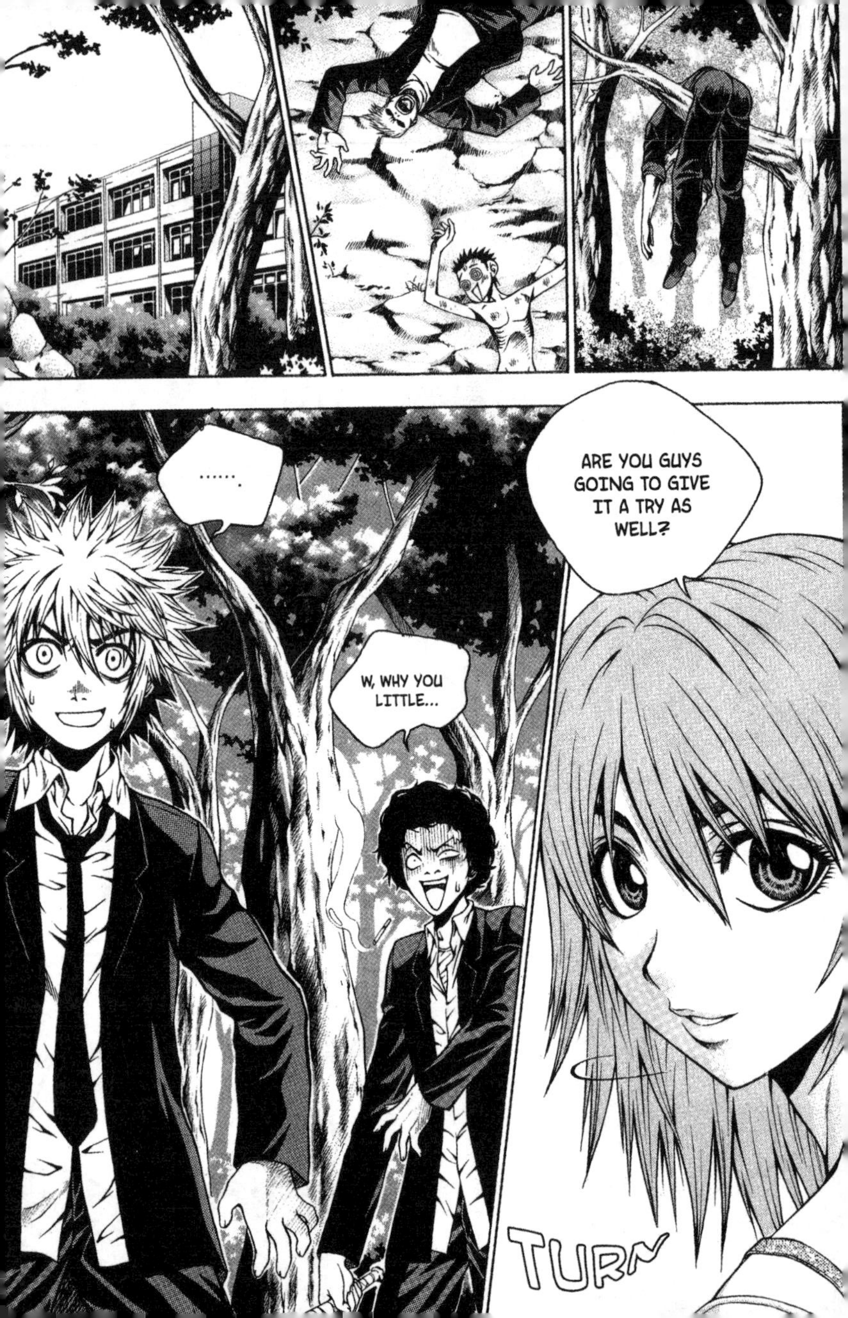
......
W, WHY YOU LITTLE...
ARE YOU GUYS GOING TO GIVE IT A TRY AS WELL?
TURN

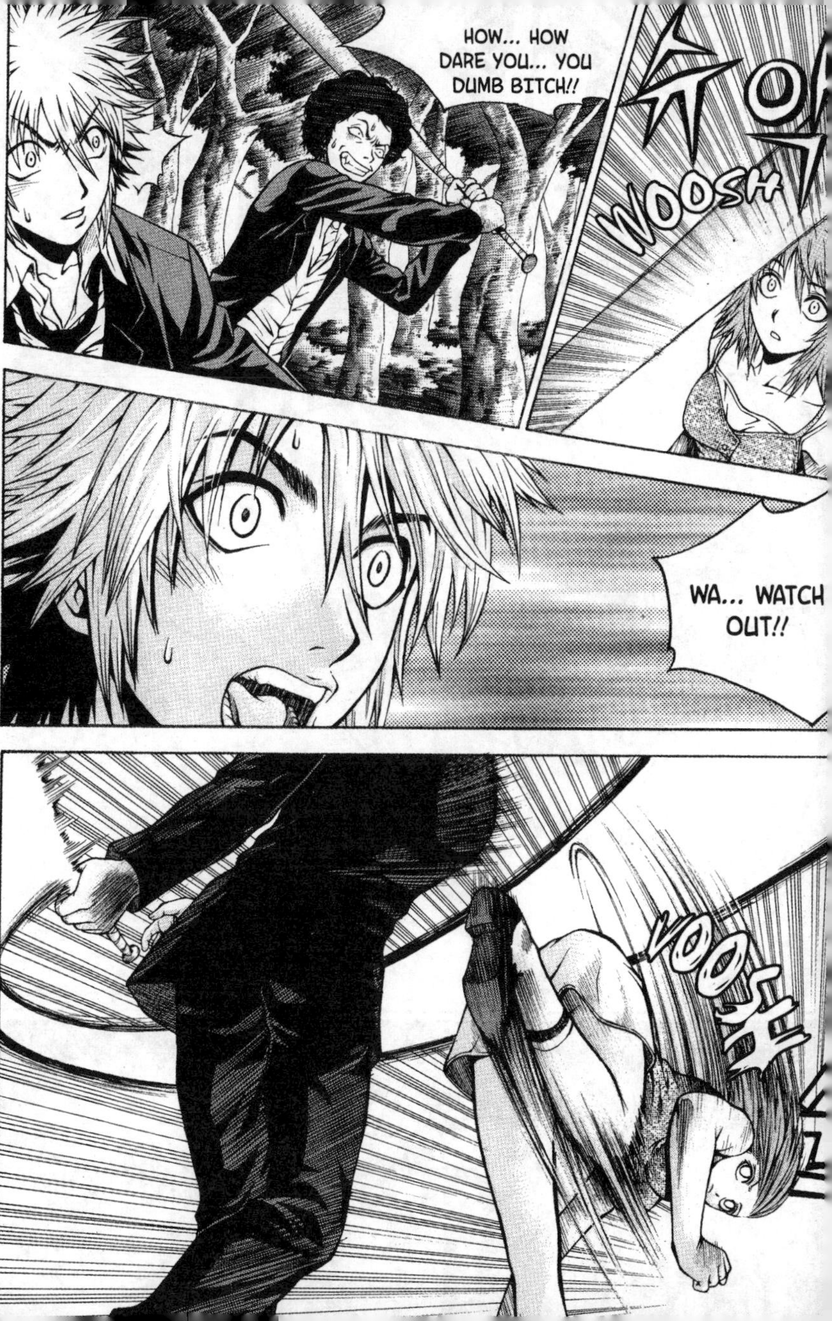
HOW... HOW DARE YOU... YOU DUMB BITCH!!
WOOSH
WA... WATCH OUT!!
WOOSH

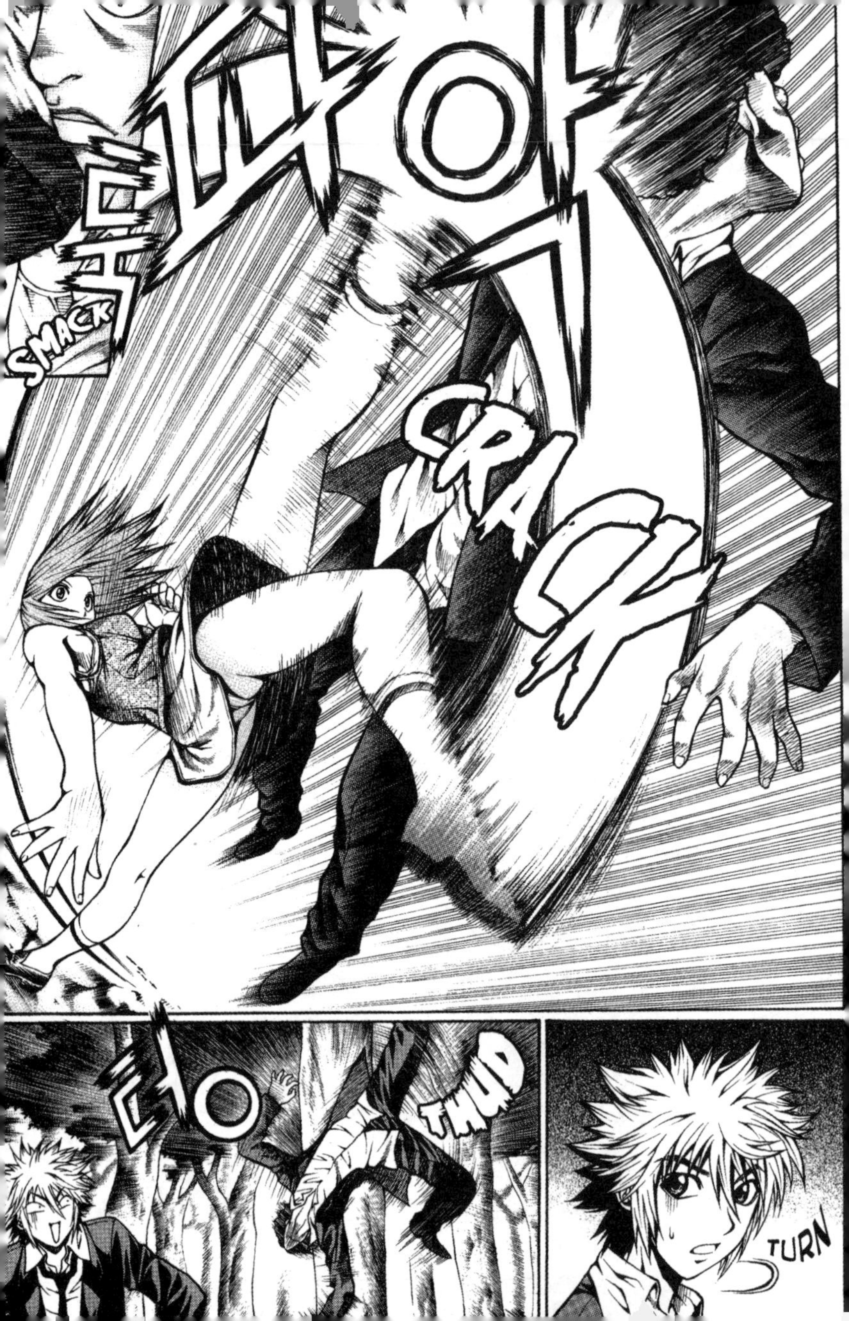
SMACK
CRACK
THUD
TURN

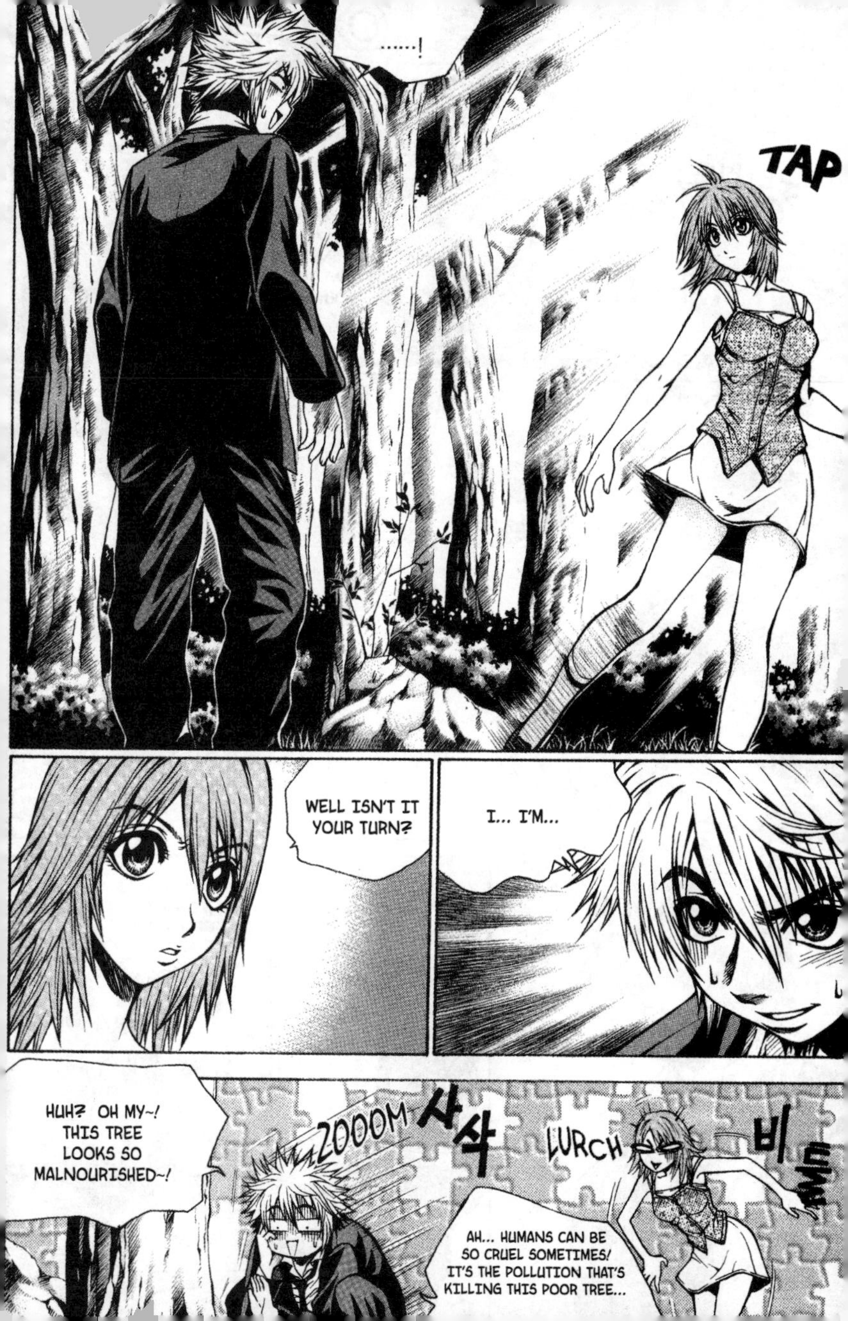
......!
TAP
WELL ISN'T IT YOUR TURN?
I... I'M...
HUH? OH MY~! THIS TREE LOOKS SO MALNOURISHED~!
ZOOOM
사삭
LURCH
비틀
AH... HUMANS CAN BE SO CRUEL SOMETIMES! IT'S THE POLLUTION THAT'S KILLING THIS POOR TREE...

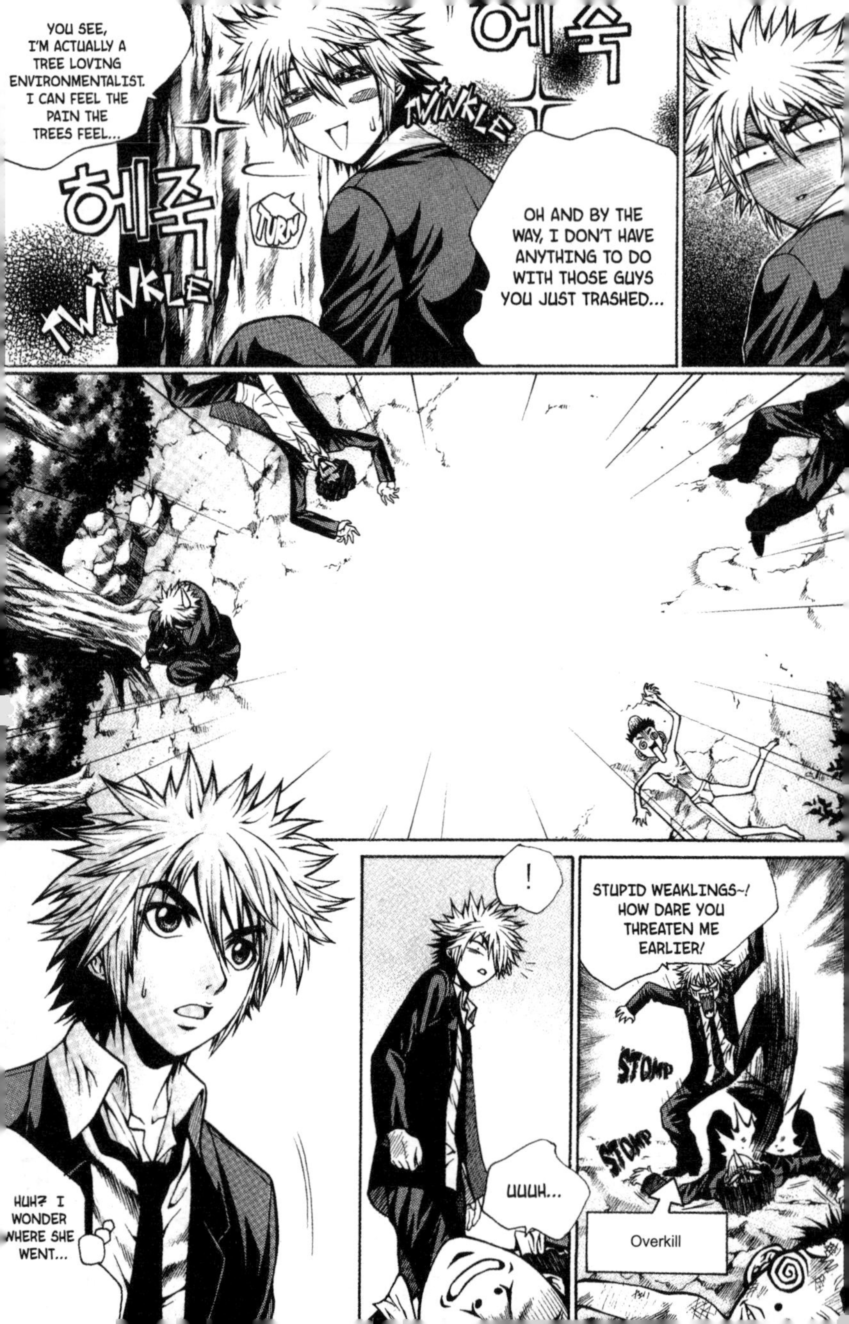
YOU SEE, I'M ACTUALLY A TREE LOVING ENVIRONMENTALIST. I CAN FEEL THE PAIN THE TREES FEEL...
헤죽
TURN
TWINKLE
TWINKLE
OH AND BY THE WAY, I DON'T HAVE ANYTHING TO DO WITH THOSE GUYS YOU JUST TRASHED...
HUH? I WONDER WHERE SHE WENT...
!
UUUH...
STUPID WEAKLINGS~! HOW DARE YOU THREATEN ME EARLIER!
STOMP
STOMP
Overkill

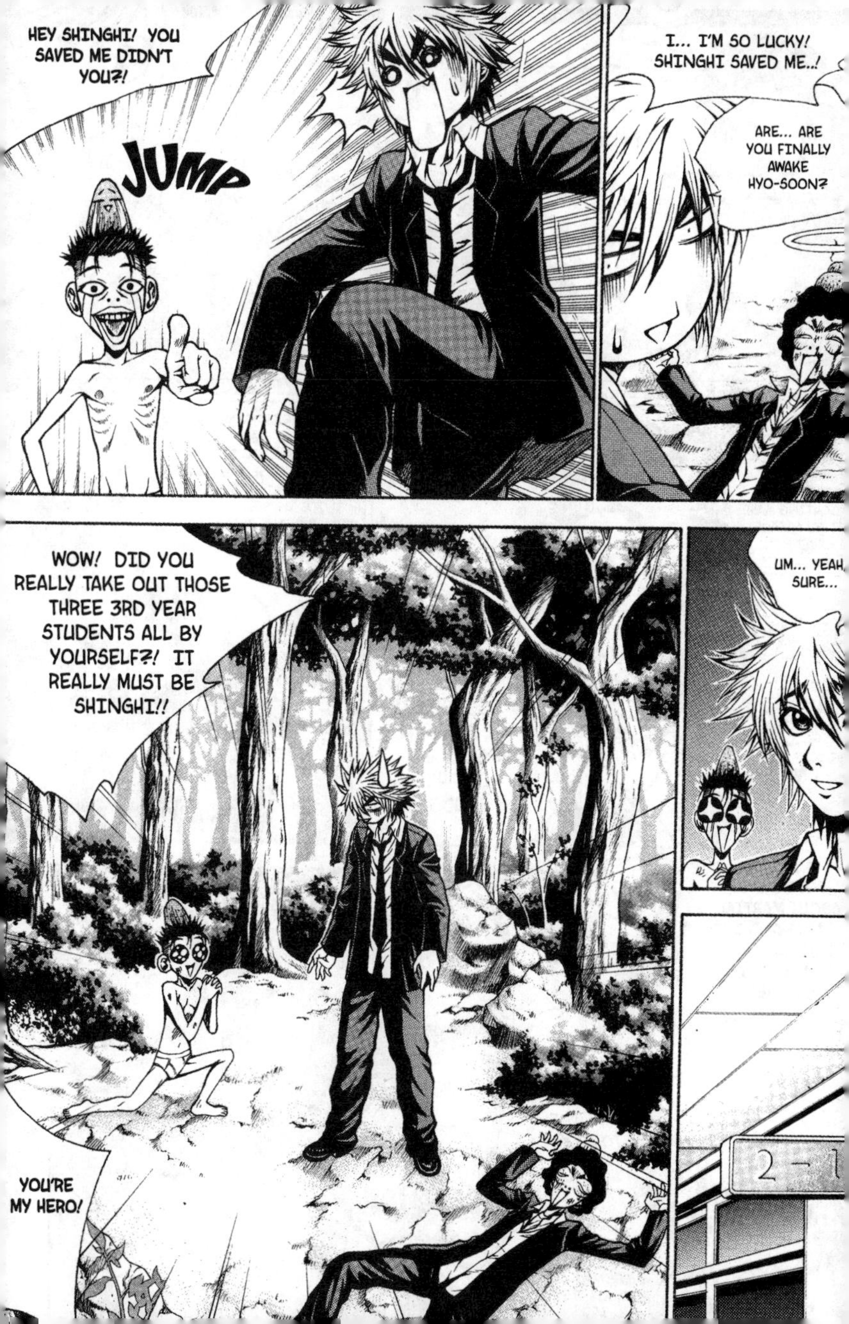

HEY SHINGHI! YOU SAVED ME DIDN'T YOU?!
JUMP
I... I'M SO LUCKY! SHINGHI SAVED ME..!
ARE... ARE YOU FINALLY AWAKE HYO-SOON?
WOW! DID YOU REALLY TAKE OUT THOSE THREE 3RD YEAR STUDENTS ALL BY YOURSELF?! IT REALLY MUST BE SHINGHI!!
YOU'RE MY HERO!
UM... YEAH, SURE...

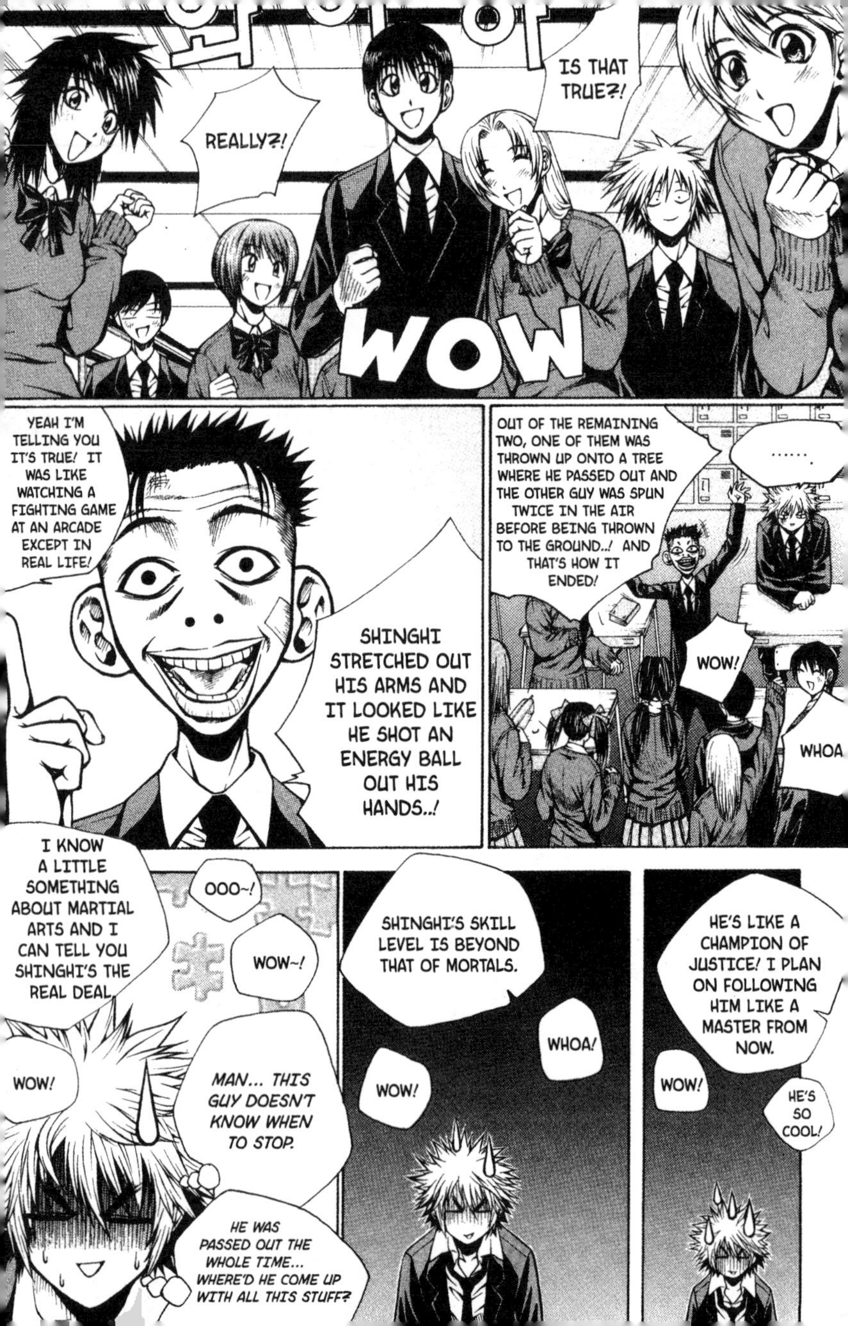
REALLY?!
IS THAT TRUE?!
WOW
YEAH I'M TELLING YOU IT'S TRUE! IT WAS LIKE WATCHING A FIGHTING GAME AT AN ARCADE EXCEPT IN REAL LIFE!
SHINGHI STRETCHED OUT HIS ARMS AND IT LOOKED LIKE HE SHOT AN ENERGY BALL OUT HIS HANDS..!
OUT OF THE REMAINING TWO, ONE OF THEM WAS THROWN UP ONTO A TREE WHERE HE PASSED OUT AND THE OTHER GUY WAS SPUN TWICE IN THE AIR BEFORE BEING THROWN TO THE GROUND..! AND THAT'S HOW IT ENDED!
....
WOW!
WHOA
I KNOW A LITTLE SOMETHING ABOUT MARTIAL ARTS AND I CAN TELL YOU SHINGHI'S THE REAL DEAL.
OOO~!
WOW~!
WOW!
MAN... THIS GUY DOESN'T KNOW WHEN TO STOP.
HE WAS PASSED OUT THE WHOLE TIME... WHERE'D HE COME UP WITH ALL THIS STUFF?
SHINGHI'S SKILL LEVEL IS BEYOND THAT OF MORTALS.
WHOA!
WOW!
HE'S LIKE A CHAMPION OF JUSTICE! I PLAN ON FOLLOWING HIM LIKE A MASTER FROM NOW.
WOW!
HE'S SO COOL!

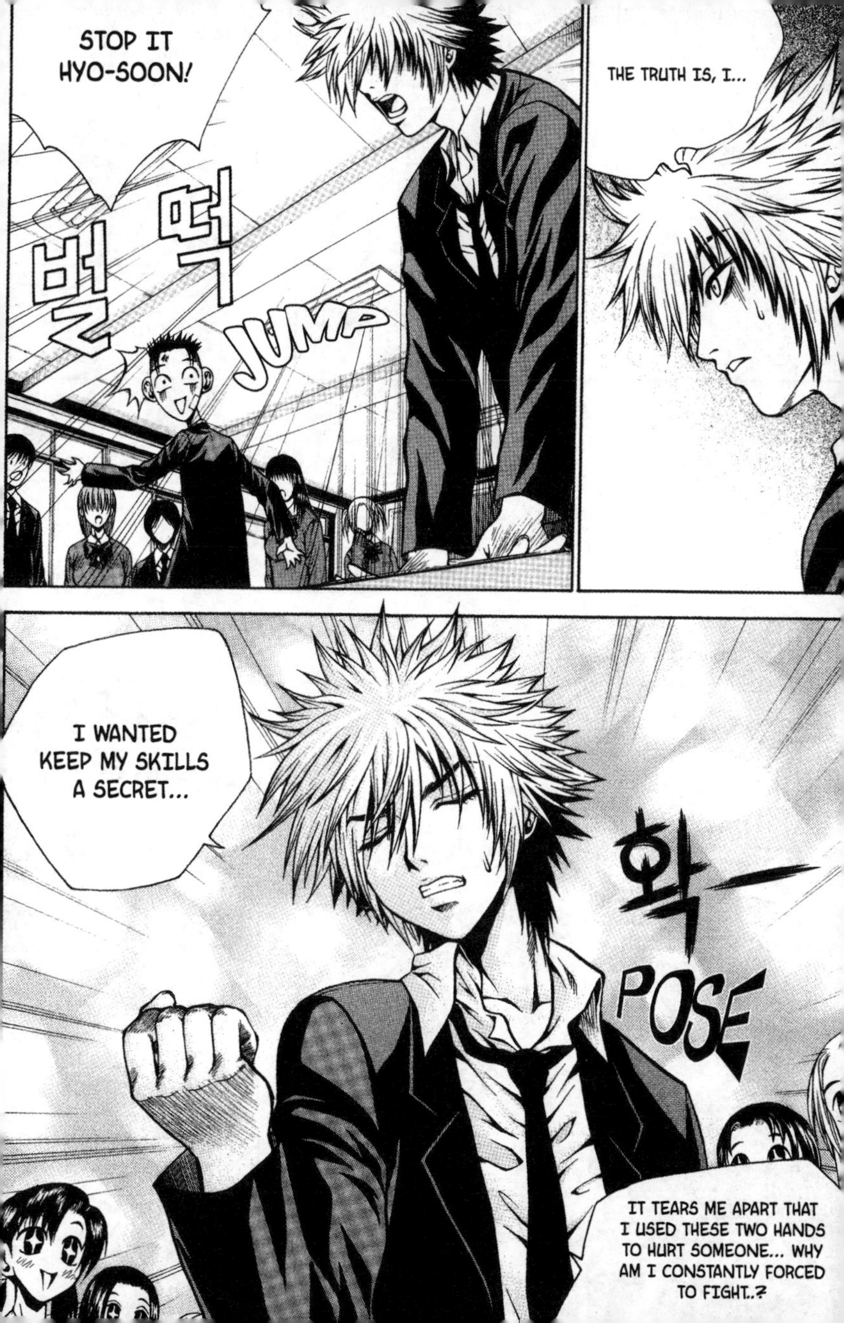
STOP IT HYO-SOON!
벌떡
JUMP
THE TRUTH IS, I...
I WANTED KEEP MY SKILLS A SECRET...
확
POSE
IT TEARS ME APART THAT I USED THESE TWO HANDS TO HURT SOMEONE... WHY AM I CONSTANTLY FORCED TO FIGHT..?

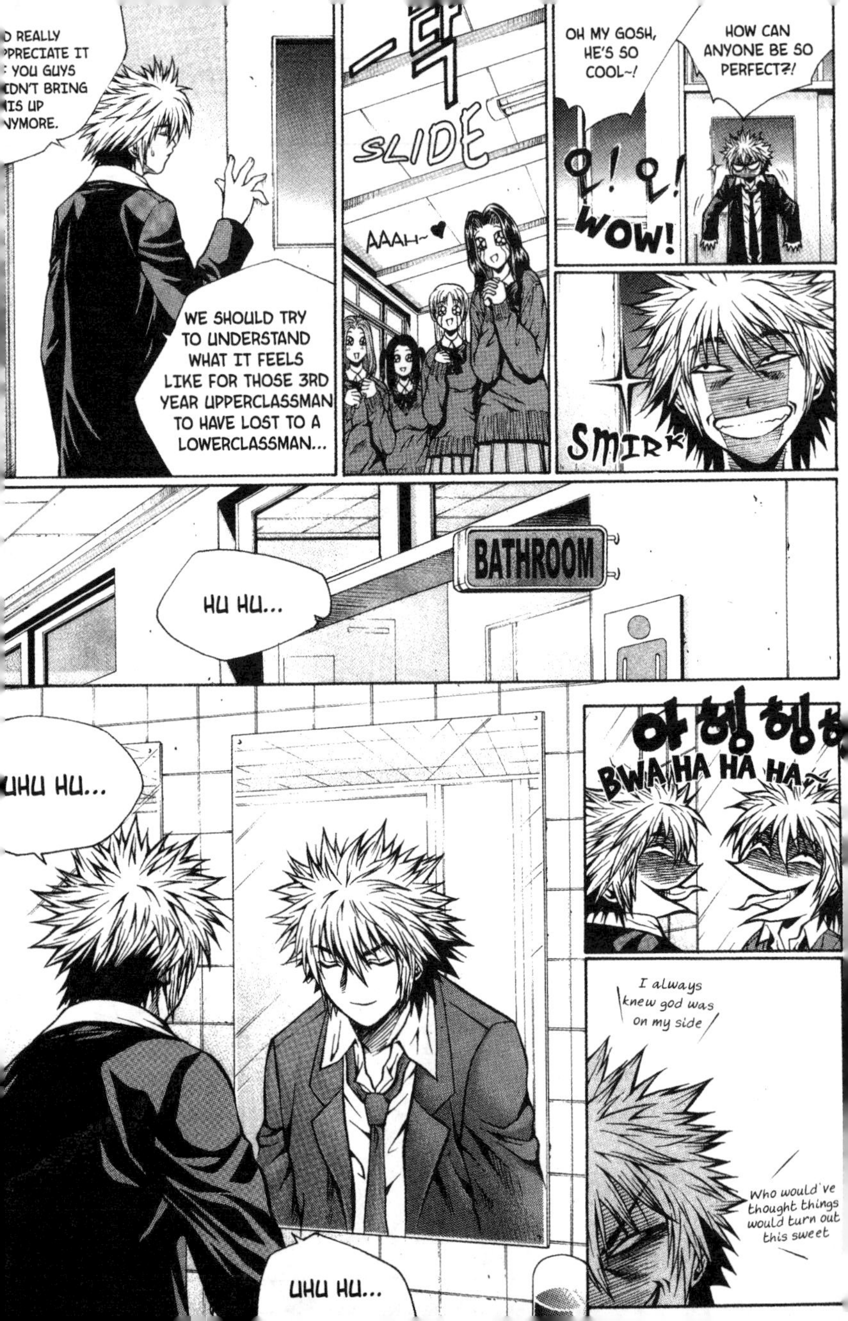
D REALLY PPRECIATE IT F YOU GUYS IDN'T BRING IS UP NYMORE.
WE SHOULD TRY TO UNDERSTAND WHAT IT FEELS LIKE FOR THOSE 3RD YEAR UPPERCLASSMAN TO HAVE LOST TO A LOWERCLASSMAN...
SLIDE
AAAH~♥
OH MY GOSH, HE'S SO COOL~!
HOW CAN ANYONE BE SO PERFECT?!
오! 오!
WOW!
SMIRK
HU HU...
BATHROOM
UHU HU...
UHU HU...
BWA HA HA HA~
I always knew god was on my side
Who would've thought things would turn out this sweet

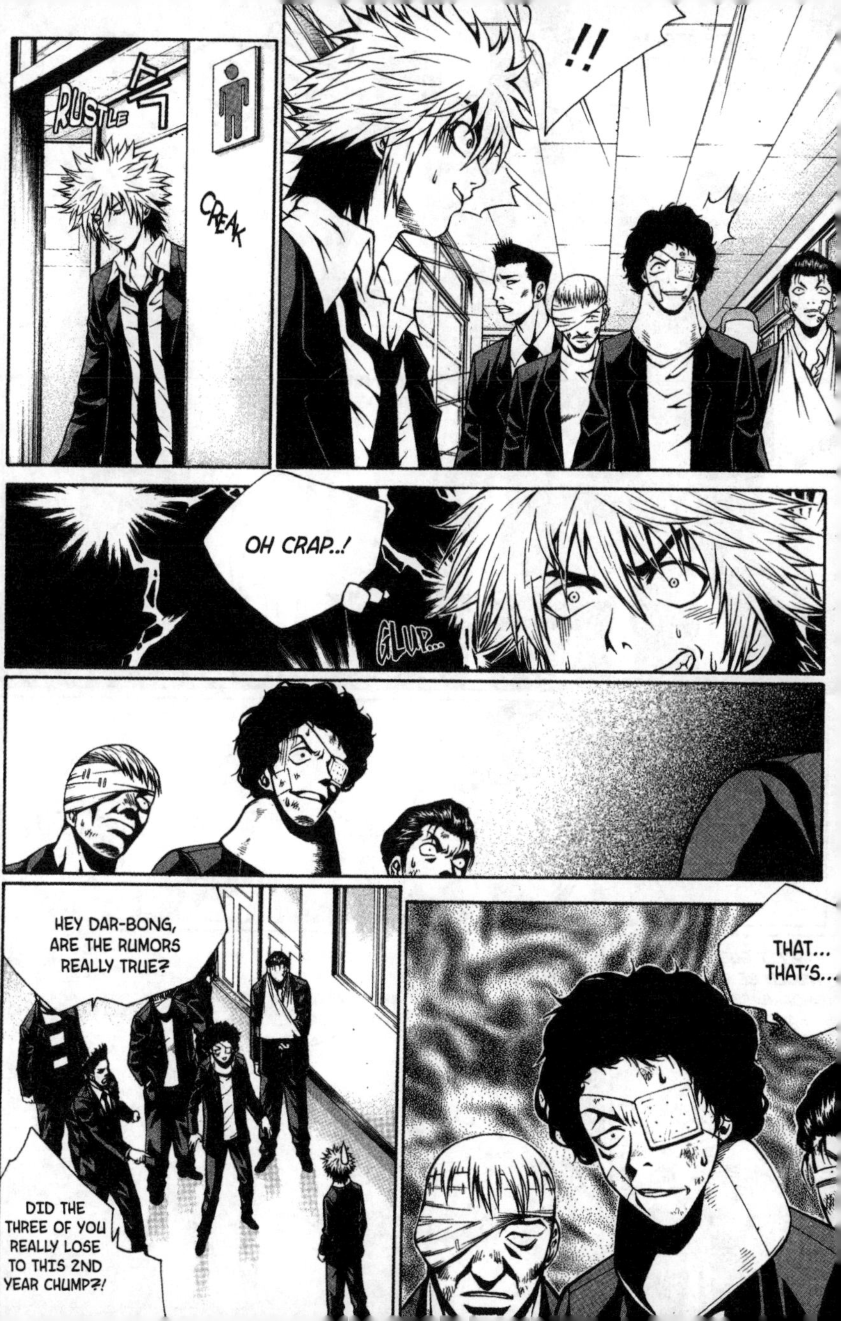
RUSTLE
CREAK
!!
OH CRAP..!
GLUP...
HEY DAR-BONG, ARE THE RUMORS REALLY TRUE?
DID THE THREE OF YOU REALLY LOSE TO THIS 2ND YEAR CHUMP?!
THAT... THAT'S...

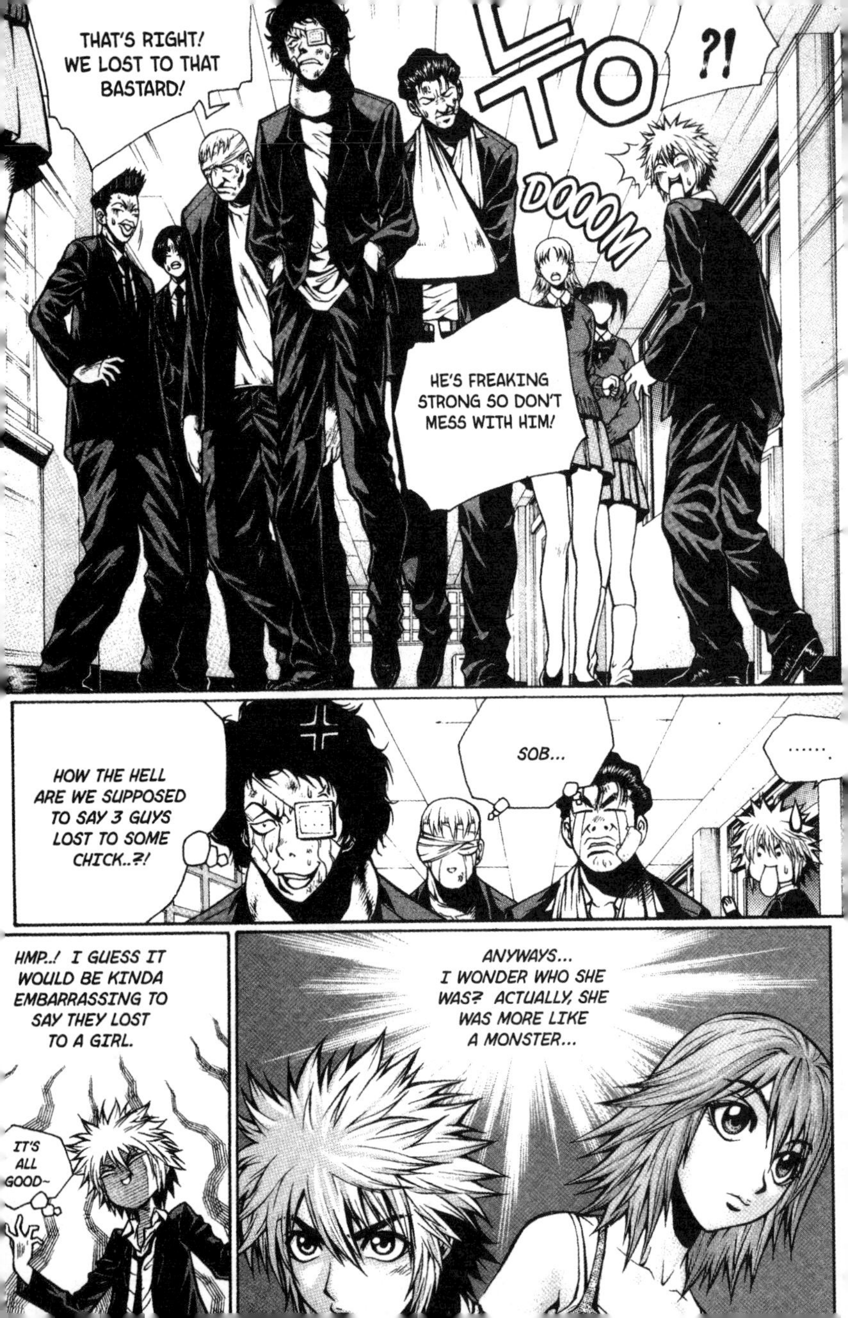
THAT'S RIGHT! WE LOST TO THAT BASTARD!
LTO
?!
DOOOM
HE'S FREAKING STRONG SO DON'T MESS WITH HIM!
HOW THE HELL ARE WE SUPPOSED TO SAY 3 GUYS LOST TO SOME CHICK..?!
SOB...
......
HMP..! I GUESS IT WOULD BE KINDA EMBARRASSING TO SAY THEY LOST TO A GIRL.
IT'S ALL GOOD~
ANYWAYS... I WONDER WHO SHE WAS? ACTUALLY, SHE WAS MORE LIKE A MONSTER...

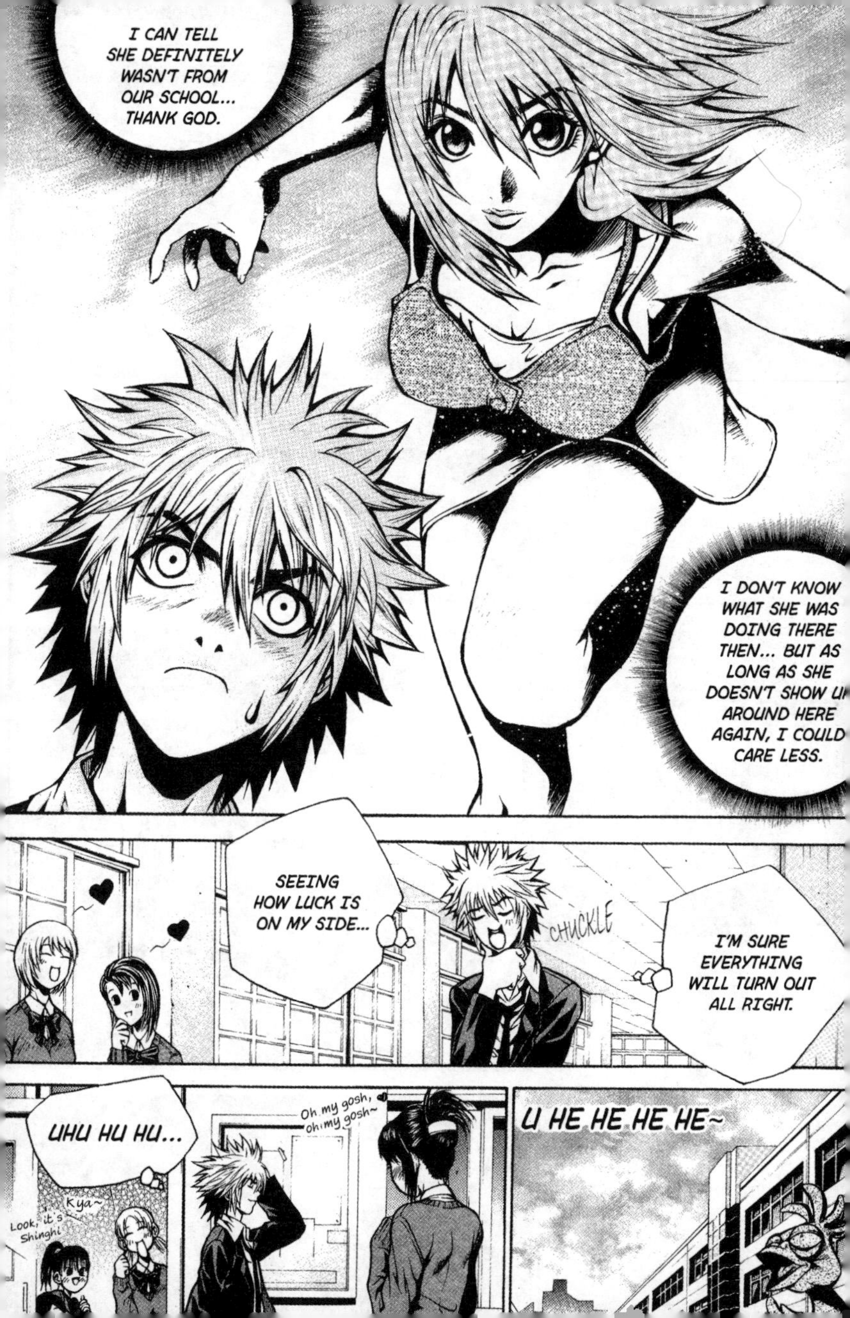
I CAN TELL SHE DEFINITELY WASN'T FROM OUR SCHOOL... THANK GOD.
I DON'T KNOW WHAT SHE WAS DOING THERE THEN... BUT AS LONG AS SHE DOESN'T SHOW U AROUND HERE AGAIN, I COULD CARE LESS.
SEEING HOW LUCK IS ON MY SIDE...
CHUCKLE
I'M SURE EVERYTHING WILL TURN OUT ALL RIGHT.
UHU HU HU...
Oh my gosh, oh my gosh~
Kya~
Look, it's Shinghi
U HE HE HE HE~

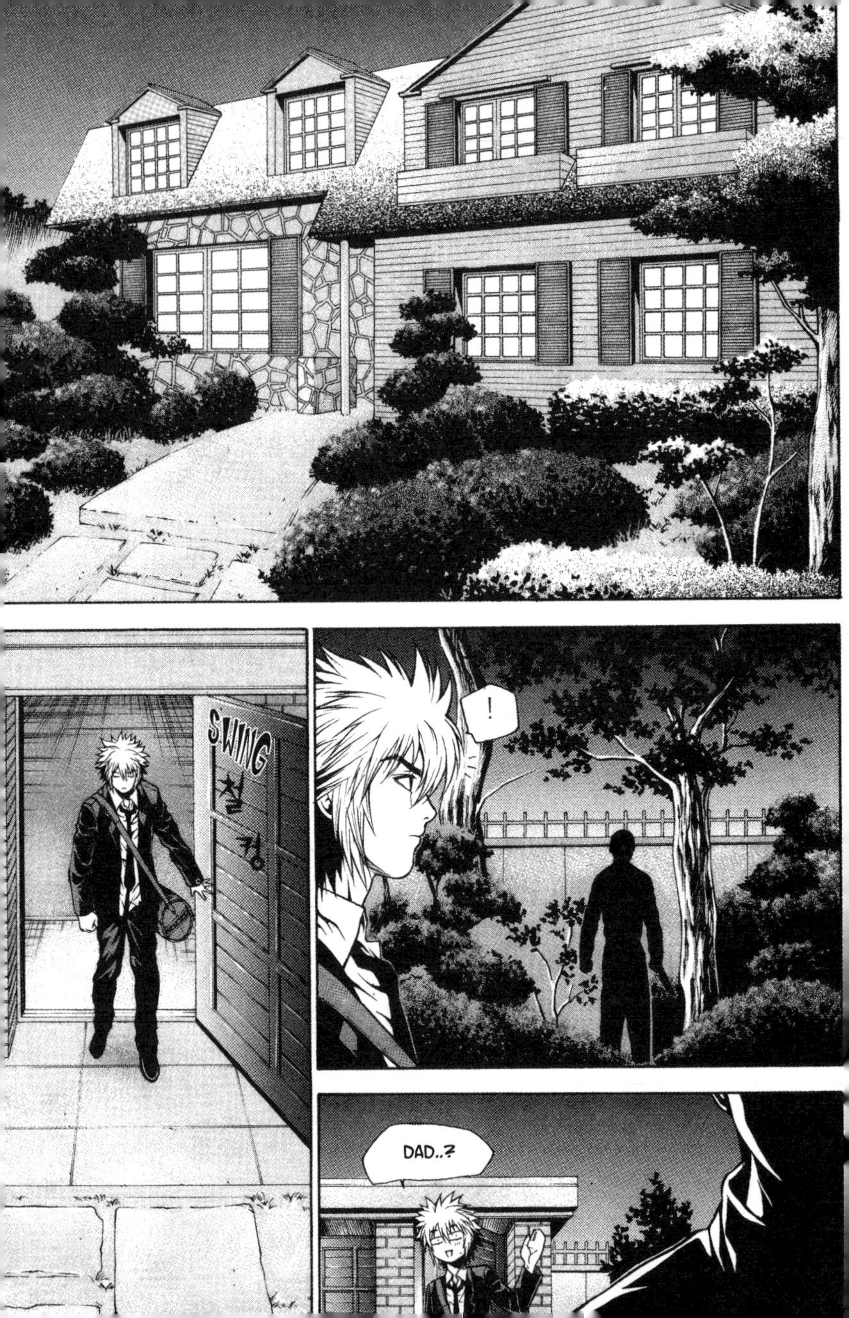
SWING
철컹
!
DAD..?

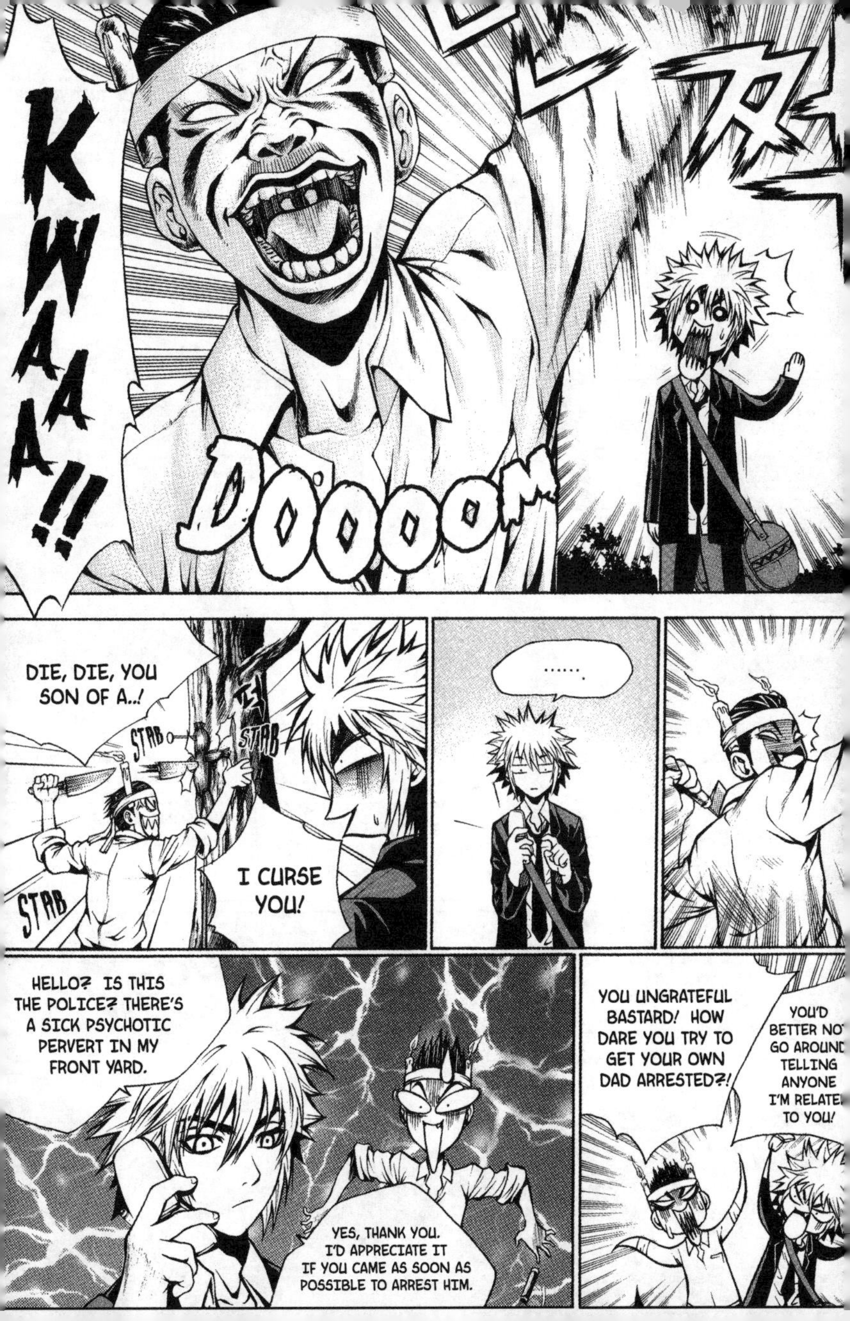
KWAAAA!!
DOOOOM
DIE, DIE, YOU SON OF A..!
STAB
STAB
STAB
I CURSE YOU!
......
HELLO? IS THIS THE POLICE? THERE'S A SICK PSYCHOTIC PERVERT IN MY FRONT YARD.
YES, THANK YOU. I'D APPRECIATE IT IF YOU CAME AS SOON AS POSSIBLE TO ARREST HIM.
YOU UNGRATEFUL BASTARD! HOW DARE YOU TRY TO GET YOUR OWN DAD ARRESTED?!
YOU'D BETTER NOT GO AROUND TELLING ANYONE I'M RELATED TO YOU!

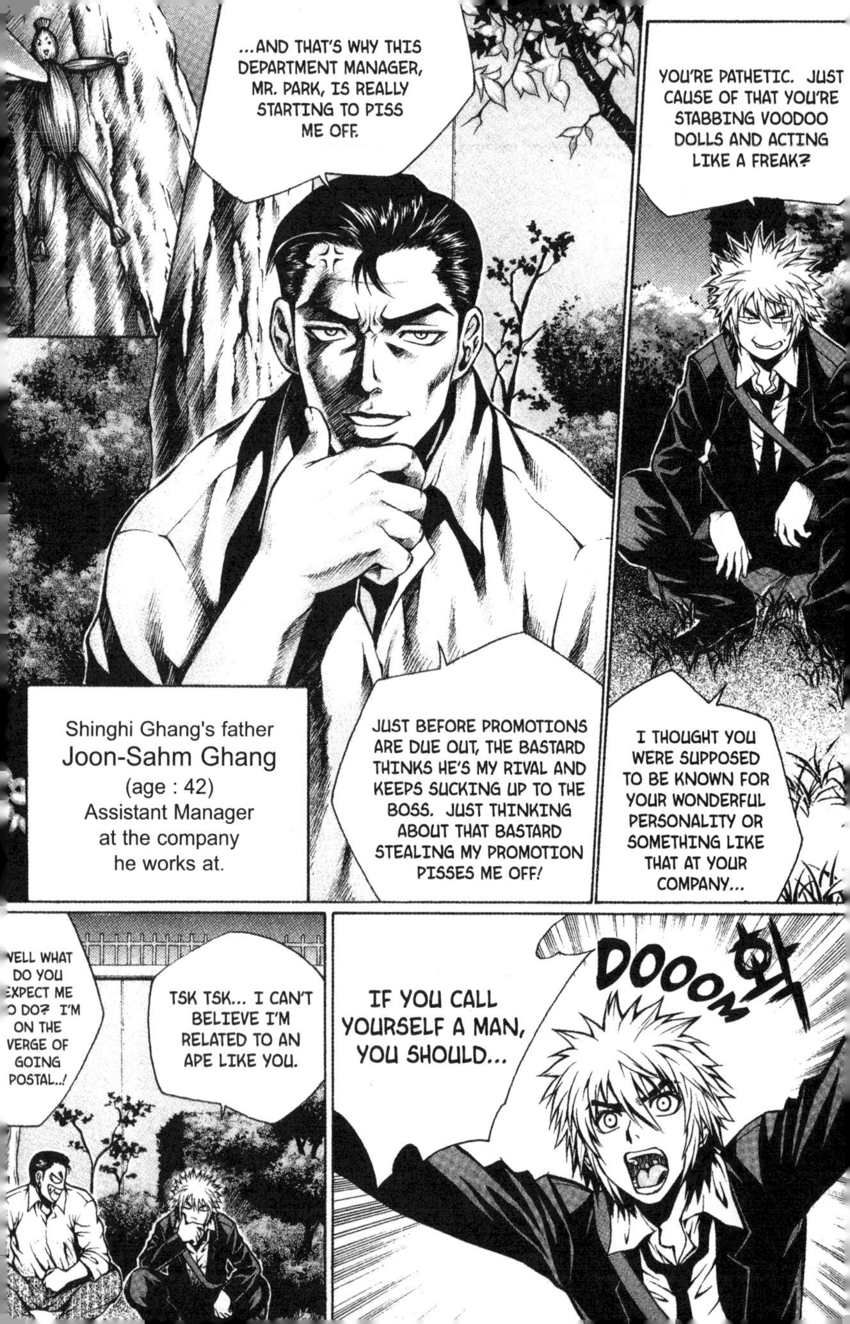
...AND THAT'S WHY THIS DEPARTMENT MANAGER, MR. PARK, IS REALLY STARTING TO PISS ME OFF.
Shinghi Ghang's father
Joon-Sahm Ghang
(age : 42)
Assistant Manager at the company he works at.
JUST BEFORE PROMOTIONS ARE DUE OUT, THE BASTARD THINKS HE'S MY RIVAL AND KEEPS SUCKING UP TO THE BOSS. JUST THINKING ABOUT THAT BASTARD STEALING MY PROMOTION PISSES ME OFF!
YOU'RE PATHETIC. JUST CAUSE OF THAT YOU'RE STABBING VOODOO DOLLS AND ACTING LIKE A FREAK?
I THOUGHT YOU WERE SUPPOSED TO BE KNOWN FOR YOUR WONDERFUL PERSONALITY OR SOMETHING LIKE THAT AT YOUR COMPANY...
VELL WHAT DO YOU EXPECT ME O DO? I'M ON THE VERGE OF GOING POSTAL..!
TSK TSK... I CAN'T BELIEVE I'M RELATED TO AN APE LIKE YOU.
IF YOU CALL YOURSELF A MAN, YOU SHOULD...
DOOOOM

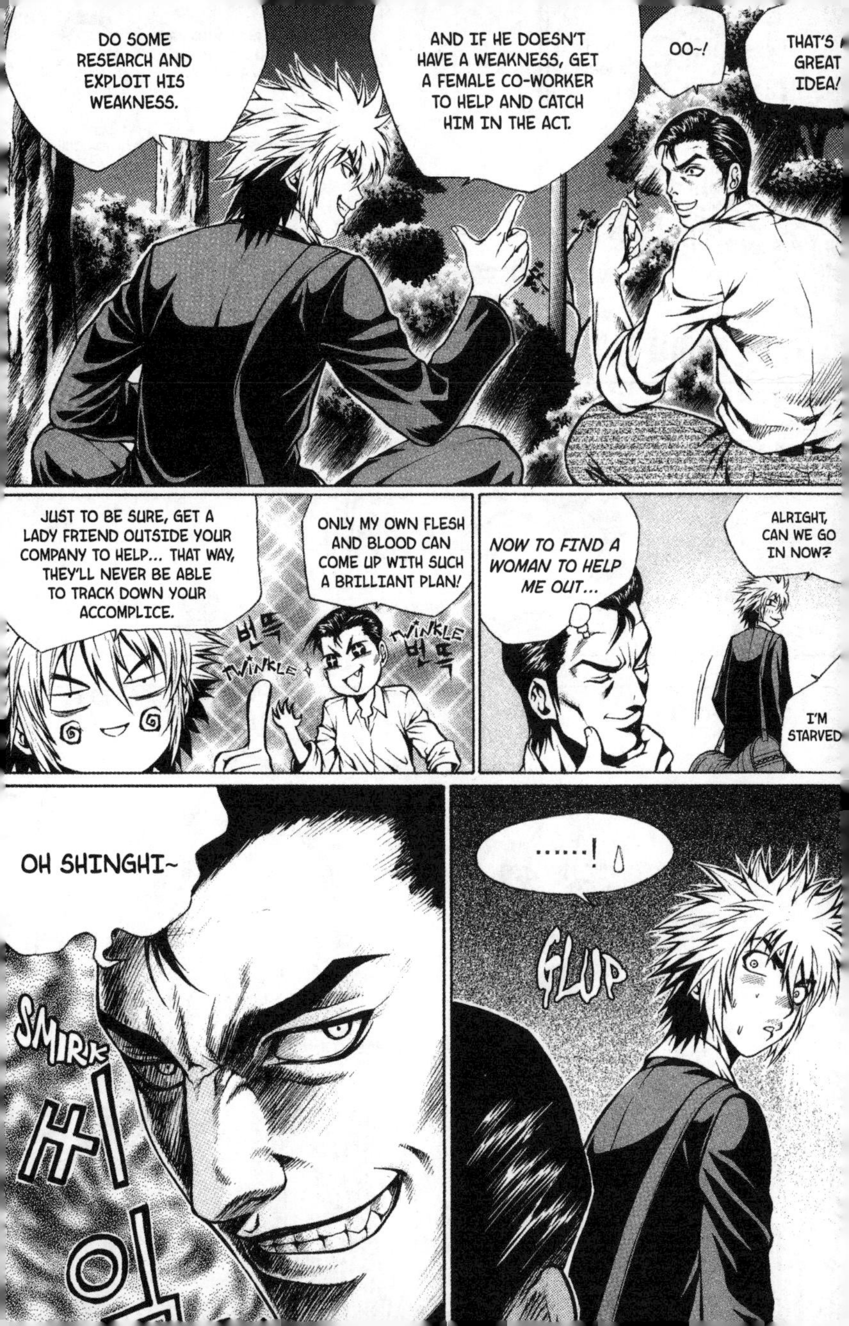
DO SOME RESEARCH AND EXPLOIT HIS WEAKNESS.
AND IF HE DOESN'T HAVE A WEAKNESS, GET A FEMALE CO-WORKER TO HELP AND CATCH HIM IN THE ACT.
OO~!
THAT'S A GREAT IDEA!
JUST TO BE SURE, GET A LADY FRIEND OUTSIDE YOUR COMPANY TO HELP... THAT WAY, THEY'LL NEVER BE ABLE TO TRACK DOWN YOUR ACCOMPLICE.
ONLY MY OWN FLESH AND BLOOD CAN COME UP WITH SUCH A BRILLIANT PLAN!
번뜩
TWINKLE
TWINKLE
번뜩
NOW TO FIND A WOMAN TO HELP ME OUT...
ALRIGHT, CAN WE GO IN NOW?
I'M STARVED
OH SHINGHI~
SMIRK
히이
......!
GLUP

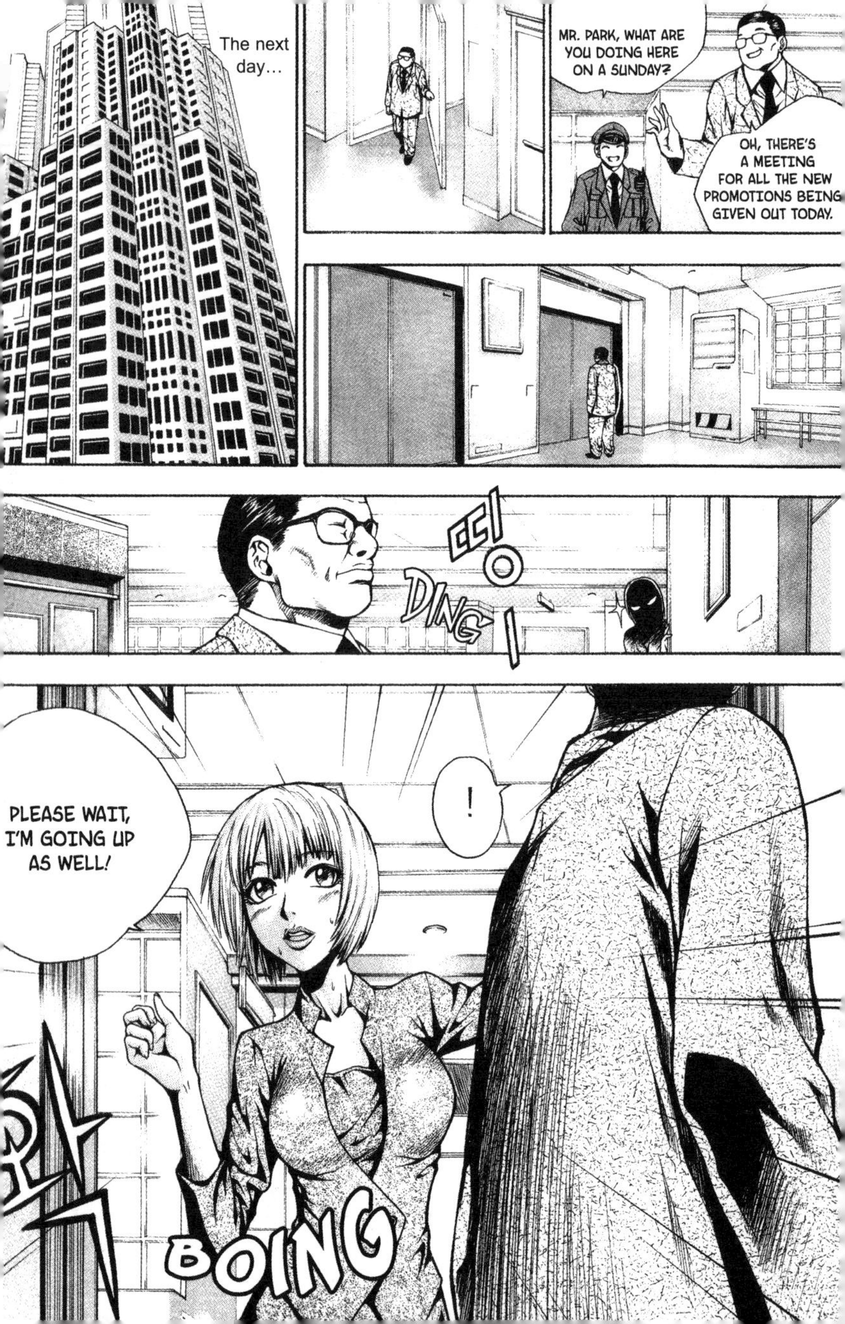
The next day...
MR. PARK, WHAT ARE YOU DOING HERE ON A SUNDAY?
OH, THERE'S A MEETING FOR ALL THE NEW PROMOTIONS BEING GIVEN OUT TODAY.
DING
PLEASE WAIT, I'M GOING UP AS WELL!
!
BOING

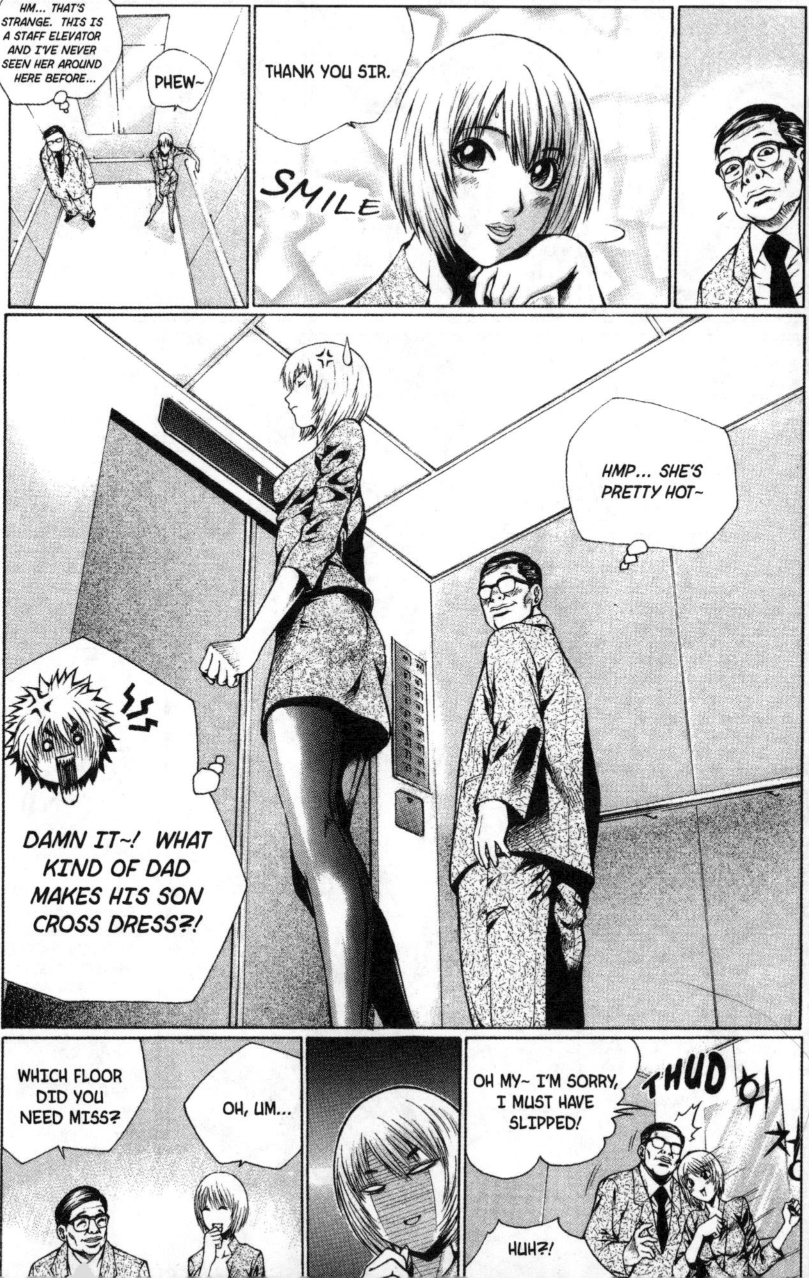
HM... THAT'S STRANGE. THIS IS A STAFF ELEVATOR AND I'VE NEVER SEEN HER AROUND HERE BEFORE...
PHEW~
THANK YOU SIR.
SMILE
HMP... SHE'S PRETTY HOT~
DAMN IT~! WHAT KIND OF DAD MAKES HIS SON CROSS DRESS?!
WHICH FLOOR DID YOU NEED MISS?
OH, UM...
OH MY~ I'M SORRY, I MUST HAVE SLIPPED!
THUD
HUH?!

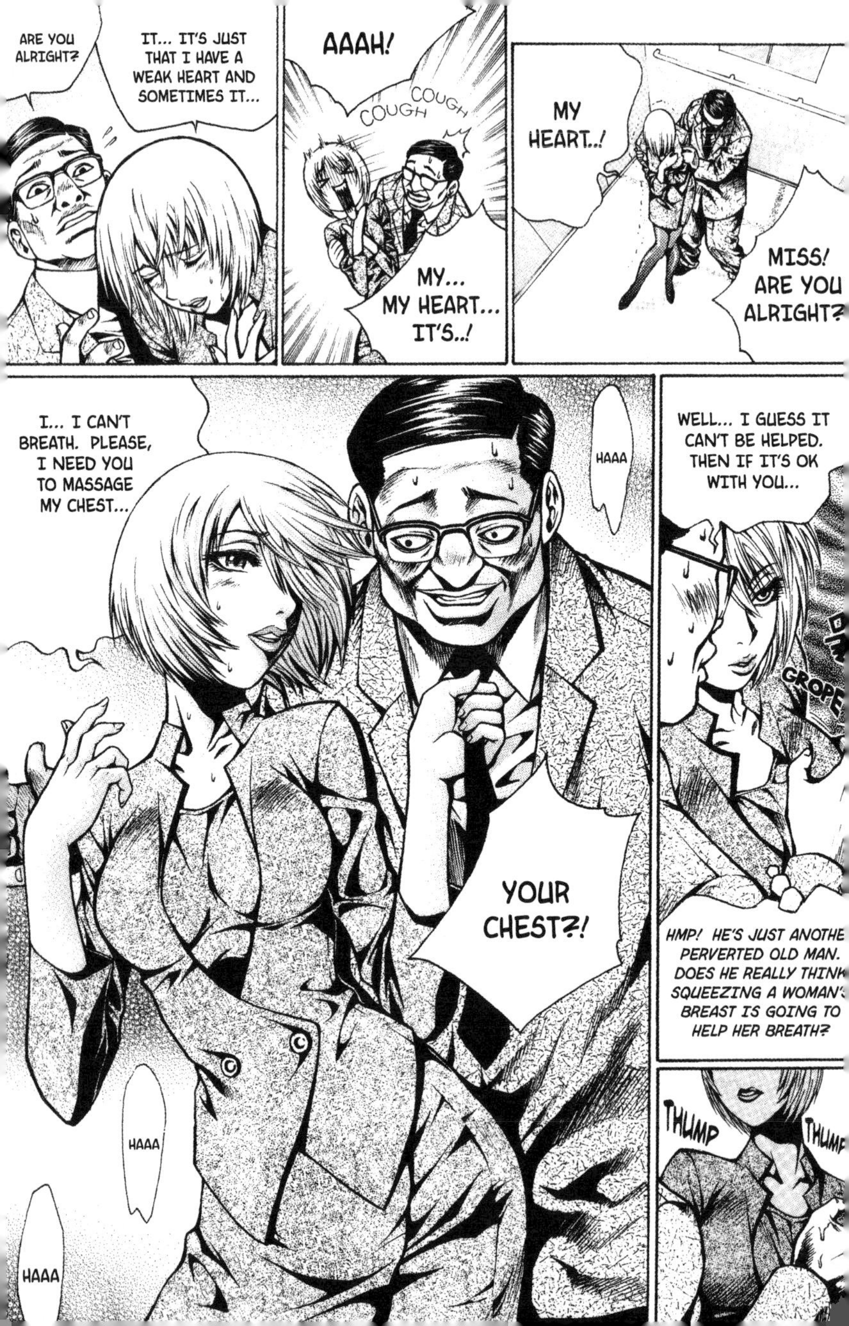

ARE YOU ALRIGHT?
IT... IT'S JUST THAT I HAVE A WEAK HEART AND SOMETIMES IT...
AAAH!
COUGH
COUGH
MY... MY HEART... IT'S..!
MY HEART..!
MISS! ARE YOU ALRIGHT?
I... I CAN'T BREATH. PLEASE, I NEED YOU TO MASSAGE MY CHEST...
HAAA
YOUR CHEST?!
HAAA
HAAA
WELL... I GUESS IT CAN'T BE HELPED. THEN IF IT'S OK WITH YOU...
GROPE
HMP! HE'S JUST ANOTHE PERVERTED OLD MAN. DOES HE REALLY THINK SQUEEZING A WOMAN'S BREAST IS GOING TO HELP HER BREATH?
THUMP
THUMP

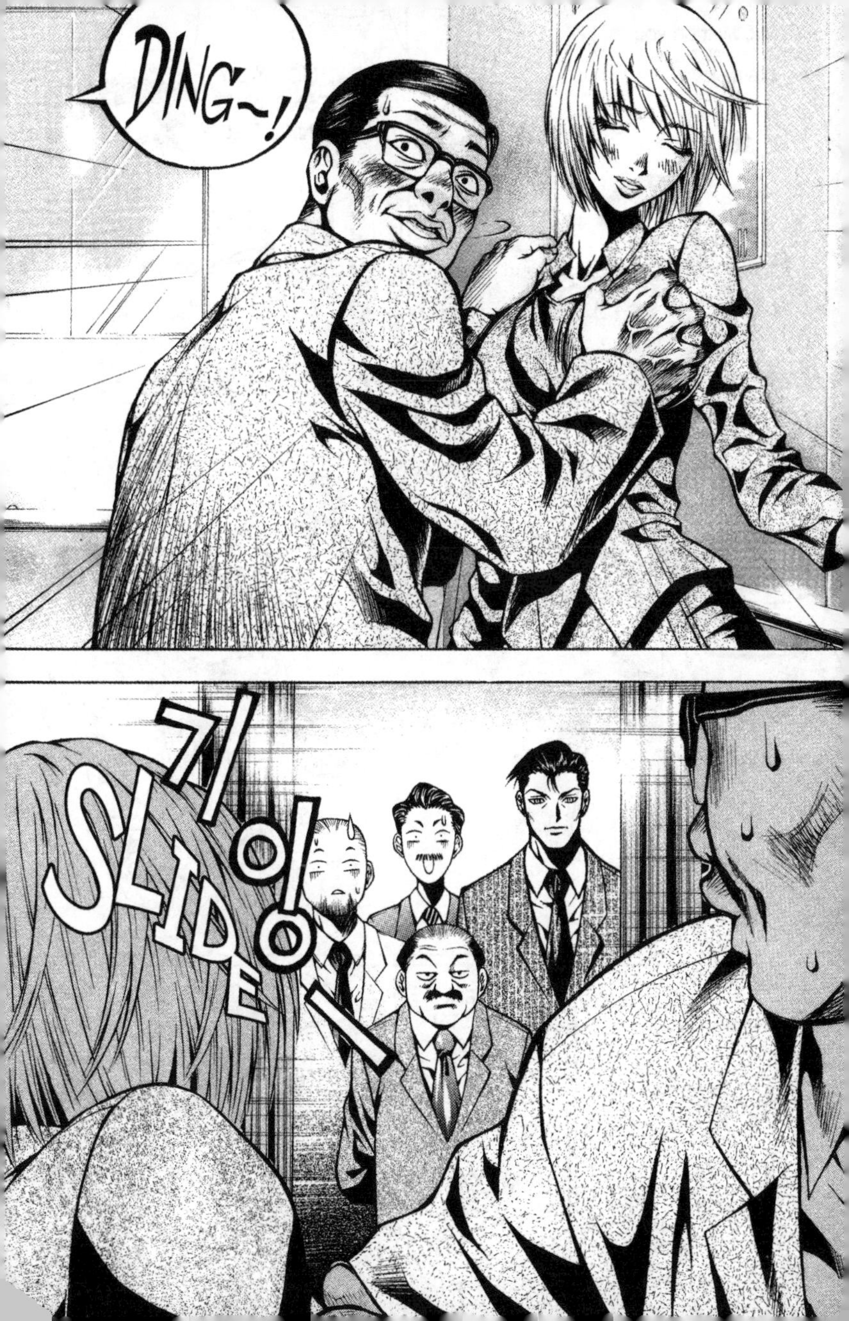
DING~!
기이이—
SLIDE

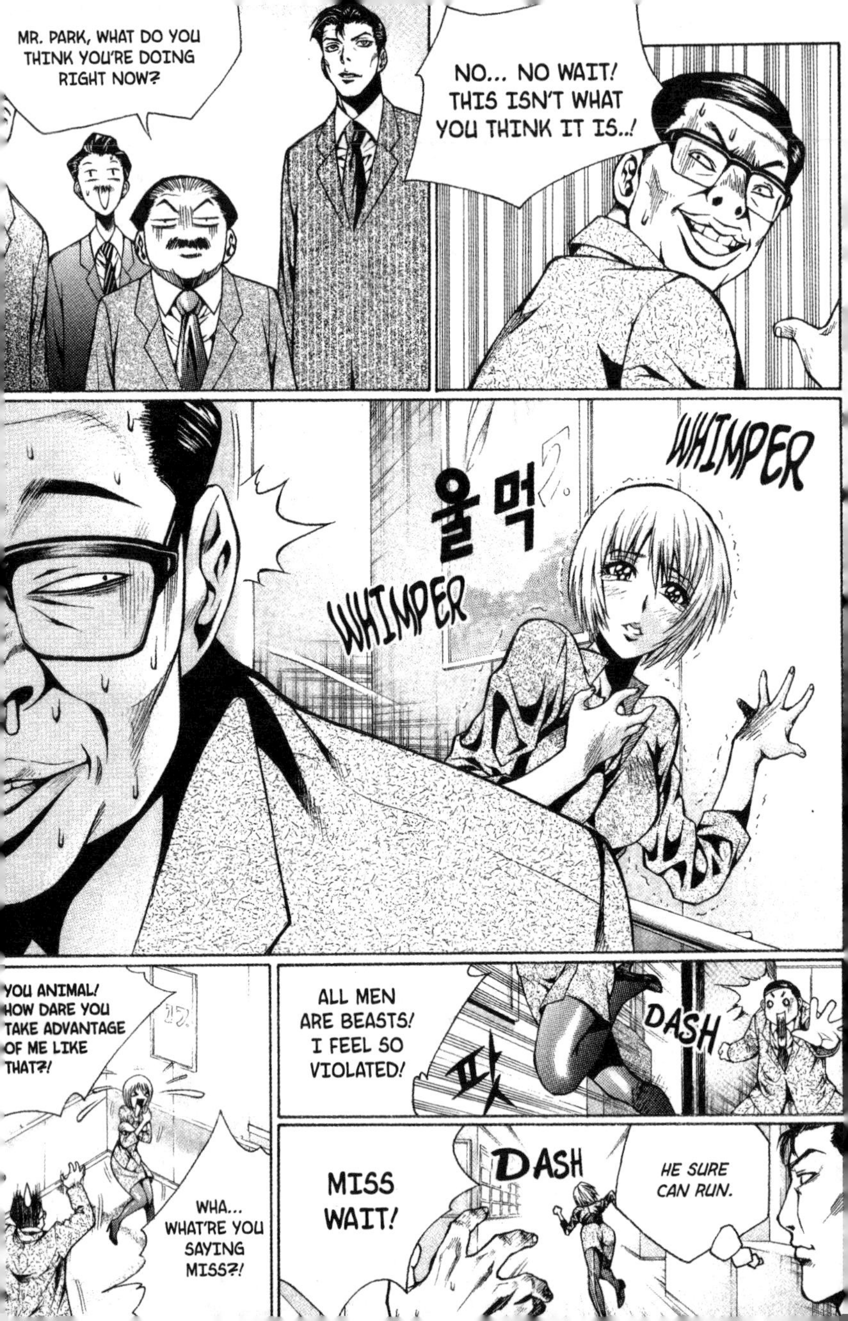
MR. PARK, WHAT DO YOU THINK YOU'RE DOING RIGHT NOW?
NO... NO WAIT! THIS ISN'T WHAT YOU THINK IT IS..!
WHIMPER
울먹
WHIMPER
YOU ANIMAL! HOW DARE YOU TAKE ADVANTAGE OF ME LIKE THAT?!
WHA... WHAT'RE YOU SAYING MISS?!
ALL MEN ARE BEASTS! I FEEL SO VIOLATED!
파
DASH
MISS WAIT!
DASH
HE SURE CAN RUN.

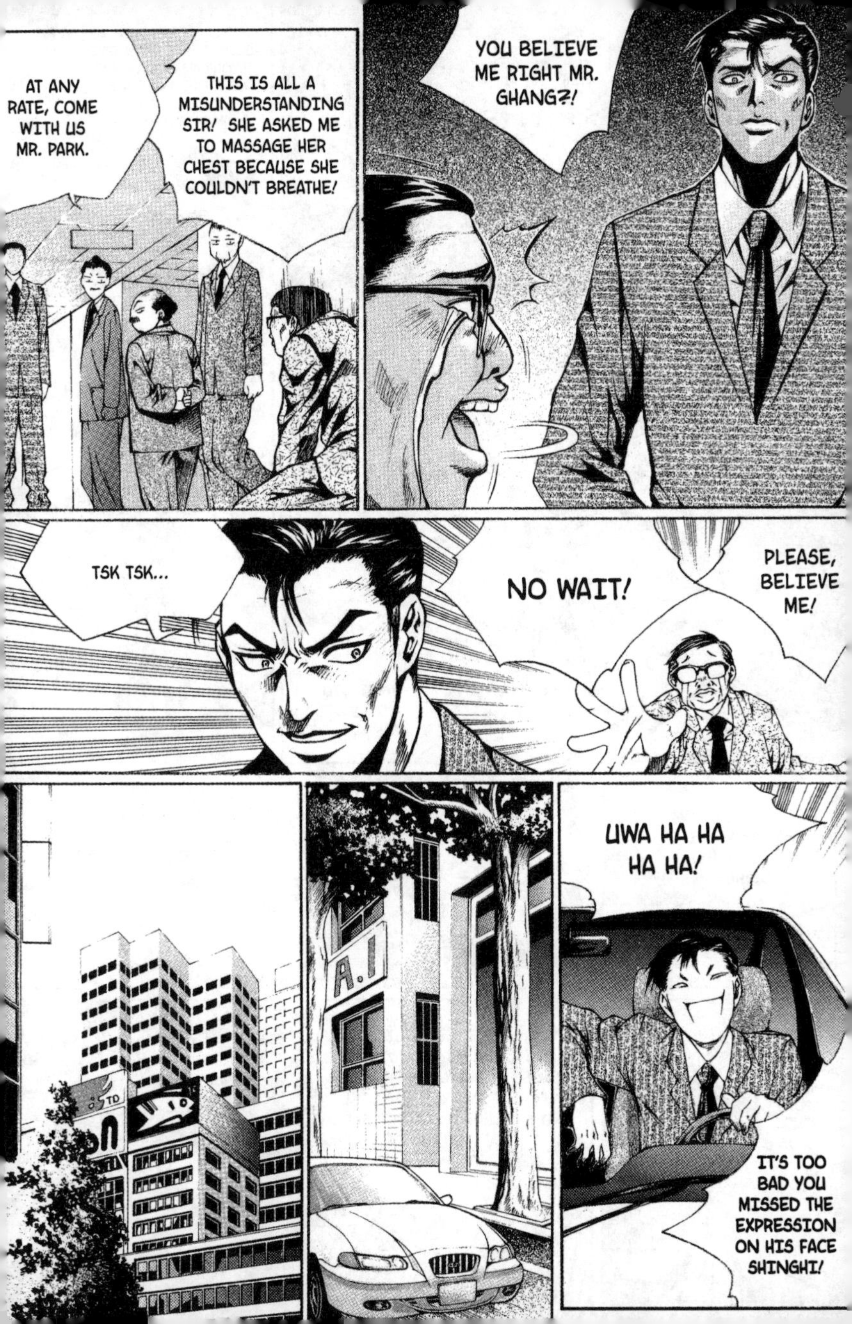
AT ANY RATE, COME WITH US MR. PARK.
THIS IS ALL A MISUNDERSTANDING SIR! SHE ASKED ME TO MASSAGE HER CHEST BECAUSE SHE COULDN'T BREATHE!
YOU BELIEVE ME RIGHT MR. GHANG?!
TSK TSK...
NO WAIT!
PLEASE, BELIEVE ME!
A.I
UWA HA HA HA HA!
IT'S TOO BAD YOU MISSED THE EXPRESSION ON HIS FACE SHINGHI!

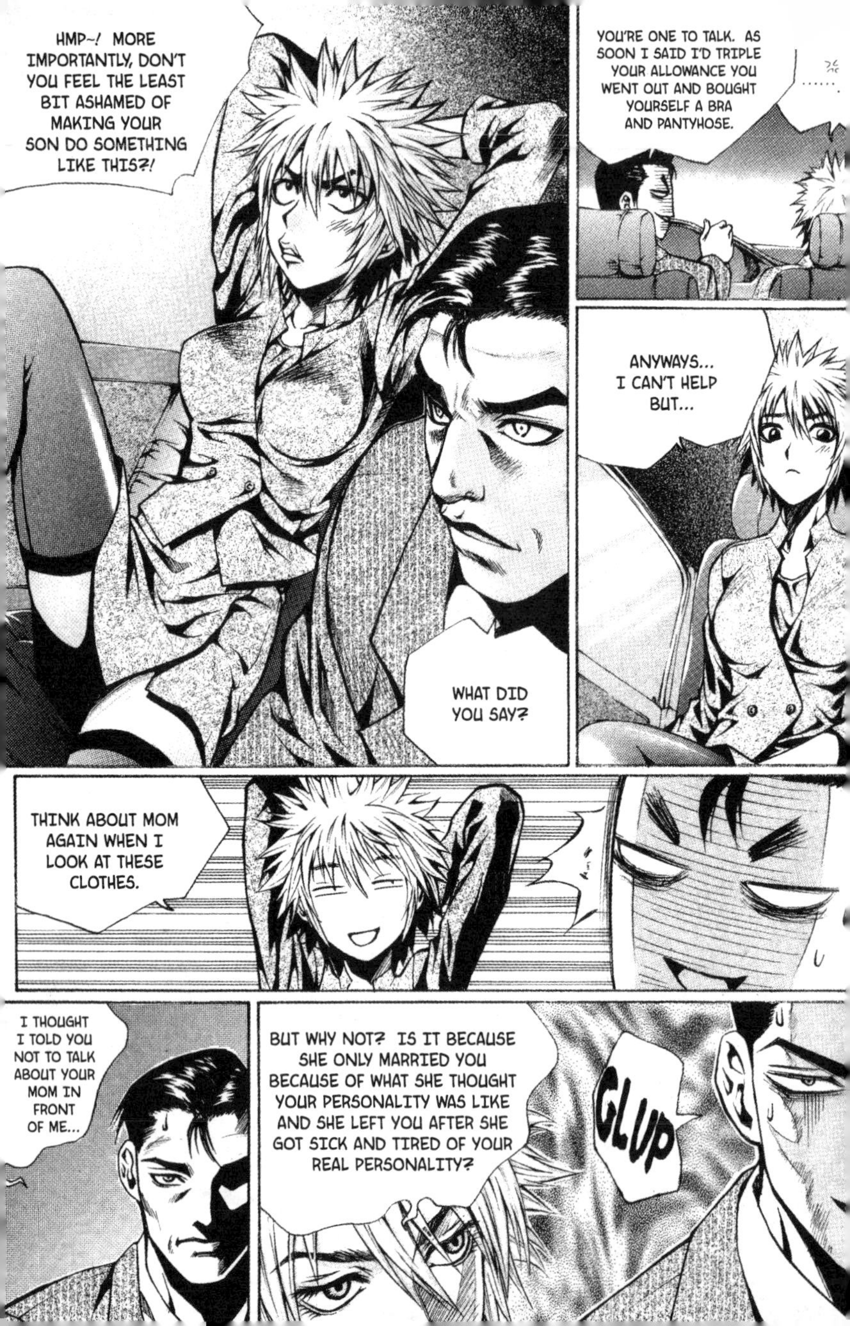
HMP~! MORE IMPORTANTLY, DON'T YOU FEEL THE LEAST BIT ASHAMED OF MAKING YOUR SON DO SOMETHING LIKE THIS?!
WHAT DID YOU SAY?
YOU'RE ONE TO TALK. AS SOON I SAID I'D TRIPLE YOUR ALLOWANCE YOU WENT OUT AND BOUGHT YOURSELF A BRA AND PANTYHOSE.
......
ANYWAYS... I CAN'T HELP BUT...
THINK ABOUT MOM AGAIN WHEN I LOOK AT THESE CLOTHES.
I THOUGHT I TOLD YOU NOT TO TALK ABOUT YOUR MOM IN FRONT OF ME...
BUT WHY NOT? IS IT BECAUSE SHE ONLY MARRIED YOU BECAUSE OF WHAT SHE THOUGHT YOUR PERSONALITY WAS LIKE AND SHE LEFT YOU AFTER SHE GOT SICK AND TIRED OF YOUR REAL PERSONALITY?
GLUP

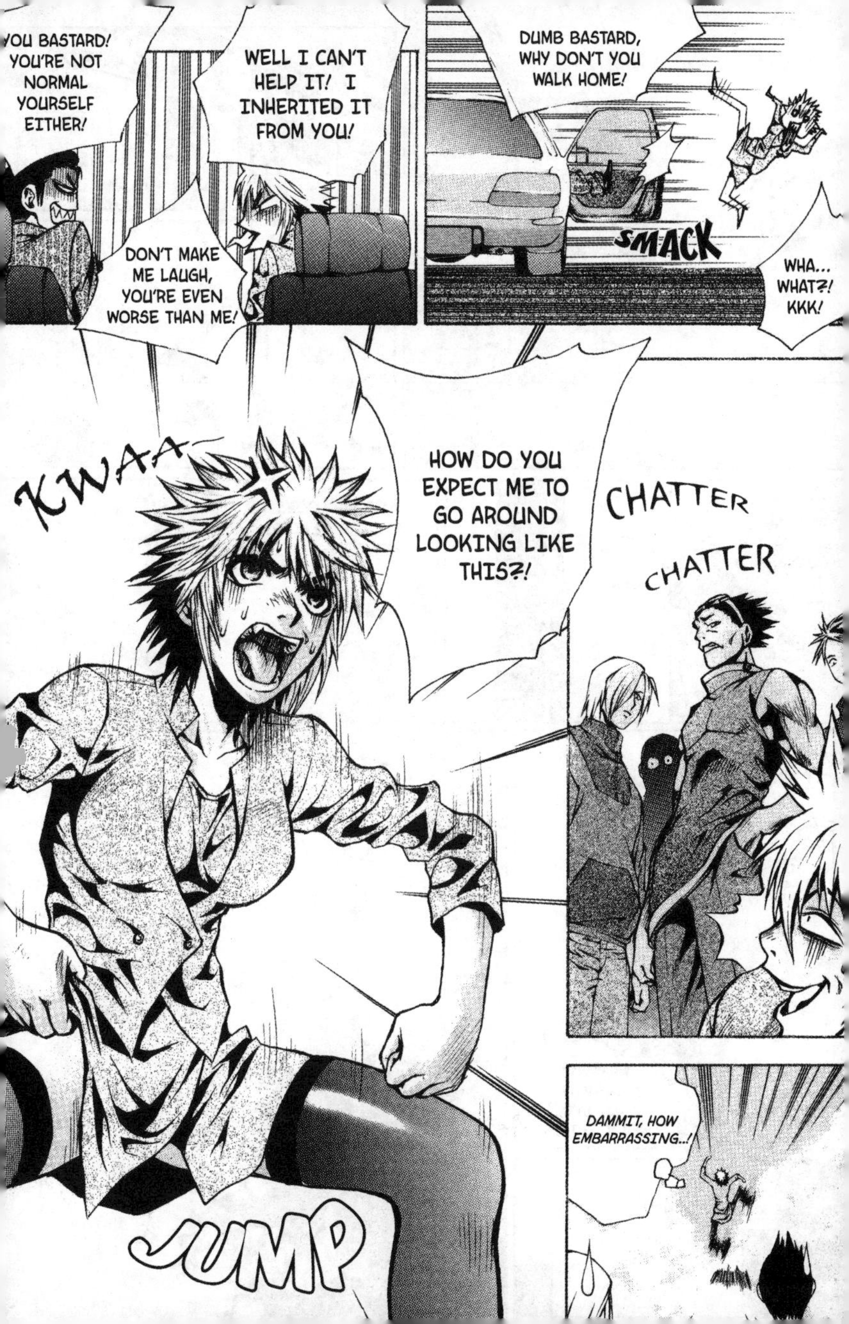
YOU BASTARD! YOU'RE NOT NORMAL YOURSELF EITHER!
WELL I CAN'T HELP IT! I INHERITED IT FROM YOU!
DON'T MAKE ME LAUGH, YOU'RE EVEN WORSE THAN ME!
DUMB BASTARD, WHY DON'T YOU WALK HOME!
SMACK
WHA... WHAT?! KKK!
KWAA
HOW DO YOU EXPECT ME TO GO AROUND LOOKING LIKE THIS?!
JUMP
CHATTER
CHATTER
DAMMIT, HOW EMBARRASSING...!

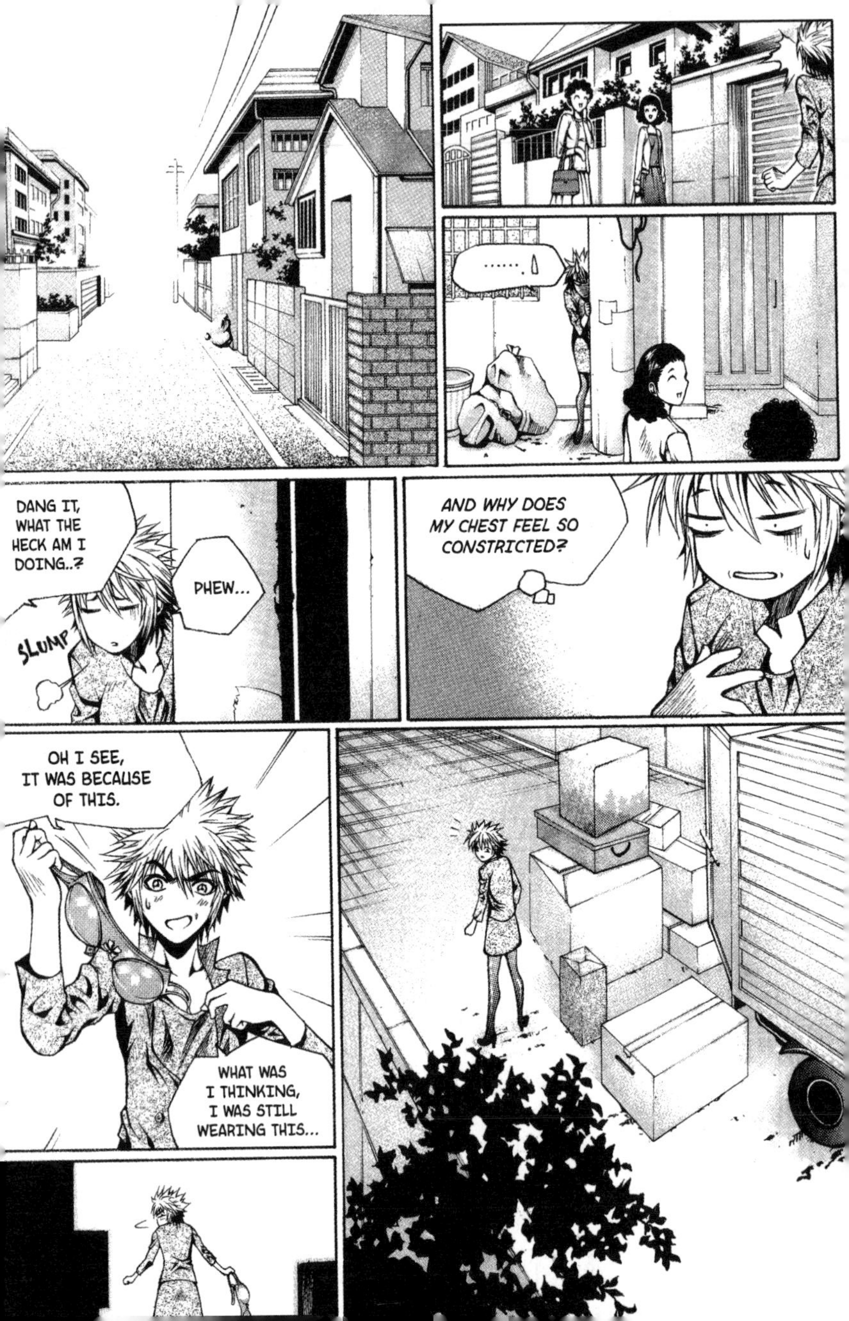

......!
DANG IT, WHAT THE HECK AM I DOING..?
SLUMP
PHEW...
AND WHY DOES MY CHEST FEEL SO CONSTRICTED?
OH I SEE, IT WAS BECAUSE OF THIS.
WHAT WAS I THINKING, I WAS STILL WEARING THIS...

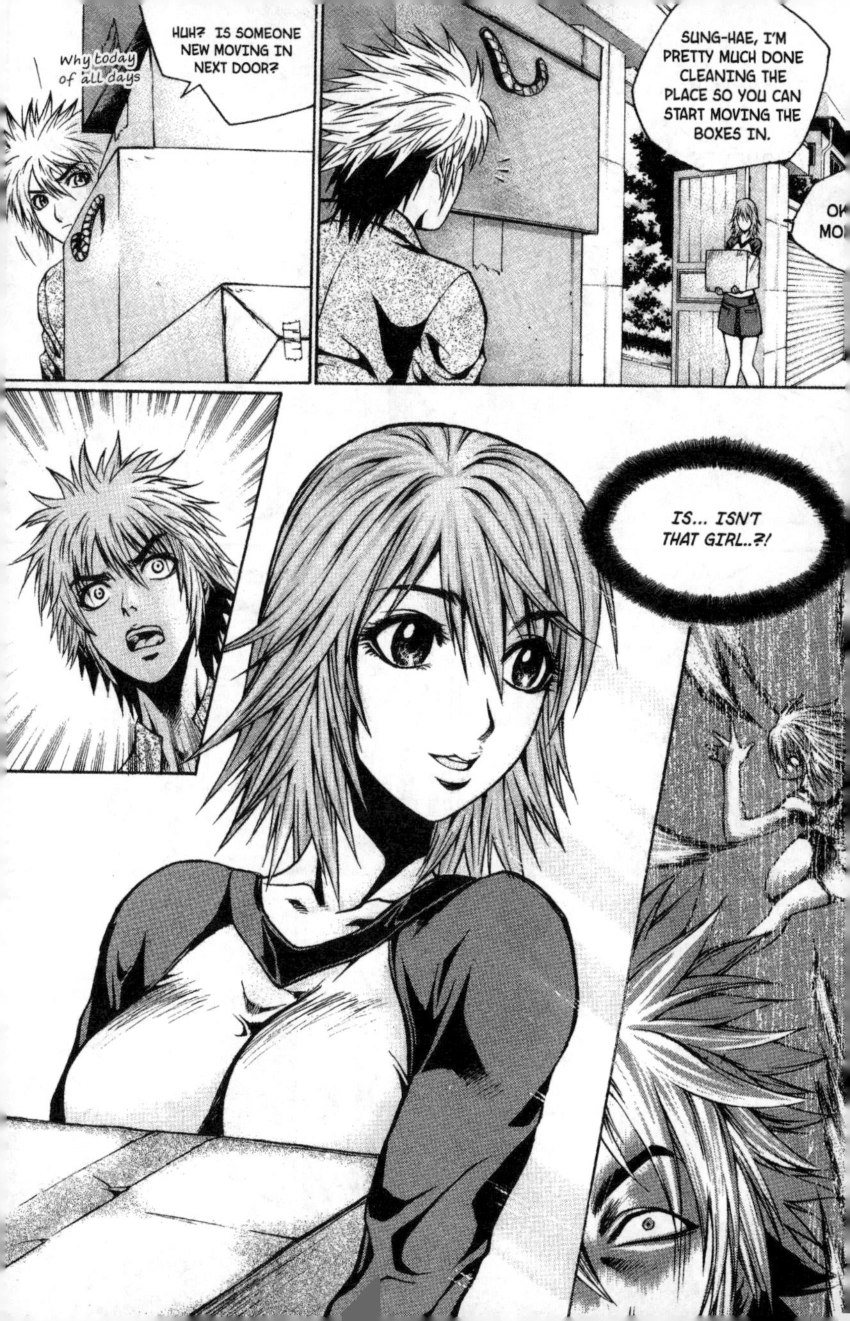
Why today of all days
HUH? IS SOMEONE NEW MOVING IN NEXT DOOR?
SUNG-HAE, I'M PRETTY MUCH DONE CLEANING THE PLACE SO YOU CAN START MOVING THE BOXES IN.
IS... ISN'T THAT GIRL..?!

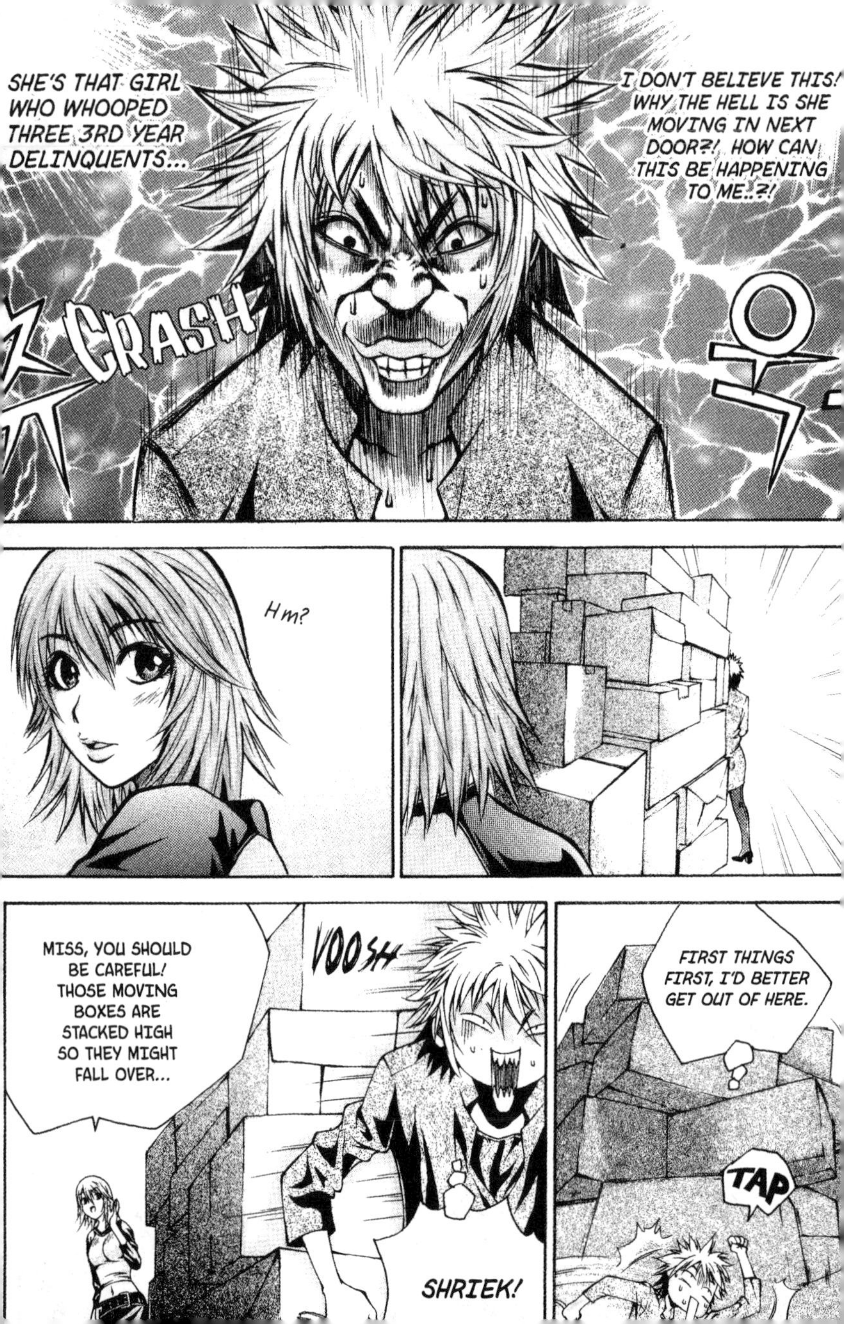
SHE'S THAT GIRL WHO WHOOPED THREE 3RD YEAR DELINQUENTS...
CRASH
I DON'T BELIEVE THIS! WHY THE HELL IS SHE MOVING IN NEXT DOOR?! HOW CAN THIS BE HAPPENING TO ME..?!
Hm?
MISS, YOU SHOULD BE CAREFUL! THOSE MOVING BOXES ARE STACKED HIGH SO THEY MIGHT FALL OVER...
VOOSH
SHRIEK!
FIRST THINGS FIRST, I'D BETTER GET OUT OF HERE.
TAP

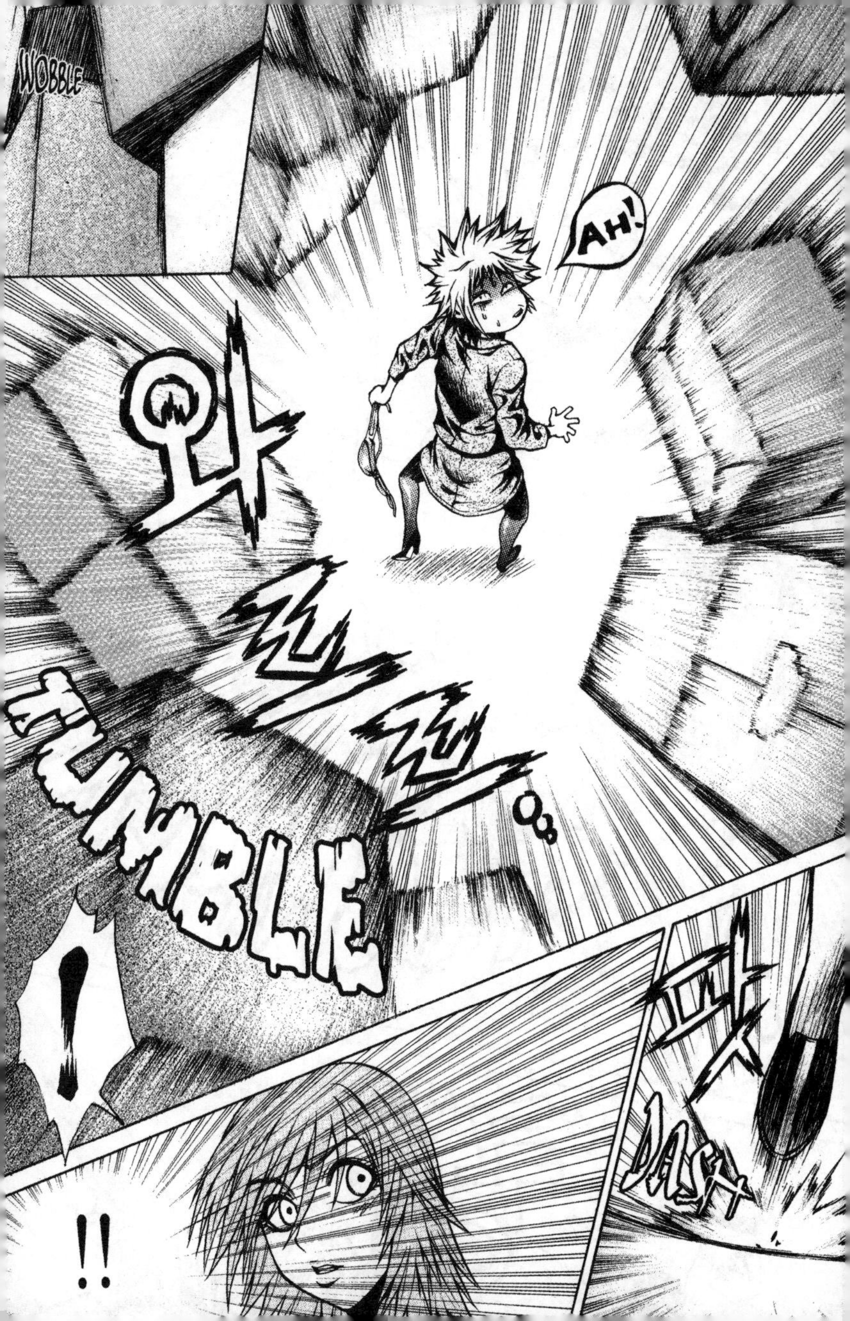
WOBBLE
AH!
TUMBLE
!
!!
DASH

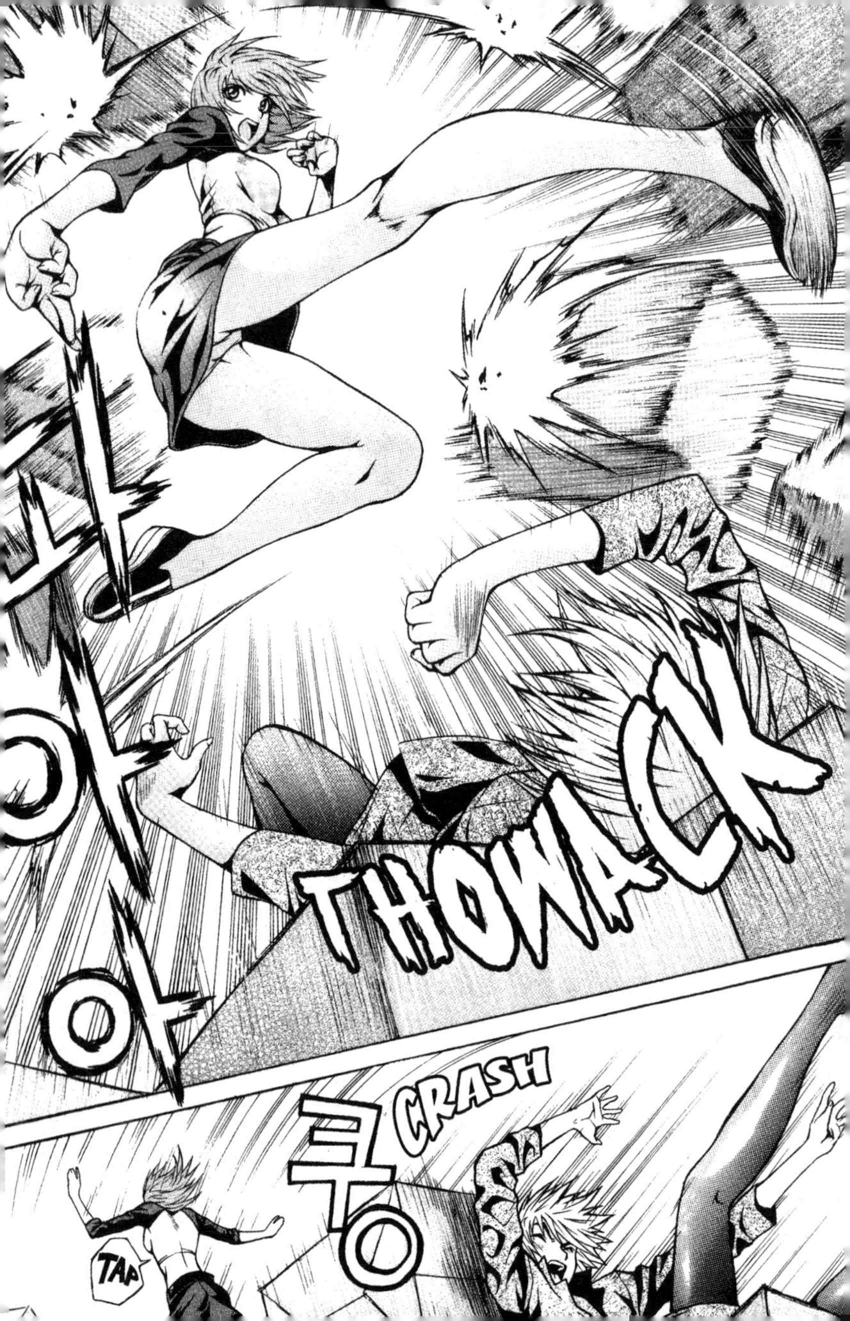
THOWACK
TAP
쿵
CRASH

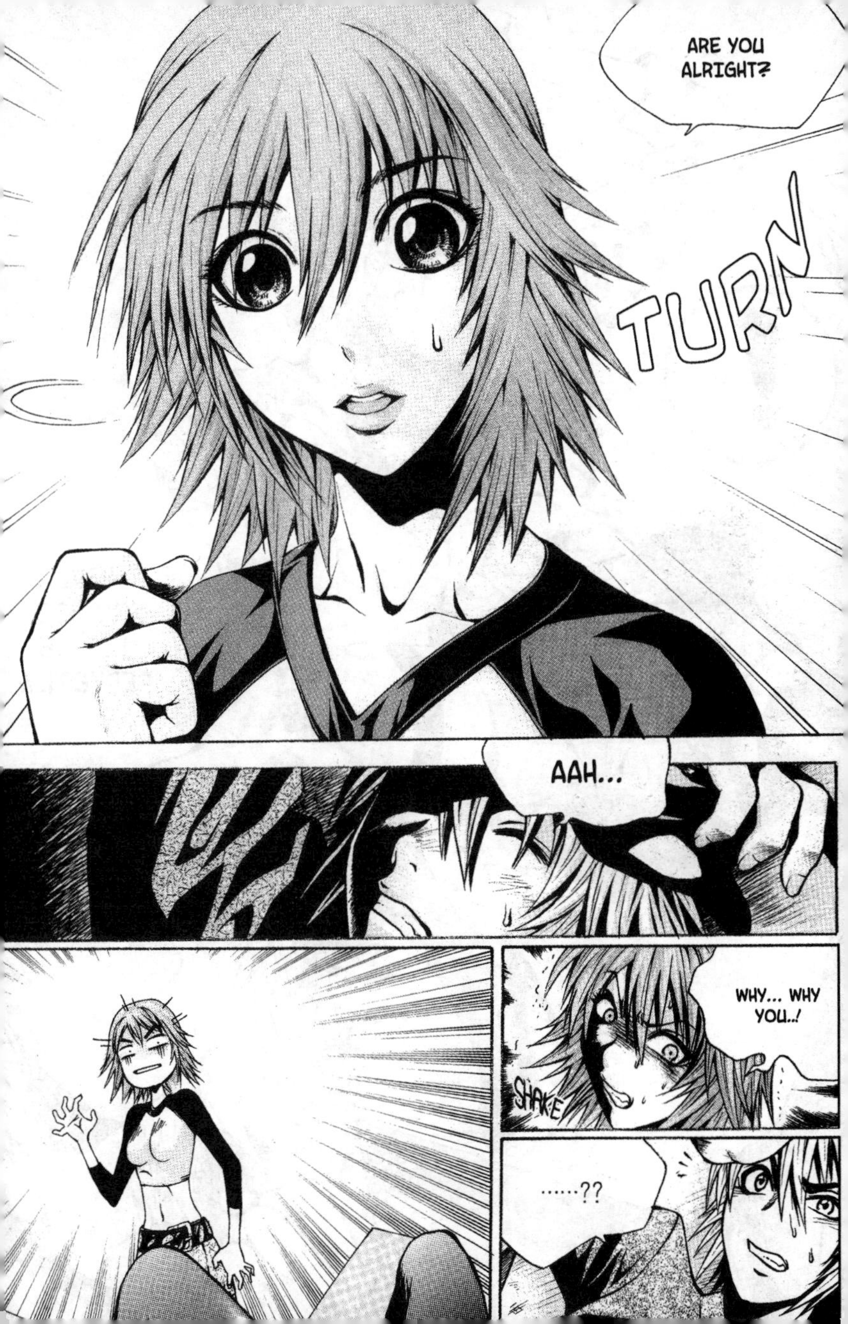
ARE YOU ALRIGHT?
TURN
AAH...
WHY... WHY YOU..!
SHAKE
......??

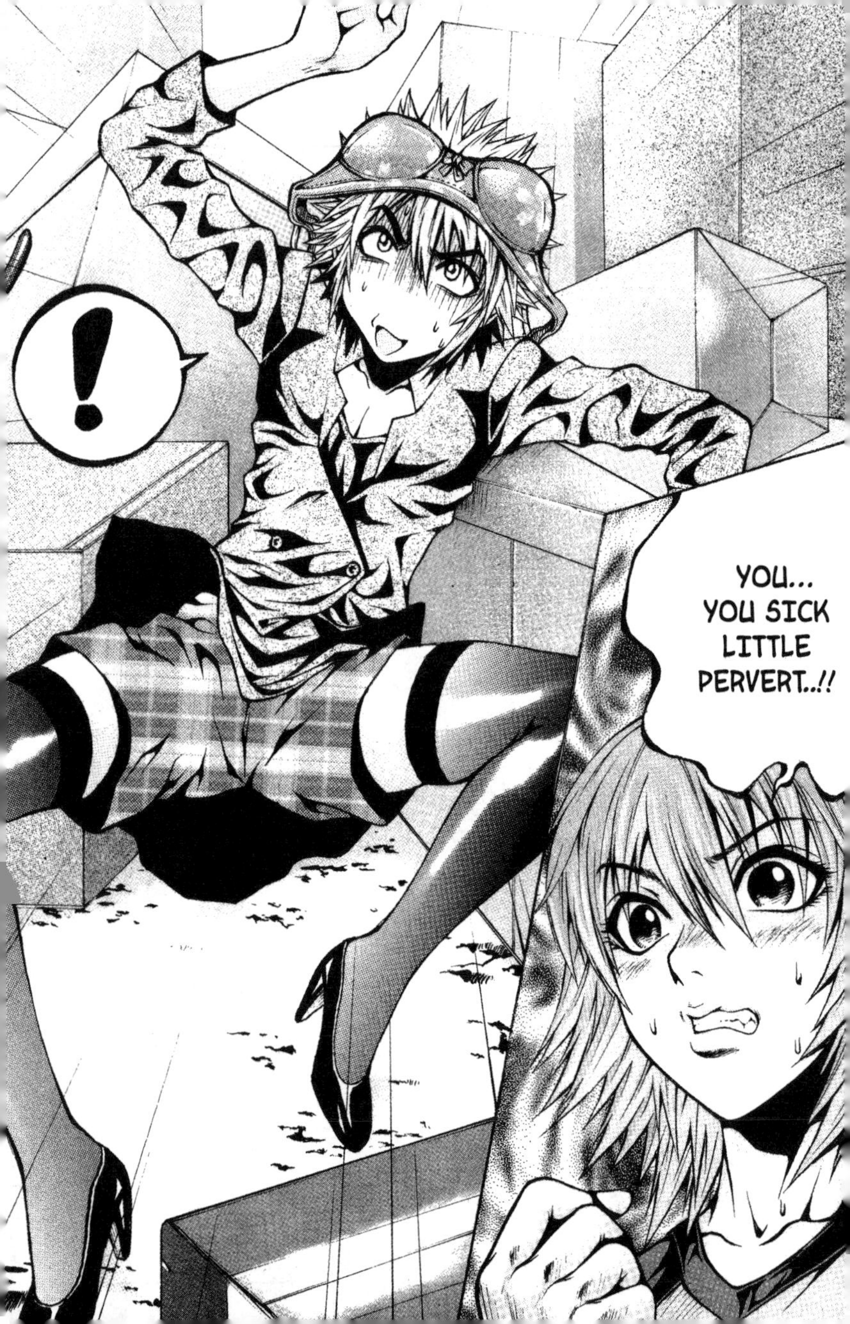
!
YOU...
YOU SICK
LITTLE
PERVERT..!!

Chapter 3 : How Could This Happen?!

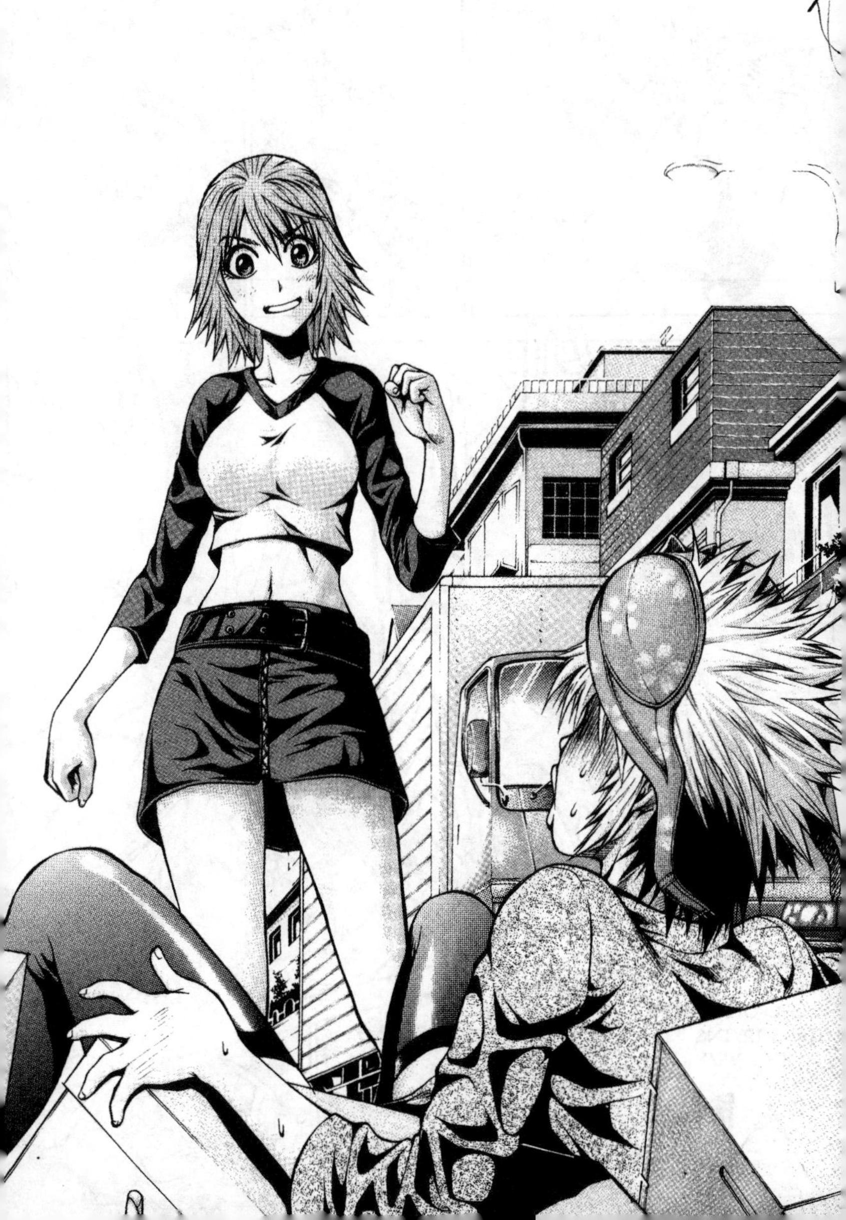

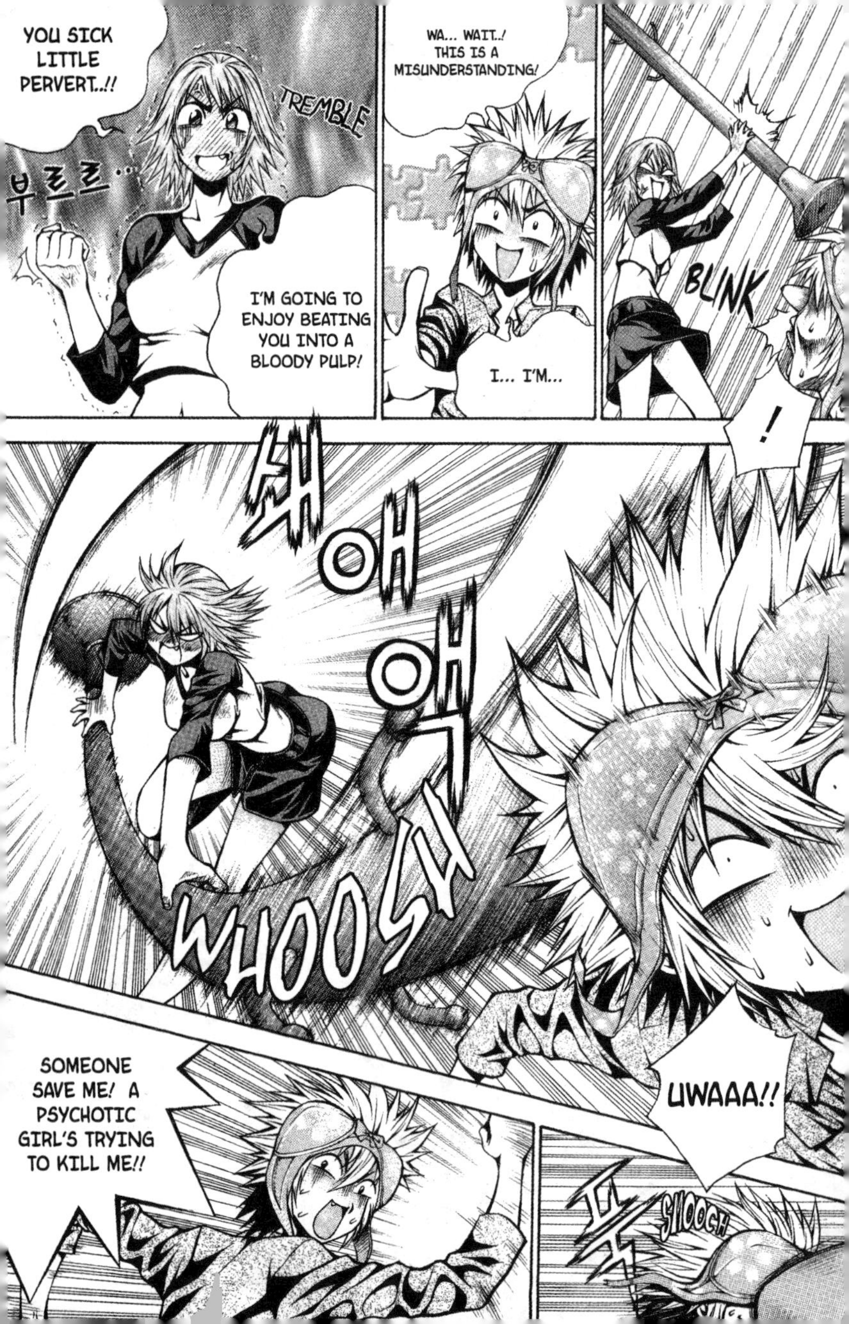
YOU SICK LITTLE PERVERT..!!
TREMBLE
부르르...
I'M GOING TO ENJOY BEATING YOU INTO A BLOODY PULP!
WA... WAIT..! THIS IS A MISUNDERSTANDING!
I... I'M...
BLINK
!
WHOOSH
SOMEONE SAVE ME! A PSYCHOTIC GIRL'S TRYING TO KILL ME!!
UWAAA!!
SWOOCH

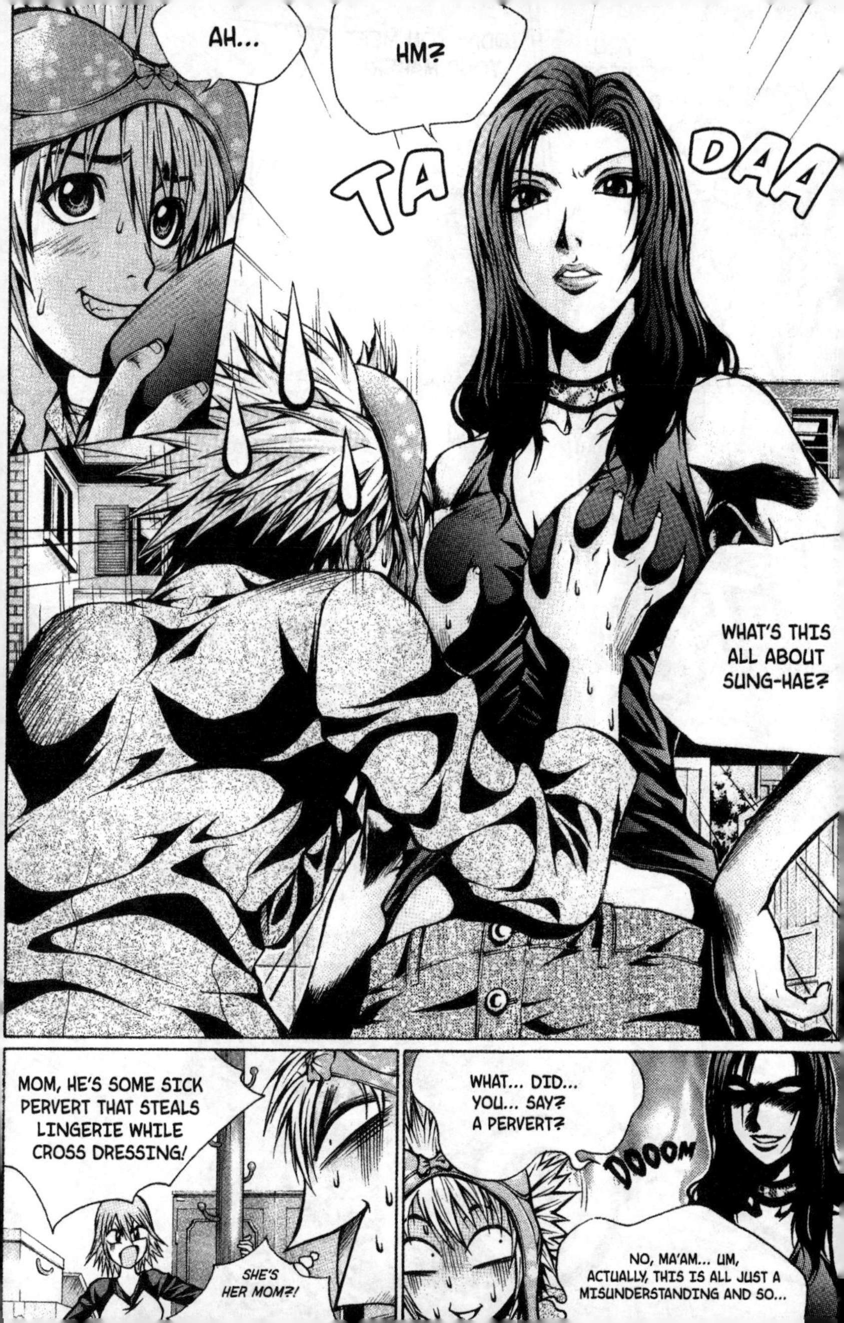
AH...
HM?
TA DAA
WHAT'S THIS ALL ABOUT SUNG-HAE?
MOM, HE'S SOME SICK PERVERT THAT STEALS LINGERIE WHILE CROSS DRESSING!
SHE'S HER MOM?!
WHAT... DID... YOU... SAY? A PERVERT?
DOOOM
NO, MA'AM... UM, ACTUALLY, THIS IS ALL JUST A MISUNDERSTANDING AND SO...

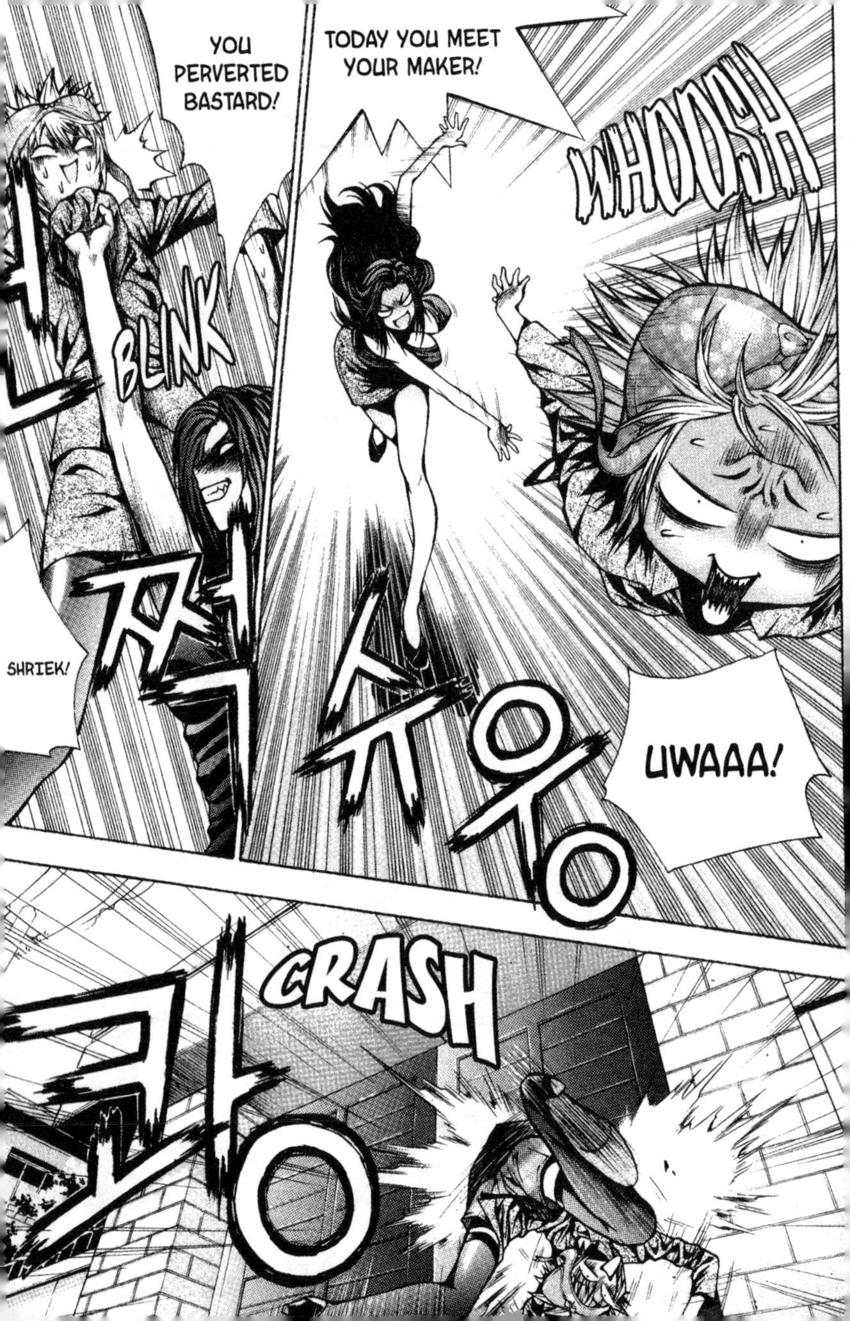
YOU PERVERTED BASTARD!
BLINK
SHRIEK!
TODAY YOU MEET YOUR MAKER!
WHOOSH
UWAAA!
CRASH

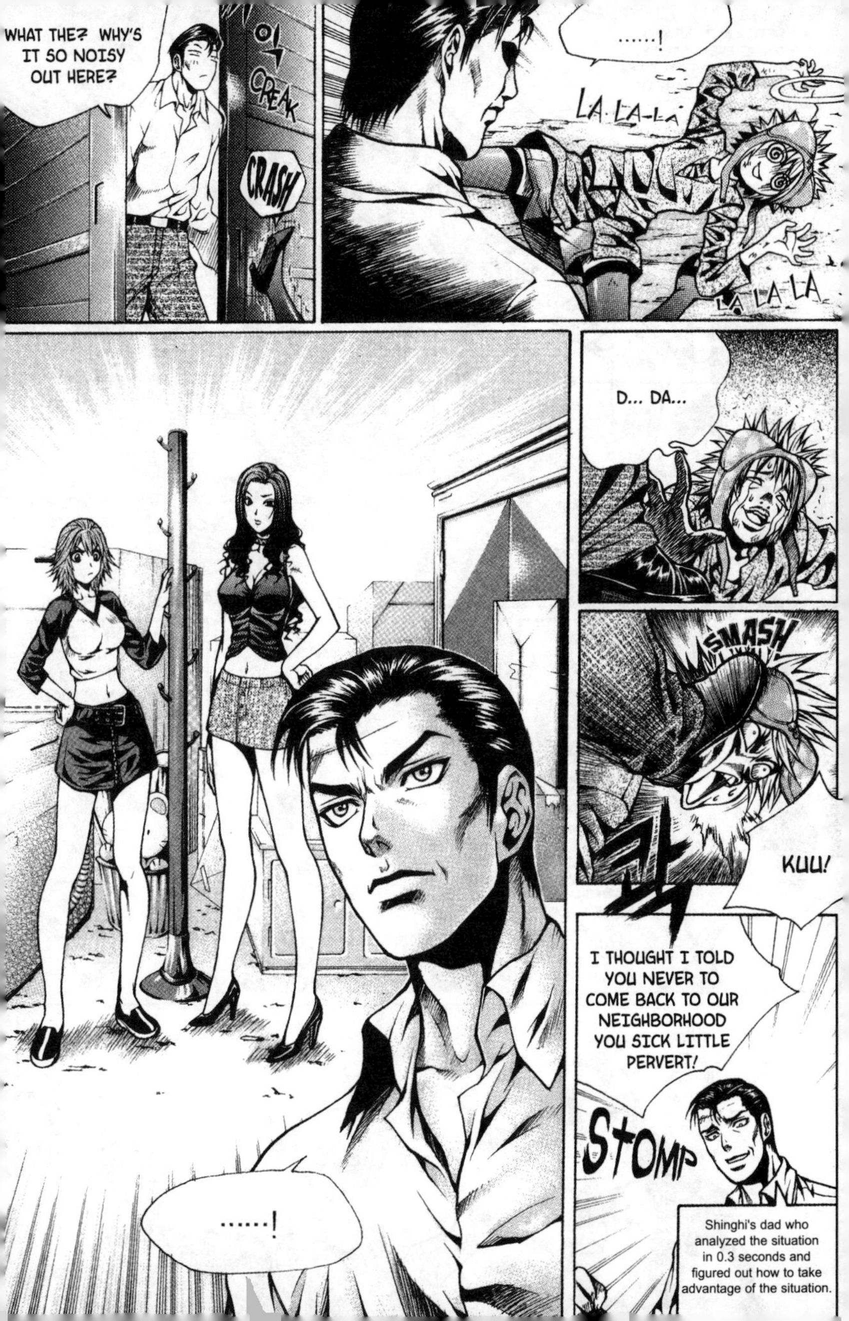
WHAT THE? WHY'S IT SO NOISY OUT HERE?
CREAK
CRASH
......!
LA-LA-LA
LA LA LA
......!
D... DA...
SMASH
KUU!
I THOUGHT I TOLD YOU NEVER TO COME BACK TO OUR NEIGHBORHOOD YOU SICK LITTLE PERVERT!
STOMP
Shinghi's dad who analyzed the situation in 0.3 seconds and figured out how to take advantage of the situation.

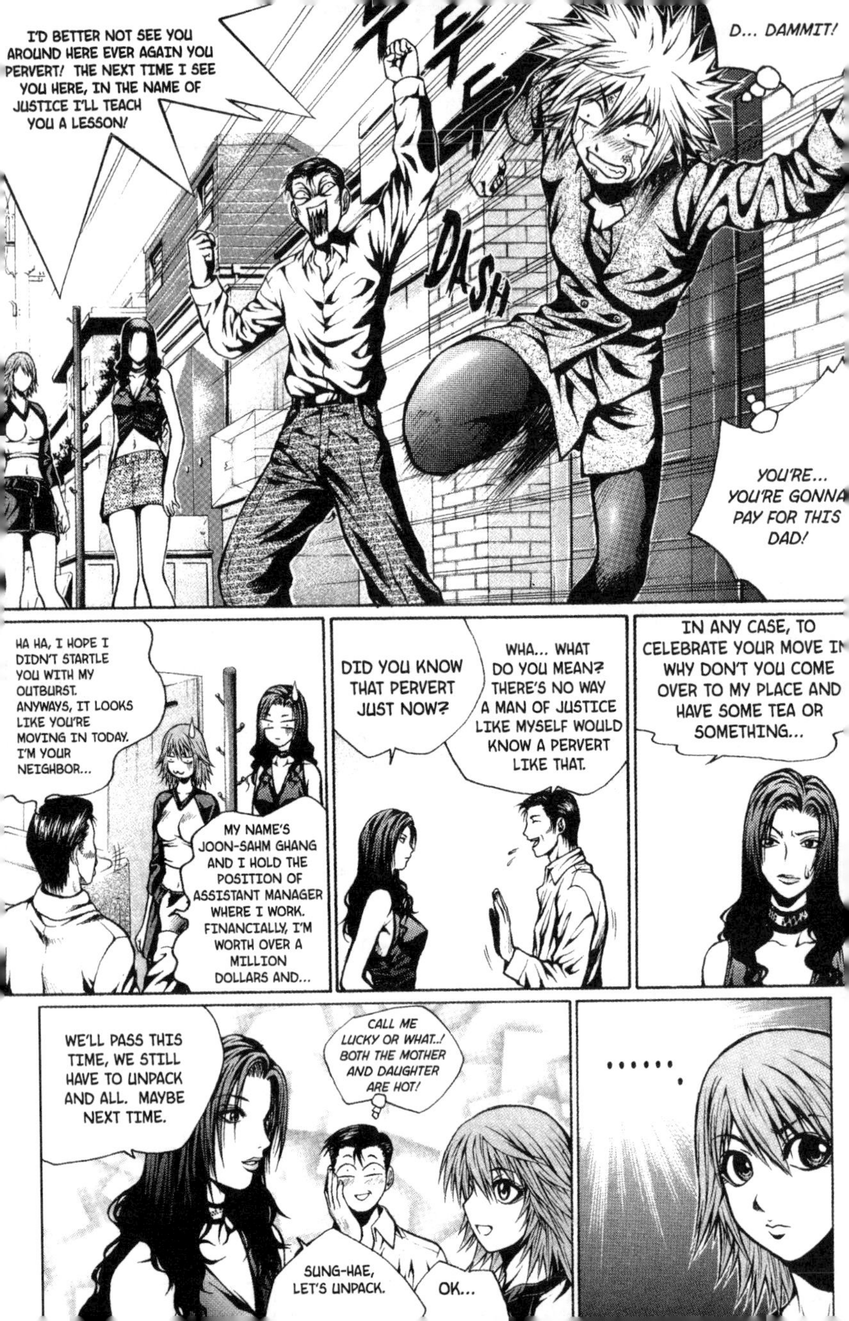
I'D BETTER NOT SEE YOU AROUND HERE EVER AGAIN YOU PERVERT! THE NEXT TIME I SEE YOU HERE, IN THE NAME OF JUSTICE I'LL TEACH YOU A LESSON!
D... DAMMIT!
DASH
YOU'RE... YOU'RE GONNA PAY FOR THIS DAD!
HA HA, I HOPE I DIDN'T STARTLE YOU WITH MY OUTBURST. ANYWAYS, IT LOOKS LIKE YOU'RE MOVING IN TODAY. I'M YOUR NEIGHBOR...
MY NAME'S JOON-SAHM GHANG AND I HOLD THE POSITION OF ASSISTANT MANAGER WHERE I WORK. FINANCIALLY, I'M WORTH OVER A MILLION DOLLARS AND...
DID YOU KNOW THAT PERVERT JUST NOW?
WHA... WHAT DO YOU MEAN? THERE'S NO WAY A MAN OF JUSTICE LIKE MYSELF WOULD KNOW A PERVERT LIKE THAT.
IN ANY CASE, TO CELEBRATE YOUR MOVE IN WHY DON'T YOU COME OVER TO MY PLACE AND HAVE SOME TEA OR SOMETHING...
WE'LL PASS THIS TIME, WE STILL HAVE TO UNPACK AND ALL. MAYBE NEXT TIME.
CALL ME LUCKY OR WHAT..! BOTH THE MOTHER AND DAUGHTER ARE HOT!
SUNG-HAE, LET'S UNPACK.
OK...
......,

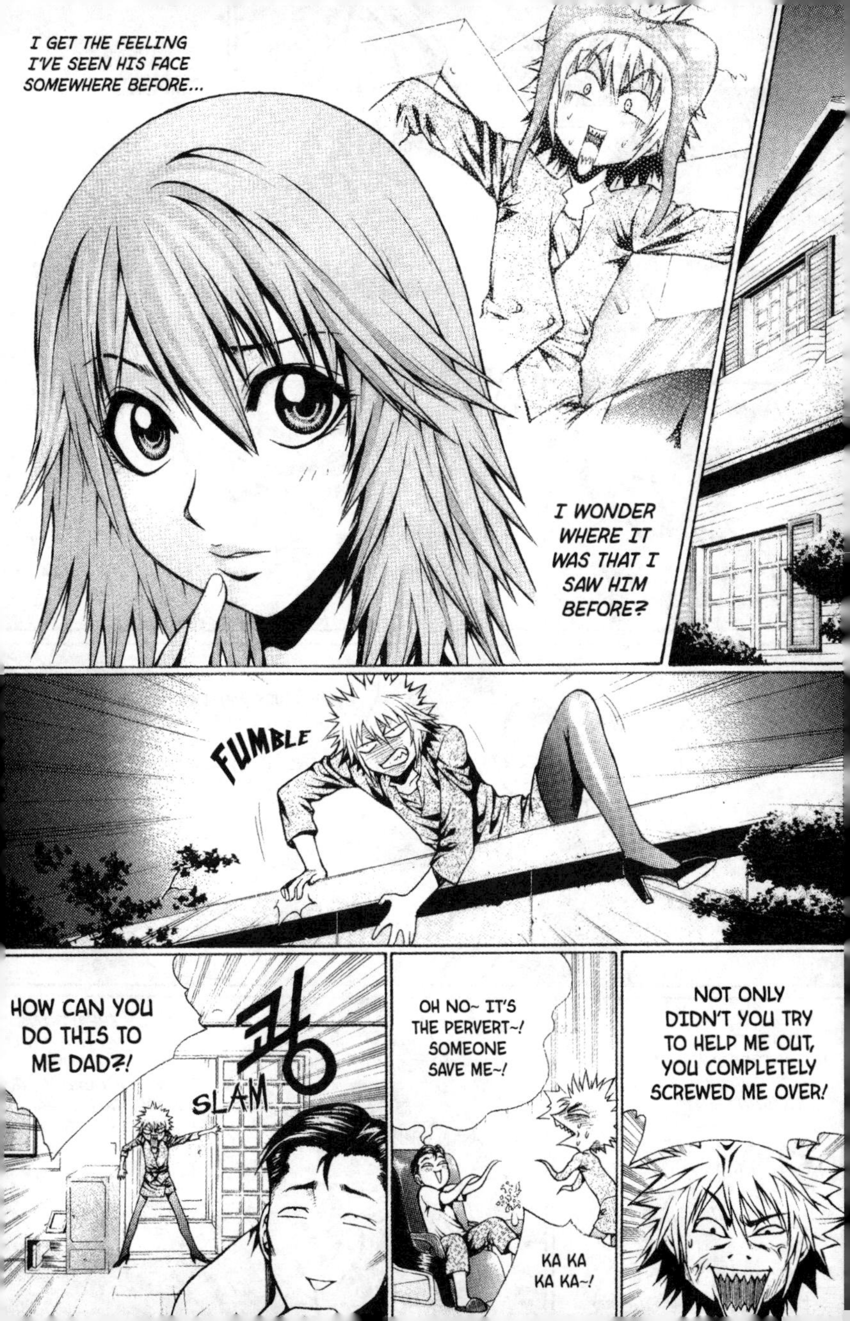
I GET THE FEELING I'VE SEEN HIS FACE SOMEWHERE BEFORE...
I WONDER WHERE IT WAS THAT I SAW HIM BEFORE?
FUMBLE
HOW CAN YOU DO THIS TO ME DAD?!
SLAM
OH NO~ IT'S THE PERVERT~! SOMEONE SAVE ME~!
KA KA KA KA~!
NOT ONLY DIDN'T YOU TRY TO HELP ME OUT, YOU COMPLETELY SCREWED ME OVER!

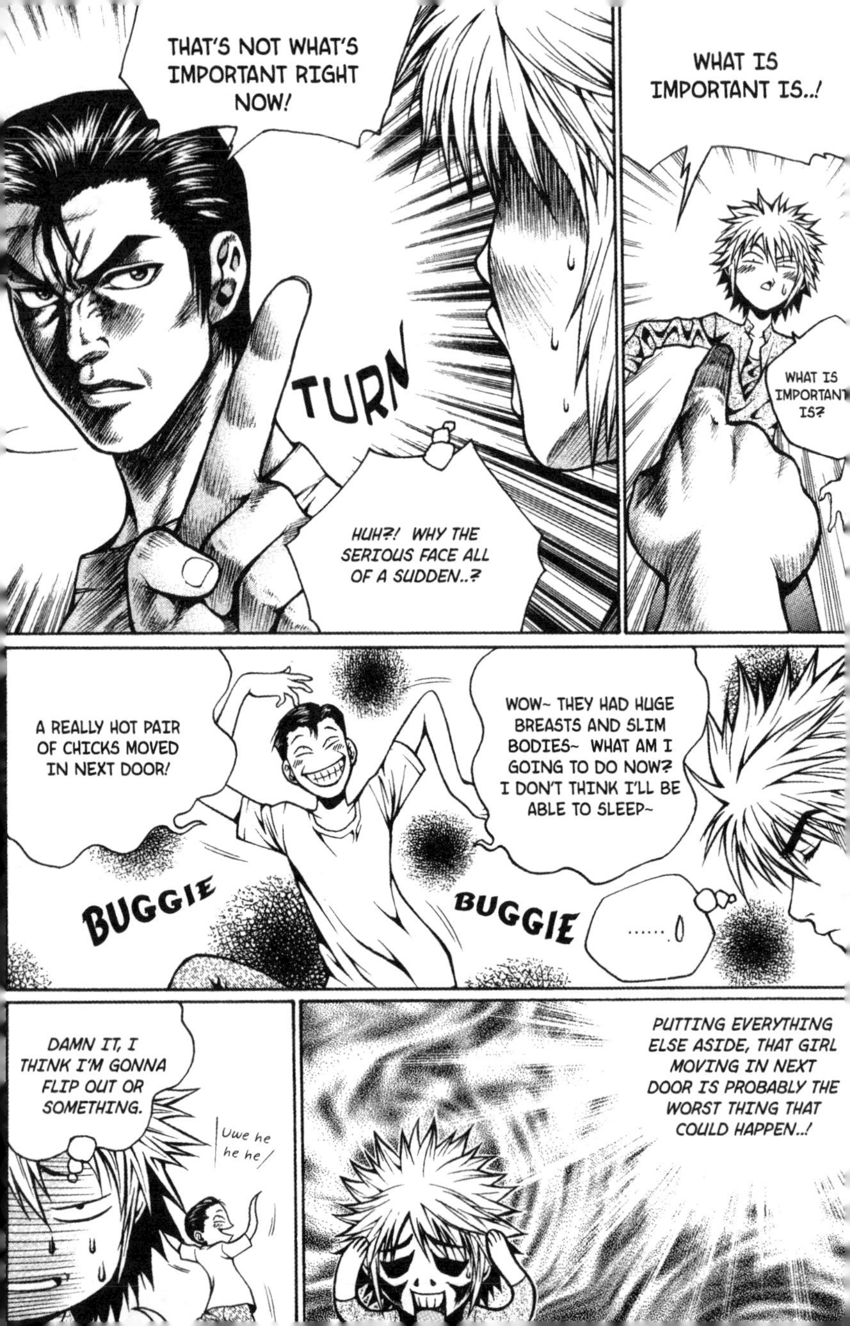
THAT'S NOT WHAT'S IMPORTANT RIGHT NOW!
TURN
HUH?! WHY THE SERIOUS FACE ALL OF A SUDDEN..?
WHAT IS IMPORTANT IS..!
WHAT IS IMPORTANT IS?
A REALLY HOT PAIR OF CHICKS MOVED IN NEXT DOOR!
BUGGIE
WOW~ THEY HAD HUGE BREASTS AND SLIM BODIES~ WHAT AM I GOING TO DO NOW? I DON'T THINK I'LL BE ABLE TO SLEEP~
BUGGIE
......!
DAMN IT, I THINK I'M GONNA FLIP OUT OR SOMETHING.
Uwe he he he!
PUTTING EVERYTHING ELSE ASIDE, THAT GIRL MOVING IN NEXT DOOR IS PROBABLY THE WORST THING THAT COULD HAPPEN..!

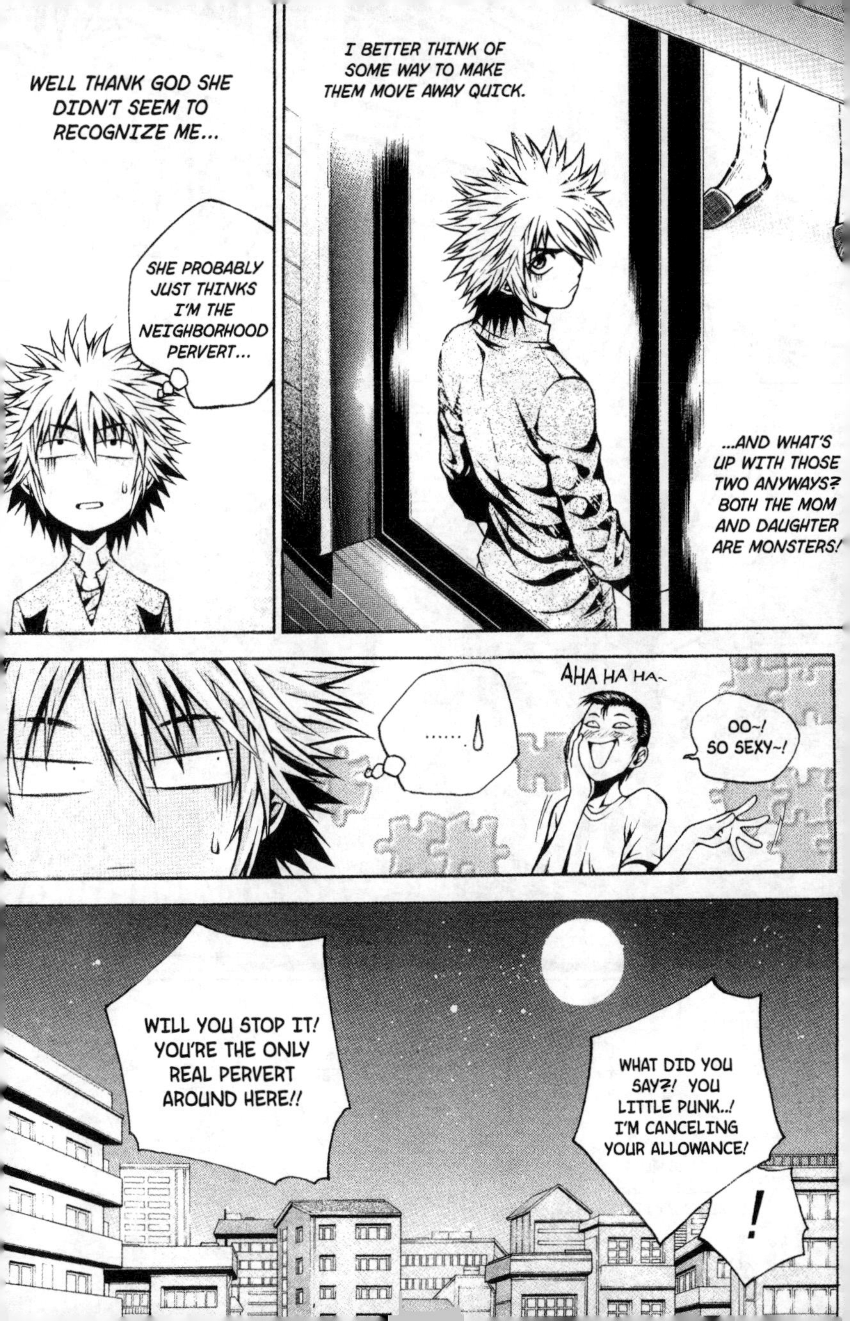
WELL THANK GOD SHE DIDN'T SEEM TO RECOGNIZE ME...
SHE PROBABLY JUST THINKS I'M THE NEIGHBORHOOD PERVERT...
I BETTER THINK OF SOME WAY TO MAKE THEM MOVE AWAY QUICK.
...AND WHAT'S UP WITH THOSE TWO ANYWAYS?! BOTH THE MOM AND DAUGHTER ARE MONSTERS!
......
AHA HA HA~
OO~! SO SEXY~!
WILL YOU STOP IT! YOU'RE THE ONLY REAL PERVERT AROUND HERE!!
WHAT DID YOU SAY?! YOU LITTLE PUNK..! I'M CANCELING YOUR ALLOWANCE!
!

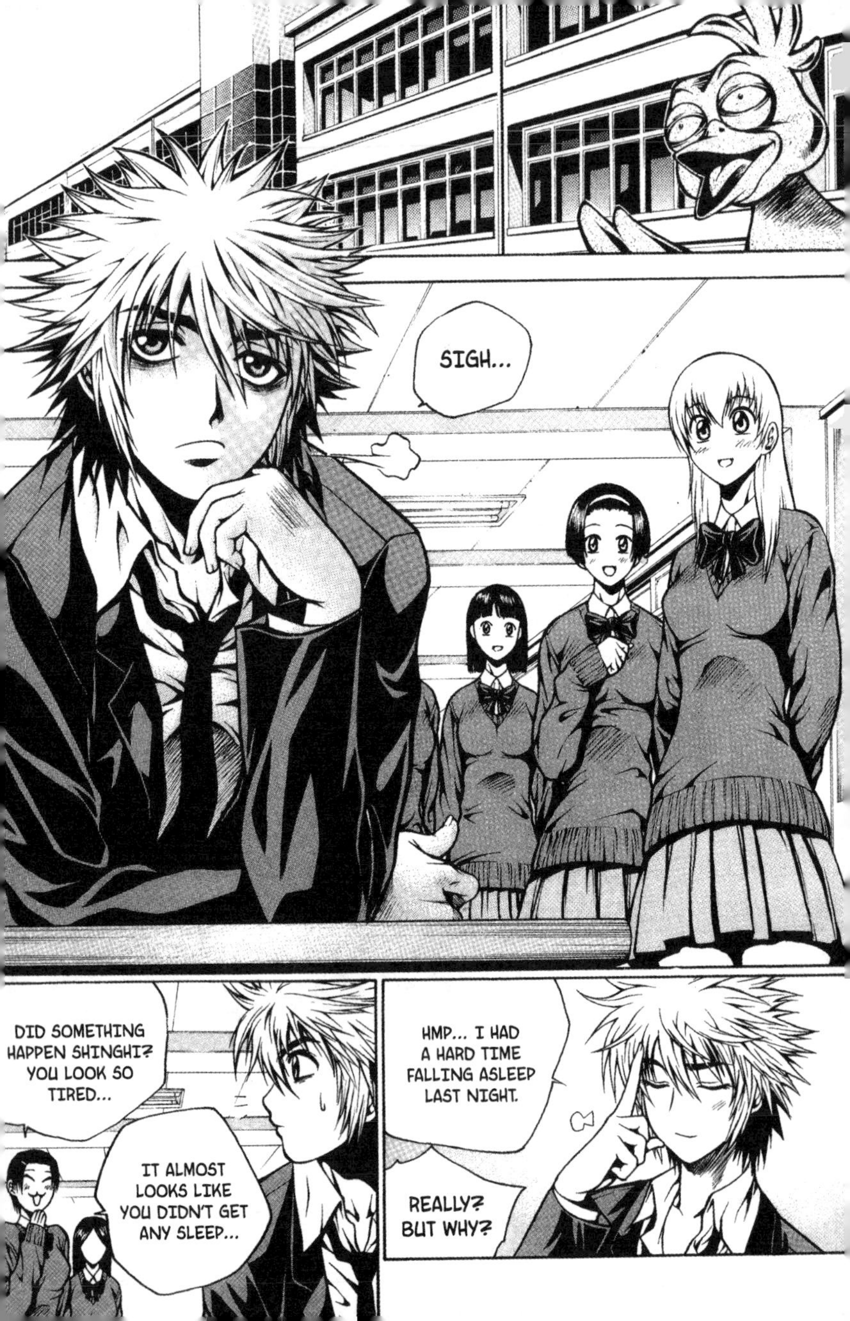
SIGH...
DID SOMETHING HAPPEN SHINGHI? YOU LOOK SO TIRED...
IT ALMOST LOOKS LIKE YOU DIDN'T GET ANY SLEEP...
HMP... I HAD A HARD TIME FALLING ASLEEP LAST NIGHT.
REALLY? BUT WHY?

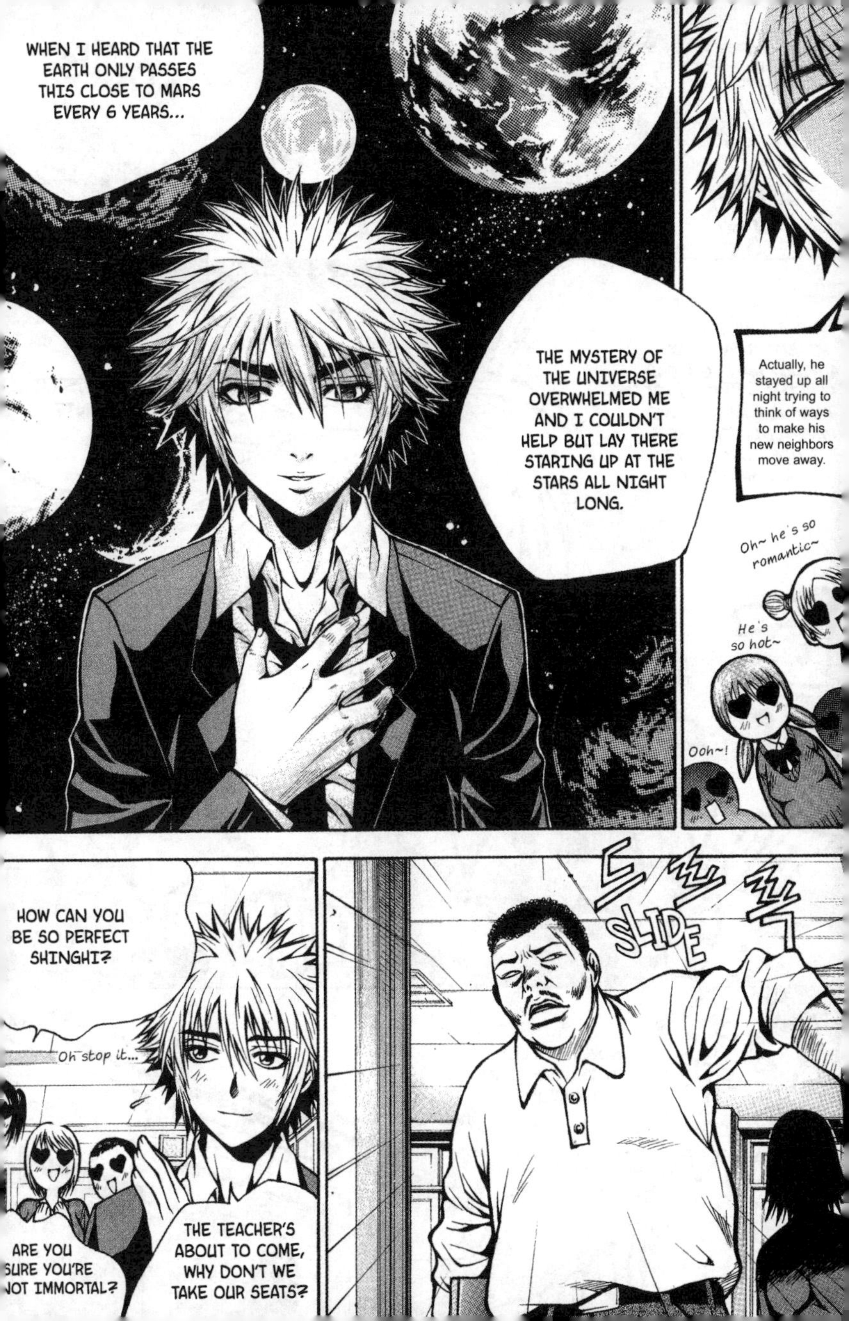
WHEN I HEARD THAT THE EARTH ONLY PASSES THIS CLOSE TO MARS EVERY 6 YEARS...
THE MYSTERY OF THE UNIVERSE OVERWHELMED ME AND I COULDN'T HELP BUT LAY THERE STARING UP AT THE STARS ALL NIGHT LONG.
Actually, he stayed up all night trying to think of ways to make his new neighbors move away.
Oh~ he's so romantic~
He's so hot~
Ooh~!
HOW CAN YOU BE SO PERFECT SHINGHI?
Oh stop it...
ARE YOU SURE YOU'RE NOT IMMORTAL?
THE TEACHER'S ABOUT TO COME, WHY DON'T WE TAKE OUR SEATS?
SLIDE

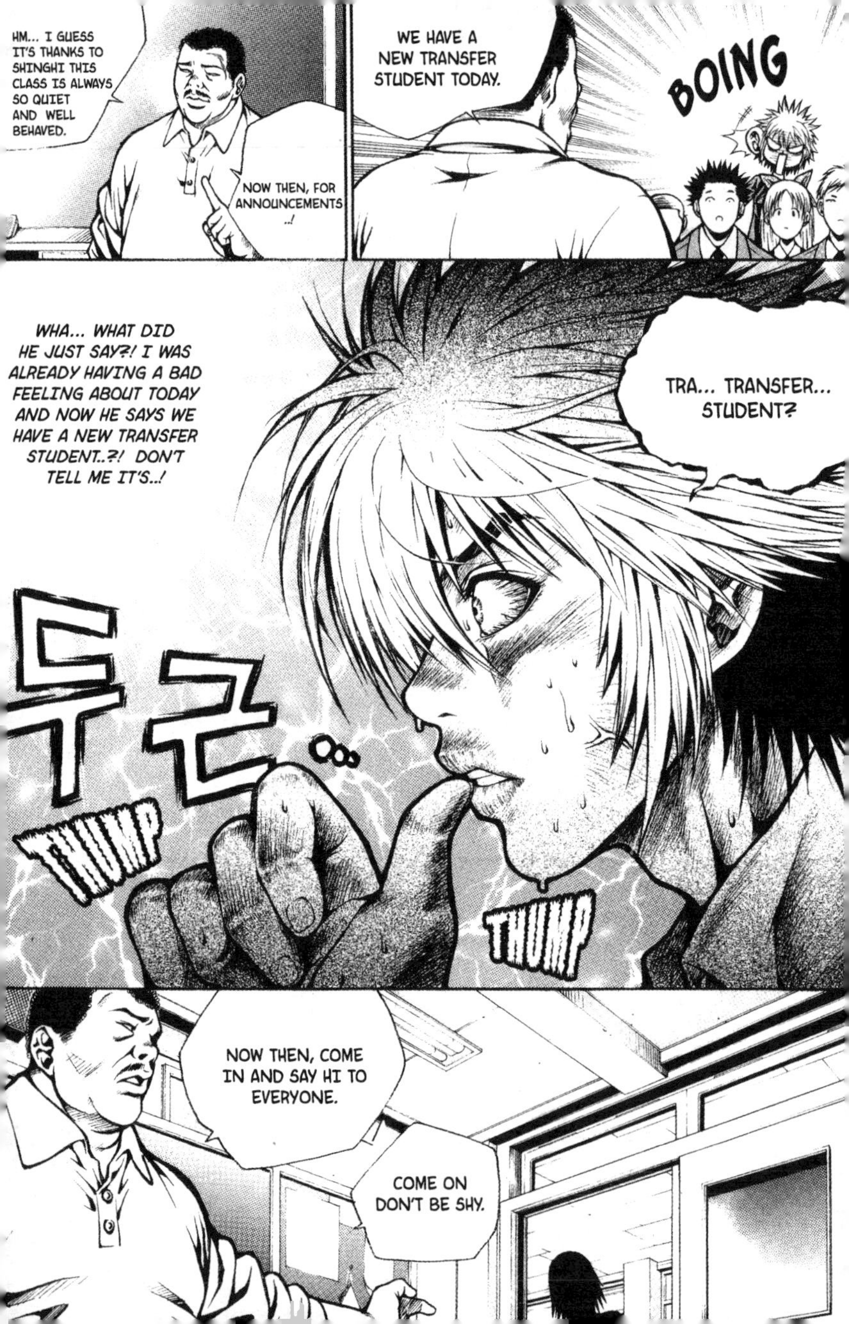
HM... I GUESS IT'S THANKS TO SHINGHI THIS CLASS IS ALWAYS SO QUIET AND WELL BEHAVED.
NOW THEN, FOR ANNOUNCEMENTS ..!
WE HAVE A NEW TRANSFER STUDENT TODAY.
BOING
TRA... TRANSFER... STUDENT?
WHA... WHAT DID HE JUST SAY?! I WAS ALREADY HAVING A BAD FEELING ABOUT TODAY AND NOW HE SAYS WE HAVE A NEW TRANSFER STUDENT..?! DON'T TELL ME IT'S..!
두근
THUMP
THUMP
NOW THEN, COME IN AND SAY HI TO EVERYONE.
COME ON DON'T BE SHY.

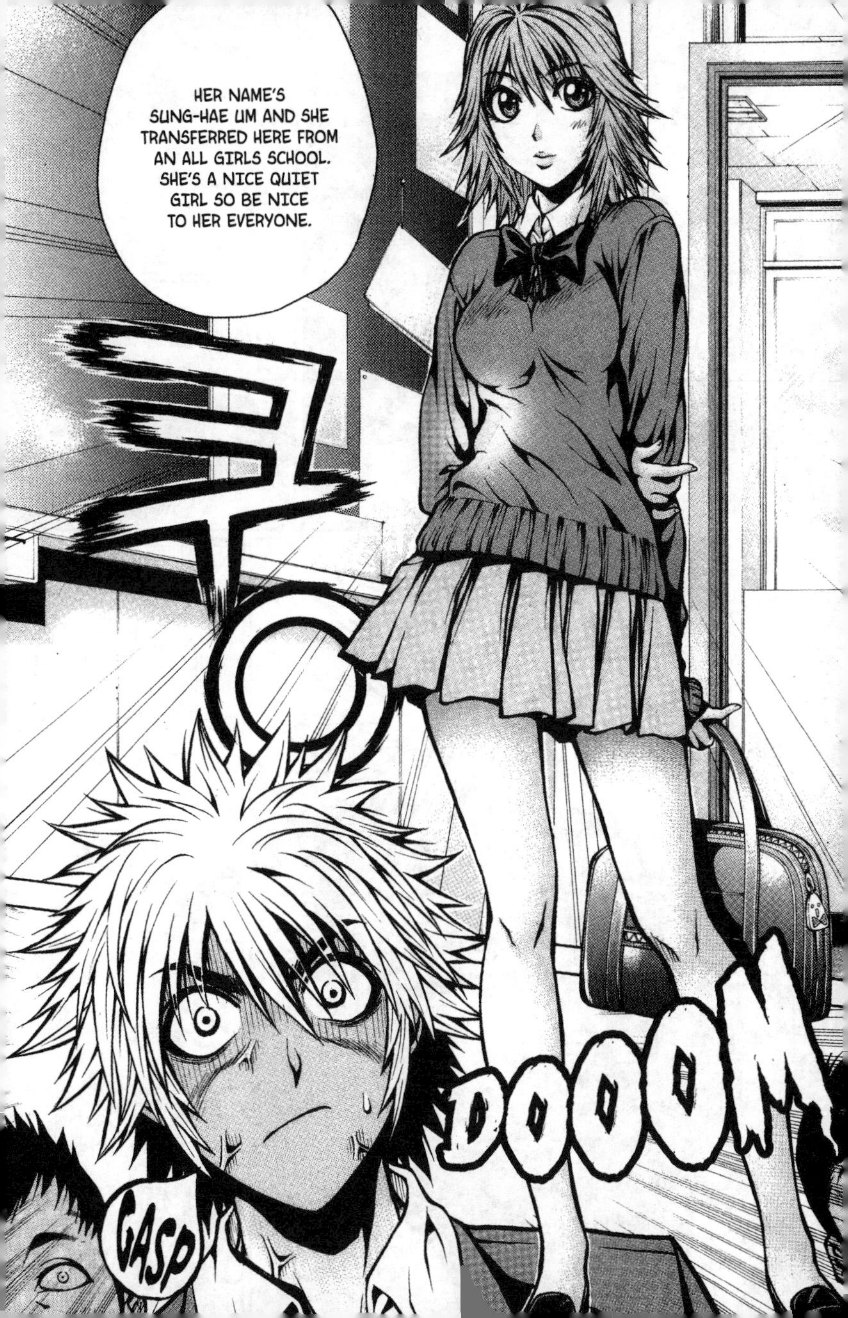
HER NAME'S SUNG-HAE UM AND SHE TRANSFERRED HERE FROM AN ALL GIRLS SCHOOL. SHE'S A NICE QUIET GIRL SO BE NICE TO HER EVERYONE.
DOOOOM
GASP

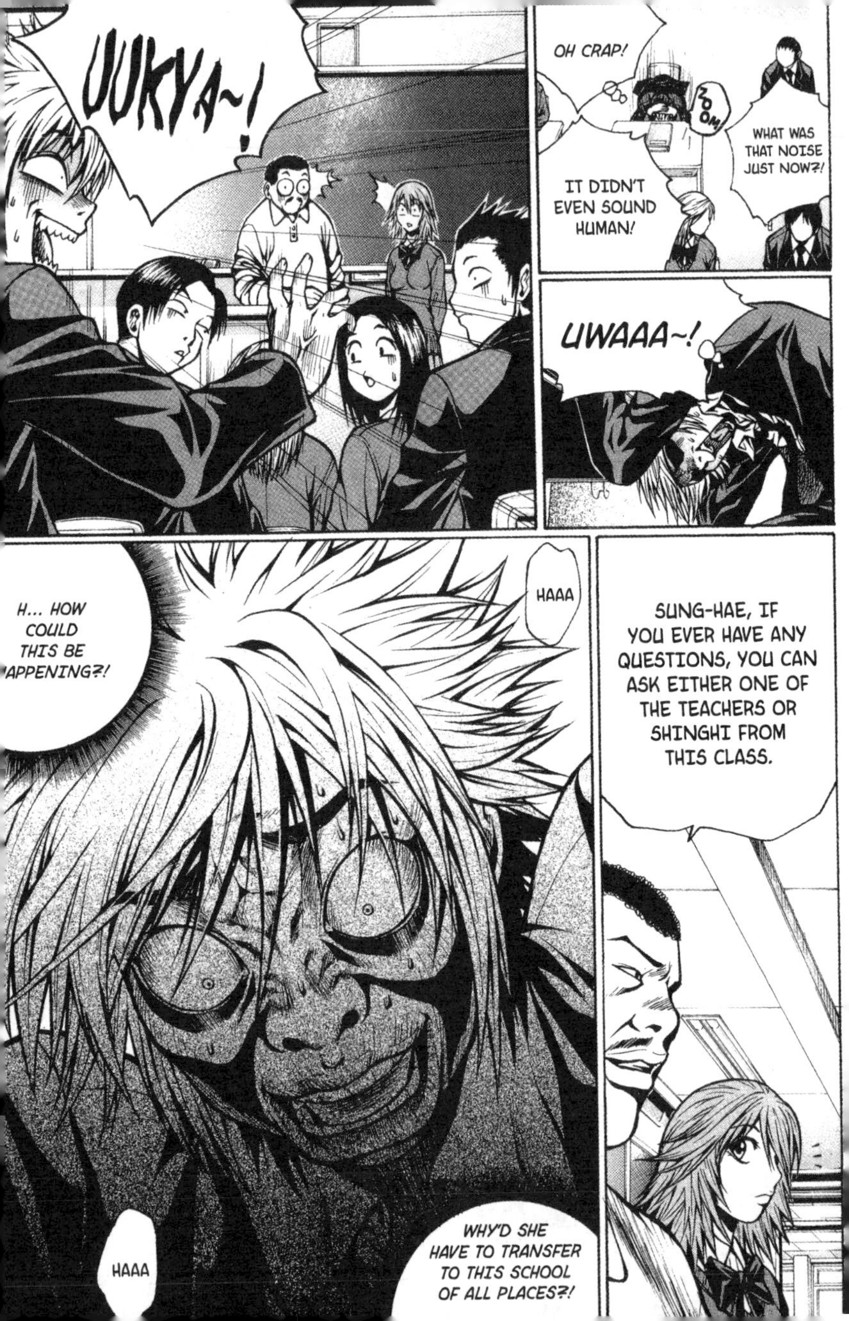
UUKYA~!
OH CRAP!
ZOOM
IT DIDN'T EVEN SOUND HUMAN!
WHAT WAS THAT NOISE JUST NOW?!
UWAAA~!
H... HOW COULD THIS BE APPENING?!
HAAA
HAAA
WHY'D SHE HAVE TO TRANSFER TO THIS SCHOOL OF ALL PLACES?!
SUNG-HAE, IF YOU EVER HAVE ANY QUESTIONS, YOU CAN ASK EITHER ONE OF THE TEACHERS OR SHINGHI FROM THIS CLASS.

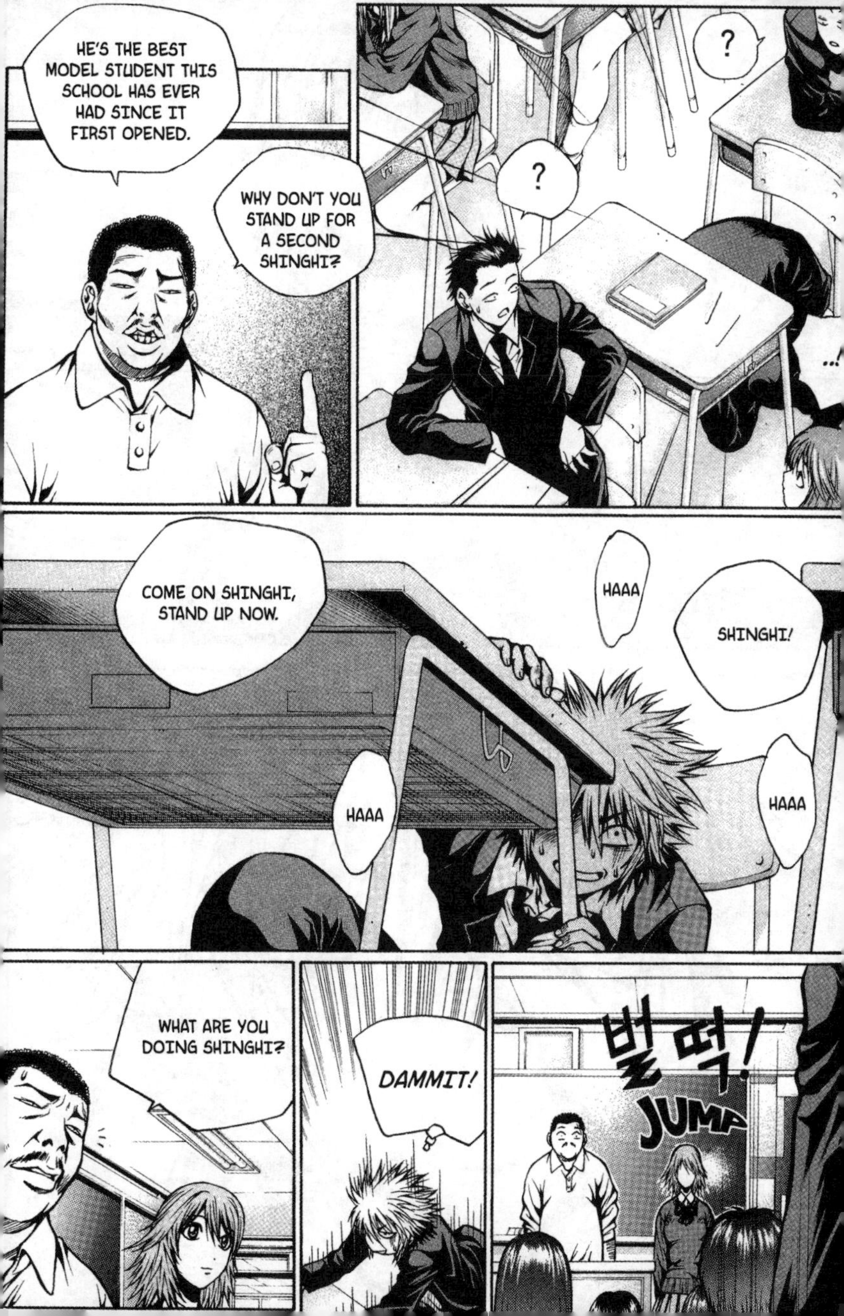
HE'S THE BEST MODEL STUDENT THIS SCHOOL HAS EVER HAD SINCE IT FIRST OPENED.
WHY DON'T YOU STAND UP FOR A SECOND SHINGHI?
?
?
..!
COME ON SHINGHI, STAND UP NOW.
HAAA
SHINGHI!
HAAA
HAAA
WHAT ARE YOU DOING SHINGHI?
DAMMIT!
벌떡!
JUMP

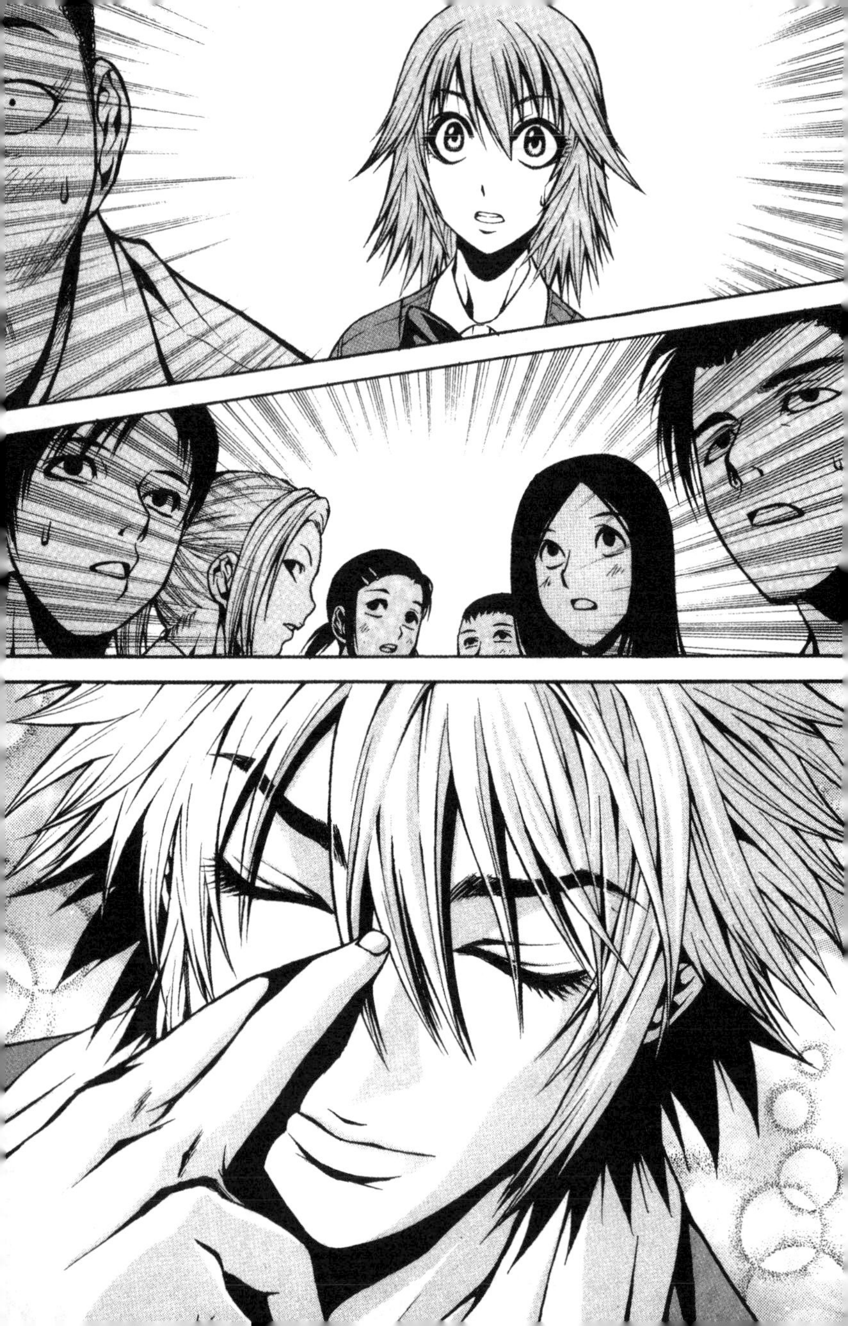

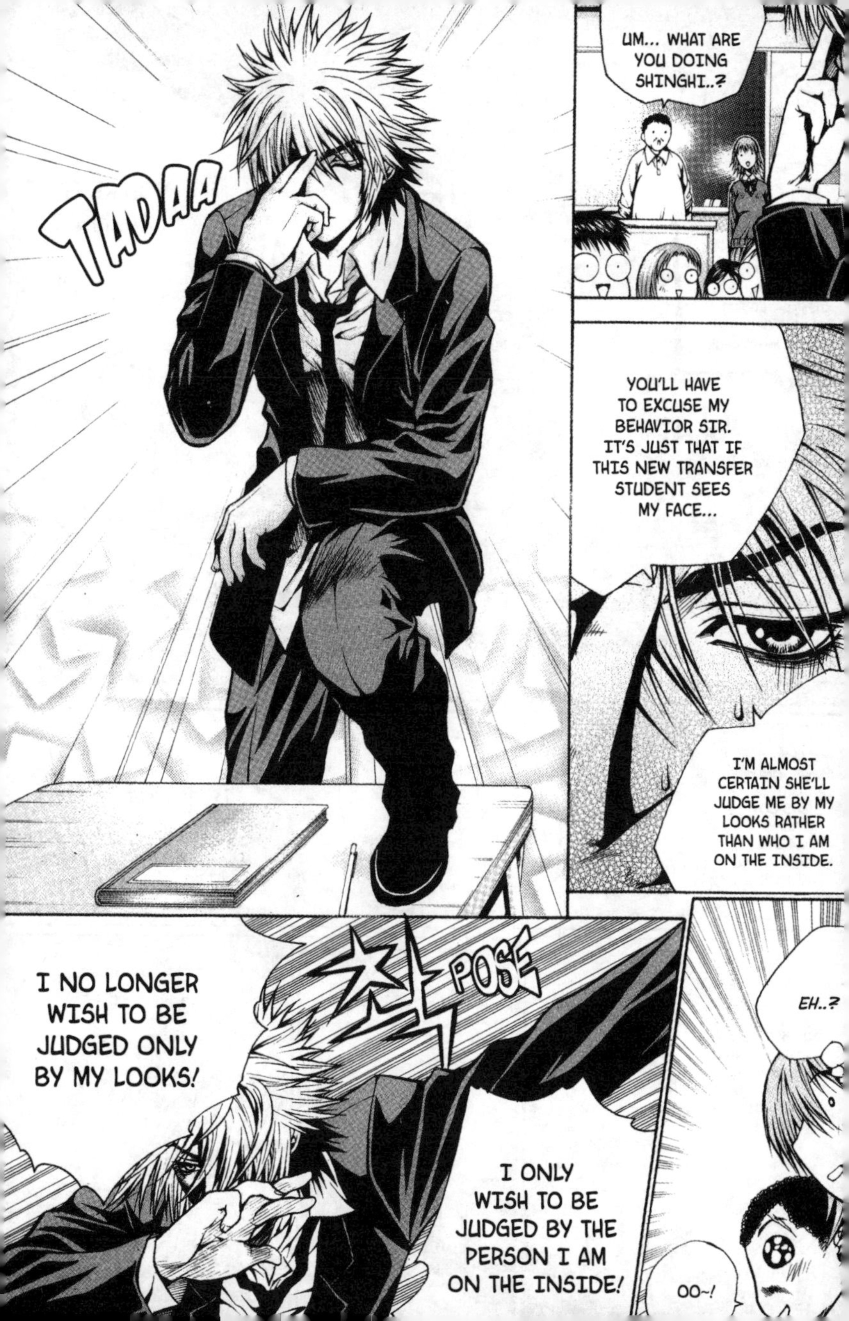
TADAA
UM... WHAT ARE YOU DOING SHINGHI..?
YOU'LL HAVE TO EXCUSE MY BEHAVIOR SIR. IT'S JUST THAT IF THIS NEW TRANSFER STUDENT SEES MY FACE...
I'M ALMOST CERTAIN SHE'LL JUDGE ME BY MY LOOKS RATHER THAN WHO I AM ON THE INSIDE.
I NO LONGER WISH TO BE JUDGED ONLY BY MY LOOKS!
POSE
I ONLY WISH TO BE JUDGED BY THE PERSON I AM ON THE INSIDE!
EH..?
OO~!

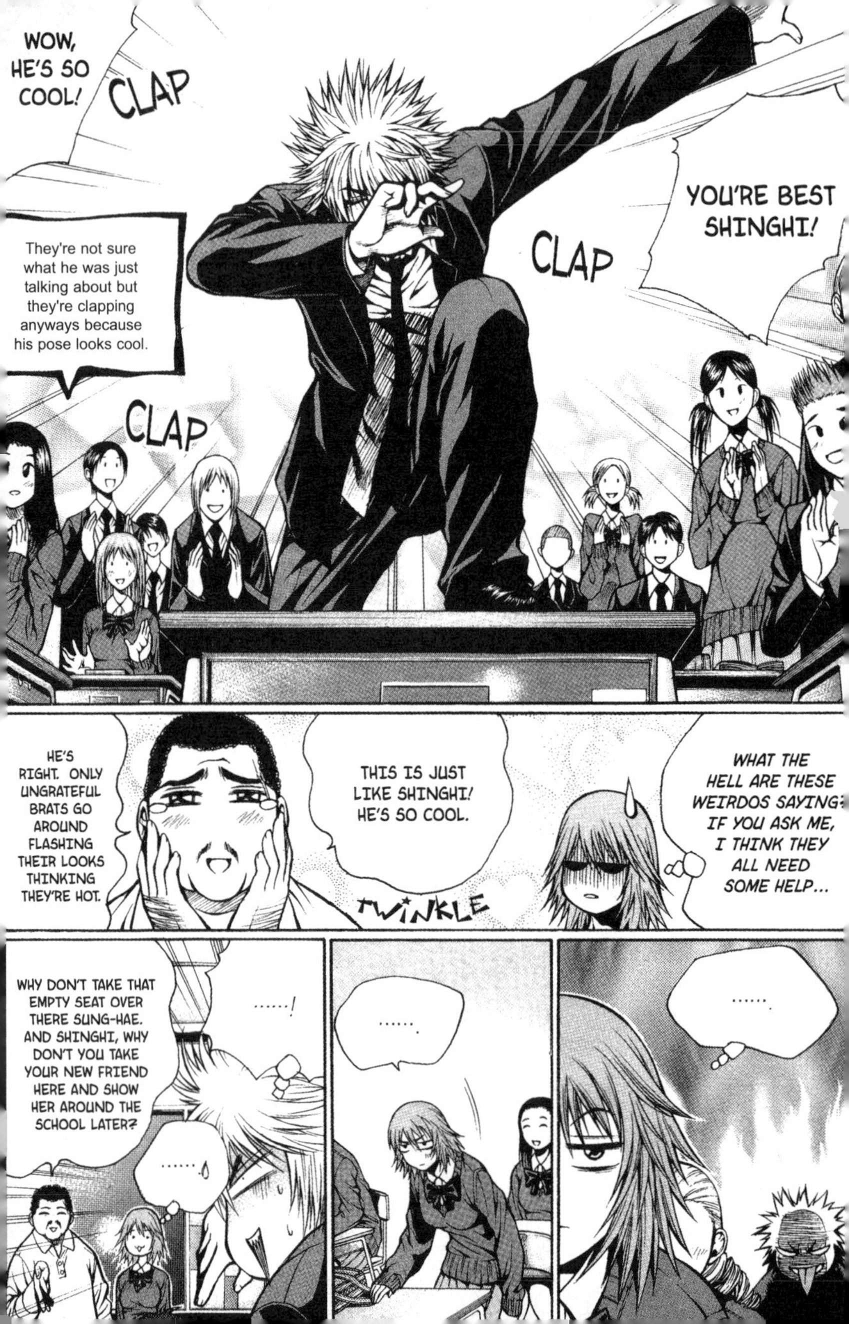
WOW, HE'S SO COOL!
CLAP
YOU'RE BEST SHINGHI!
They're not sure what he was just talking about but they're clapping anyways because his pose looks cool.
CLAP
CLAP
HE'S RIGHT. ONLY UNGRATEFUL BRATS GO AROUND FLASHING THEIR LOOKS THINKING THEY'RE HOT.
THIS IS JUST LIKE SHINGHI! HE'S SO COOL.
TWINKLE
WHAT THE HELL ARE THESE WEIRDOS SAYING? IF YOU ASK ME, I THINK THEY ALL NEED SOME HELP...
WHY DON'T TAKE THAT EMPTY SEAT OVER THERE SUNG-HAE. AND SHINGHI, WHY DON'T YOU TAKE YOUR NEW FRIEND HERE AND SHOW HER AROUND THE SCHOOL LATER?
......!
....
....
....

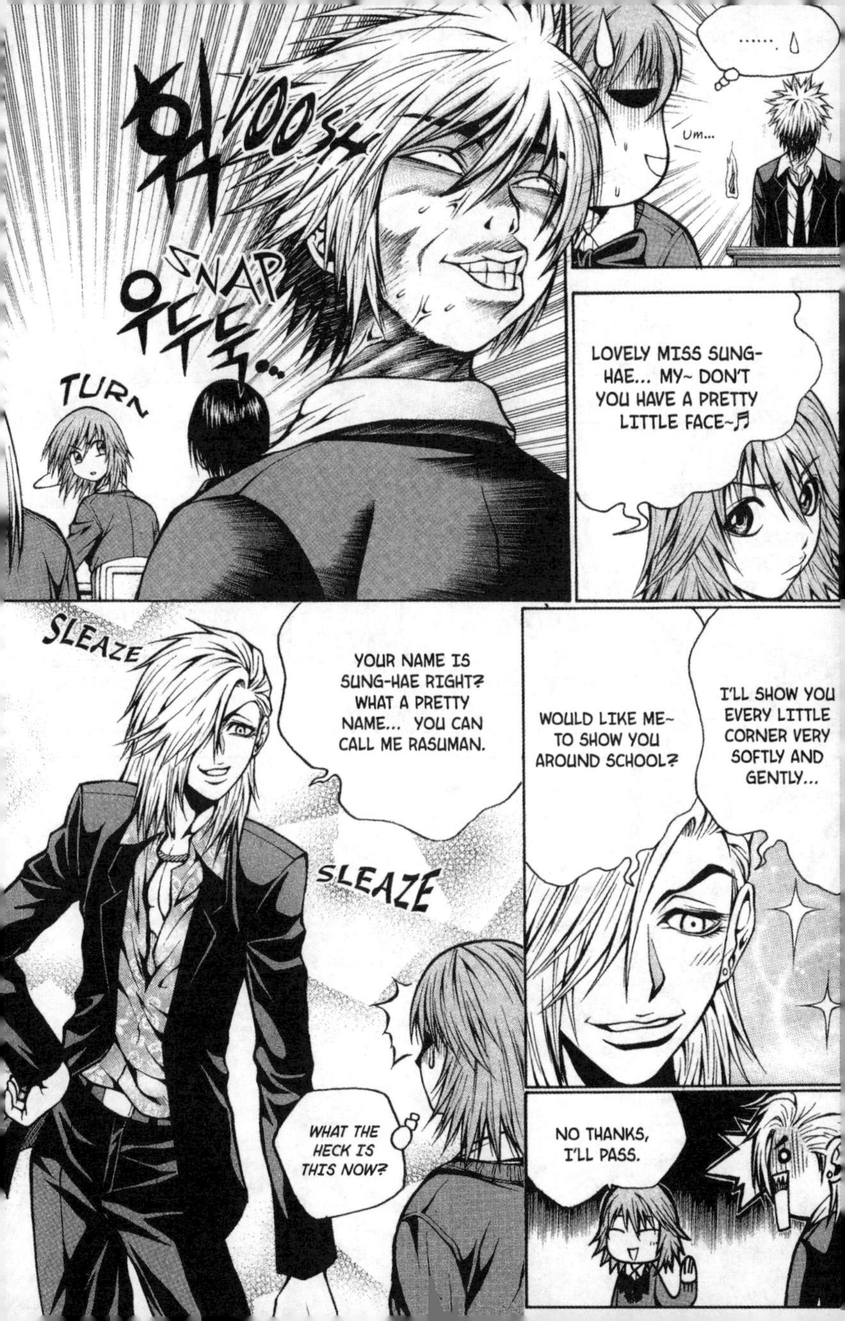
WHOOSH
SNAP
우두둑...
TURN
....
UM...
LOVELY MISS SUNG-HAE... MY~ DON'T YOU HAVE A PRETTY LITTLE FACE~♬
SLEAZE
YOUR NAME IS SUNG-HAE RIGHT? WHAT A PRETTY NAME... YOU CAN CALL ME RASUMAN.
SLEAZE
WHAT THE HECK IS THIS NOW?
WOULD LIKE ME~ TO SHOW YOU AROUND SCHOOL?
I'LL SHOW YOU EVERY LITTLE CORNER VERY SOFTLY AND GENTLY...
NO THANKS, I'LL PASS.

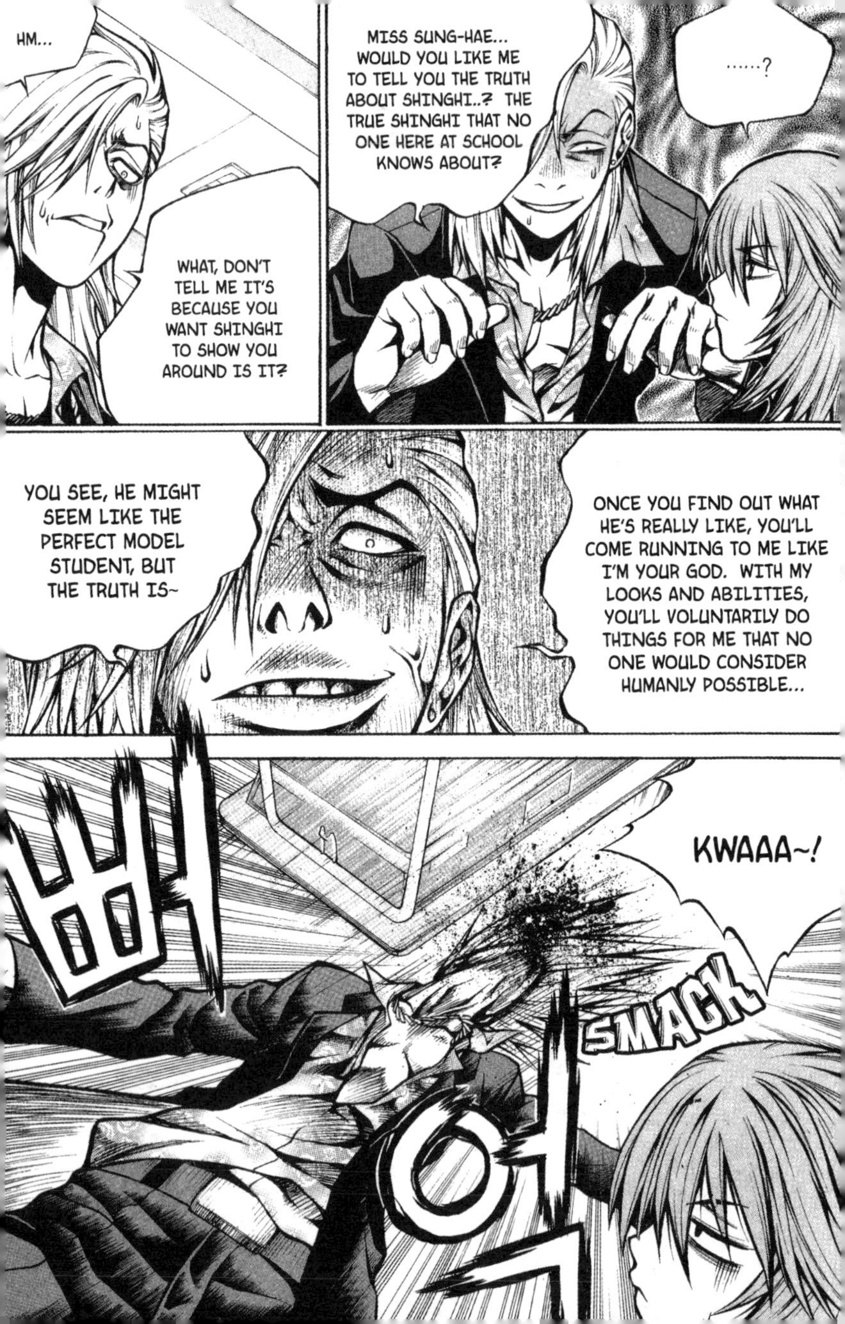
HM...
WHAT, DON'T TELL ME IT'S BECAUSE YOU WANT SHINGHI TO SHOW YOU AROUND IS IT?
MISS SUNG-HAE... WOULD YOU LIKE ME TO TELL YOU THE TRUTH ABOUT SHINGHI..? THE TRUE SHINGHI THAT NO ONE HERE AT SCHOOL KNOWS ABOUT?
......?
YOU SEE, HE MIGHT SEEM LIKE THE PERFECT MODEL STUDENT, BUT THE TRUTH IS~
ONCE YOU FIND OUT WHAT HE'S REALLY LIKE, YOU'LL COME RUNNING TO ME LIKE I'M YOUR GOD. WITH MY LOOKS AND ABILITIES, YOU'LL VOLUNTARILY DO THINGS FOR ME THAT NO ONE WOULD CONSIDER HUMANLY POSSIBLE...
KWAAA~!
SMACK

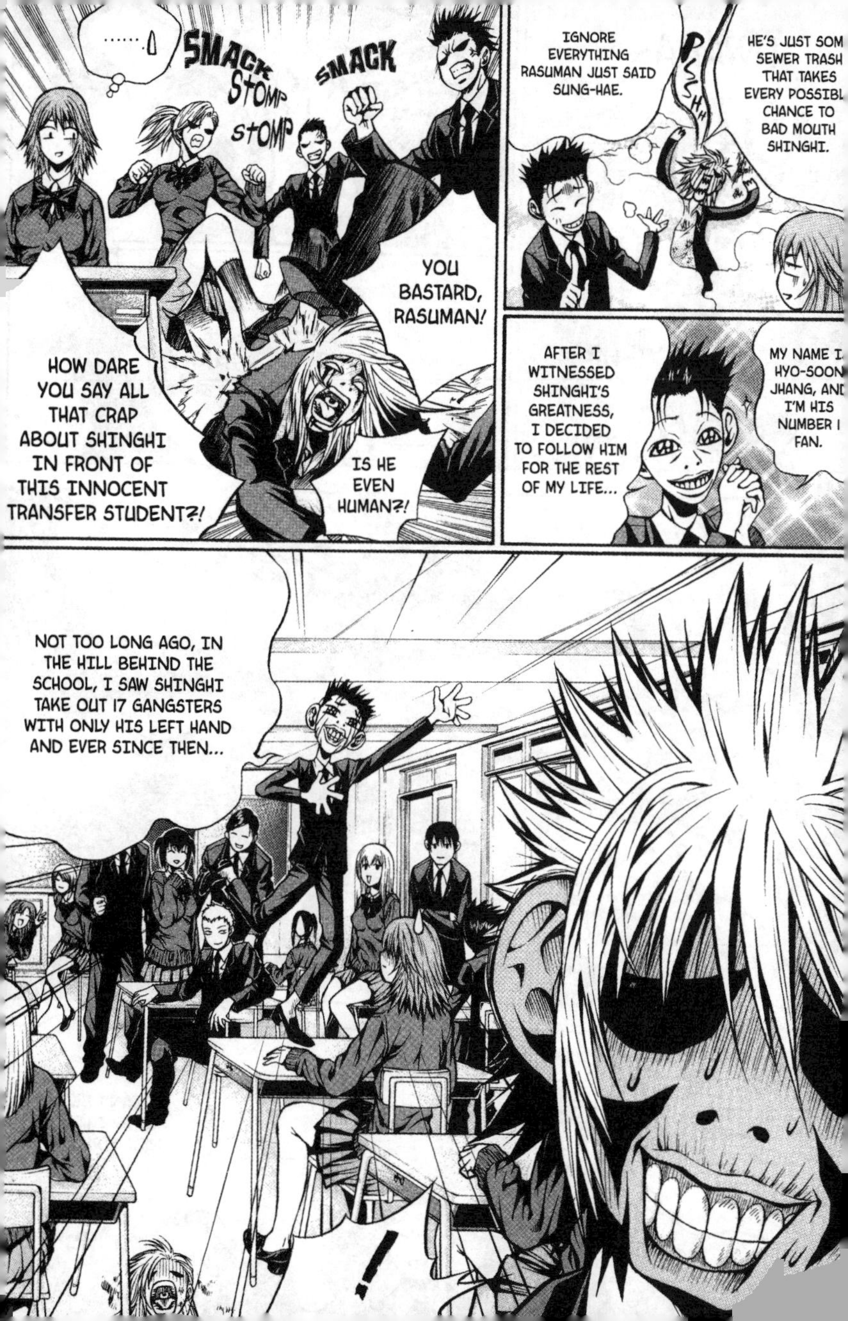
......!
SMACK
STOMP
SMACK
STOMP
YOU BASTARD, RASUMAN!
HOW DARE YOU SAY ALL THAT CRAP ABOUT SHINGHI IN FRONT OF THIS INNOCENT TRANSFER STUDENT?!
IS HE EVEN HUMAN?!
IGNORE EVERYTHING RASUMAN JUST SAID SUNG-HAE.
PUSHH
HE'S JUST SOM SEWER TRASH THAT TAKES EVERY POSSIBL CHANCE TO BAD MOUTH SHINGHI.
AFTER I WITNESSED SHINGHI'S GREATNESS, I DECIDED TO FOLLOW HIM FOR THE REST OF MY LIFE...
MY NAME I HYO-SOON JHANG, AND I'M HIS NUMBER 1 FAN.
NOT TOO LONG AGO, IN THE HILL BEHIND THE SCHOOL, I SAW SHINGHI TAKE OUT 17 GANGSTERS WITH ONLY HIS LEFT HAND AND EVER SINCE THEN...
!

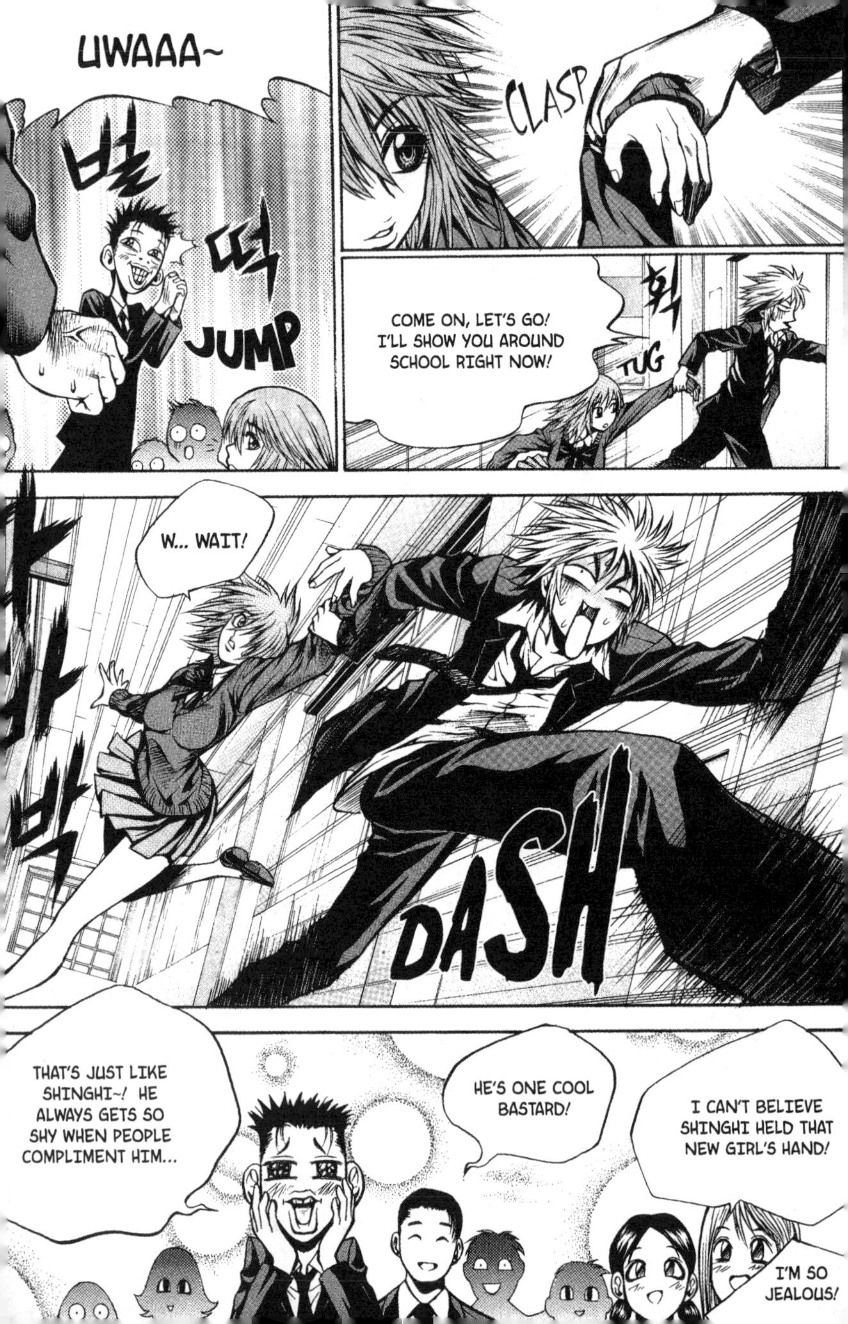
UWAAA~
JUMP
CLASP
COME ON, LET'S GO! I'LL SHOW YOU AROUND SCHOOL RIGHT NOW!
TUG
W... WAIT!
DASH
THAT'S JUST LIKE SHINGHI~! HE ALWAYS GETS SO SHY WHEN PEOPLE COMPLIMENT HIM...
HE'S ONE COOL BASTARD!
I CAN'T BELIEVE SHINGHI HELD THAT NEW GIRL'S HAND!
I'M SO JEALOUS!

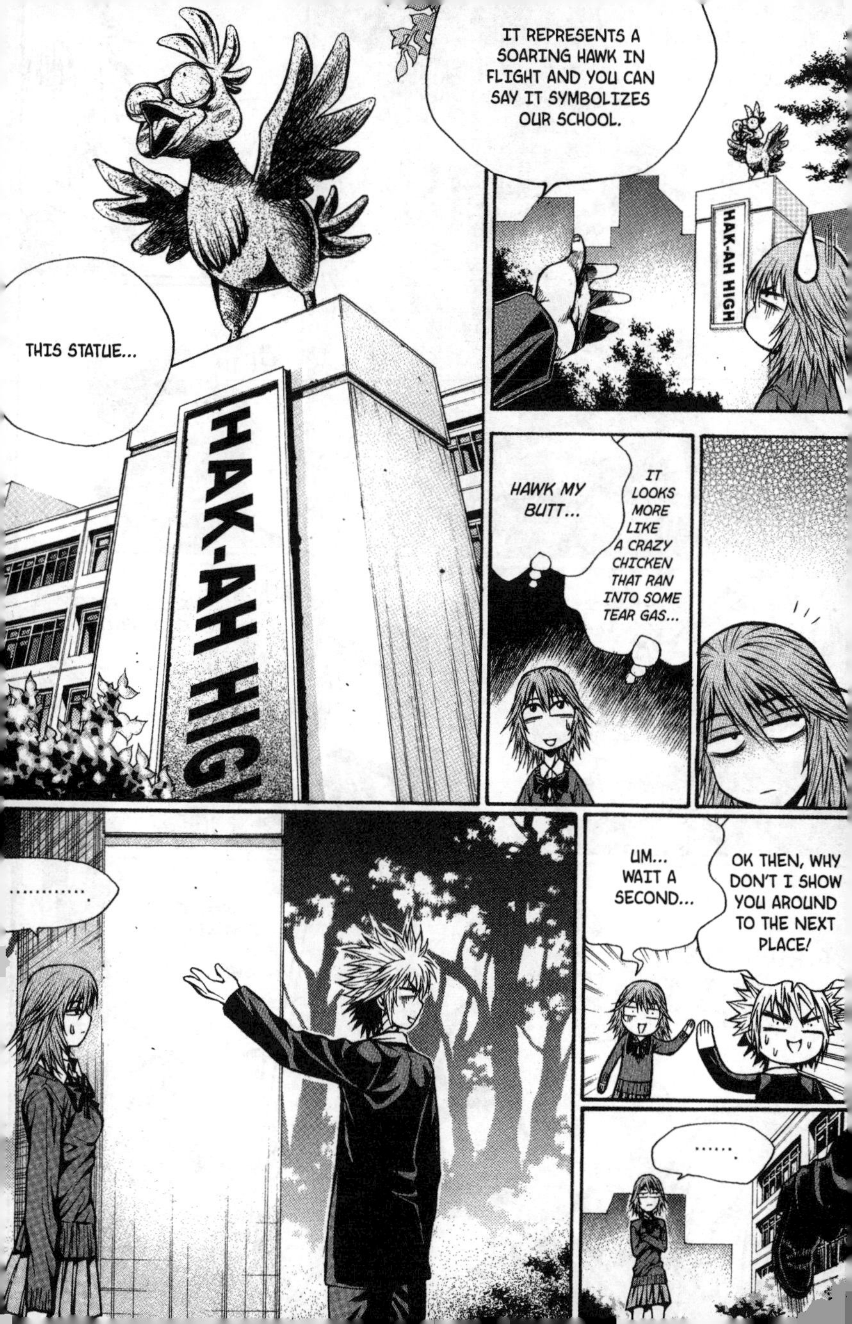

THIS STATUE...
IT REPRESENTS A SOARING HAWK IN FLIGHT AND YOU CAN SAY IT SYMBOLIZES OUR SCHOOL.
HAK-AH HIGH
HAK-AH HIGH
HAWK MY BUTT...
IT LOOKS MORE LIKE A CRAZY CHICKEN THAT RAN INTO SOME TEAR GAS...
....
OK THEN, WHY DON'T I SHOW YOU AROUND TO THE NEXT PLACE!
UM... WAIT A SECOND...
....

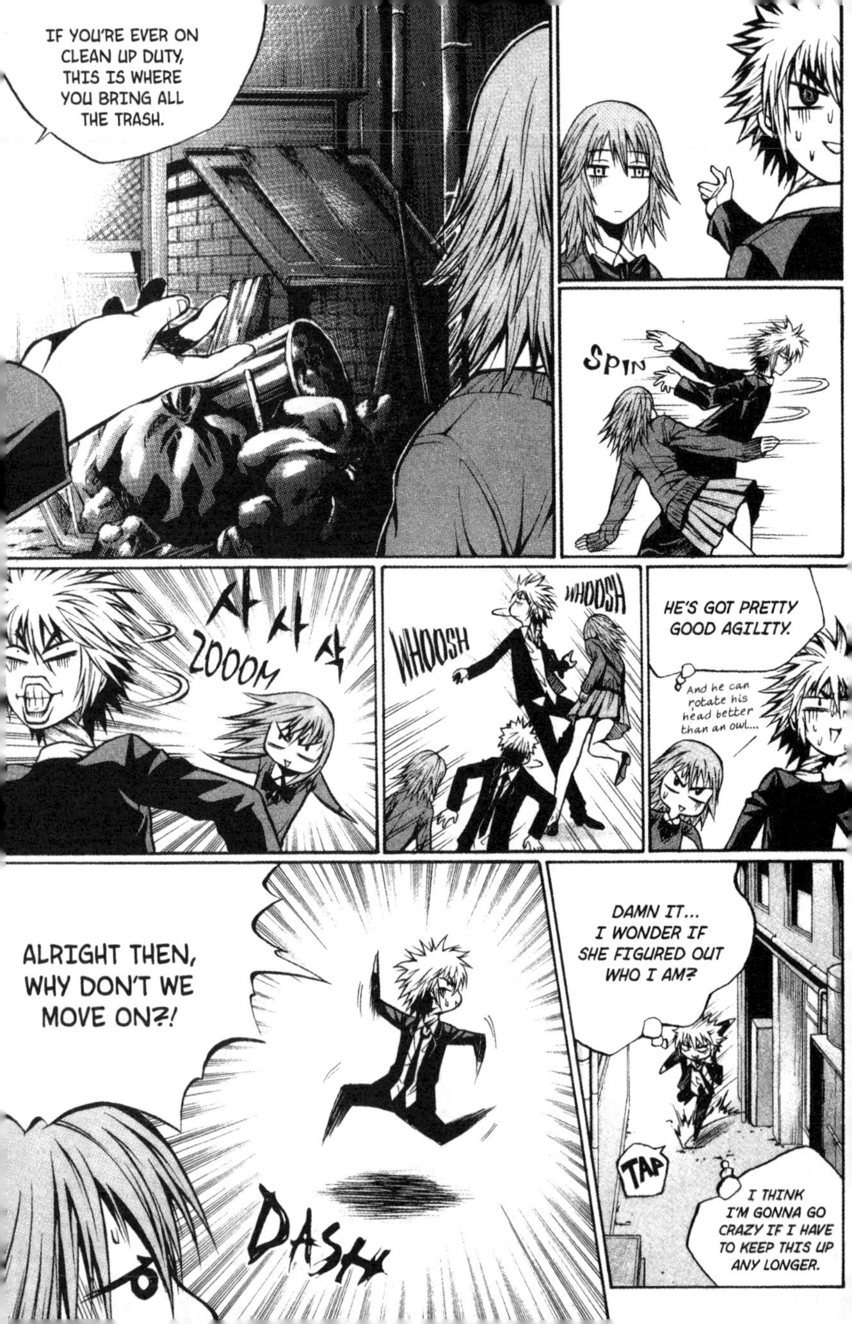
IF YOU'RE EVER ON CLEAN UP DUTY, THIS IS WHERE YOU BRING ALL THE TRASH.
SPIN
ZOOOM
WHOOSH
WHOOSH
HE'S GOT PRETTY GOOD AGILITY.
And he can rotate his head better than an owl...
ALRIGHT THEN, WHY DON'T WE MOVE ON?!
DASH
DAMN IT... I WONDER IF SHE FIGURED OUT WHO I AM?
TAP
I THINK I'M GONNA GO CRAZY IF I HAVE TO KEEP THIS UP ANY LONGER.

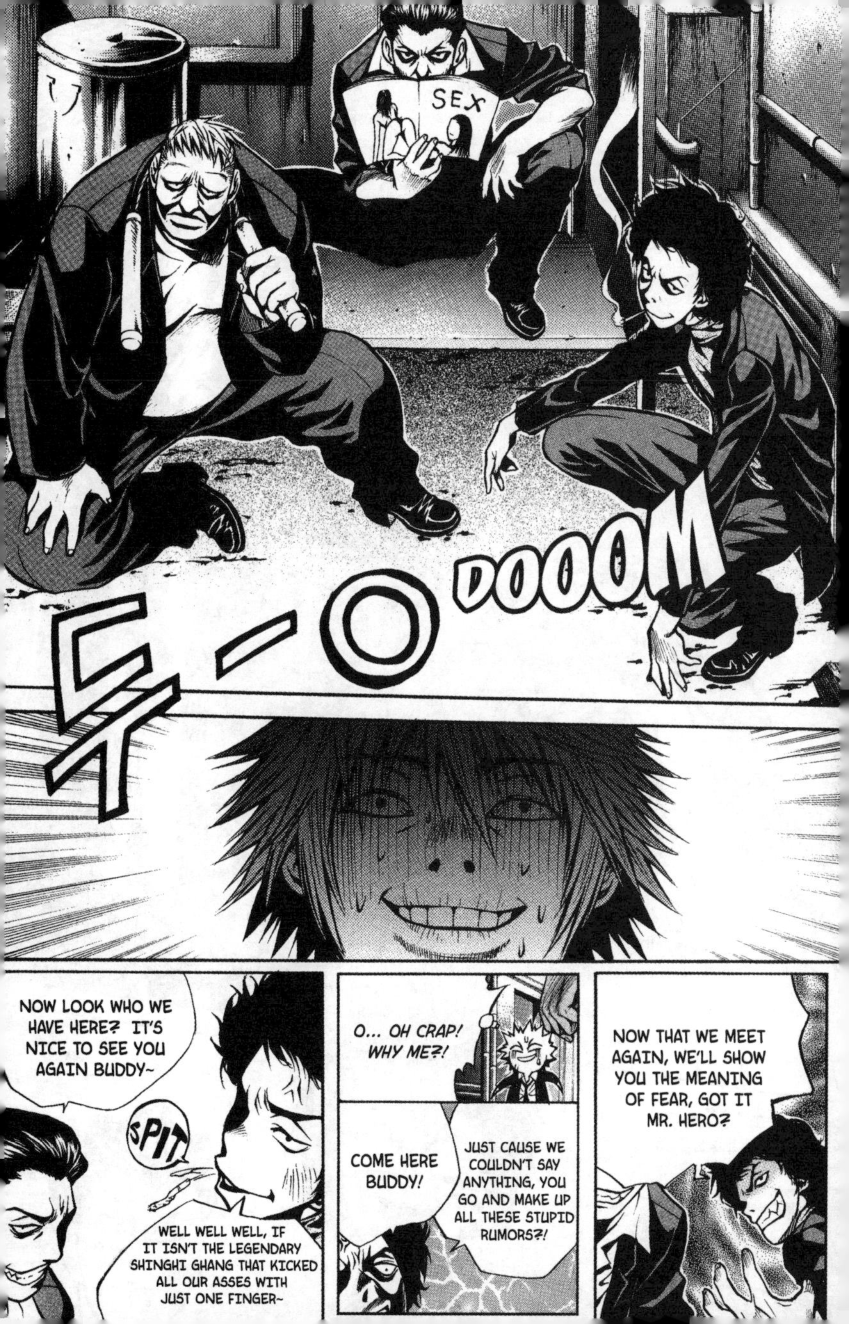
SEX
DOOOM
NOW LOOK WHO WE HAVE HERE? IT'S NICE TO SEE YOU AGAIN BUDDY~
SPIT
WELL WELL WELL, IF IT ISN'T THE LEGENDARY SHINGHI GHANG THAT KICKED ALL OUR ASSES WITH JUST ONE FINGER~
O... OH CRAP! WHY ME?!
COME HERE BUDDY!
JUST CAUSE WE COULDN'T SAY ANYTHING, YOU GO AND MAKE UP ALL THESE STUPID RUMORS?!
NOW THAT WE MEET AGAIN, WE'LL SHOW YOU THE MEANING OF FEAR, GOT IT MR. HERO?

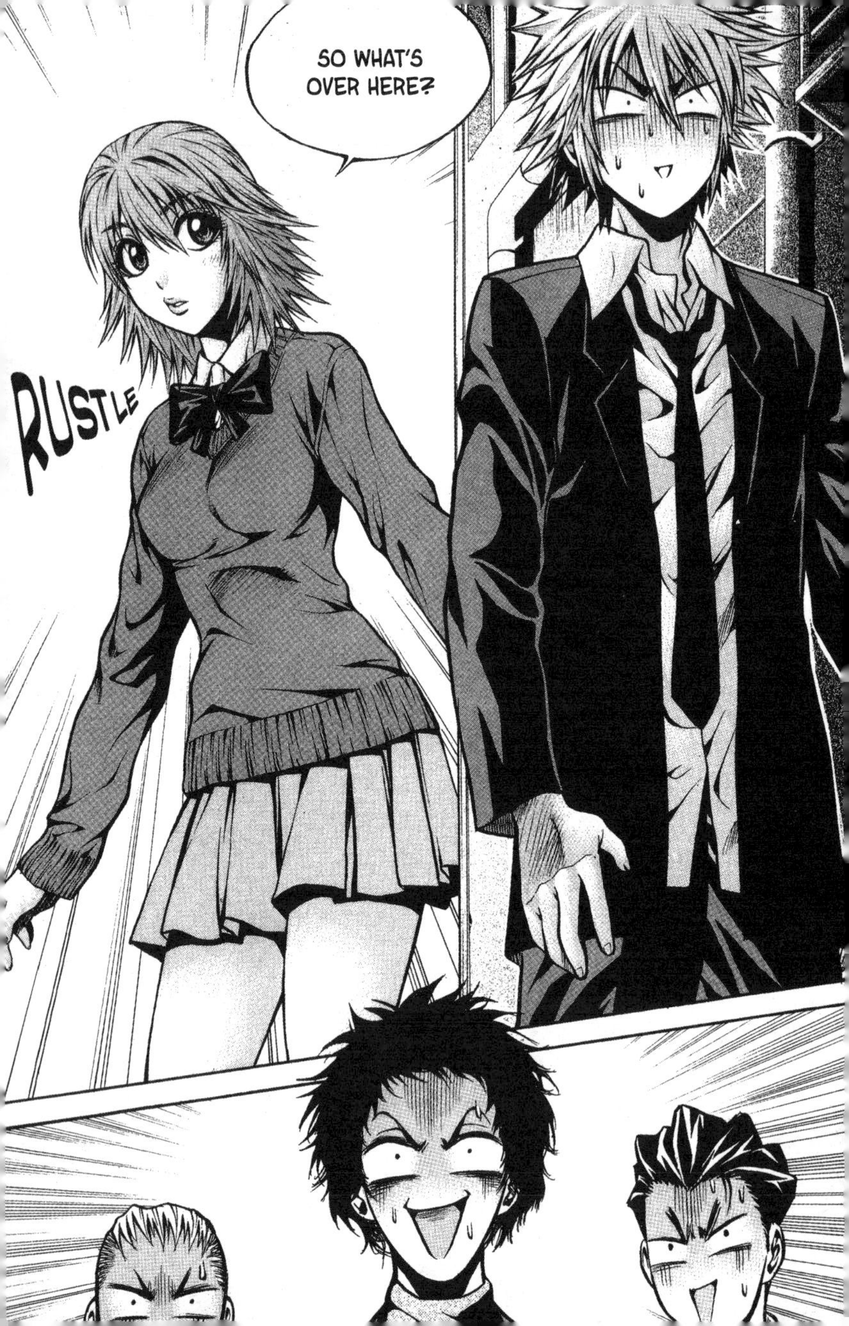
SO WHAT'S OVER HERE?
RUSTLE

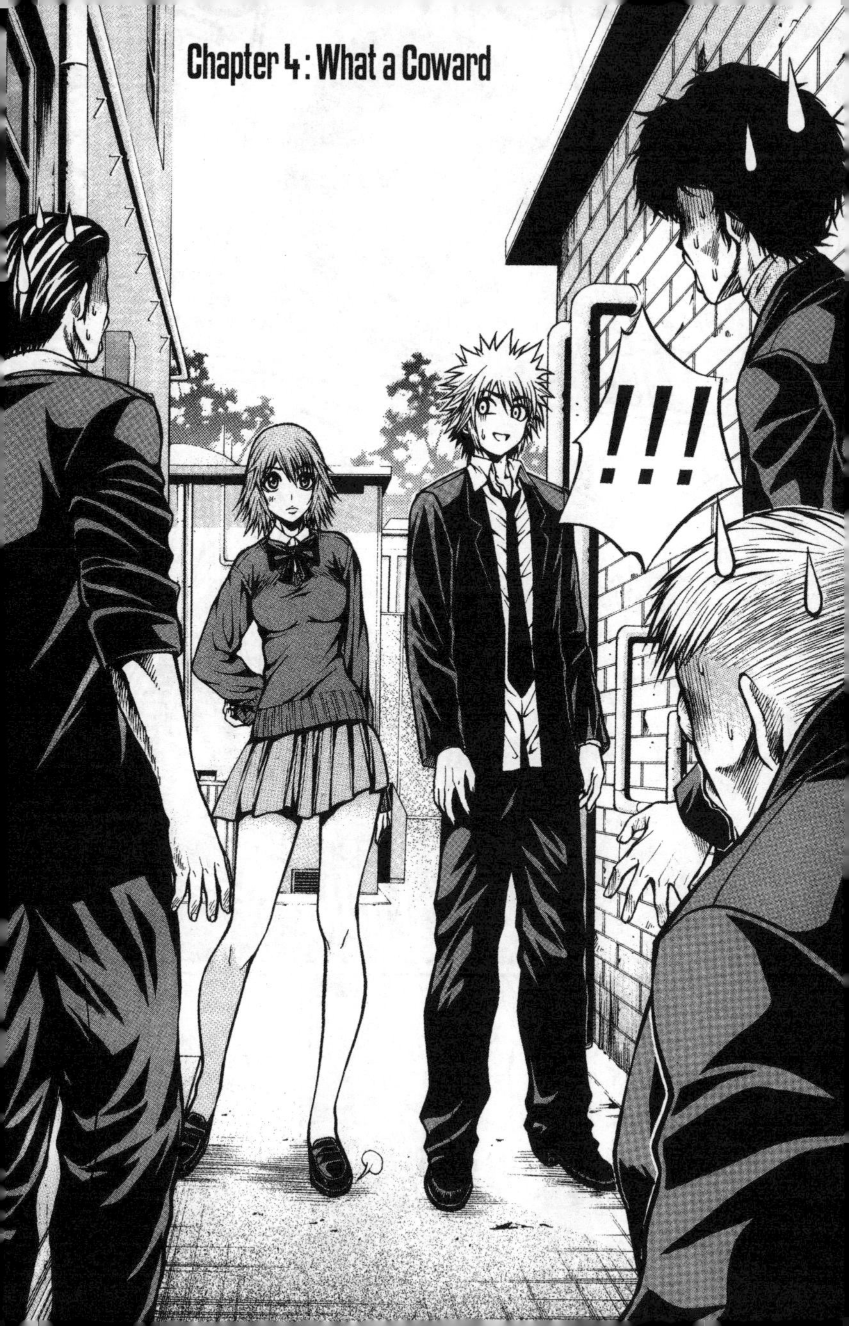
Chapter 4 : What a Coward
!!!

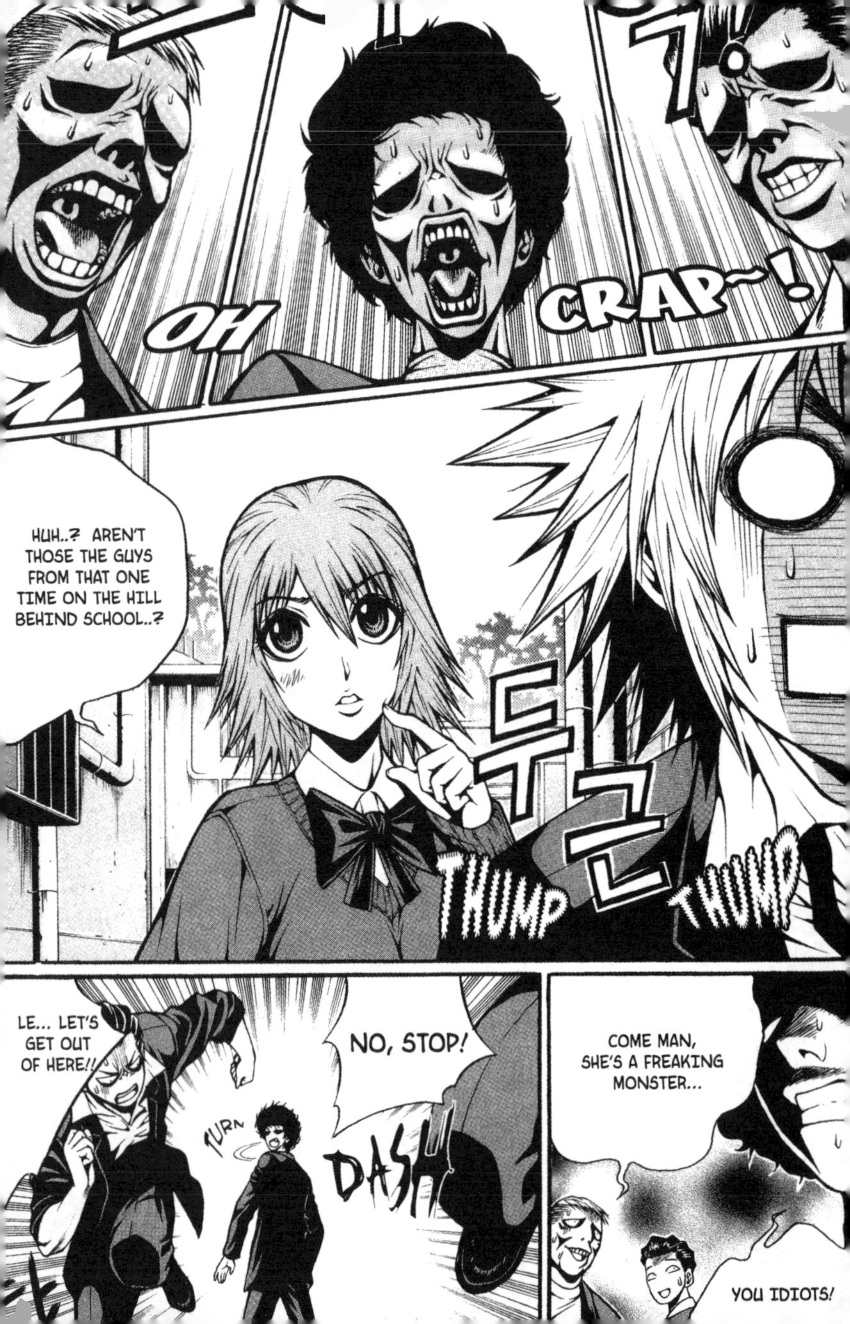
OH
CRAP~-!
HUH..? AREN'T THOSE THE GUYS FROM THAT ONE TIME ON THE HILL BEHIND SCHOOL..?
THUMP
THUMP
LE... LET'S GET OUT OF HERE!!
NO, STOP!
TURN
DASH
COME MAN, SHE'S A FREAKING MONSTER...
YOU IDIOTS!

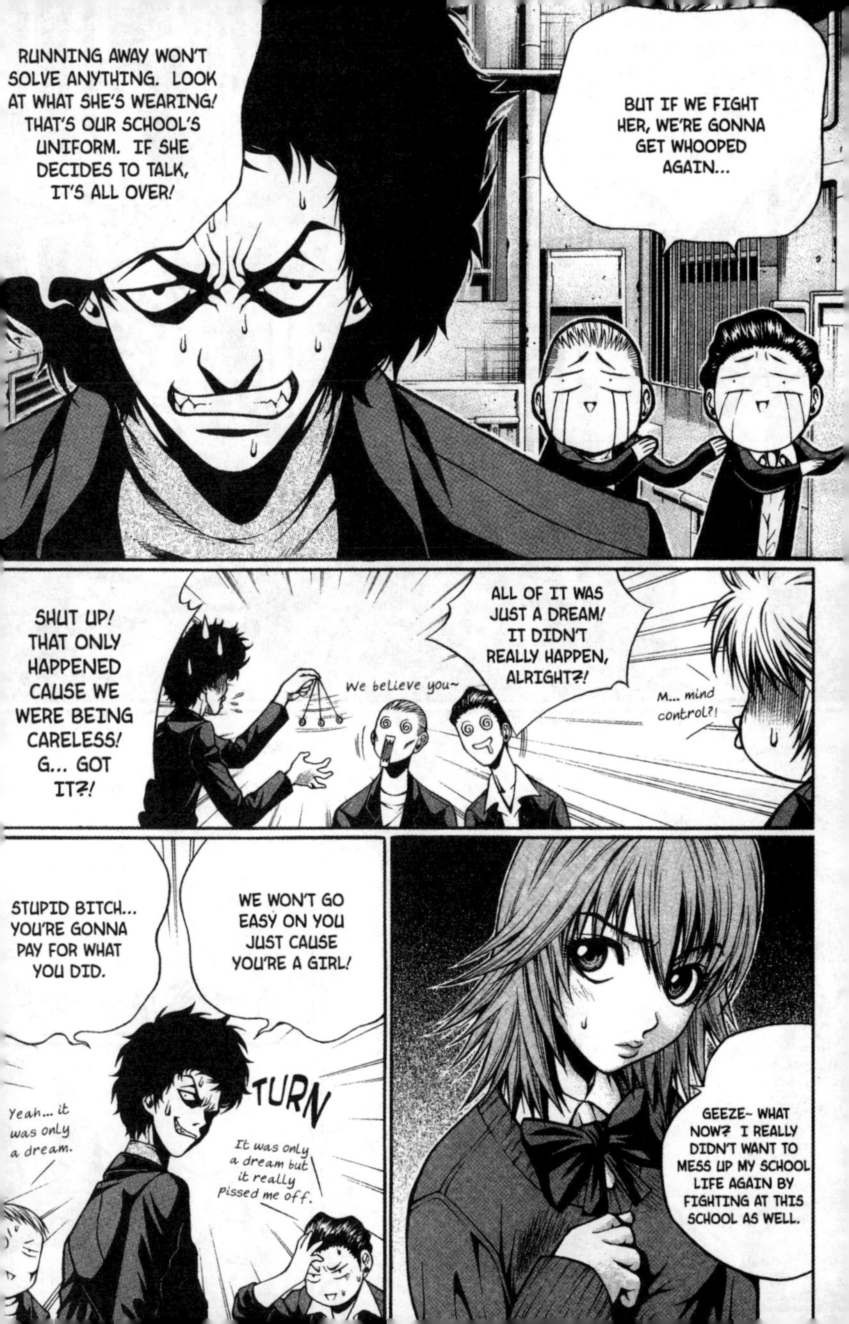
RUNNING AWAY WON'T SOLVE ANYTHING. LOOK AT WHAT SHE'S WEARING! THAT'S OUR SCHOOL'S UNIFORM. IF SHE DECIDES TO TALK, IT'S ALL OVER!
BUT IF WE FIGHT HER, WE'RE GONNA GET WHOOPED AGAIN...
SHUT UP! THAT ONLY HAPPENED CAUSE WE WERE BEING CARELESS! G... GOT IT?!
We believe you~
ALL OF IT WAS JUST A DREAM! IT DIDN'T REALLY HAPPEN, ALRIGHT?!
M... mind control?!
STUPID BITCH... YOU'RE GONNA PAY FOR WHAT YOU DID.
WE WON'T GO EASY ON YOU JUST CAUSE YOU'RE A GIRL!
TURN
Yeah... it was only a dream.
It was only a dream but it really pissed me off.
GEEZE~ WHAT NOW? I REALLY DIDN'T WANT TO MESS UP MY SCHOOL LIFE AGAIN BY FIGHTING AT THIS SCHOOL AS WELL.

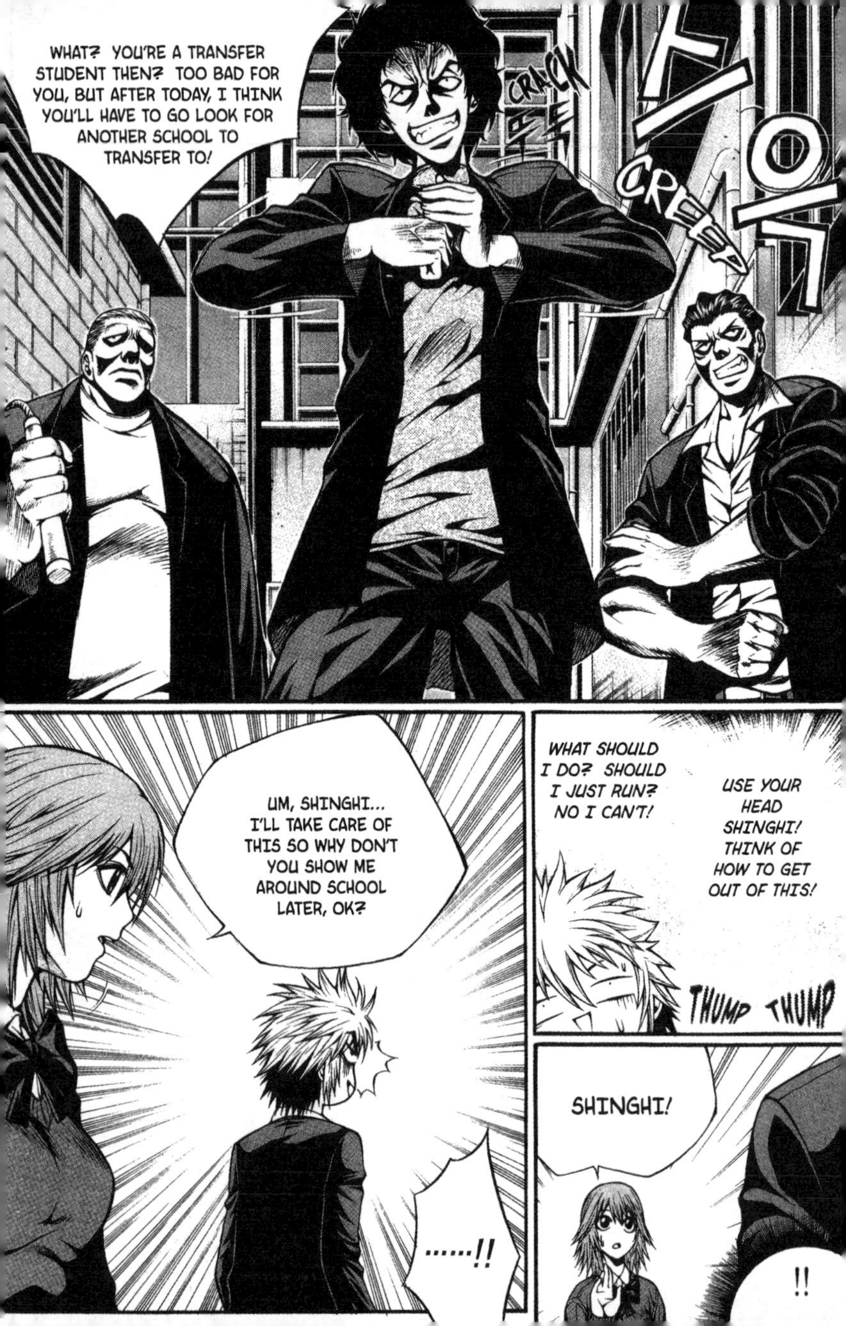
WHAT? YOU'RE A TRANSFER STUDENT THEN? TOO BAD FOR YOU, BUT AFTER TODAY, I THINK YOU'LL HAVE TO GO LOOK FOR ANOTHER SCHOOL TO TRANSFER TO!
CRACK
UM, SHINGHI... I'LL TAKE CARE OF THIS SO WHY DON'T YOU SHOW ME AROUND SCHOOL LATER, OK?
......!!
WHAT SHOULD I DO? SHOULD I JUST RUN? NO I CAN'T!
USE YOUR HEAD SHINGHI! THINK OF HOW TO GET OUT OF THIS!
THUMP THUMP
SHINGHI!
!!

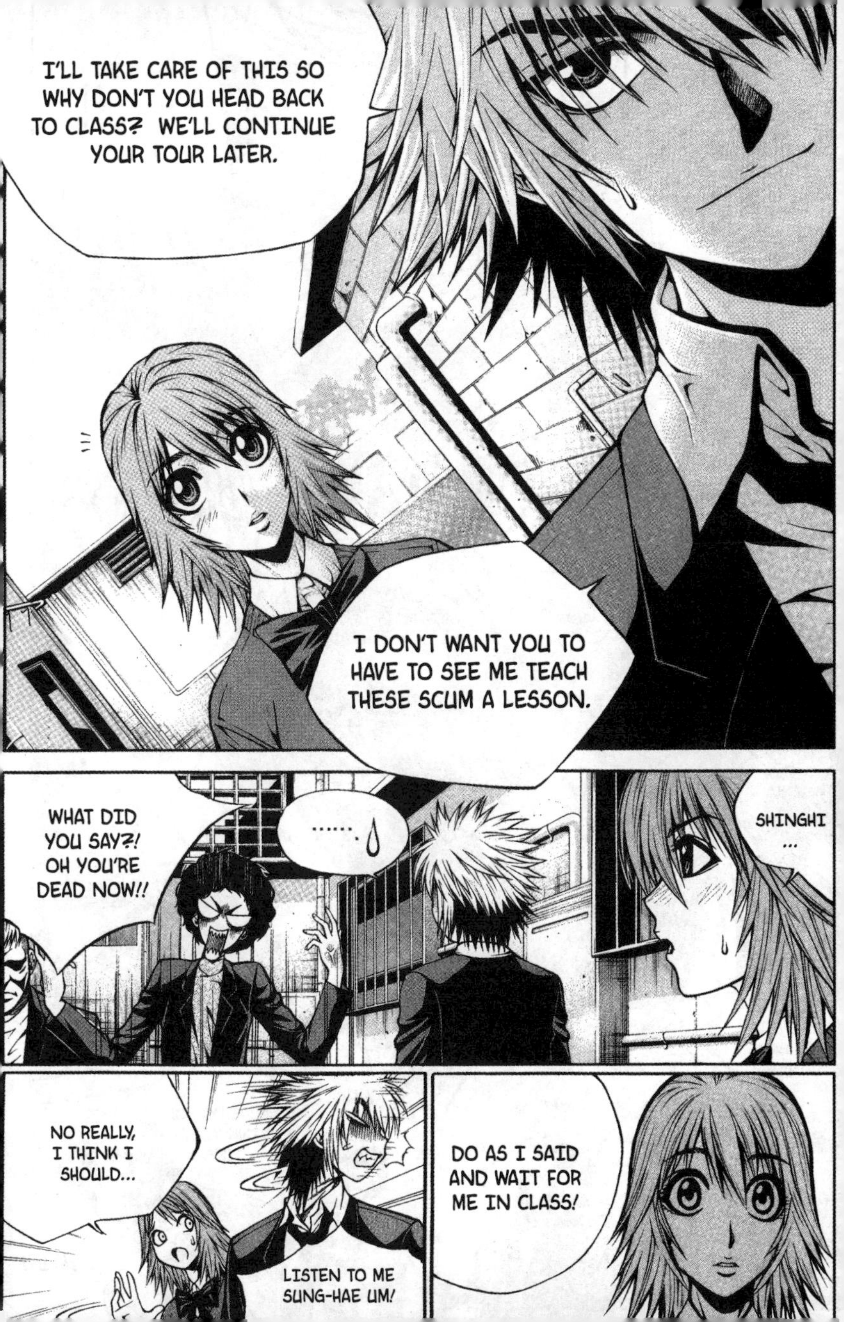
I'LL TAKE CARE OF THIS SO WHY DON'T YOU HEAD BACK TO CLASS? WE'LL CONTINUE YOUR TOUR LATER.
I DON'T WANT YOU TO HAVE TO SEE ME TEACH THESE SCUM A LESSON.
WHAT DID YOU SAY?! OH YOU'RE DEAD NOW!!
......
SHINGHI ...
NO REALLY, I THINK I SHOULD...
LISTEN TO ME SUNG-HAE UM!
DO AS I SAID AND WAIT FOR ME IN CLASS!

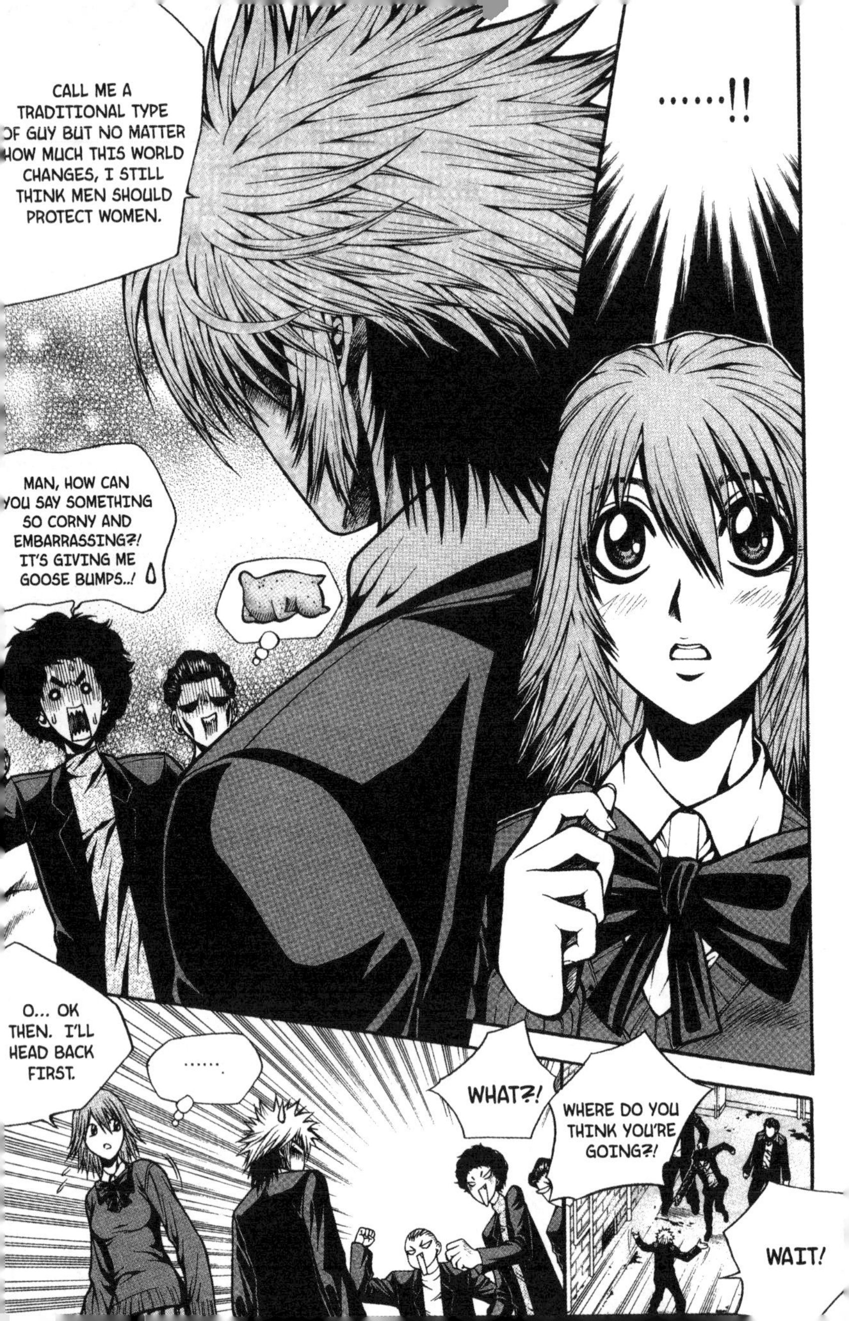
CALL ME A TRADITIONAL TYPE OF GUY BUT NO MATTER HOW MUCH THIS WORLD CHANGES, I STILL THINK MEN SHOULD PROTECT WOMEN.
......!!
MAN, HOW CAN YOU SAY SOMETHING SO CORNY AND EMBARRASSING?! IT'S GIVING ME GOOSE BUMPS..!
O... OK THEN. I'LL HEAD BACK FIRST.
....
WHAT?!
WHERE DO YOU THINK YOU'RE GOING?!
WAIT!

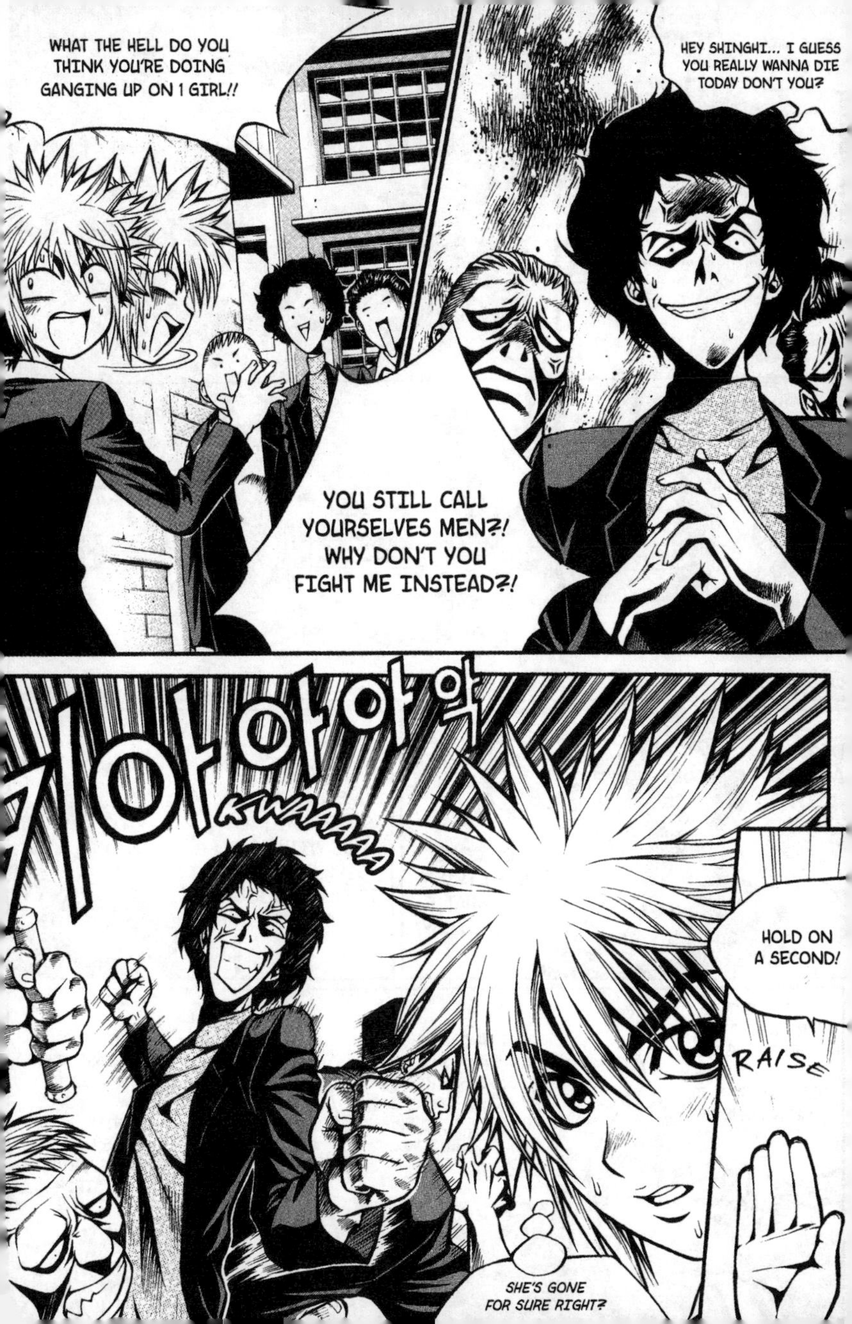
WHAT THE HELL DO YOU THINK YOU'RE DOING GANGING UP ON 1 GIRL!!
YOU STILL CALL YOURSELVES MEN?! WHY DON'T YOU FIGHT ME INSTEAD?!
HEY SHINGHI... I GUESS YOU REALLY WANNA DIE TODAY DON'T YOU?
아아아악
KWAAAAA
HOLD ON A SECOND!
RAISE
SHE'S GONE FOR SURE RIGHT?

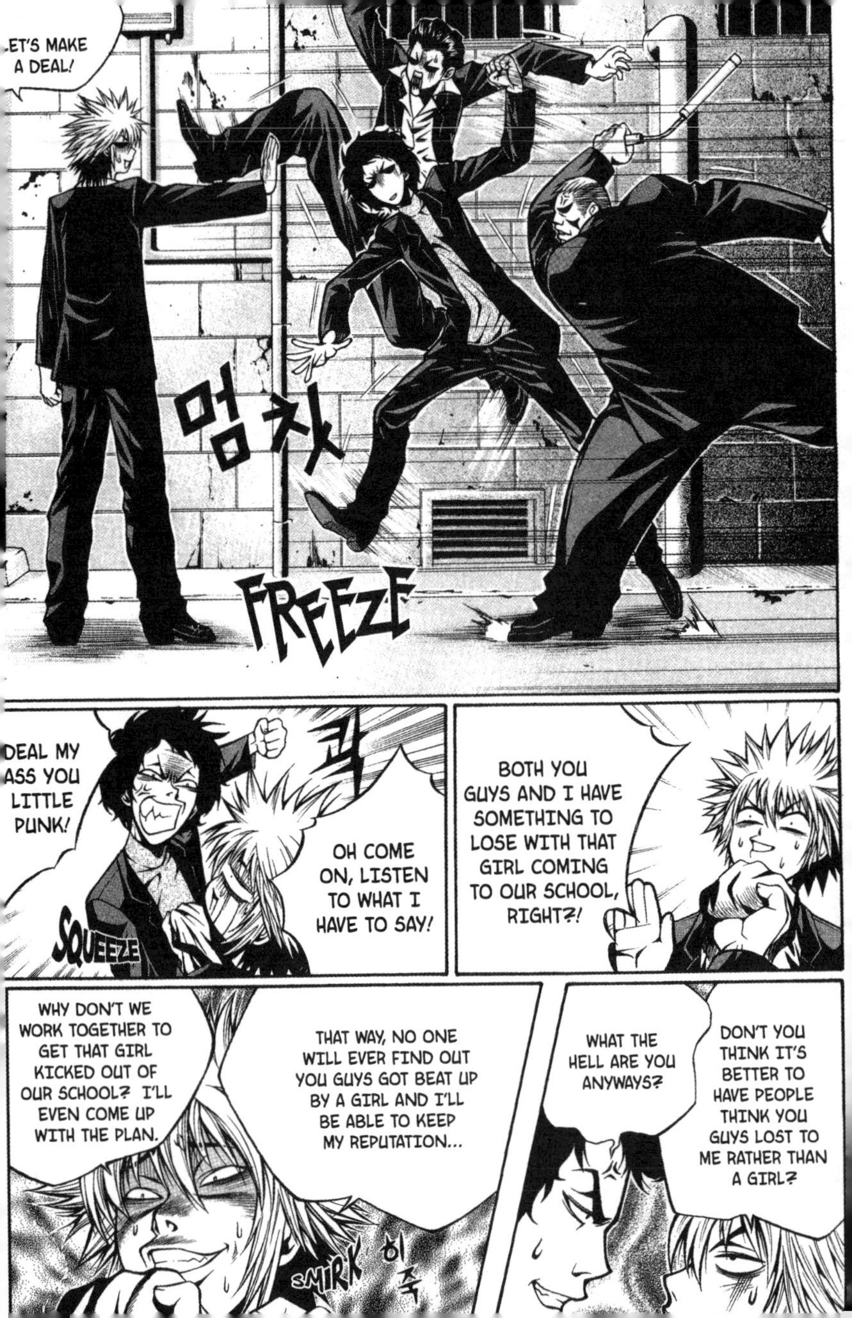

ET'S MAKE A DEAL!
멈찻
FREEZE
DEAL MY ASS YOU LITTLE PUNK!
콱
OH COME ON, LISTEN TO WHAT I HAVE TO SAY!
SQUEEZE
BOTH YOU GUYS AND I HAVE SOMETHING TO LOSE WITH THAT GIRL COMING TO OUR SCHOOL, RIGHT?!
WHY DON'T WE WORK TOGETHER TO GET THAT GIRL KICKED OUT OF OUR SCHOOL? I'LL EVEN COME UP WITH THE PLAN.
THAT WAY, NO ONE WILL EVER FIND OUT YOU GUYS GOT BEAT UP BY A GIRL AND I'LL BE ABLE TO KEEP MY REPUTATION...
SMIRK
히죽
WHAT THE HELL ARE YOU ANYWAYS?
DON'T YOU THINK IT'S BETTER TO HAVE PEOPLE THINK YOU GUYS LOST TO ME RATHER THAN A GIRL?

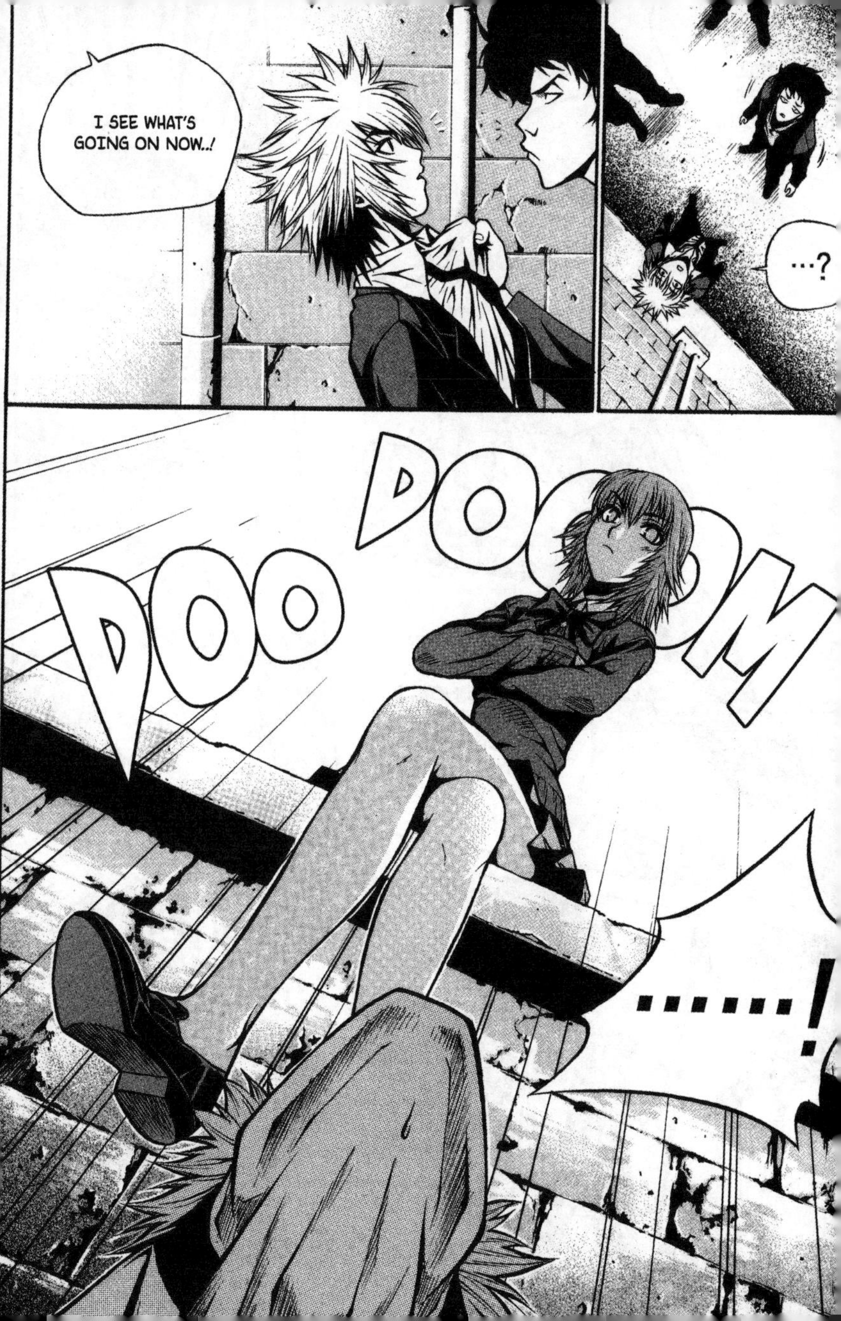
I SEE WHAT'S GOING ON NOW..!
...?
DOO DOOOM
......!

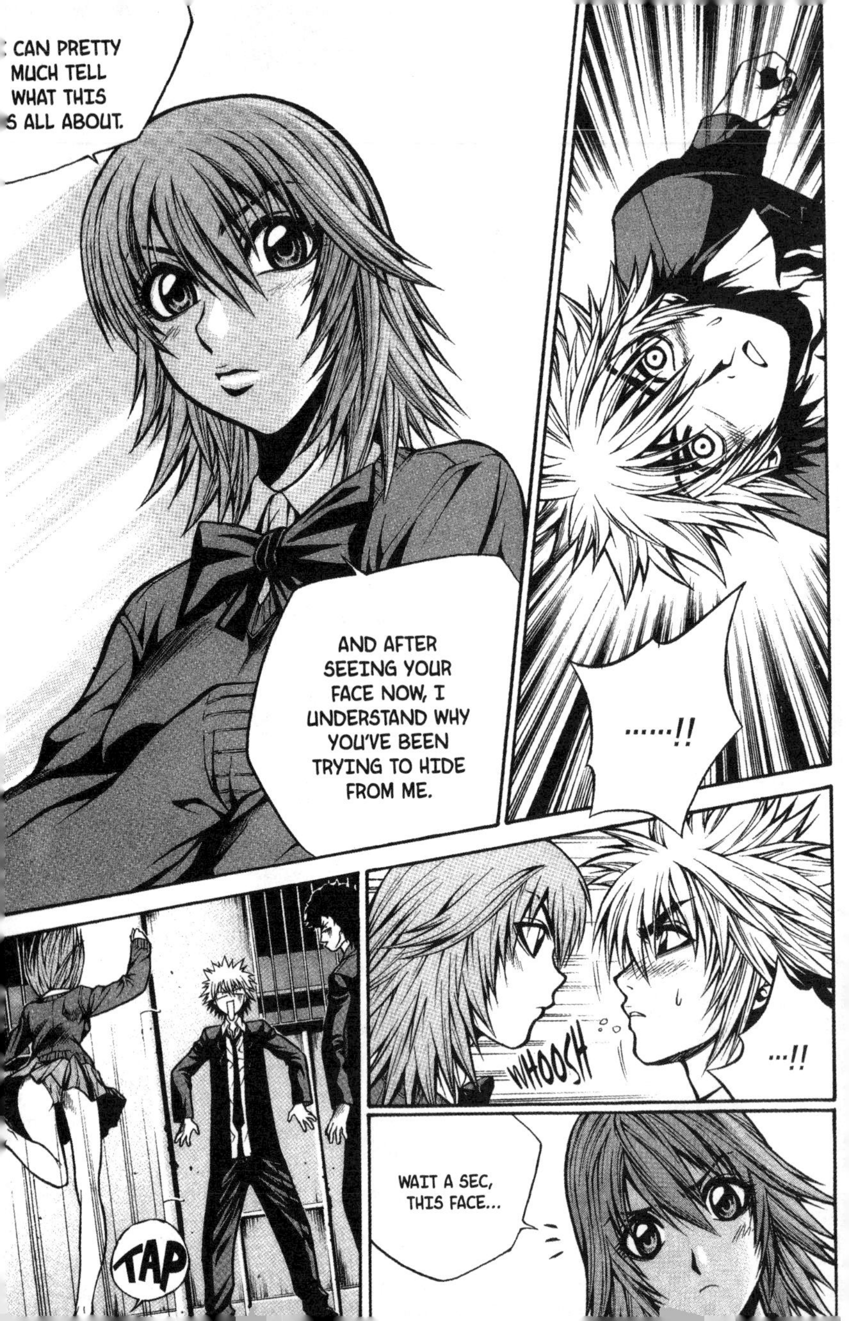
CAN PRETTY MUCH TELL WHAT THIS S ALL ABOUT.
AND AFTER SEEING YOUR FACE NOW, I UNDERSTAND WHY YOU'VE BEEN TRYING TO HIDE FROM ME.
......!!
TAP
WHOOSH
...!!
WAIT A SEC, THIS FACE...

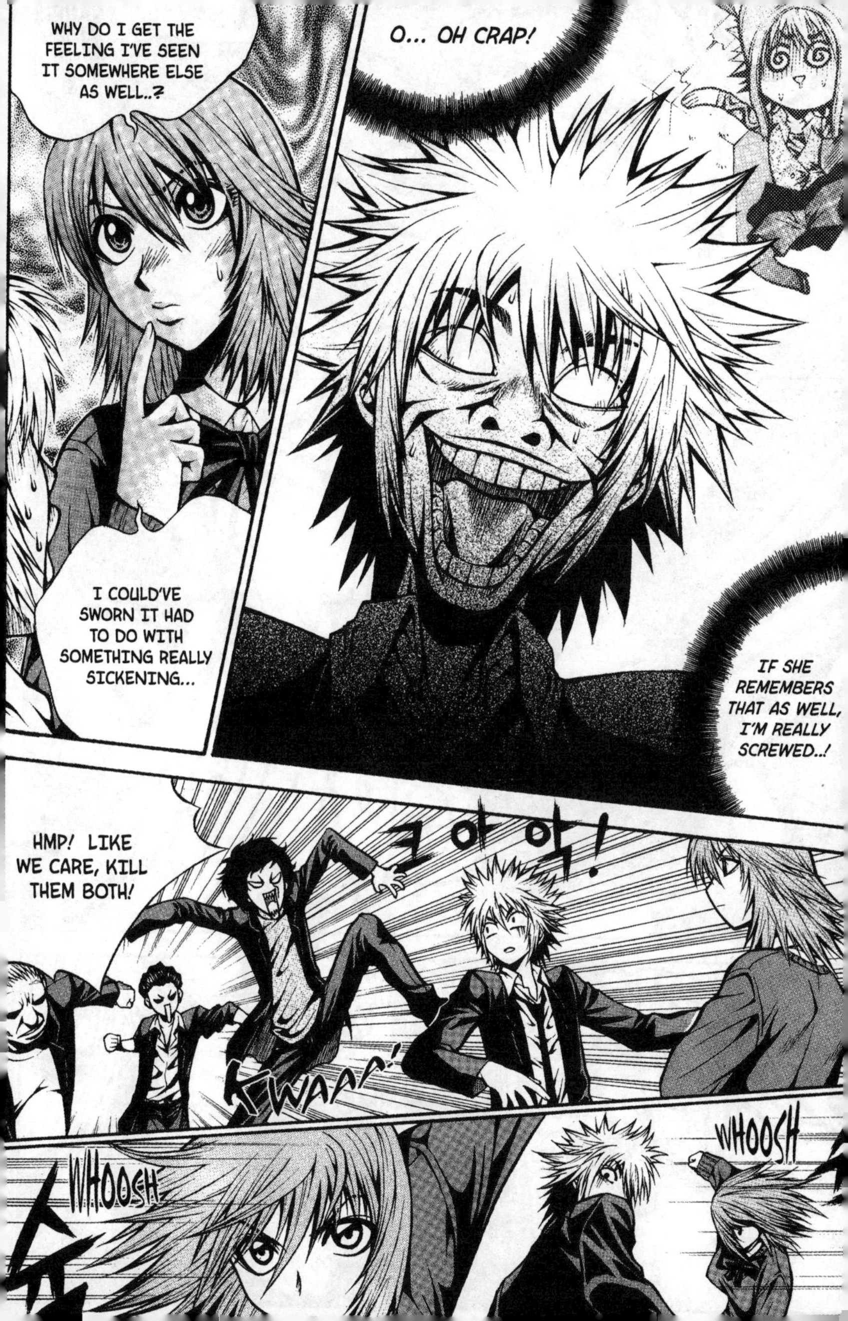
WHY DO I GET THE FEELING I'VE SEEN IT SOMEWHERE ELSE AS WELL..?
I COULD'VE SWORN IT HAD TO DO WITH SOMETHING REALLY SICKENING...
O... OH CRAP!
IF SHE REMEMBERS THAT AS WELL, I'M REALLY SCREWED..!
HMP! LIKE WE CARE, KILL THEM BOTH!
크아악!
KWAAA!
WHOOSH
WHOOSH

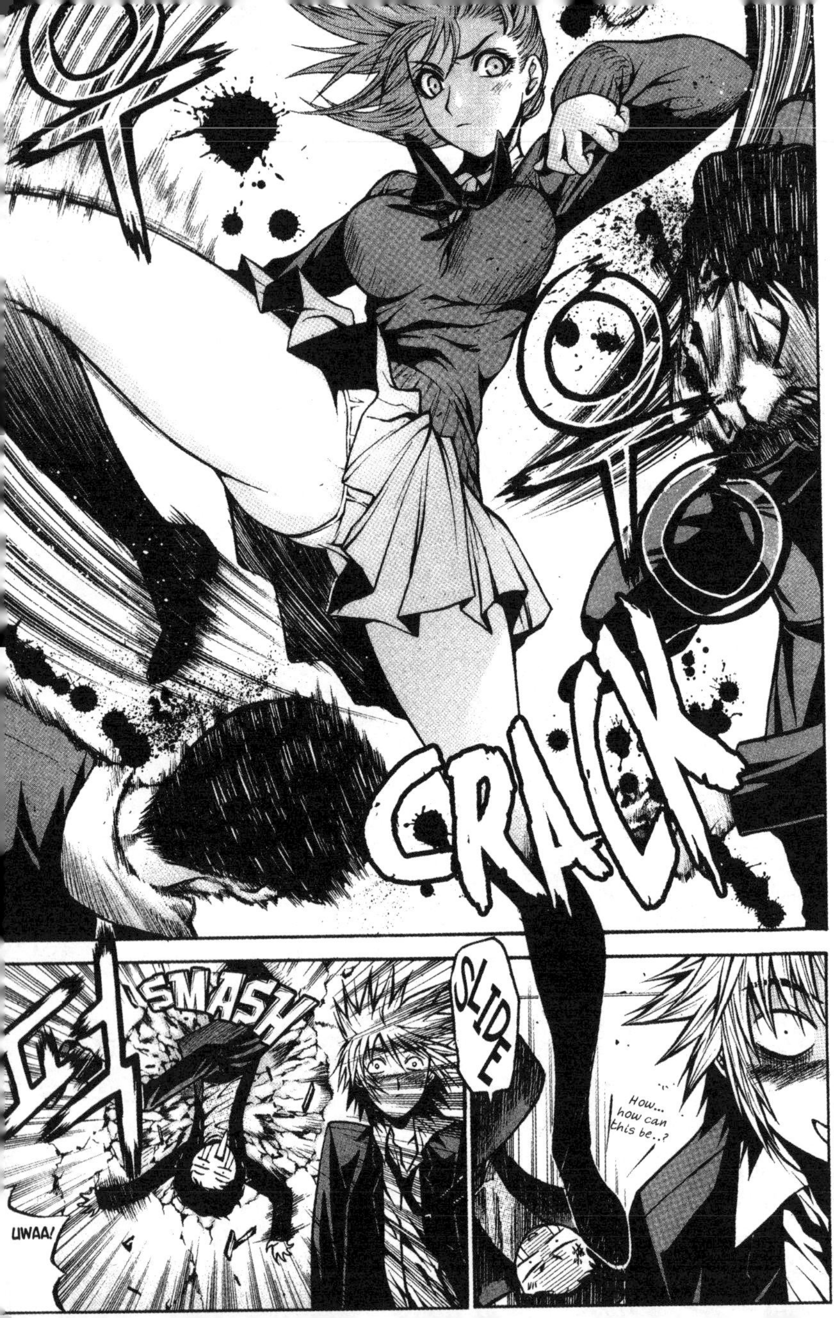
CRACK
SMASH
UWAA!
SLIDE
How... how can this be..?

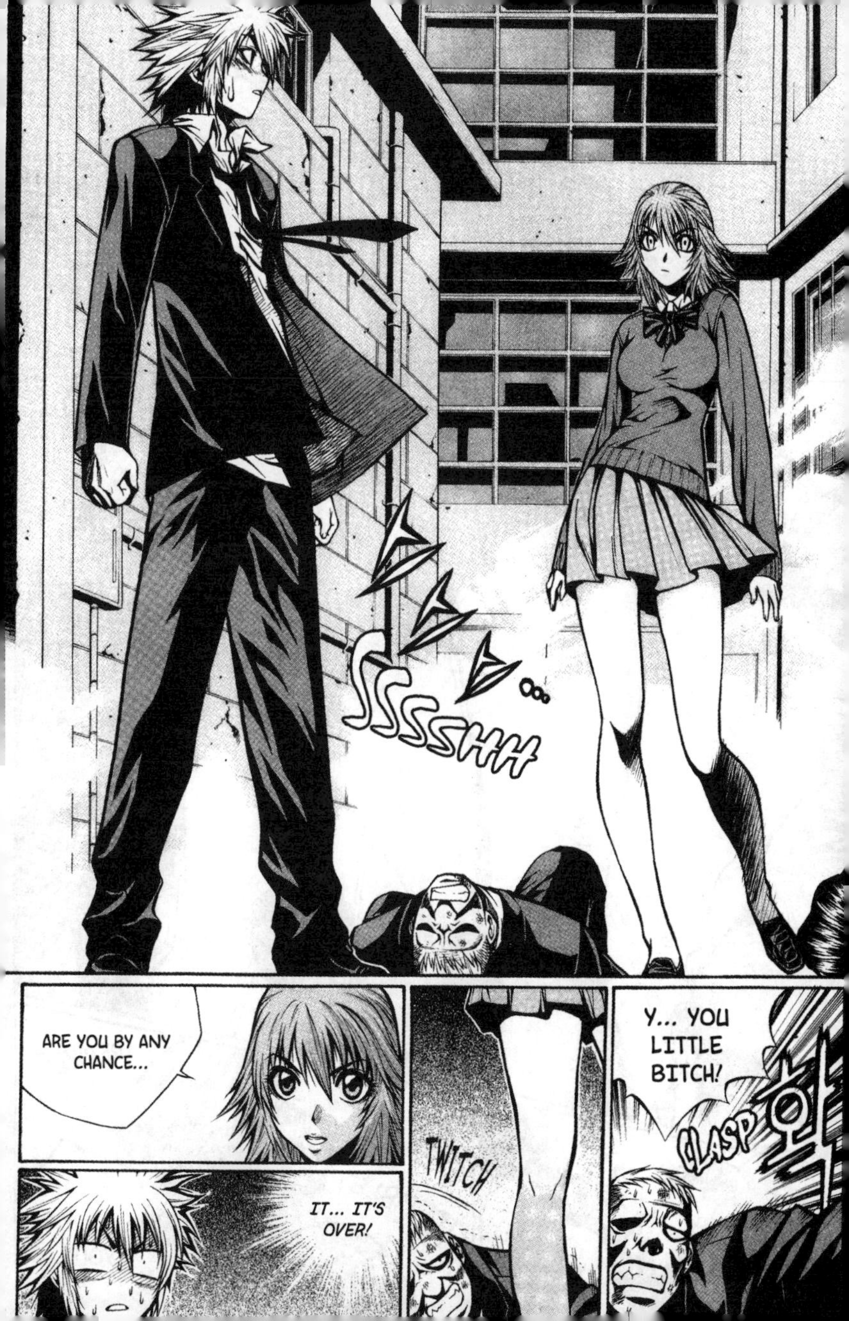
SSSSHH
ARE YOU BY ANY CHANCE...
IT... IT'S OVER!
TWITCH
Y... YOU LITTLE BITCH!
CLASP

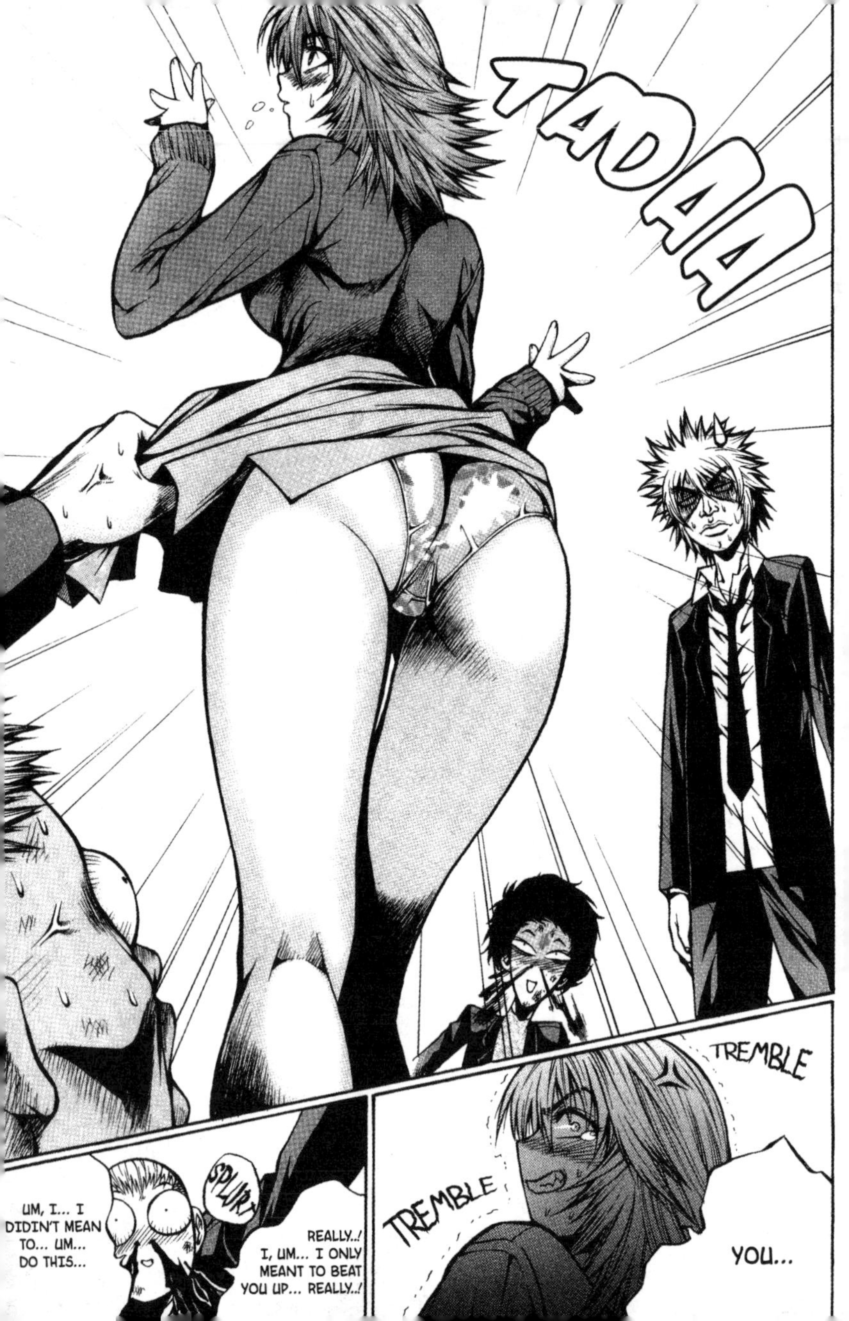
TADAAA
UM, I... I DIDIN'T MEAN TO... UM... DO THIS...
SPLURT
REALLY..! I, UM... I ONLY MEANT TO BEAT YOU UP... REALLY..!
TREMBLE
TREMBLE
YOU...

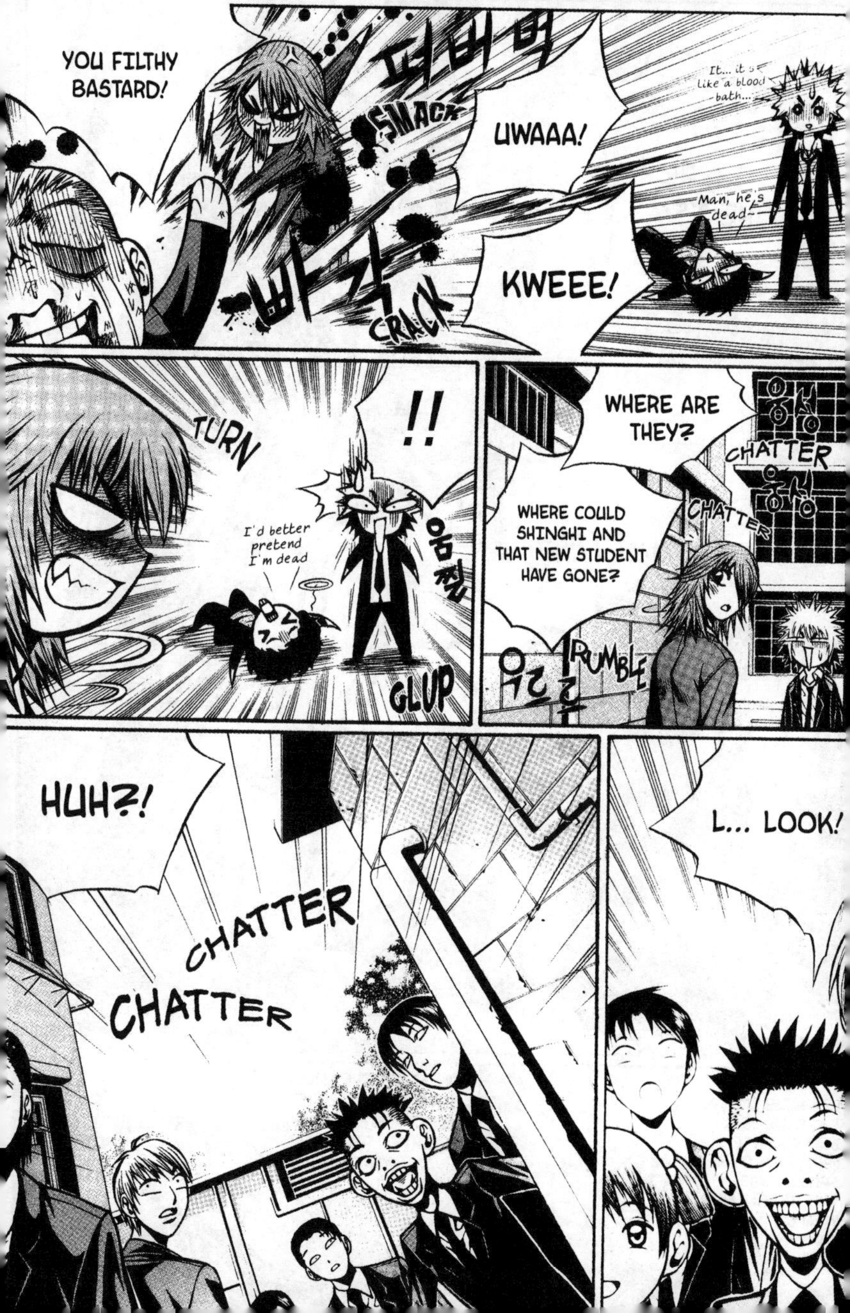
YOU FILTHY BASTARD!
퍼버벅
SMACK
빠각
CRACK
UWAAA!
KWEEE!
It... it's like a blood bath...
Man, he's dead~
TURN
!!
I'd better pretend I'm dead
움찔
GLUP
WHERE ARE THEY?
웅성
CHATTER
웅성
CHATTER
WHERE COULD SHINGHI AND THAT NEW STUDENT HAVE GONE?
우르르
RUMBLE
HUH?!
CHATTER
CHATTER
L... LOOK!

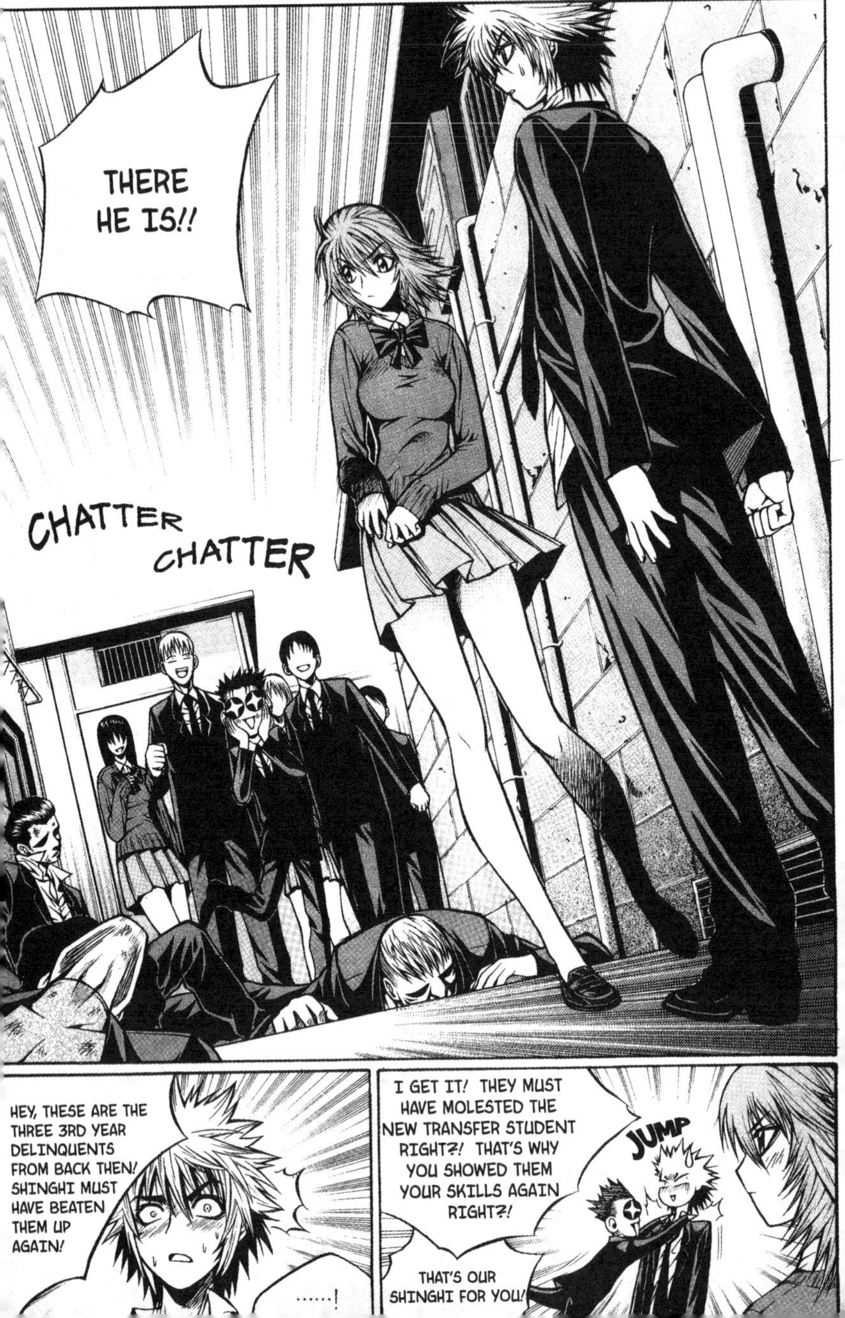
THERE HE IS!!
CHATTER CHATTER
HEY, THESE ARE THE THREE 3RD YEAR DELINQUENTS FROM BACK THEN! SHINGHI MUST HAVE BEATEN THEM UP AGAIN!
......!
I GET IT! THEY MUST HAVE MOLESTED THE NEW TRANSFER STUDENT RIGHT?! THAT'S WHY YOU SHOWED THEM YOUR SKILLS AGAIN RIGHT?!
JUMP
THAT'S OUR SHINGHI FOR YOU!

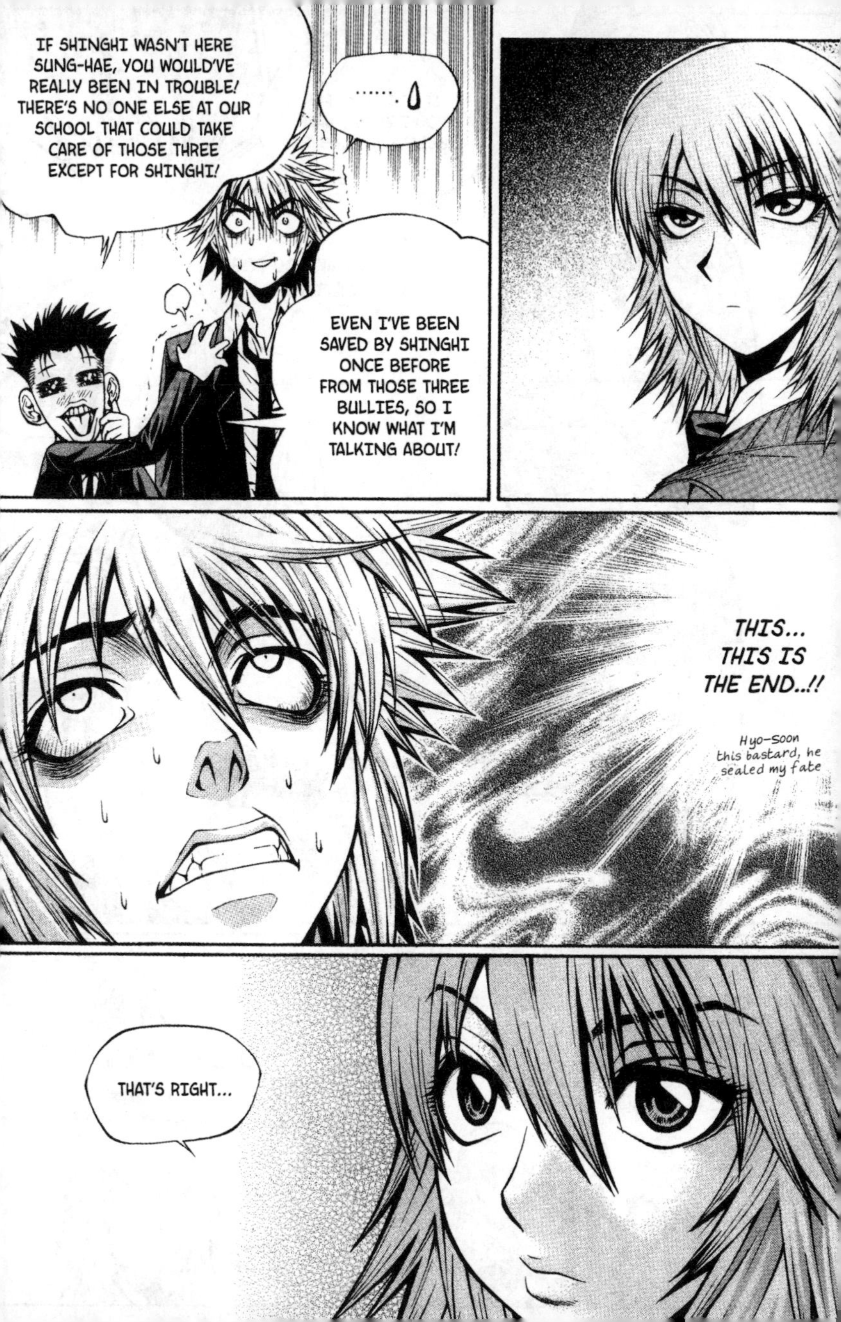
IF SHINGHI WASN'T HERE SUNG-HAE, YOU WOULD'VE REALLY BEEN IN TROUBLE! THERE'S NO ONE ELSE AT OUR SCHOOL THAT COULD TAKE CARE OF THOSE THREE EXCEPT FOR SHINGHI!
......
EVEN I'VE BEEN SAVED BY SHINGHI ONCE BEFORE FROM THOSE THREE BULLIES, SO I KNOW WHAT I'M TALKING ABOUT!
THIS... THIS IS THE END..!!
Hyo-Soon this bastard, he sealed my fate
THAT'S RIGHT...

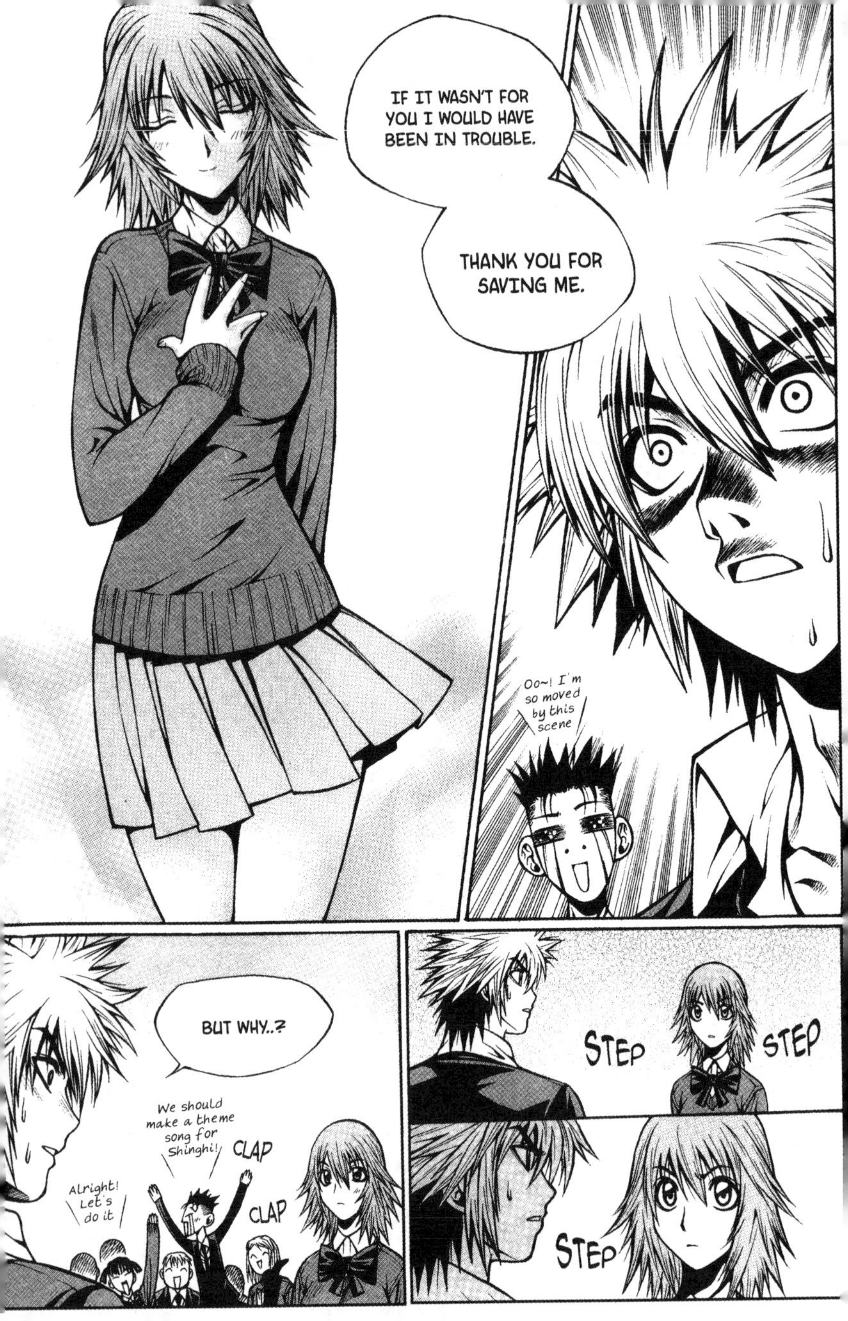
IF IT WASN'T FOR YOU I WOULD HAVE BEEN IN TROUBLE.
THANK YOU FOR SAVING ME.
Oo~! I'm so moved by this scene
BUT WHY..?
We should make a theme song for Shinghi!
CLAP
Alright! Let's do it
CLAP
STEP
STEP
STEP

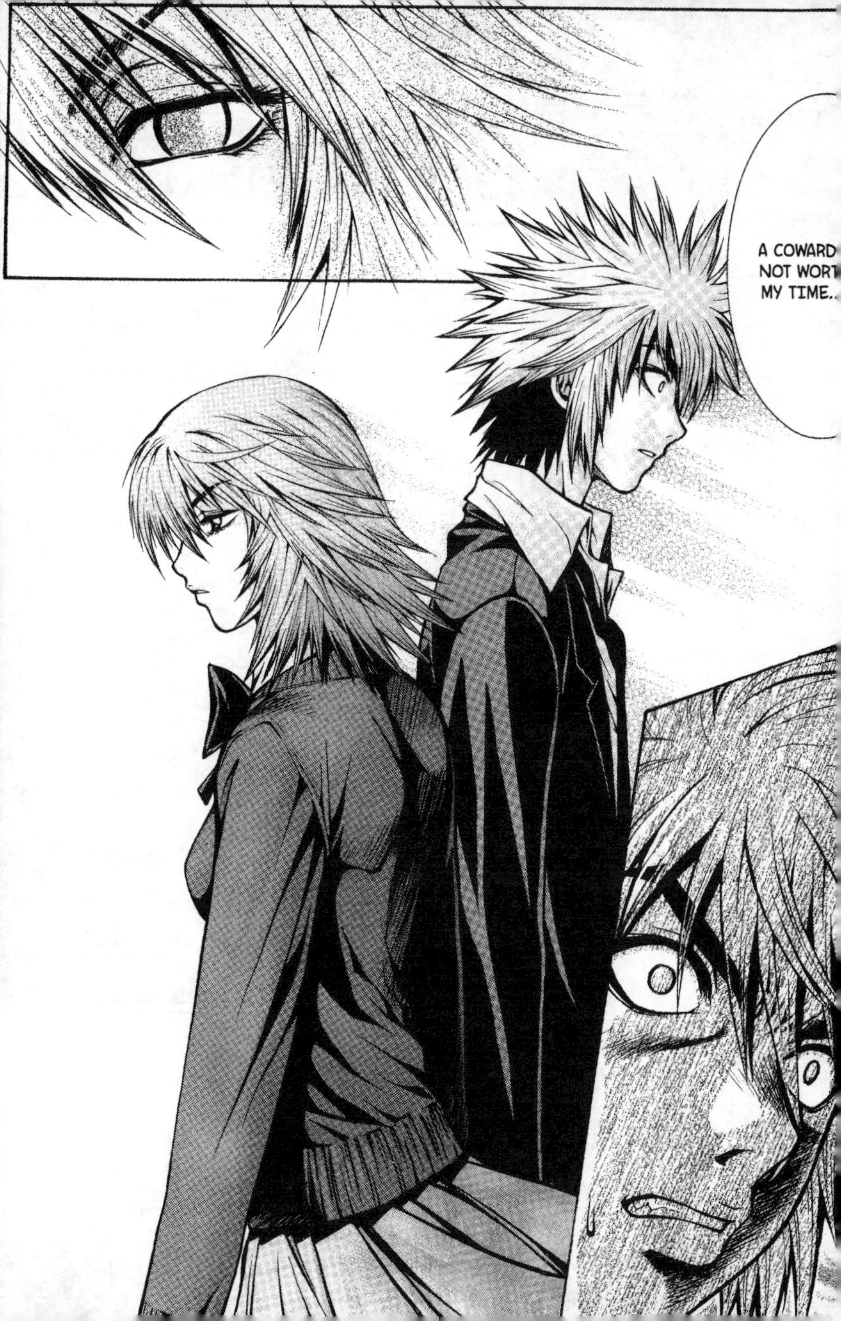
A COWARD
NOT WORT
MY TIME..

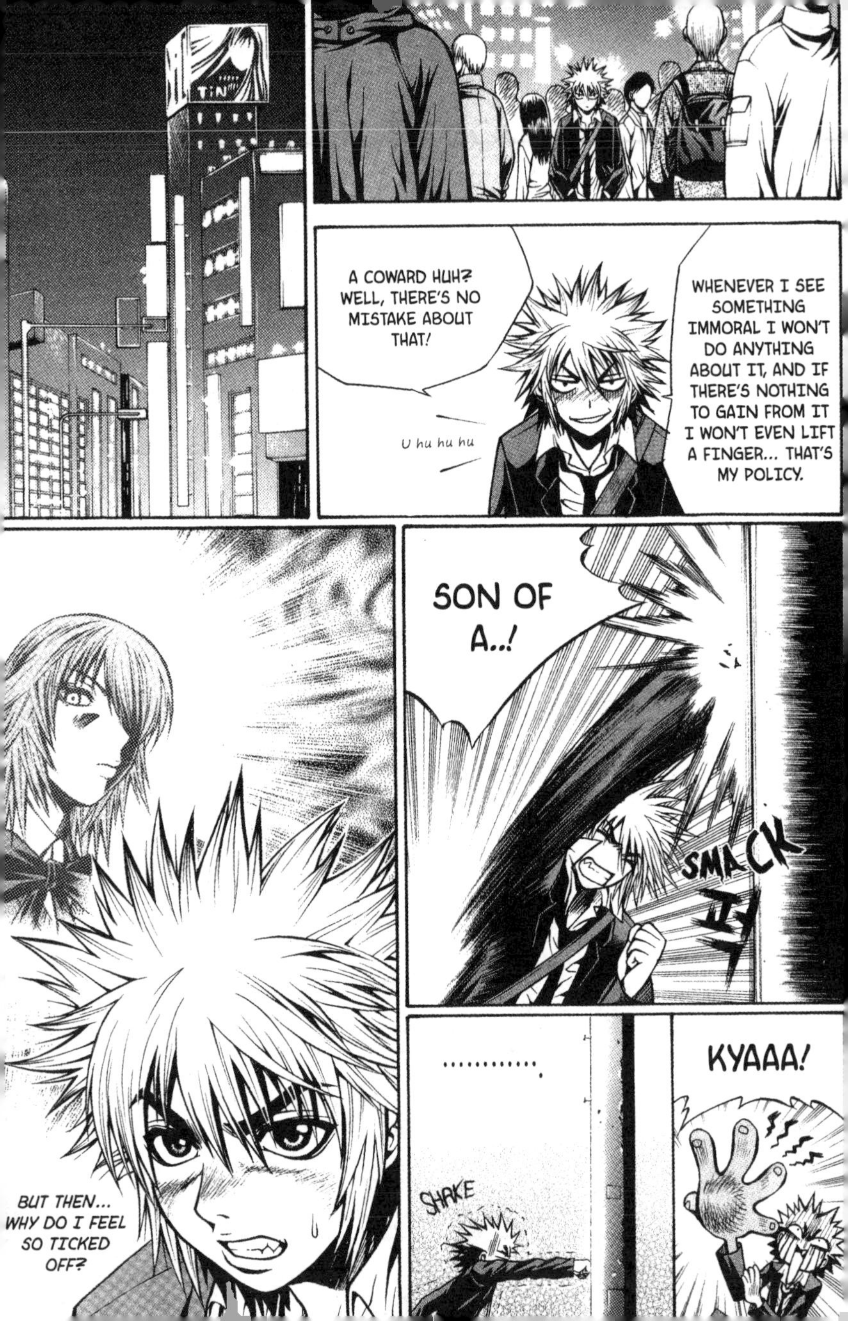
TiN
A COWARD HUH? WELL, THERE'S NO MISTAKE ABOUT THAT!
U hu hu hu
WHENEVER I SEE SOMETHING IMMORAL I WON'T DO ANYTHING ABOUT IT, AND IF THERE'S NOTHING TO GAIN FROM IT I WON'T EVEN LIFT A FINGER... THAT'S MY POLICY.
BUT THEN... WHY DO I FEEL SO TICKED OFF?
SON OF A..!
SMACK
....
SHAKE
KYAAA!

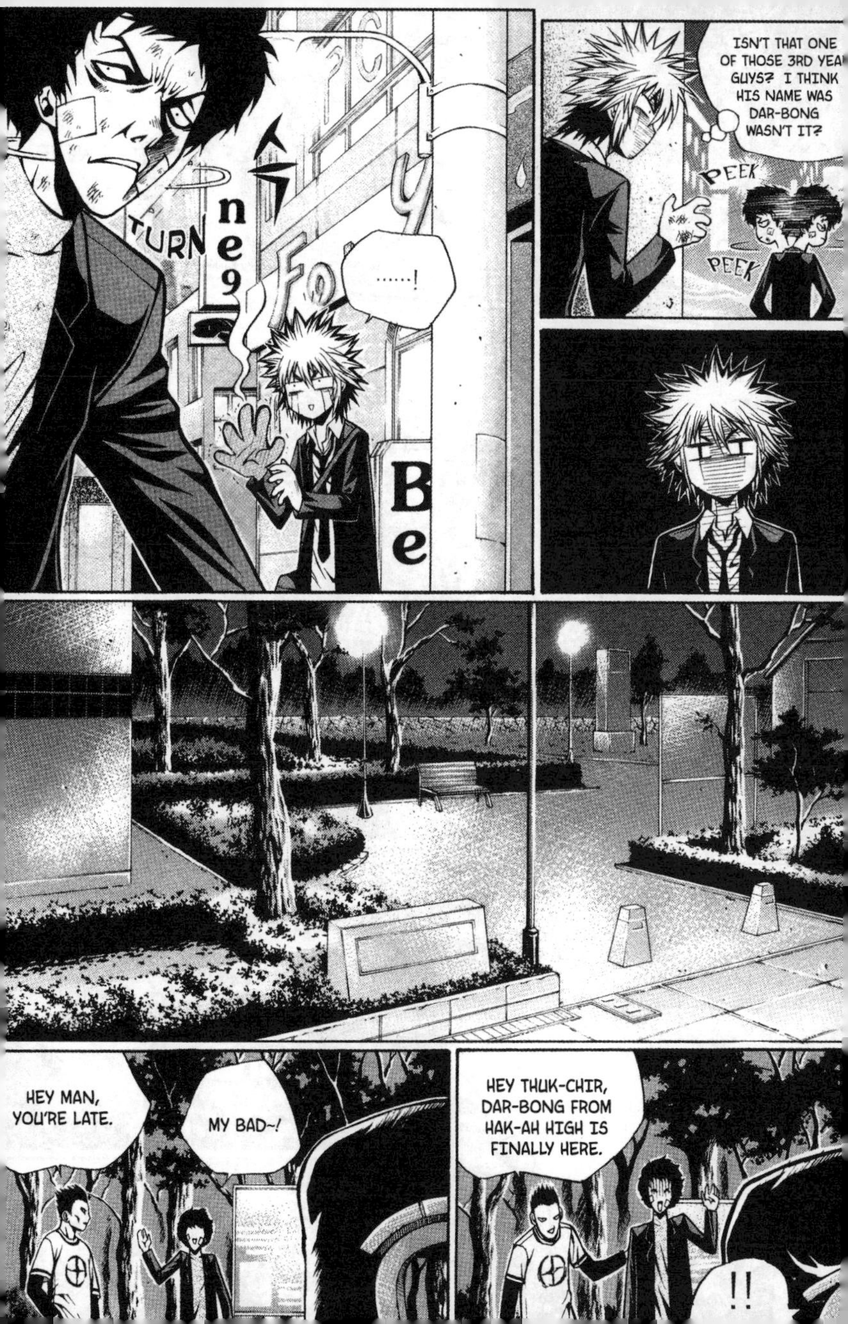
TURN
......!
ISN'T THAT ONE OF THOSE 3RD YEA GUYS? I THINK HIS NAME WAS DAR-BONG WASN'T IT?
PEEK
PEEK
HEY MAN, YOU'RE LATE.
MY BAD~!
HEY THUK-CHIR, DAR-BONG FROM HAK-AH HIGH IS FINALLY HERE.
!!

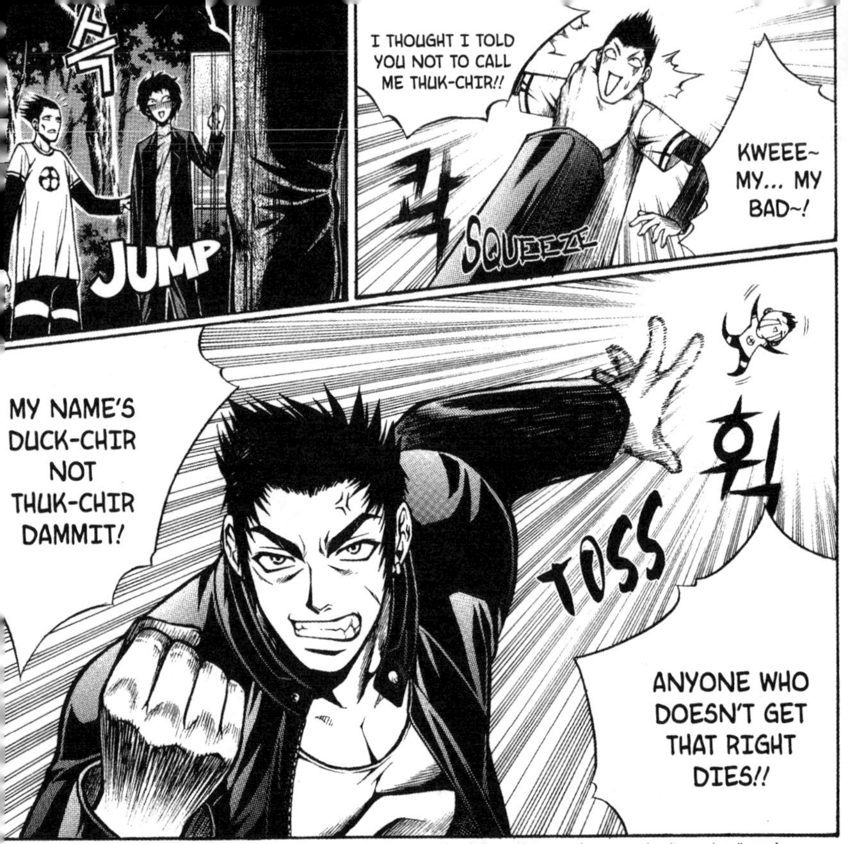
JUMP
I THOUGHT I TOLD YOU NOT TO CALL ME THUK-CHIR!!
꾹
SQUEEZE
KWEEE~ MY... MY BAD~!
MY NAME'S DUCK-CHIR NOT THUK-CHIR DAMMIT!
휙
TOSS
ANYONE WHO DOESN'T GET THAT RIGHT DIES!!

Note : In Korean, Thuck is the word for a Korean pastry. Incorporating that word into a guy's name makes it sound really goofy.

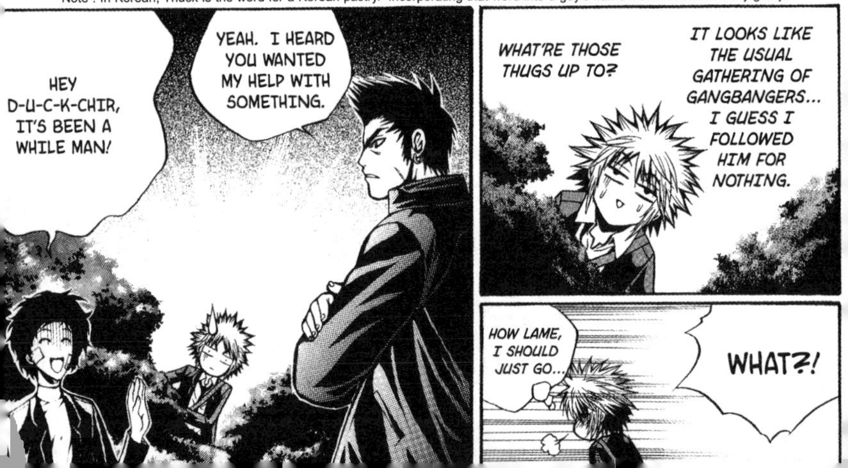
HEY D-U-C-K-CHIR, IT'S BEEN A WHILE MAN!
YEAH. I HEARD YOU WANTED MY HELP WITH SOMETHING.
WHAT'RE THOSE THUGS UP TO?
IT LOOKS LIKE THE USUAL GATHERING OF GANGBANGERS... I GUESS I FOLLOWED HIM FOR NOTHING.
HOW LAME, I SHOULD JUST GO...
WHAT?!

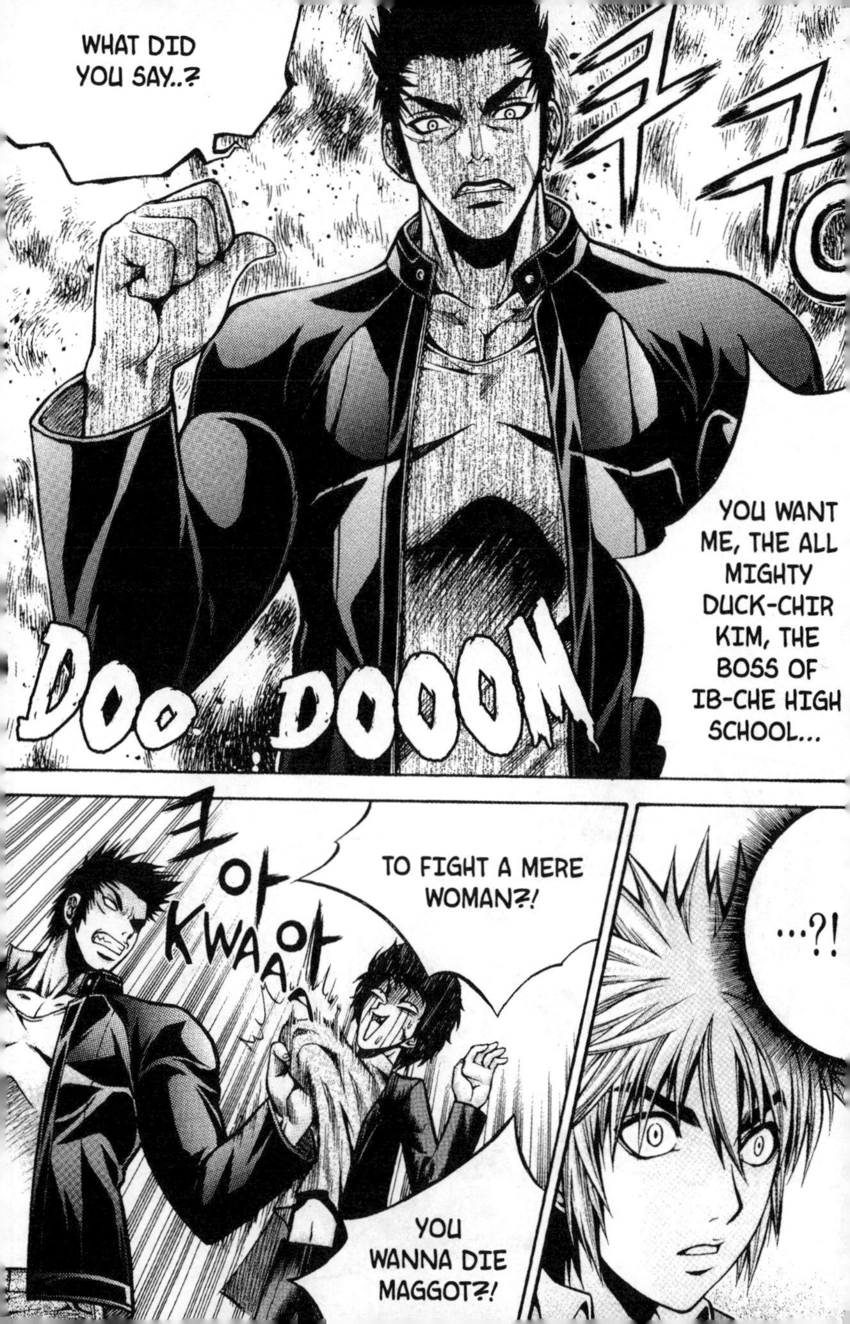
WHAT DID YOU SAY..?
DOO DOOOOM
YOU WANT ME, THE ALL MIGHTY DUCK-CHIR KIM, THE BOSS OF IB-CHE HIGH SCHOOL...
TO FIGHT A MERE WOMAN?!
KWAAA
YOU WANNA DIE MAGGOT?!
...?!

Chapter 5 : Shinghi is in a Bind

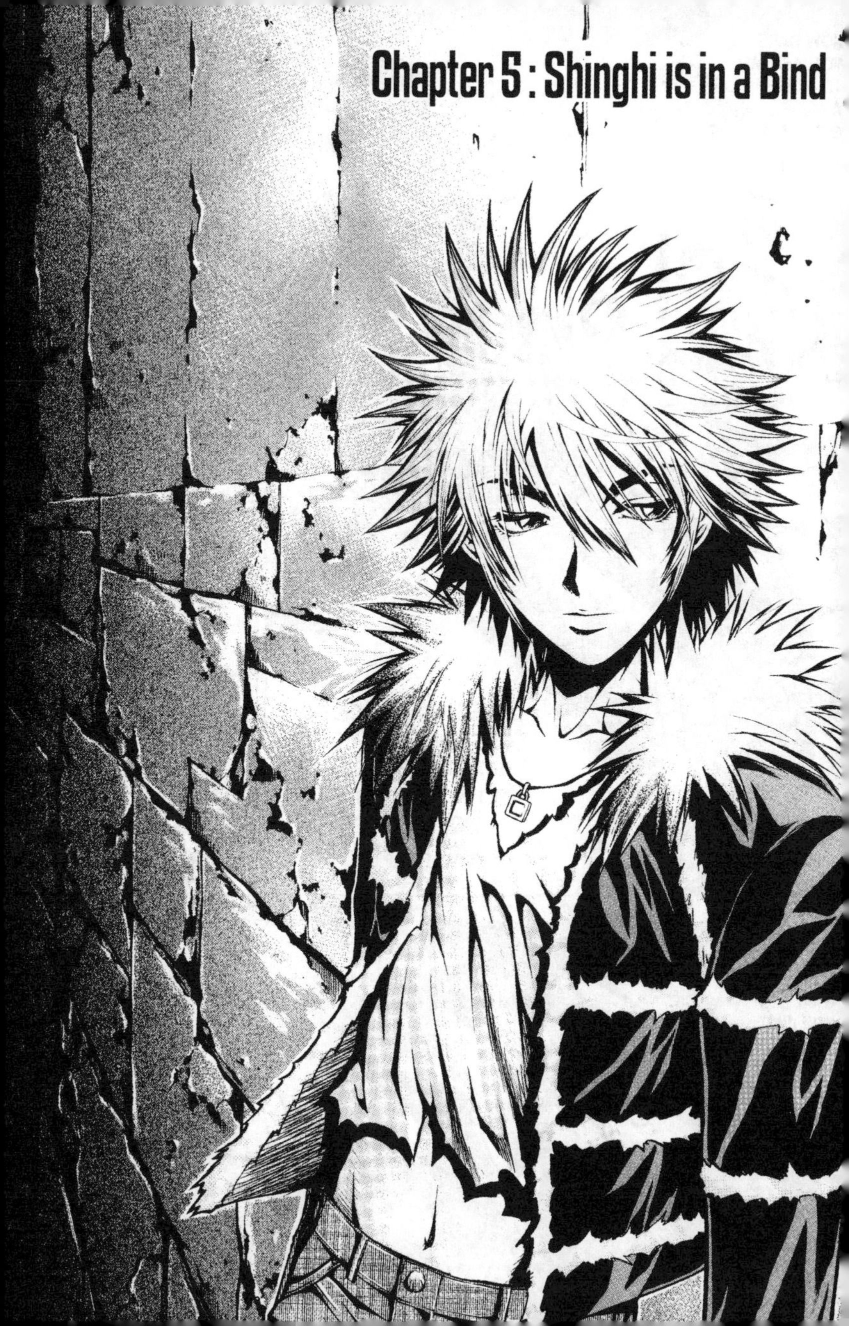

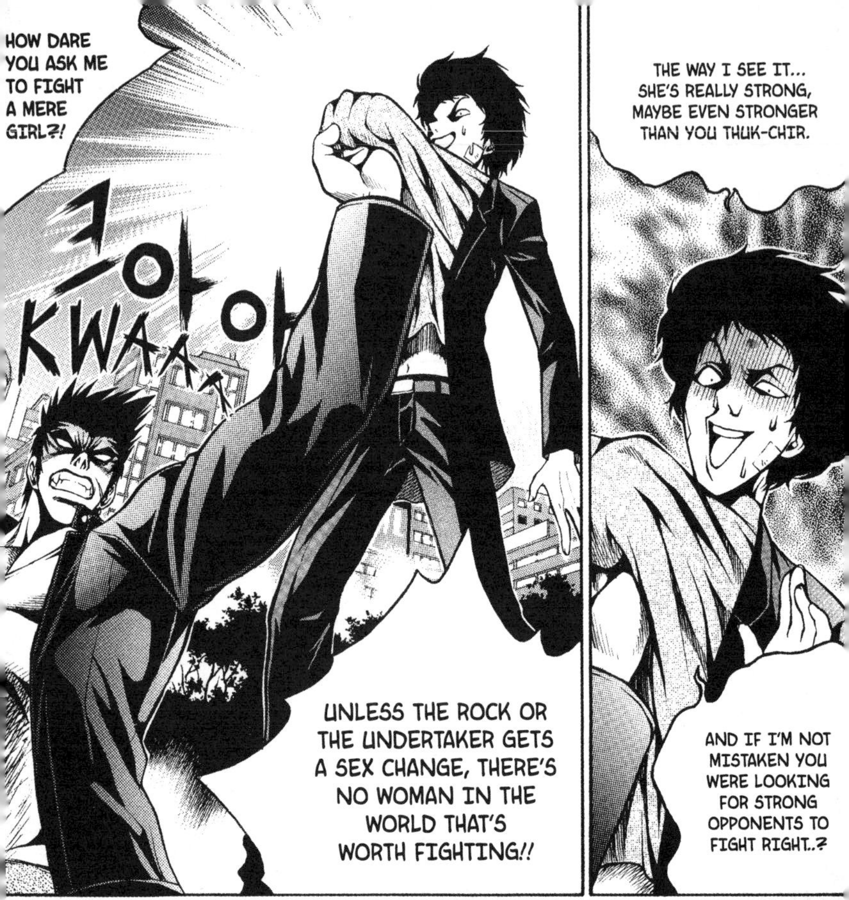
HOW DARE YOU ASK ME TO FIGHT A MERE GIRL?!
KWAA
UNLESS THE ROCK OR THE UNDERTAKER GETS A SEX CHANGE, THERE'S NO WOMAN IN THE WORLD THAT'S WORTH FIGHTING!!
THE WAY I SEE IT... SHE'S REALLY STRONG, MAYBE EVEN STRONGER THAN YOU THUK-CHIR.
AND IF I'M NOT MISTAKEN YOU WERE LOOKING FOR STRONG OPPONENTS TO FIGHT RIGHT..?

Note : Both the Rock and the Undertaker are professional wrestlers.

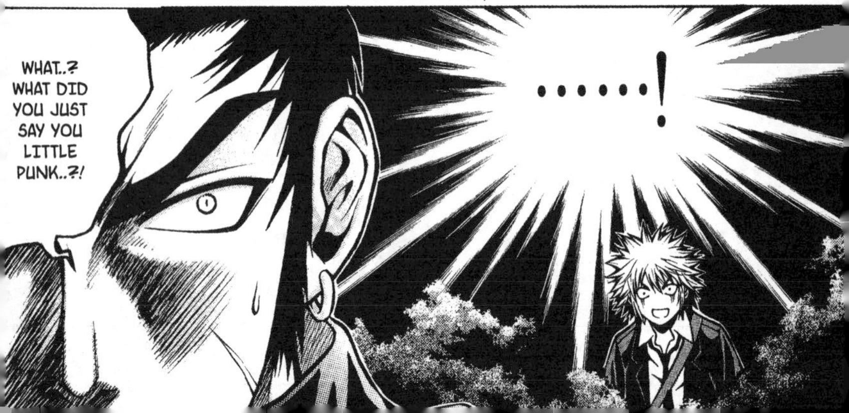
WHAT..? WHAT DID YOU JUST SAY YOU LITTLE PUNK..?!
......!

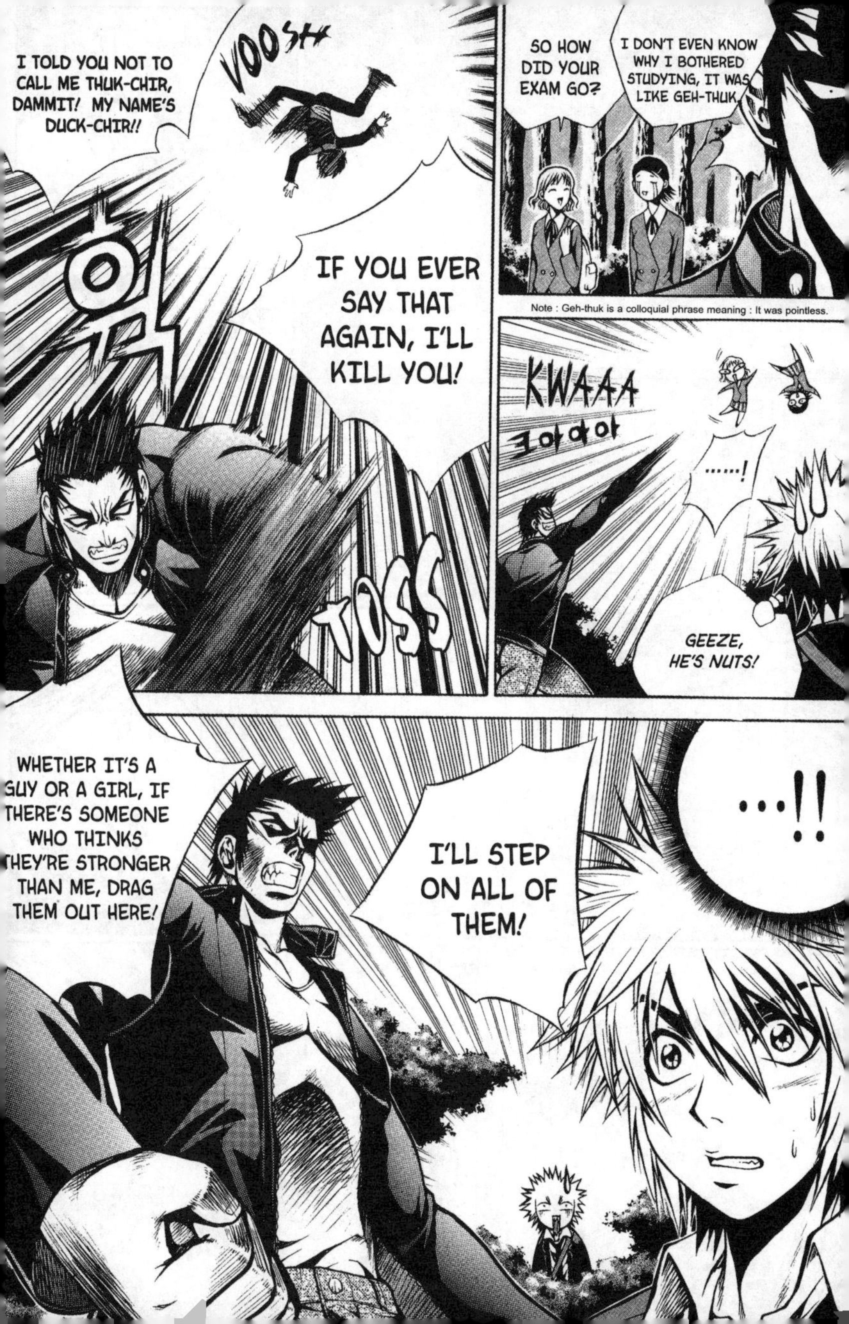
I TOLD YOU NOT TO CALL ME THUK-CHIR, DAMMIT! MY NAME'S DUCK-CHIR!!
VOOSH
IF YOU EVER SAY THAT AGAIN, I'LL KILL YOU!
TOSS
SO HOW DID YOUR EXAM GO?
I DON'T EVEN KNOW WHY I BOTHERED STUDYING, IT WAS LIKE GEH-THUK.
KWAAA
......!
GEEZE, HE'S NUTS!
WHETHER IT'S A GUY OR A GIRL, IF THERE'S SOMEONE WHO THINKS THEY'RE STRONGER THAN ME, DRAG THEM OUT HERE!
I'LL STEP ON ALL OF THEM!
...!!
Note : Geh-thuk is a colloquial phrase meaning : It was pointless.

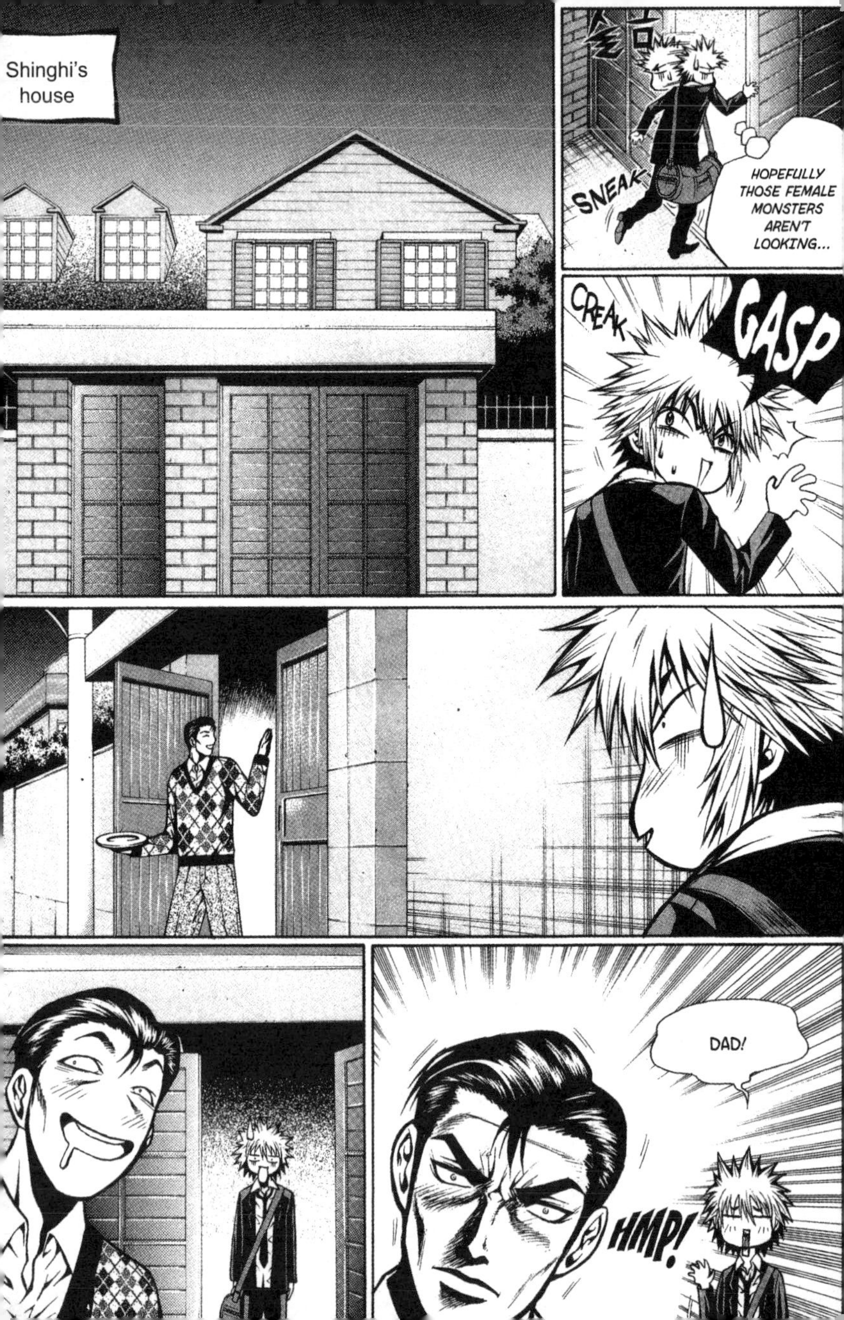
Shinghi's house
SNEAK
HOPEFULLY THOSE FEMALE MONSTERS AREN'T LOOKING...
CREAK
GASP
DAD!
HMP!

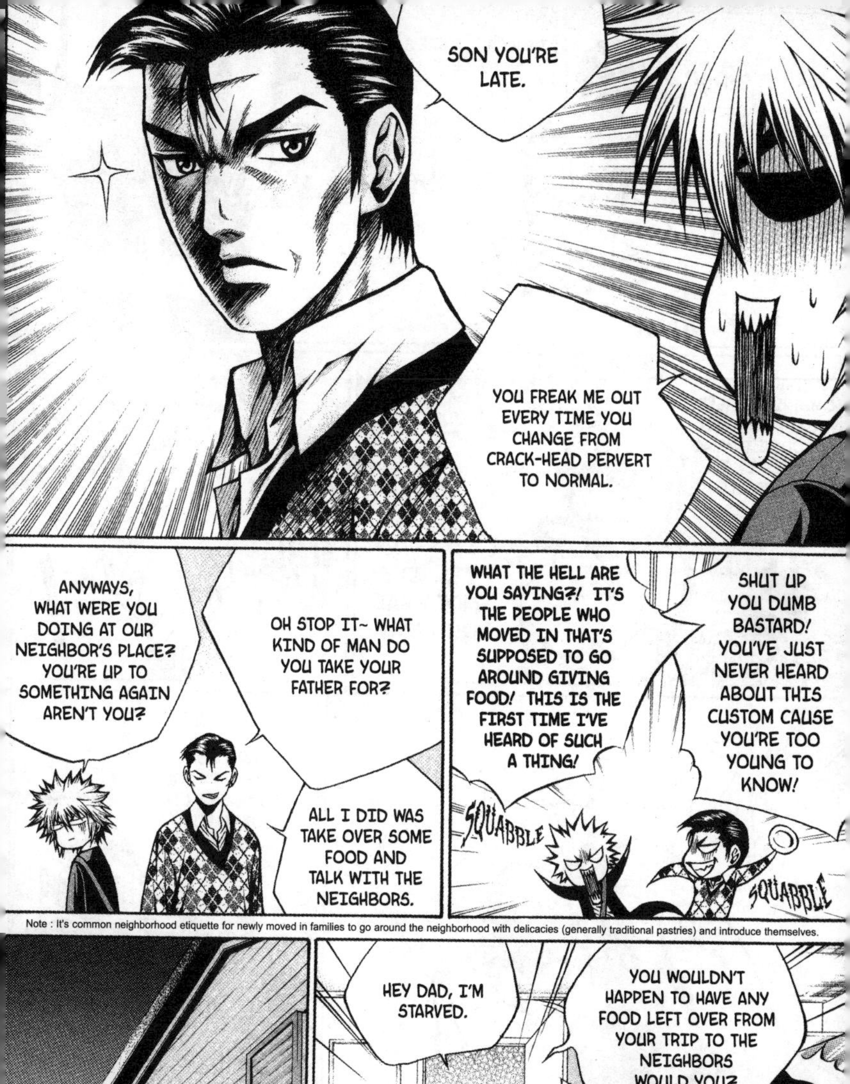
SON YOU'RE LATE.
YOU FREAK ME OUT EVERY TIME YOU CHANGE FROM CRACK-HEAD PERVERT TO NORMAL.
ANYWAYS, WHAT WERE YOU DOING AT OUR NEIGHBOR'S PLACE? YOU'RE UP TO SOMETHING AGAIN AREN'T YOU?
OH STOP IT~ WHAT KIND OF MAN DO YOU TAKE YOUR FATHER FOR?
ALL I DID WAS TAKE OVER SOME FOOD AND TALK WITH THE NEIGHBORS.
WHAT THE HELL ARE YOU SAYING?! IT'S THE PEOPLE WHO MOVED IN THAT'S SUPPOSED TO GO AROUND GIVING FOOD! THIS IS THE FIRST TIME I'VE HEARD OF SUCH A THING!
SHUT UP YOU DUMB BASTARD! YOU'VE JUST NEVER HEARD ABOUT THIS CUSTOM CAUSE YOU'RE TOO YOUNG TO KNOW!
SQUABBLE
SQUABBLE

Note : It's common neighborhood etiquette for newly moved in families to go around the neighborhood with delicacies (generally traditional pastries) and introduce themselves.

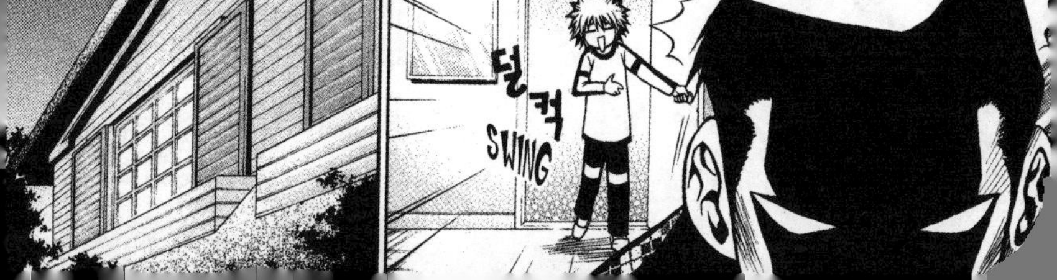
HEY DAD, I'M STARVED.
덜컥
SWING
YOU WOULDN'T HAPPEN TO HAVE ANY FOOD LEFT OVER FROM YOUR TRIP TO THE NEIGHBORS WOULD YOU?

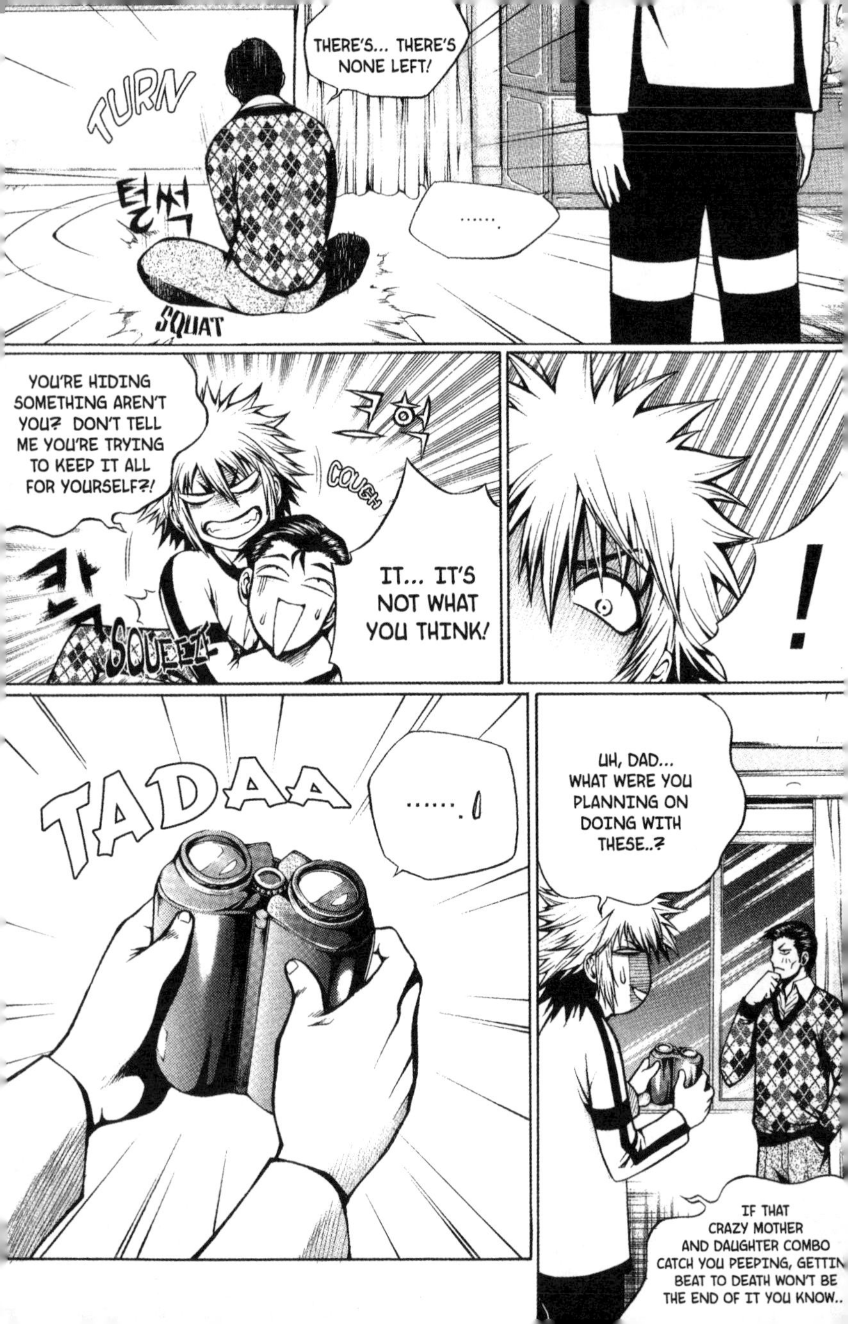
TURN
털썩
SQUAT
THERE'S... THERE'S NONE LEFT!
....
YOU'RE HIDING SOMETHING AREN'T YOU? DON'T TELL ME YOU'RE TRYING TO KEEP IT ALL FOR YOURSELF?!
COUGH
SQUEEZE
IT... IT'S NOT WHAT YOU THINK!
!
TADAA
....
UH, DAD... WHAT WERE YOU PLANNING ON DOING WITH THESE..?
IF THAT CRAZY MOTHER AND DAUGHTER COMBO CATCH YOU PEEPING, GETTIN BEAT TO DEATH WON'T BE THE END OF IT YOU KNOW..

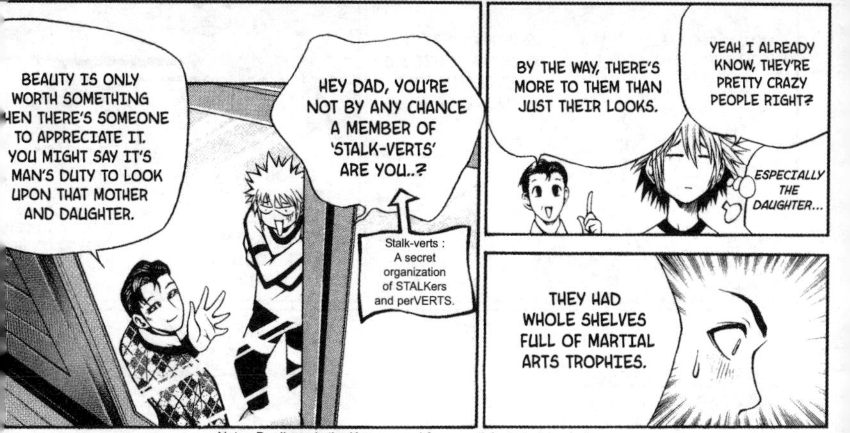
BEAUTY IS ONLY WORTH SOMETHING HEN THERE'S SOMEONE TO APPRECIATE IT. YOU MIGHT SAY IT'S MAN'S DUTY TO LOOK UPON THAT MOTHER AND DAUGHTER.
HEY DAD, YOU'RE NOT BY ANY CHANCE A MEMBER OF 'STALK-VERTS' ARE YOU..?
Stalk-verts : A secret organization of STALKers and perVERTS.
BY THE WAY, THERE'S MORE TO THEM THAN JUST THEIR LOOKS.
YEAH I ALREADY KNOW, THEY'RE PRETTY CRAZY PEOPLE RIGHT?
ESPECIALLY THE DAUGHTER...
THEY HAD WHOLE SHELVES FULL OF MARTIAL ARTS TROPHIES.

Note : Do-Jhang is the Korean word for a martial arts training hall.

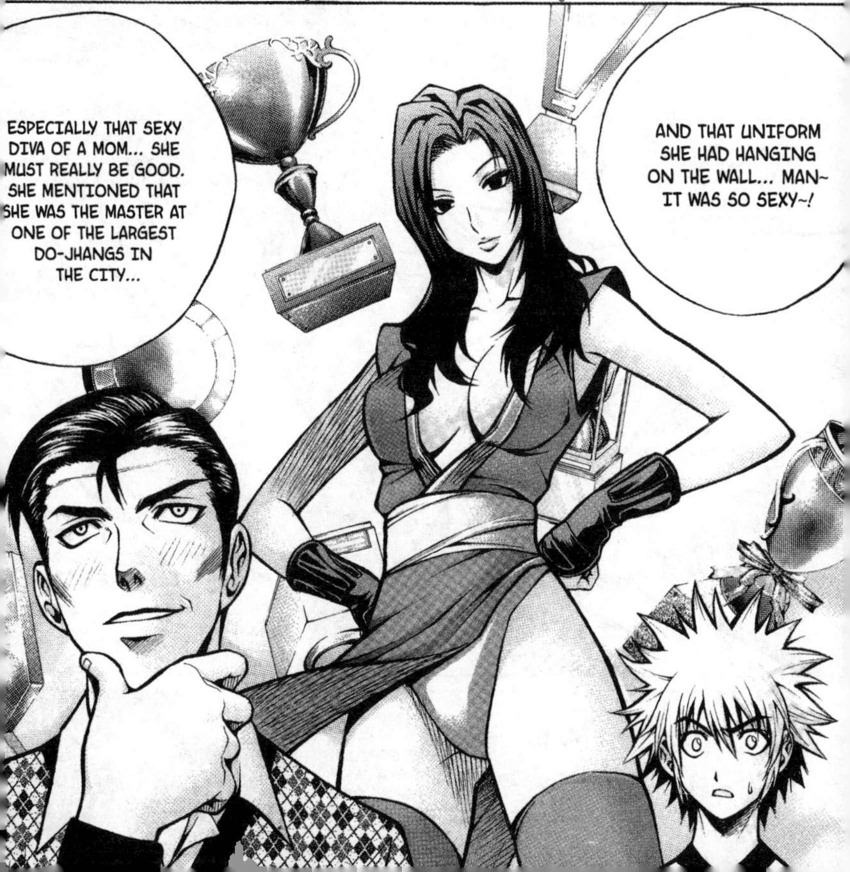
ESPECIALLY THAT SEXY DIVA OF A MOM... SHE MUST REALLY BE GOOD. SHE MENTIONED THAT SHE WAS THE MASTER AT ONE OF THE LARGEST DO-JHANGS IN THE CITY...
AND THAT UNIFORM SHE HAD HANGING ON THE WALL... MAN~ IT WAS SO SEXY~!

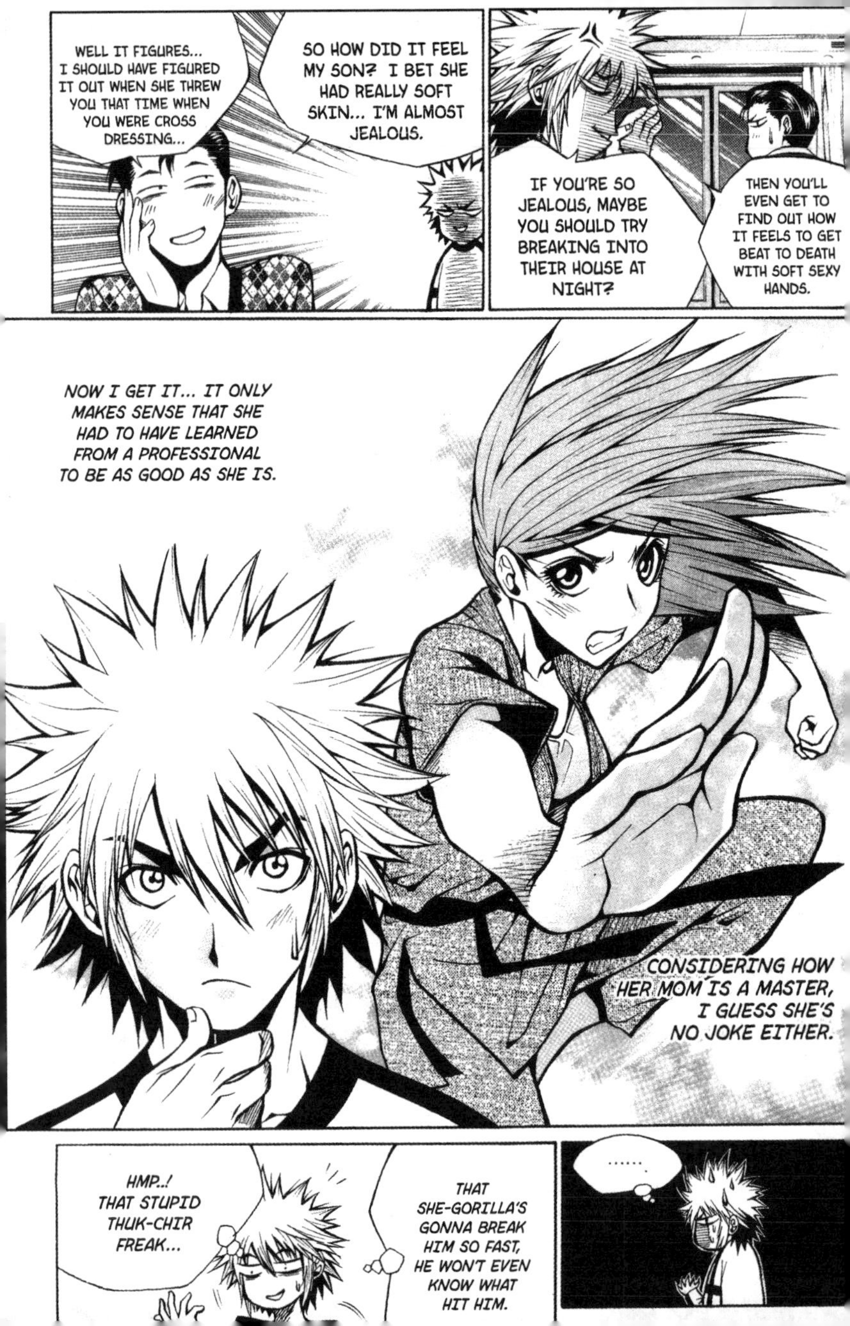

WELL IT FIGURES... I SHOULD HAVE FIGURED IT OUT WHEN SHE THREW YOU THAT TIME WHEN YOU WERE CROSS DRESSING...
SO HOW DID IT FEEL MY SON? I BET SHE HAD REALLY SOFT SKIN... I'M ALMOST JEALOUS.
IF YOU'RE SO JEALOUS, MAYBE YOU SHOULD TRY BREAKING INTO THEIR HOUSE AT NIGHT?
THEN YOU'LL EVEN GET TO FIND OUT HOW IT FEELS TO GET BEAT TO DEATH WITH SOFT SEXY HANDS.
NOW I GET IT... IT ONLY MAKES SENSE THAT SHE HAD TO HAVE LEARNED FROM A PROFESSIONAL TO BE AS GOOD AS SHE IS.
CONSIDERING HOW HER MOM IS A MASTER, I GUESS SHE'S NO JOKE EITHER.
HMP..! THAT STUPID THUK-CHIR FREAK...
THAT SHE-GORILLA'S GONNA BREAK HIM SO FAST, HE WON'T EVEN KNOW WHAT HIT HIM.
......

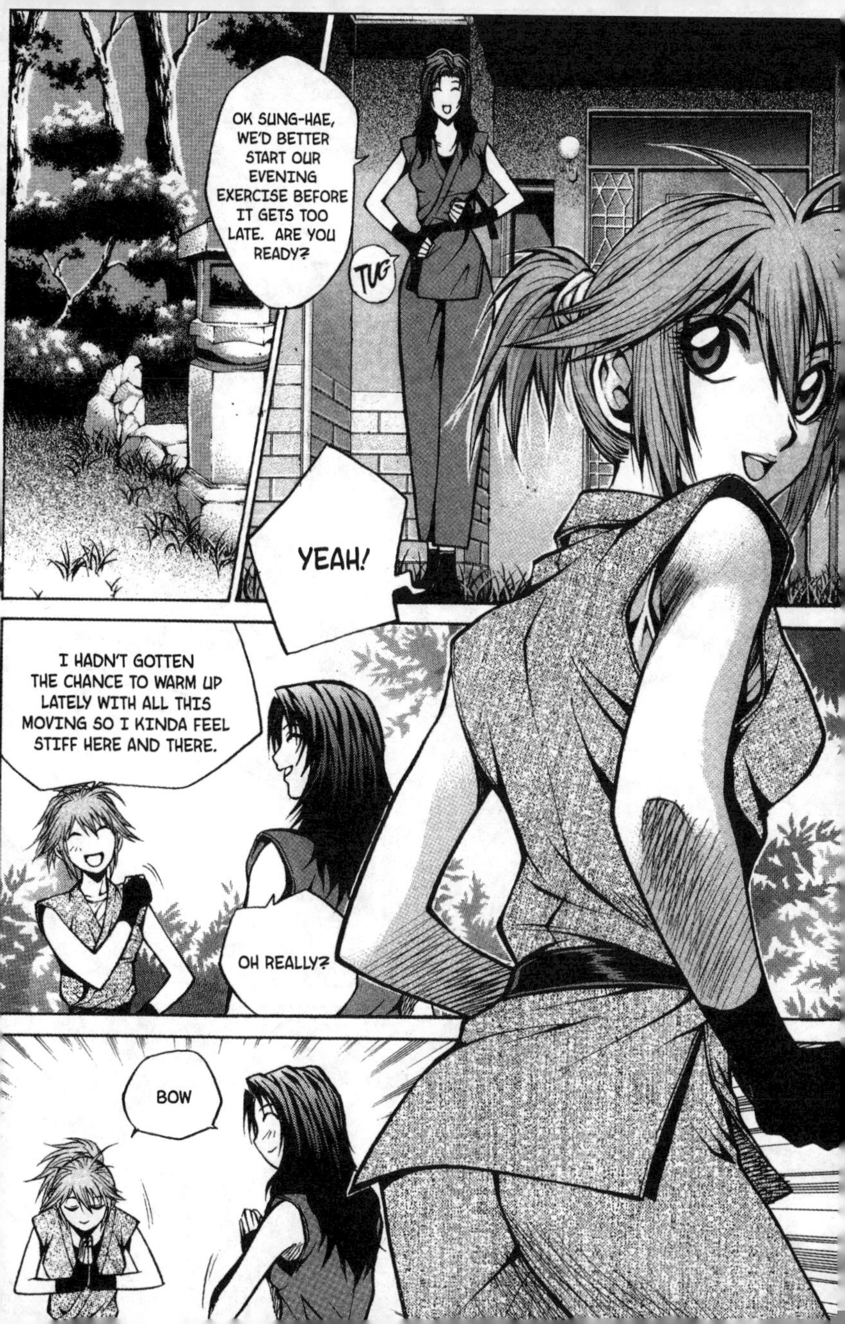
OK SUNG-HAE, WE'D BETTER START OUR EVENING EXERCISE BEFORE IT GETS TOO LATE. ARE YOU READY?
TUG
YEAH!
I HADN'T GOTTEN THE CHANCE TO WARM UP LATELY WITH ALL THIS MOVING SO I KINDA FEEL STIFF HERE AND THERE.
OH REALLY?
BOW

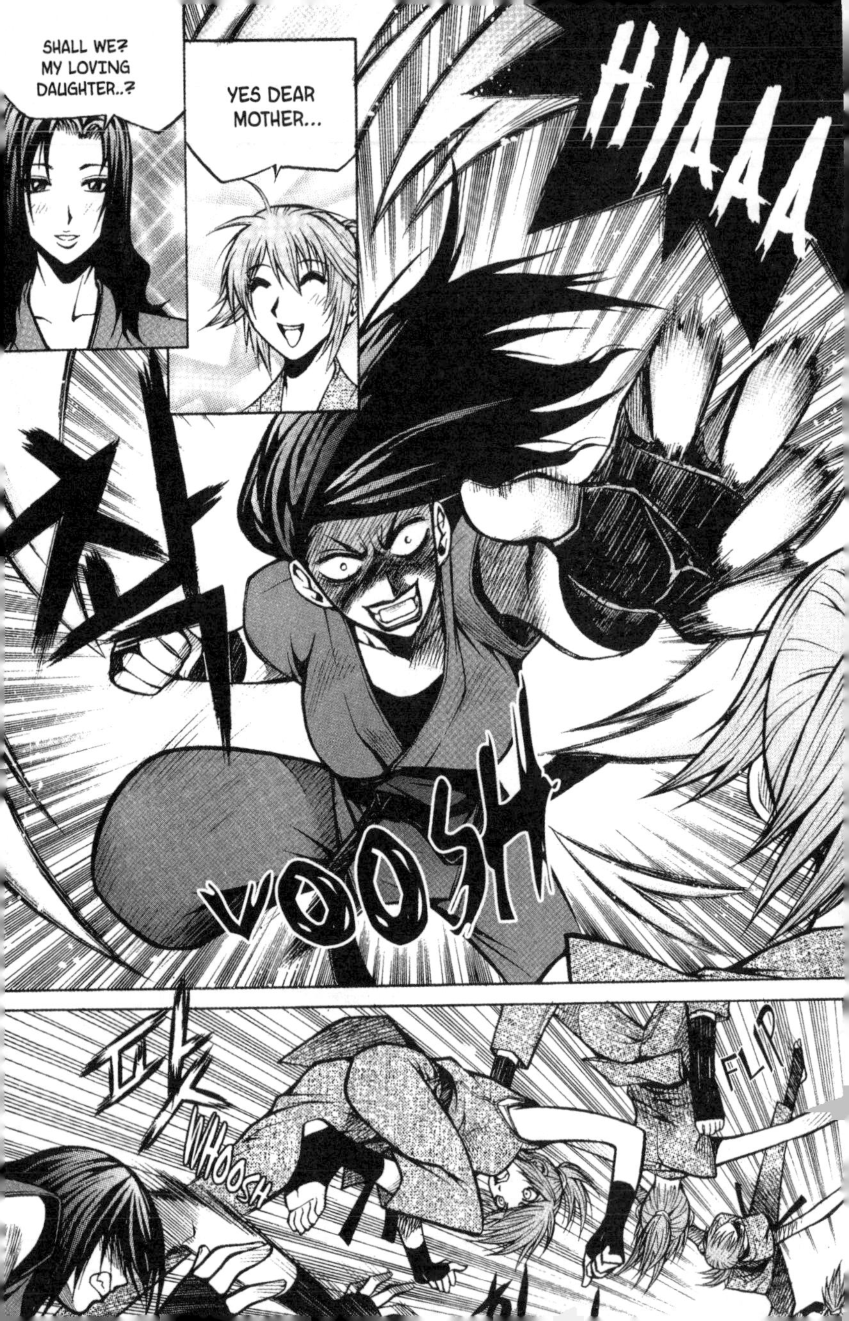
SHALL WE? MY LOVING DAUGHTER..?
YES DEAR MOTHER...
HYAAA
VOOSH
WHOOSH
FLIP

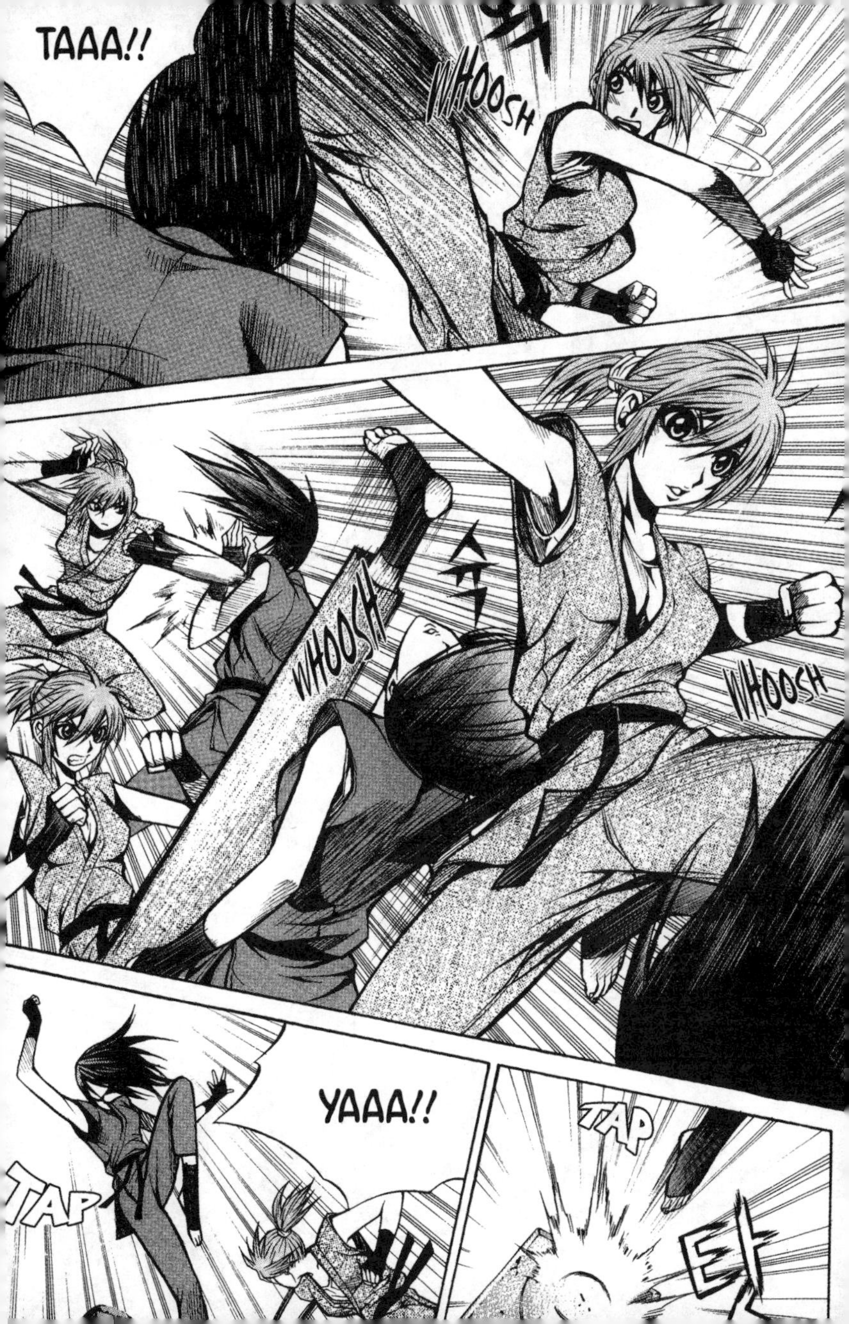
TAAA!!
WHOOSH
WHOOSH
WHOOSH
TAP
YAAA!!
TAP

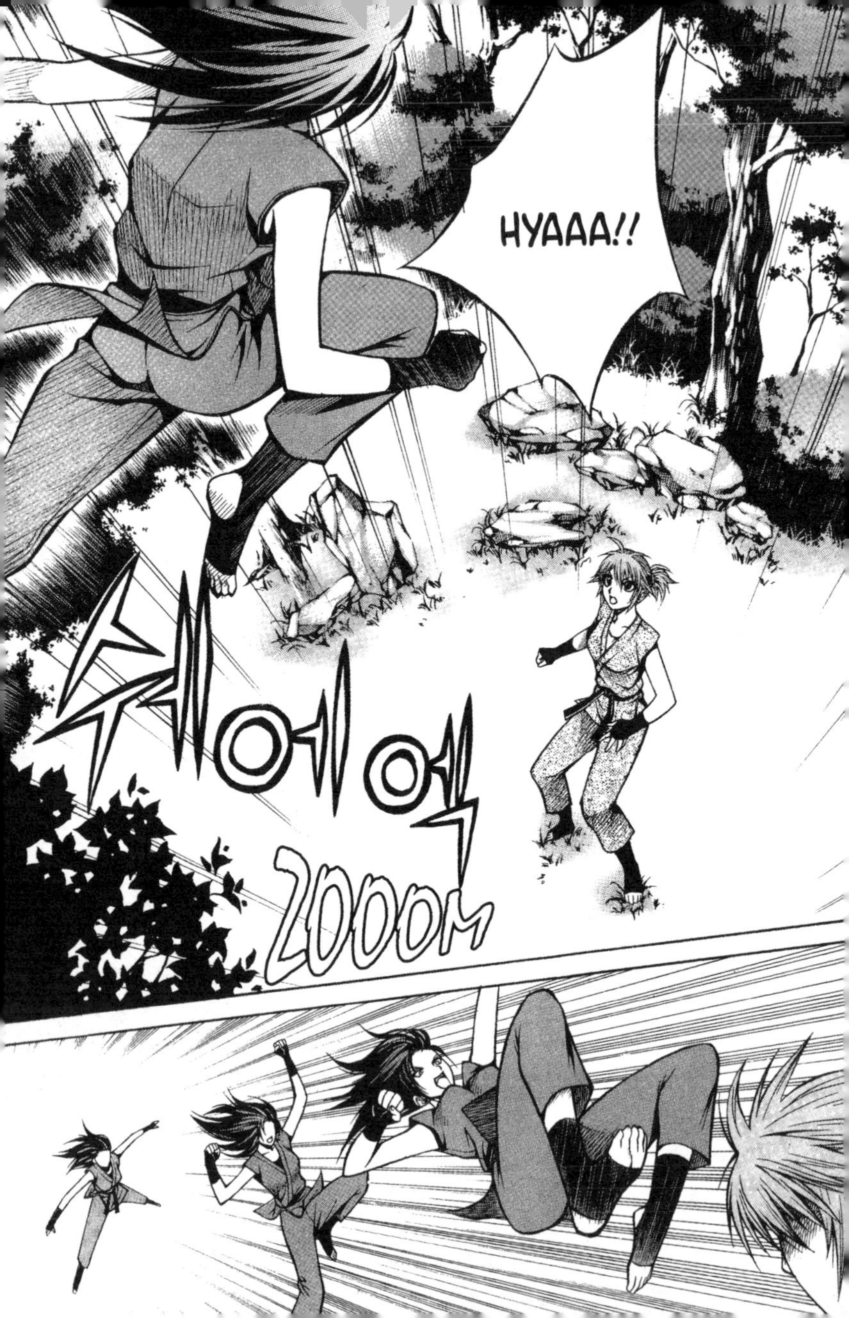
HYAAA!!
ZOOOM

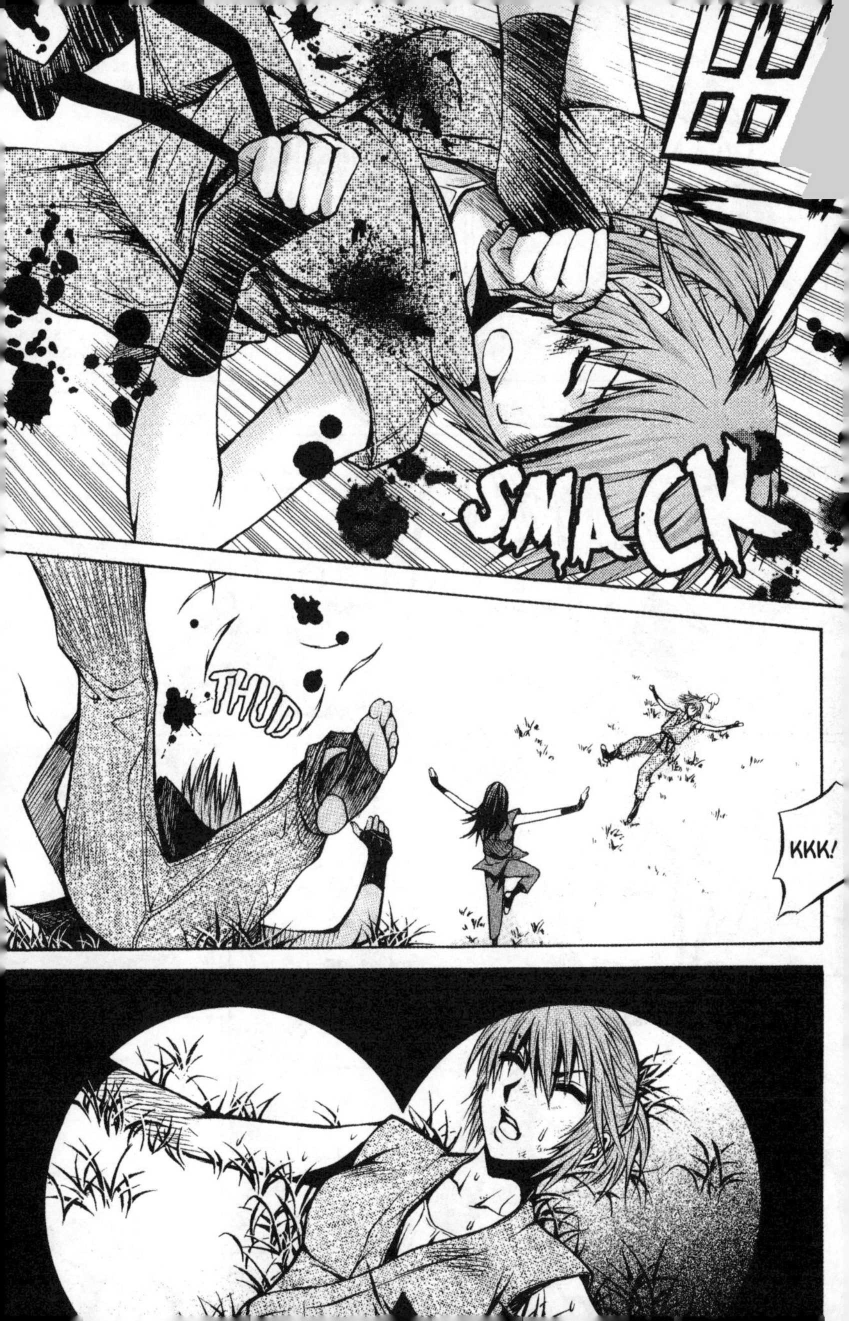
SMACK
THUD
KKK!

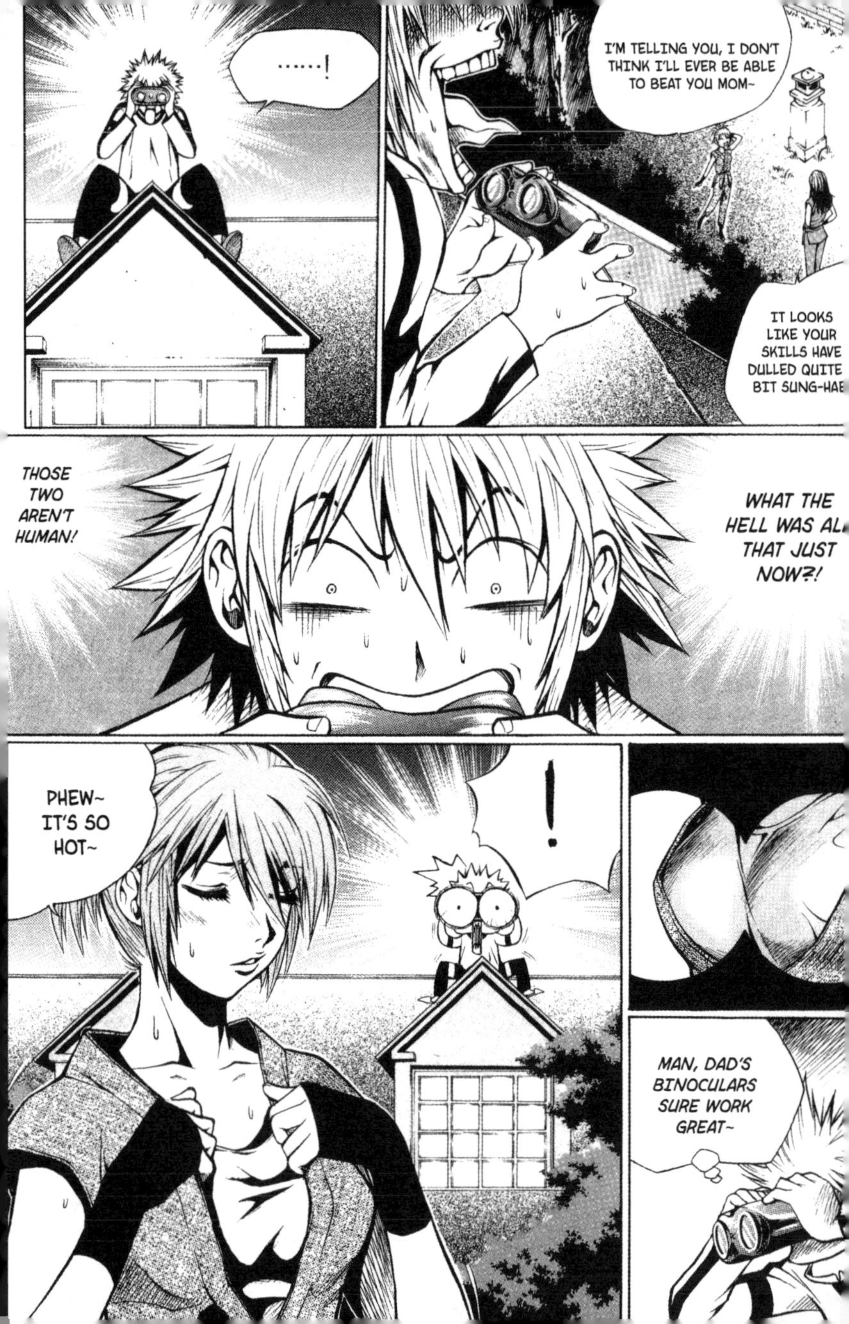
......!
I'M TELLING YOU, I DON'T THINK I'LL EVER BE ABLE TO BEAT YOU MOM~
IT LOOKS LIKE YOUR SKILLS HAVE DULLED QUITE BIT SUNG-HAE
THOSE TWO AREN'T HUMAN!
WHAT THE HELL WAS ALL THAT JUST NOW?!
PHEW~ IT'S SO HOT~
!
MAN, DAD'S BINOCULARS SURE WORK GREAT~

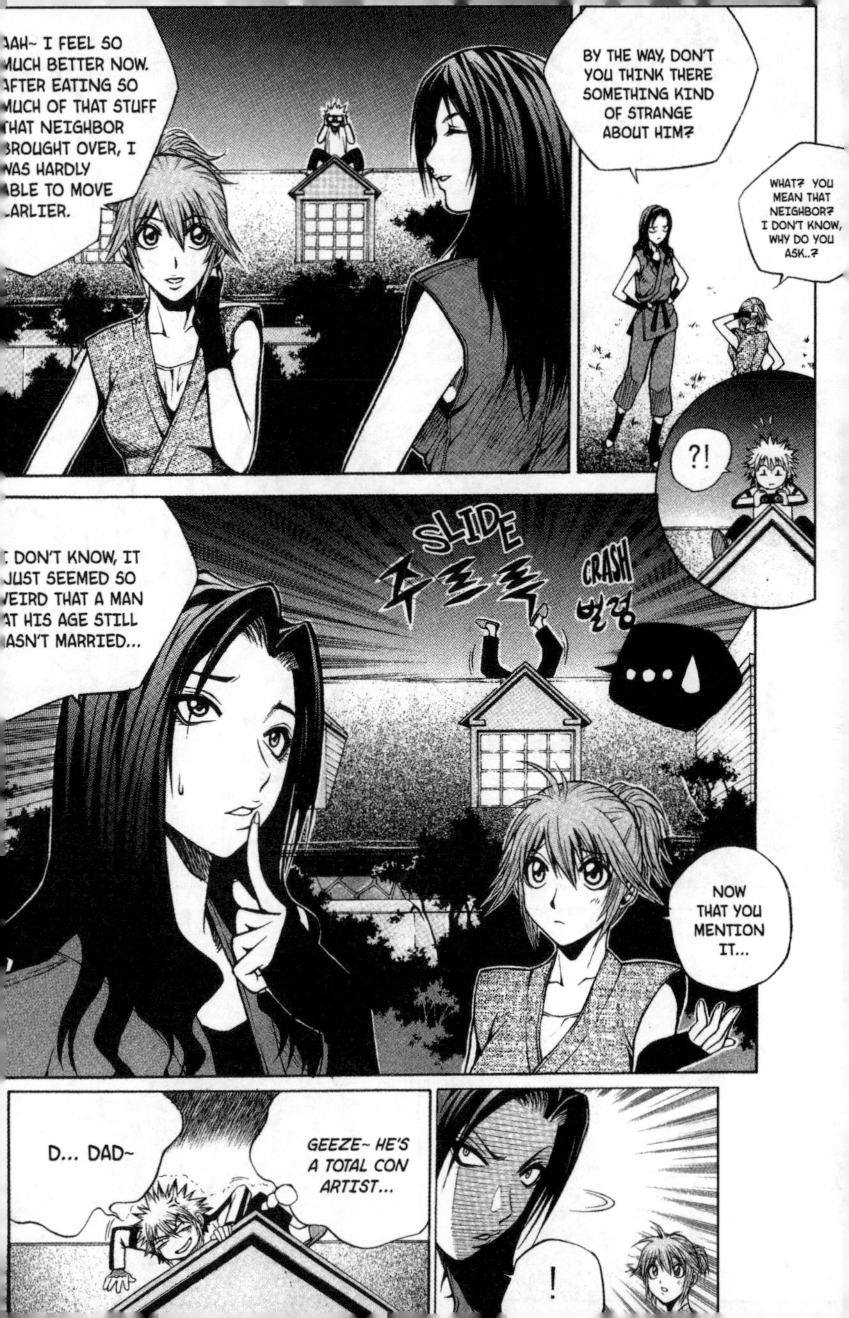
AAH~ I FEEL SO MUCH BETTER NOW. AFTER EATING SO MUCH OF THAT STUFF THAT NEIGHBOR BROUGHT OVER, I WAS HARDLY ABLE TO MOVE EARLIER.
BY THE WAY, DON'T YOU THINK THERE SOMETHING KIND OF STRANGE ABOUT HIM?
WHAT? YOU MEAN THAT NEIGHBOR? I DON'T KNOW, WHY DO YOU ASK..?
?!
I DON'T KNOW, IT JUST SEEMED SO WEIRD THAT A MAN AT HIS AGE STILL WASN'T MARRIED...
SLIDE
CRASH
...
NOW THAT YOU MENTION IT...
D... DAD~
GEEZE~ HE'S A TOTAL CON ARTIST...
!

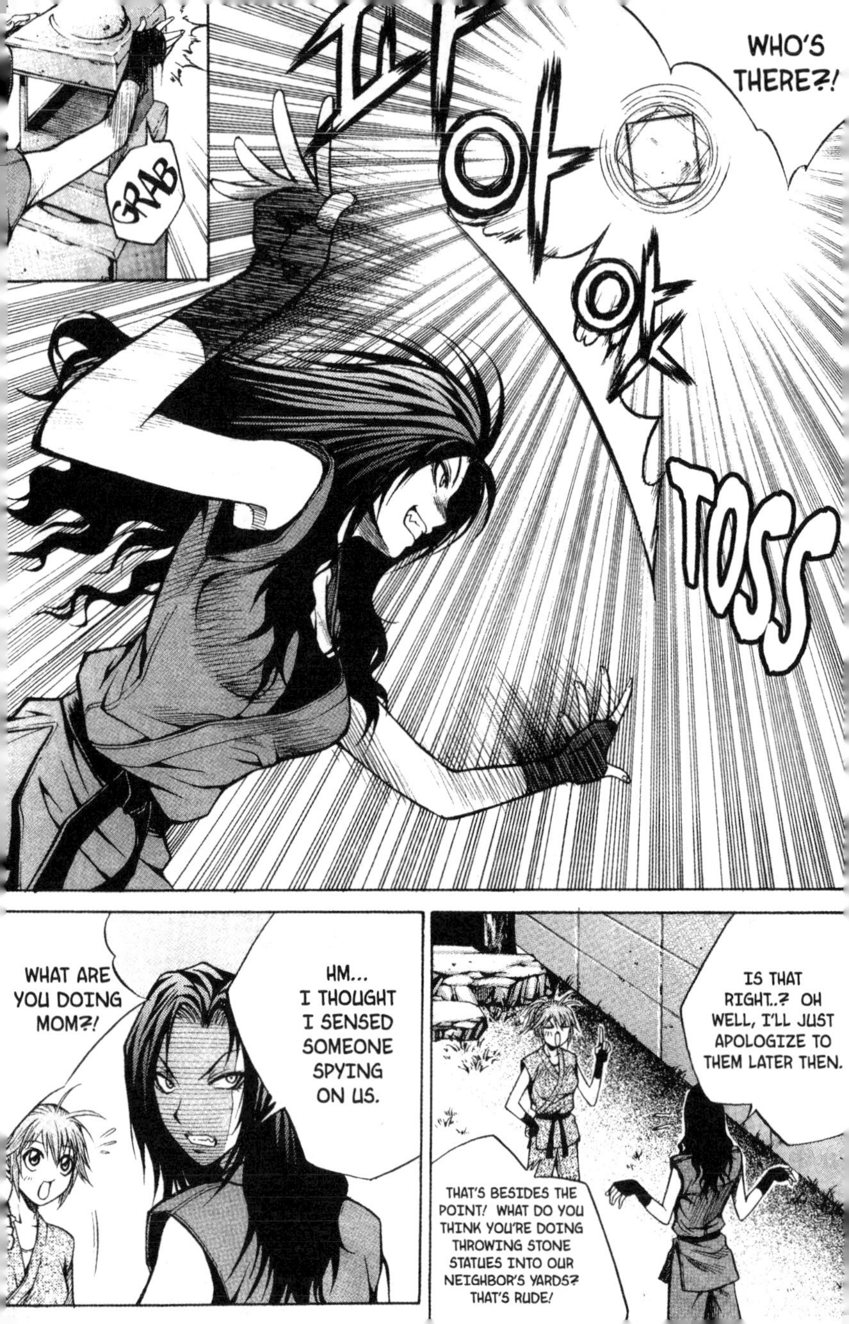
GRAB
WHO'S THERE?!
TOSS
WHAT ARE YOU DOING MOM?!
HM... I THOUGHT I SENSED SOMEONE SPYING ON US.
IS THAT RIGHT..? OH WELL, I'LL JUST APOLOGIZE TO THEM LATER THEN.
THAT'S BESIDES THE POINT! WHAT DO YOU THINK YOU'RE DOING THROWING STONE STATUES INTO OUR NEIGHBOR'S YARDS? THAT'S RUDE!

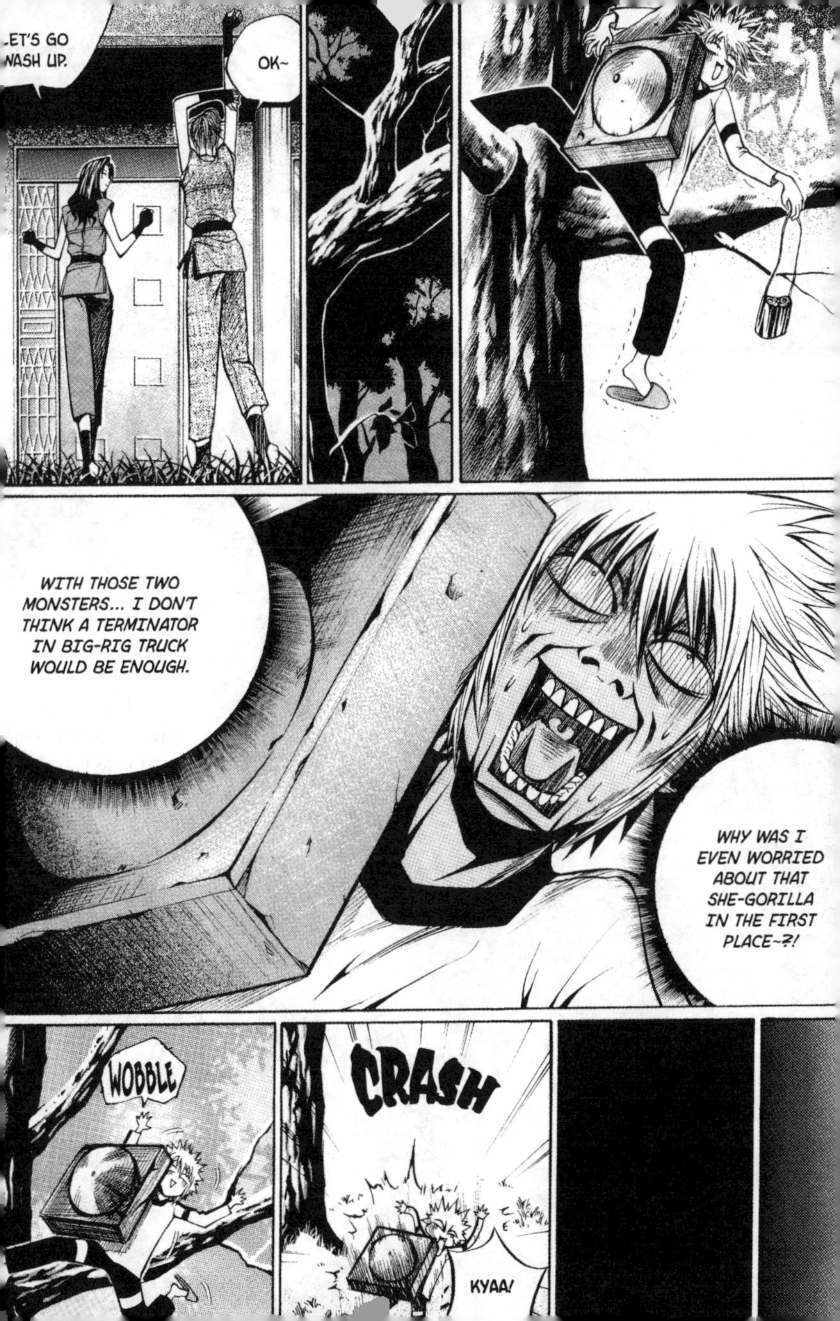
LET'S GO WASH UP.
OK~
WITH THOSE TWO MONSTERS... I DON'T THINK A TERMINATOR IN BIG-RIG TRUCK WOULD BE ENOUGH.
WHY WAS I EVEN WORRIED ABOUT THAT SHE-GORILLA IN THE FIRST PLACE~?!
WOBBLE
CRASH
KYAA!

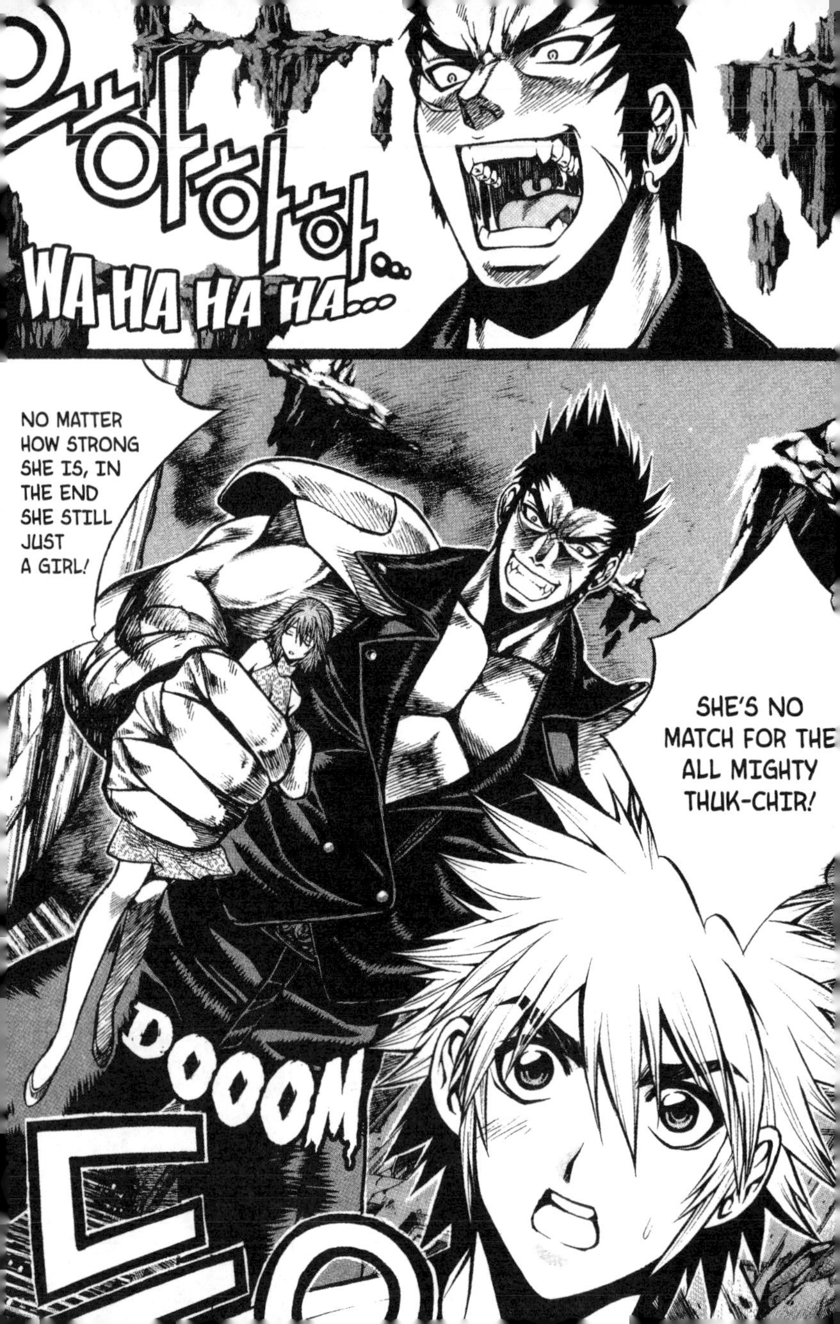
으하하하...
WA HA HA HA...
NO MATTER HOW STRONG SHE IS, IN THE END SHE STILL JUST A GIRL!
SHE'S NO MATCH FOR THE ALL MIGHTY THUK-CHIR!
DOOOM

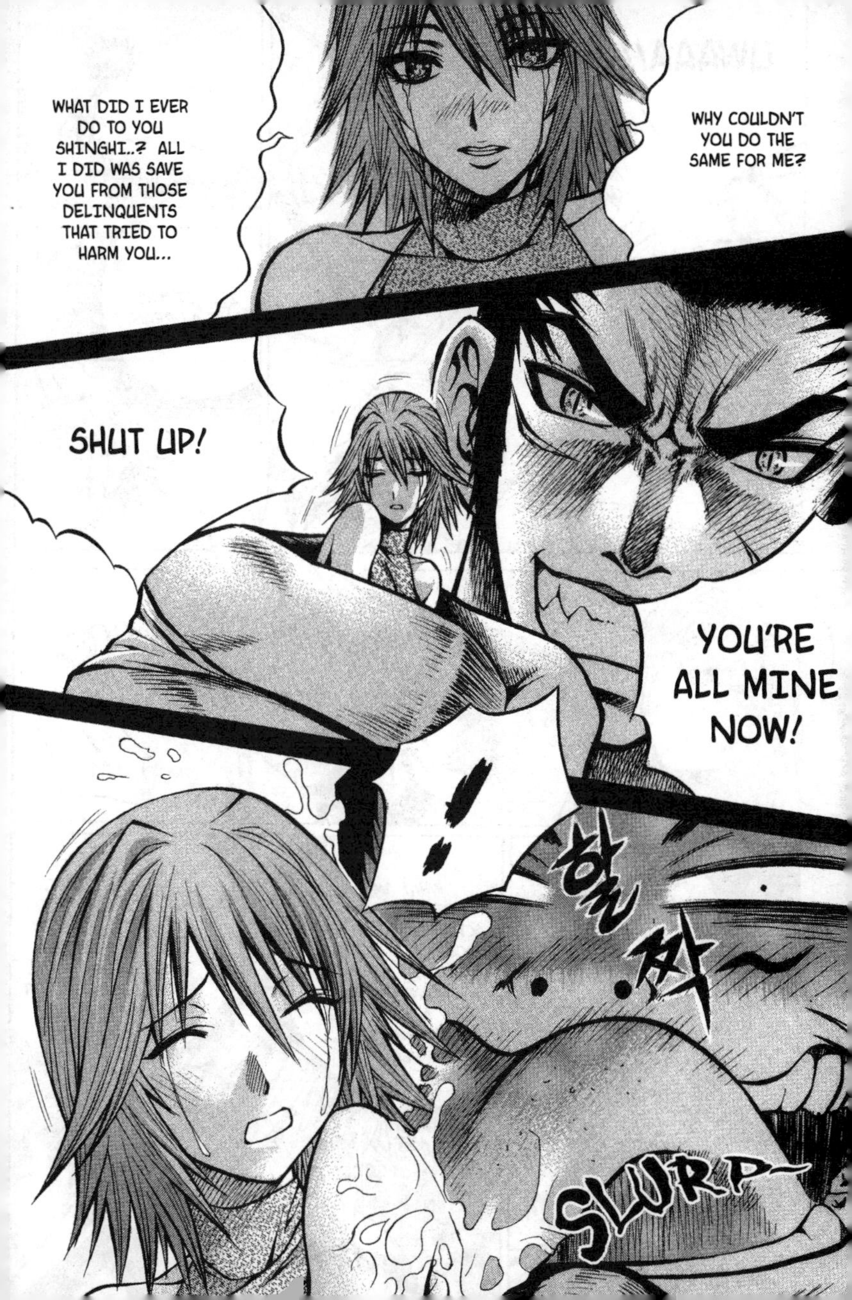
WHAT DID I EVER DO TO YOU SHINGHI..? ALL I DID WAS SAVE YOU FROM THOSE DELINQUENTS THAT TRIED TO HARM YOU...
WHY COULDN'T YOU DO THE SAME FOR ME?
SHUT UP!
YOU'RE ALL MINE NOW!
SLURP-

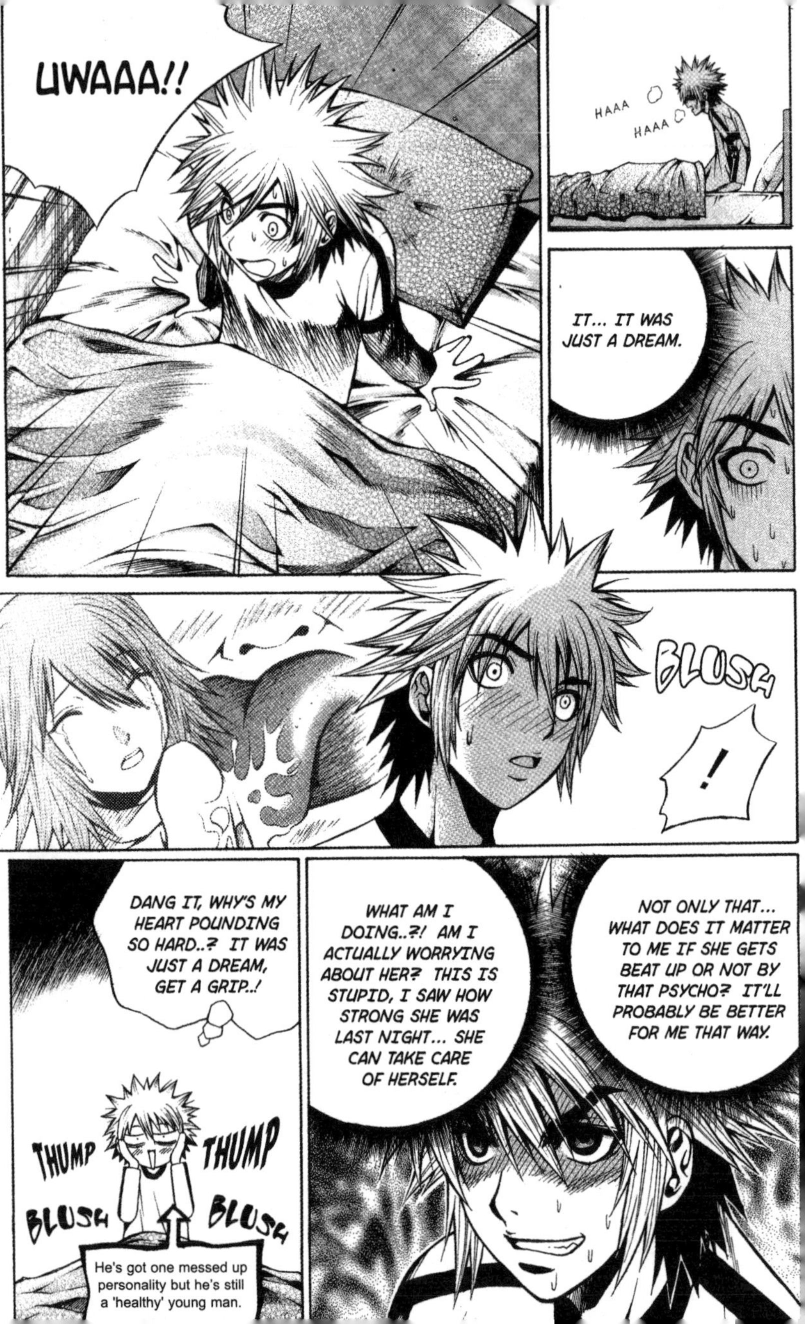
UWAAA!!
HAAA
HAAA
IT... IT WAS JUST A DREAM.
BLUSH
!
DANG IT, WHY'S MY HEART POUNDING SO HARD..? IT WAS JUST A DREAM, GET A GRIP..!
THUMP
THUMP
BLUSH
BLUSH
He's got one messed up personality but he's still a 'healthy' young man.
WHAT AM I DOING..?! AM I ACTUALLY WORRYING ABOUT HER? THIS IS STUPID, I SAW HOW STRONG SHE WAS LAST NIGHT... SHE CAN TAKE CARE OF HERSELF.
NOT ONLY THAT... WHAT DOES IT MATTER TO ME IF SHE GETS BEAT UP OR NOT BY THAT PSYCHO? IT'LL PROBABLY BE BETTER FOR ME THAT WAY.

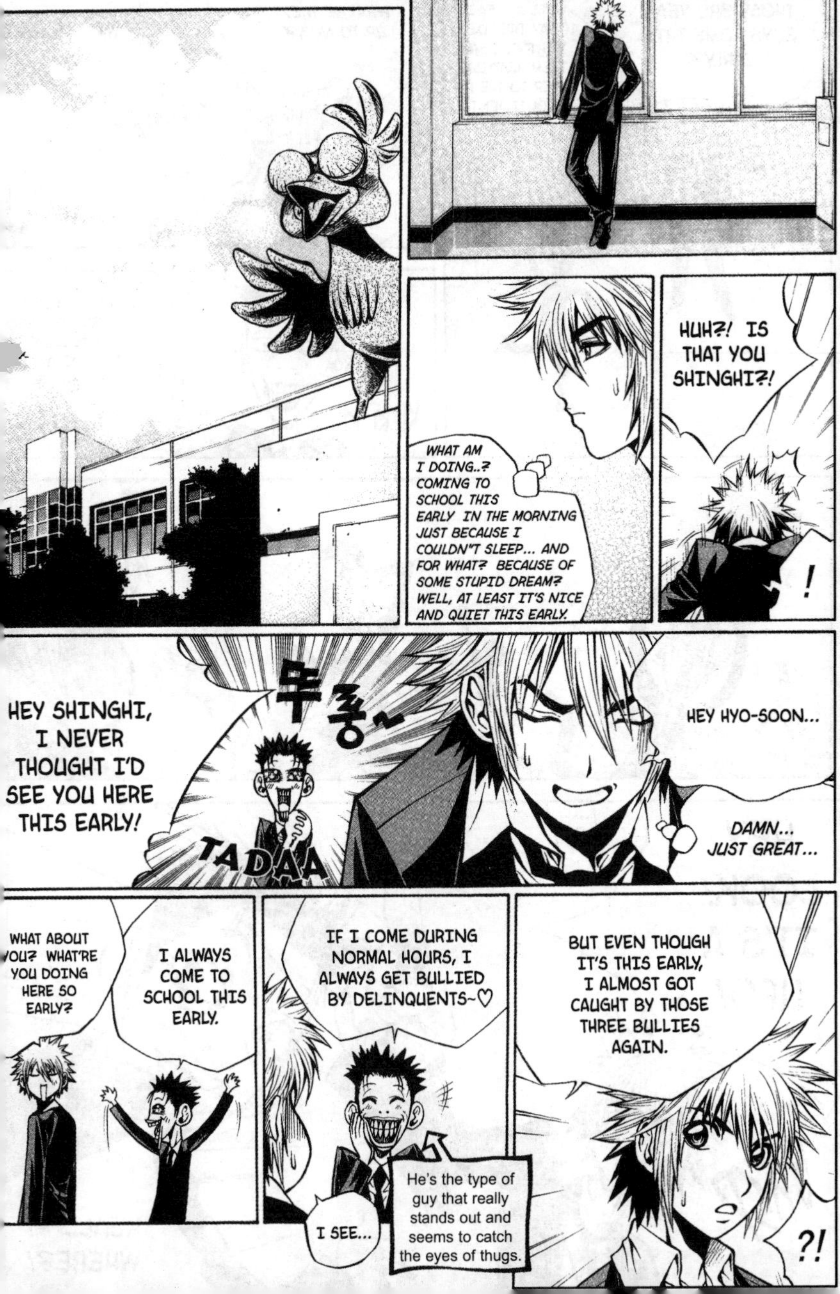
WHAT AM I DOING..? COMING TO SCHOOL THIS EARLY IN THE MORNING JUST BECAUSE I COULDN'T SLEEP... AND FOR WHAT? BECAUSE OF SOME STUPID DREAM? WELL, AT LEAST IT'S NICE AND QUIET THIS EARLY.
HUH?! IS THAT YOU SHINGHI?!
!
HEY SHINGHI, I NEVER THOUGHT I'D SEE YOU HERE THIS EARLY!
TADAA
HEY HYO-SOON...
DAMN... JUST GREAT...
WHAT ABOUT YOU? WHAT'RE YOU DOING HERE SO EARLY?
I ALWAYS COME TO SCHOOL THIS EARLY.
IF I COME DURING NORMAL HOURS, I ALWAYS GET BULLIED BY DELINQUENTS~♡
I SEE...
He's the type of guy that really stands out and seems to catch the eyes of thugs.
BUT EVEN THOUGH IT'S THIS EARLY, I ALMOST GOT CAUGHT BY THOSE THREE BULLIES AGAIN.
?!

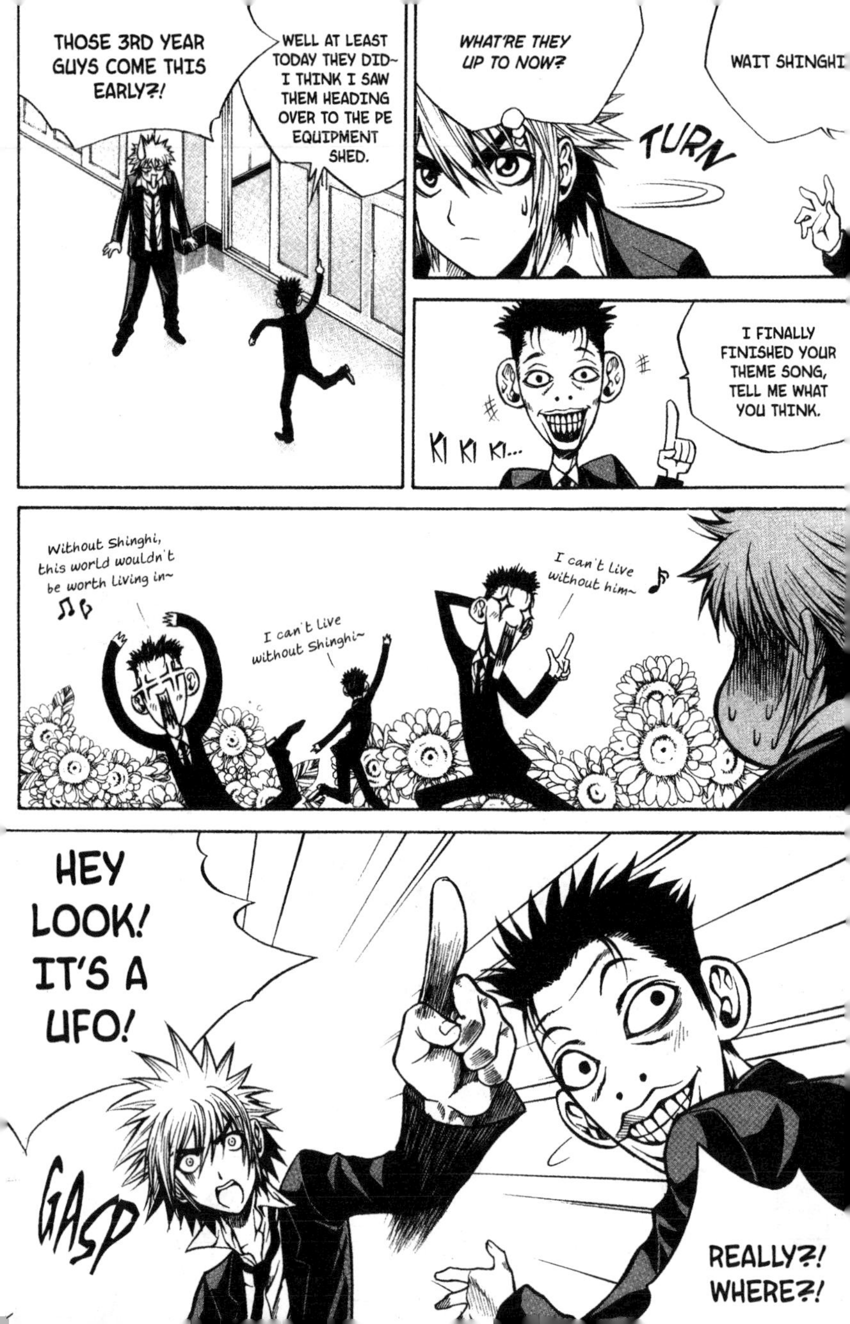
THOSE 3RD YEAR GUYS COME THIS EARLY?!
WELL AT LEAST TODAY THEY DID~ I THINK I SAW THEM HEADING OVER TO THE PE EQUIPMENT SHED.
WHAT'RE THEY UP TO NOW?
TURN
WAIT SHINGHI
KI KI KI...
I FINALLY FINISHED YOUR THEME SONG, TELL ME WHAT YOU THINK.
Without Shinghi, this world wouldn't be worth living in~
I can't live without Shinghi~
I can't live without him~
HEY LOOK! IT'S A UFO!
GASP
REALLY?! WHERE?!

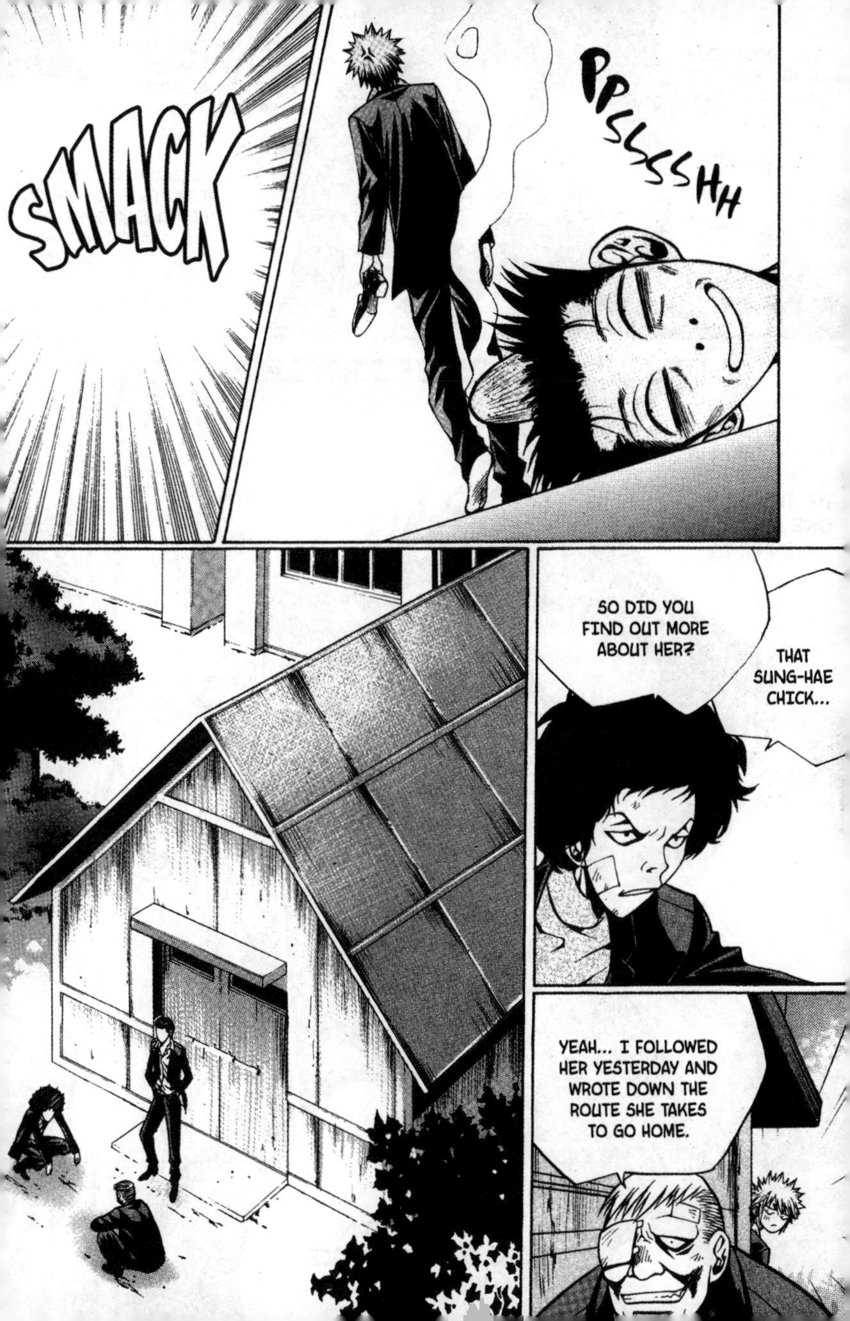
SMACK
PPSSSSHH
SO DID YOU FIND OUT MORE ABOUT HER?
THAT SUNG-HAE CHICK...
YEAH... I FOLLOWED HER YESTERDAY AND WROTE DOWN THE ROUTE SHE TAKES TO GO HOME.

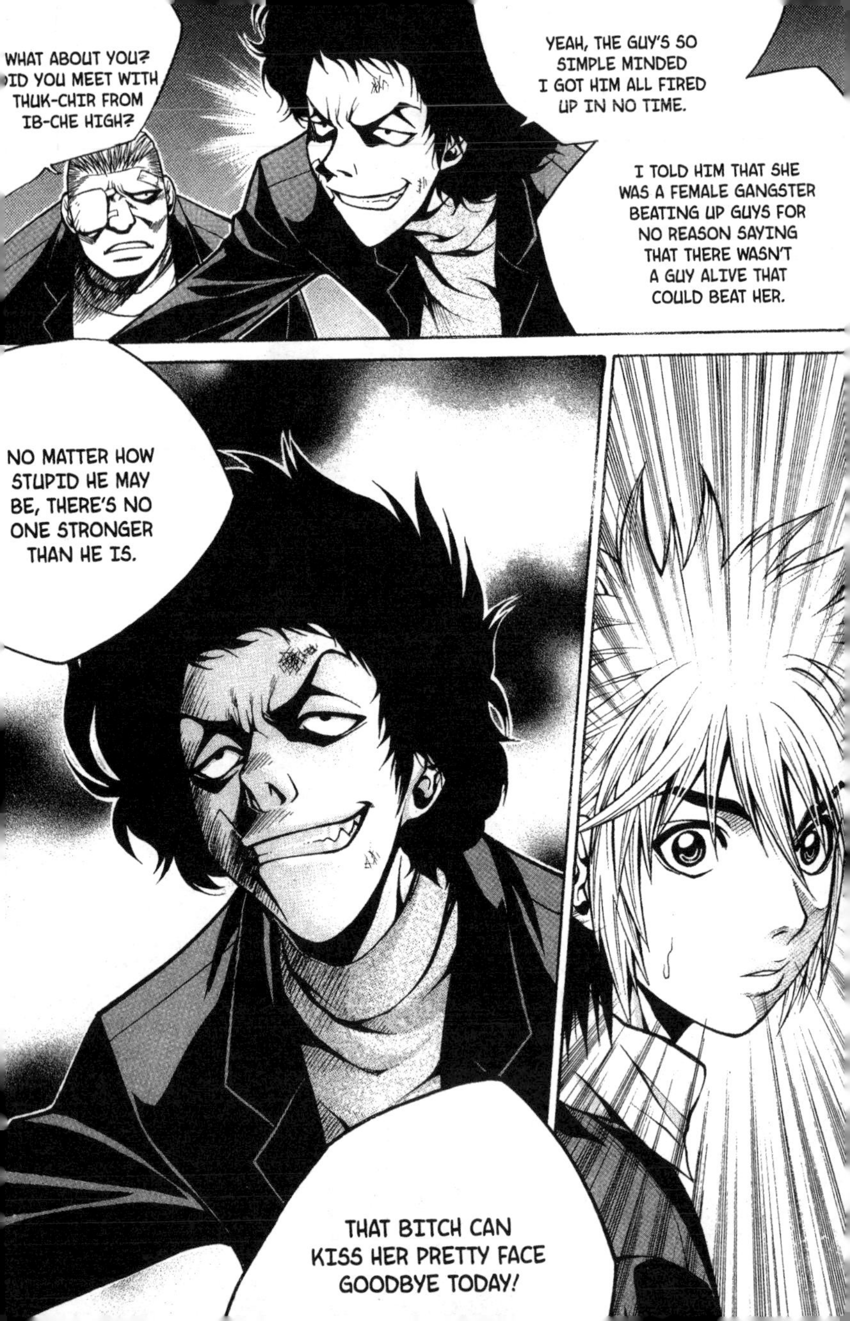
WHAT ABOUT YOU? DID YOU MEET WITH THUK-CHIR FROM IB-CHE HIGH?
YEAH, THE GUY'S SO SIMPLE MINDED I GOT HIM ALL FIRED UP IN NO TIME.
I TOLD HIM THAT SHE WAS A FEMALE GANGSTER BEATING UP GUYS FOR NO REASON SAYING THAT THERE WASN'T A GUY ALIVE THAT COULD BEAT HER.
NO MATTER HOW STUPID HE MAY BE, THERE'S NO ONE STRONGER THAN HE IS.
THAT BITCH CAN KISS HER PRETTY FACE GOODBYE TODAY!

Chapter 6 : Should I Protect Her or Not?

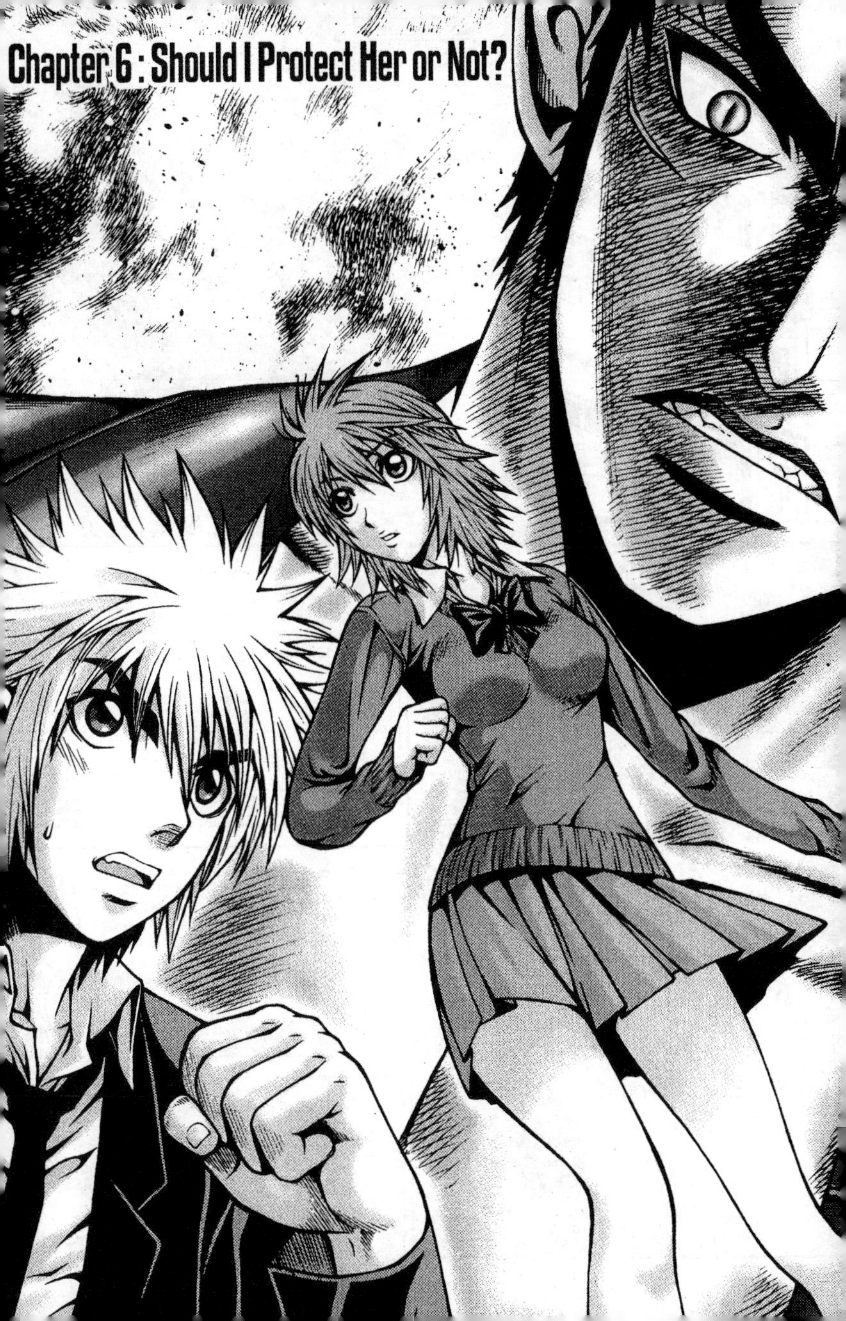

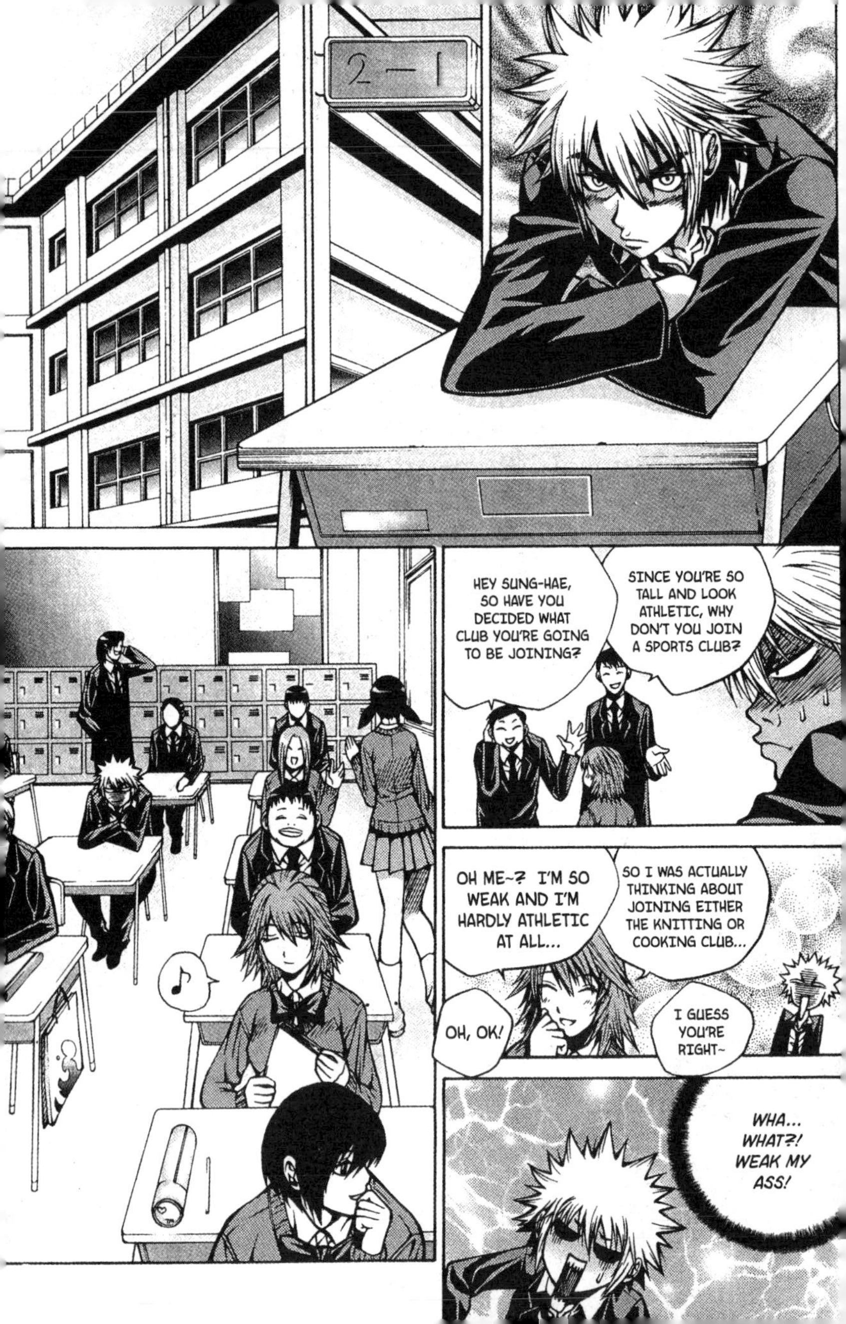
2-1
♪
HEY SUNG-HAE, SO HAVE YOU DECIDED WHAT CLUB YOU'RE GOING TO BE JOINING?
SINCE YOU'RE SO TALL AND LOOK ATHLETIC, WHY DON'T YOU JOIN A SPORTS CLUB?
OH ME~? I'M SO WEAK AND I'M HARDLY ATHLETIC AT ALL...
SO I WAS ACTUALLY THINKING ABOUT JOINING EITHER THE KNITTING OR COOKING CLUB...
OH, OK!
I GUESS YOU'RE RIGHT~
WHA... WHAT?! WEAK MY ASS!

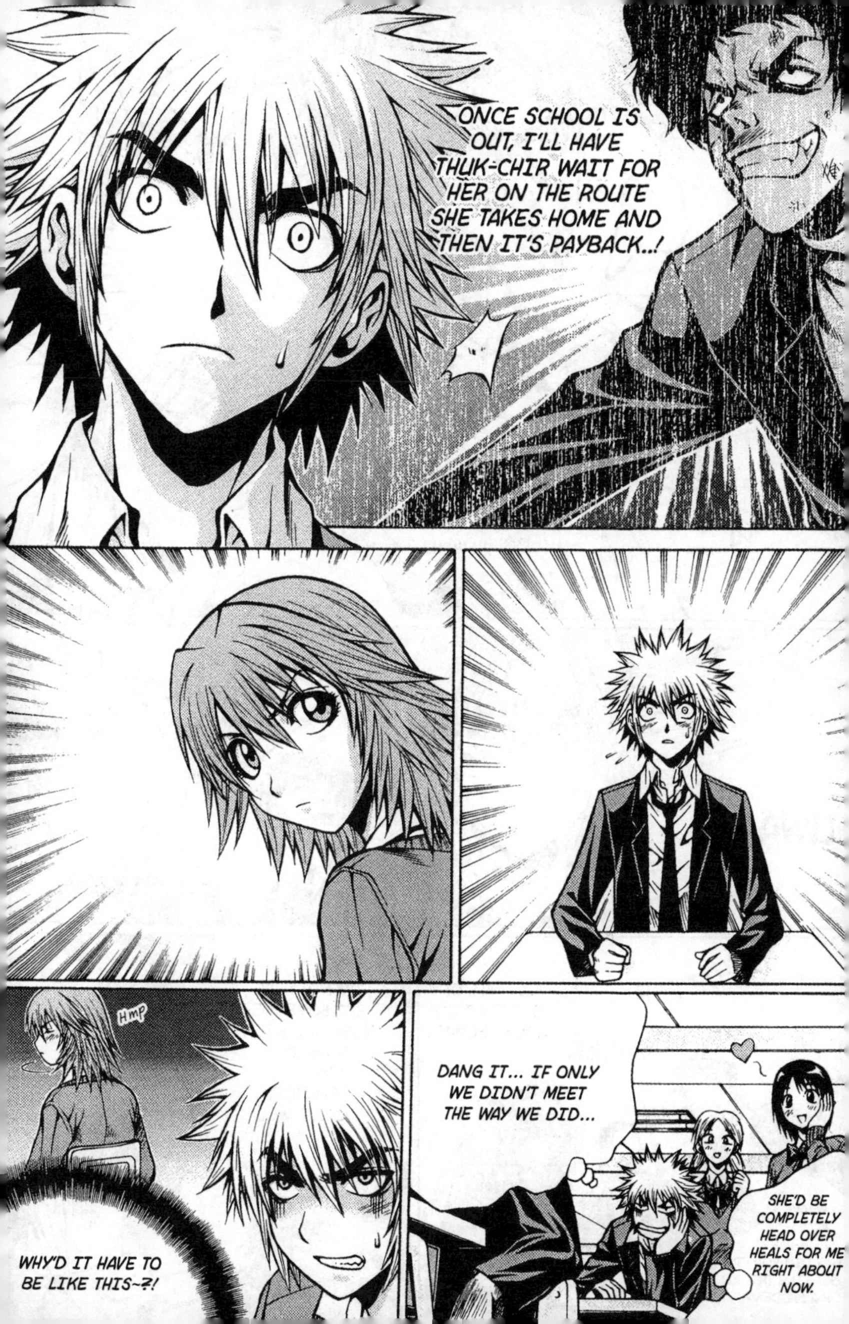
ONCE SCHOOL IS OUT, I'LL HAVE THUK-CHIR WAIT FOR HER ON THE ROUTE SHE TAKES HOME AND THEN IT'S PAYBACK..!
Hmp
WHY'D IT HAVE TO BE LIKE THIS~?!
DANG IT... IF ONLY WE DIDN'T MEET THE WAY WE DID...
SHE'D BE COMPLETELY HEAD OVER HEALS FOR ME RIGHT ABOUT NOW.

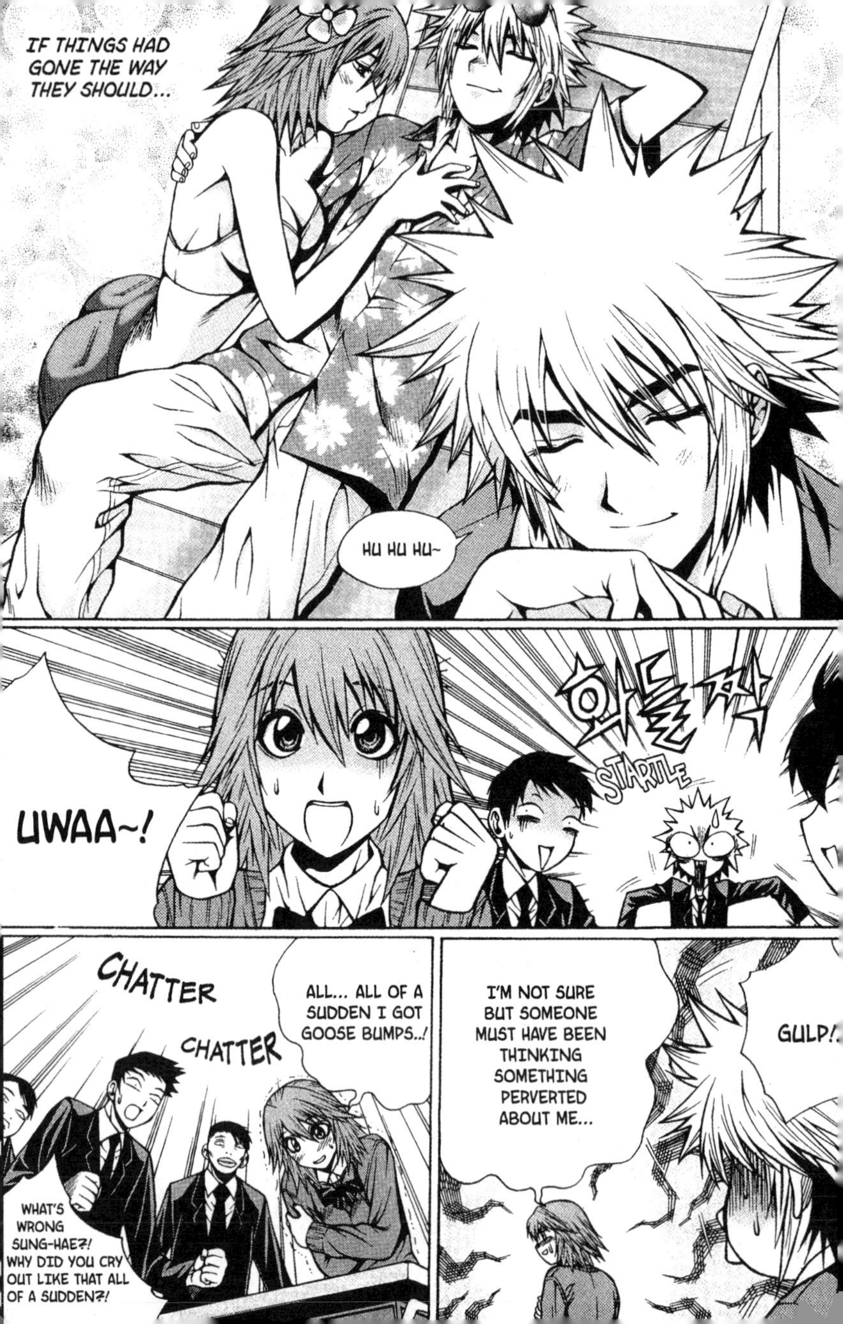

IF THINGS HAD GONE THE WAY THEY SHOULD...
HU HU HU~
UWAA~!
STARTLE
CHATTER
CHATTER
ALL... ALL OF A SUDDEN I GOT GOOSE BUMPS..!
WHAT'S WRONG SUNG-HAE?! WHY DID YOU CRY OUT LIKE THAT ALL OF A SUDDEN?!
I'M NOT SURE BUT SOMEONE MUST HAVE BEEN THINKING SOMETHING PERVERTED ABOUT ME...
GULP!.

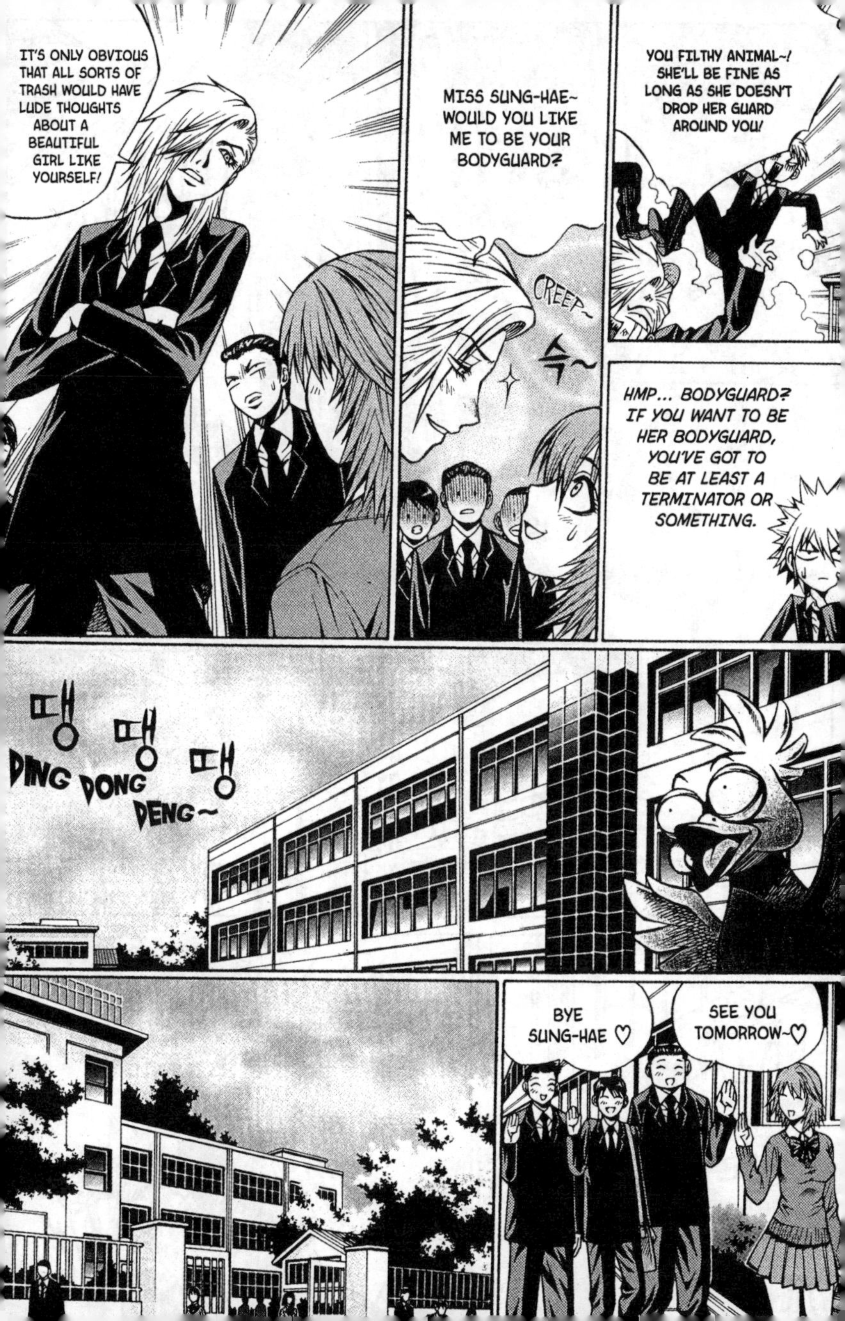
IT'S ONLY OBVIOUS THAT ALL SORTS OF TRASH WOULD HAVE LUDE THOUGHTS ABOUT A BEAUTIFUL GIRL LIKE YOURSELF!
MISS SUNG-HAE~ WOULD YOU LIKE ME TO BE YOUR BODYGUARD?
CREEP~
YOU FILTHY ANIMAL~! SHE'LL BE FINE AS LONG AS SHE DOESN'T DROP HER GUARD AROUND YOU!
HMP... BODYGUARD? IF YOU WANT TO BE HER BODYGUARD, YOU'VE GOT TO BE AT LEAST A TERMINATOR OR SOMETHING.
DING DONG DENG~
BYE SUNG-HAE ♡
SEE YOU TOMORROW~♡

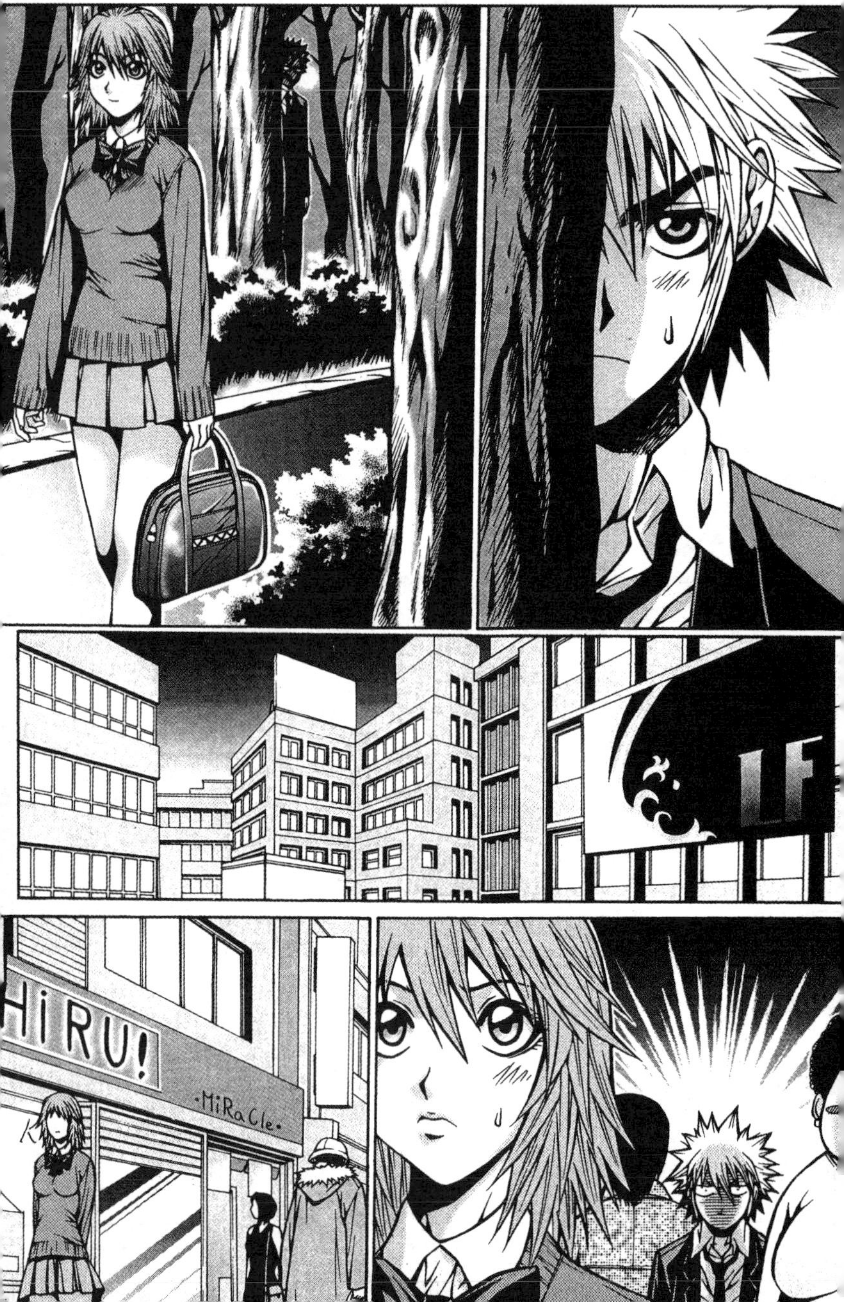
HiRU!
-MiRaCle-

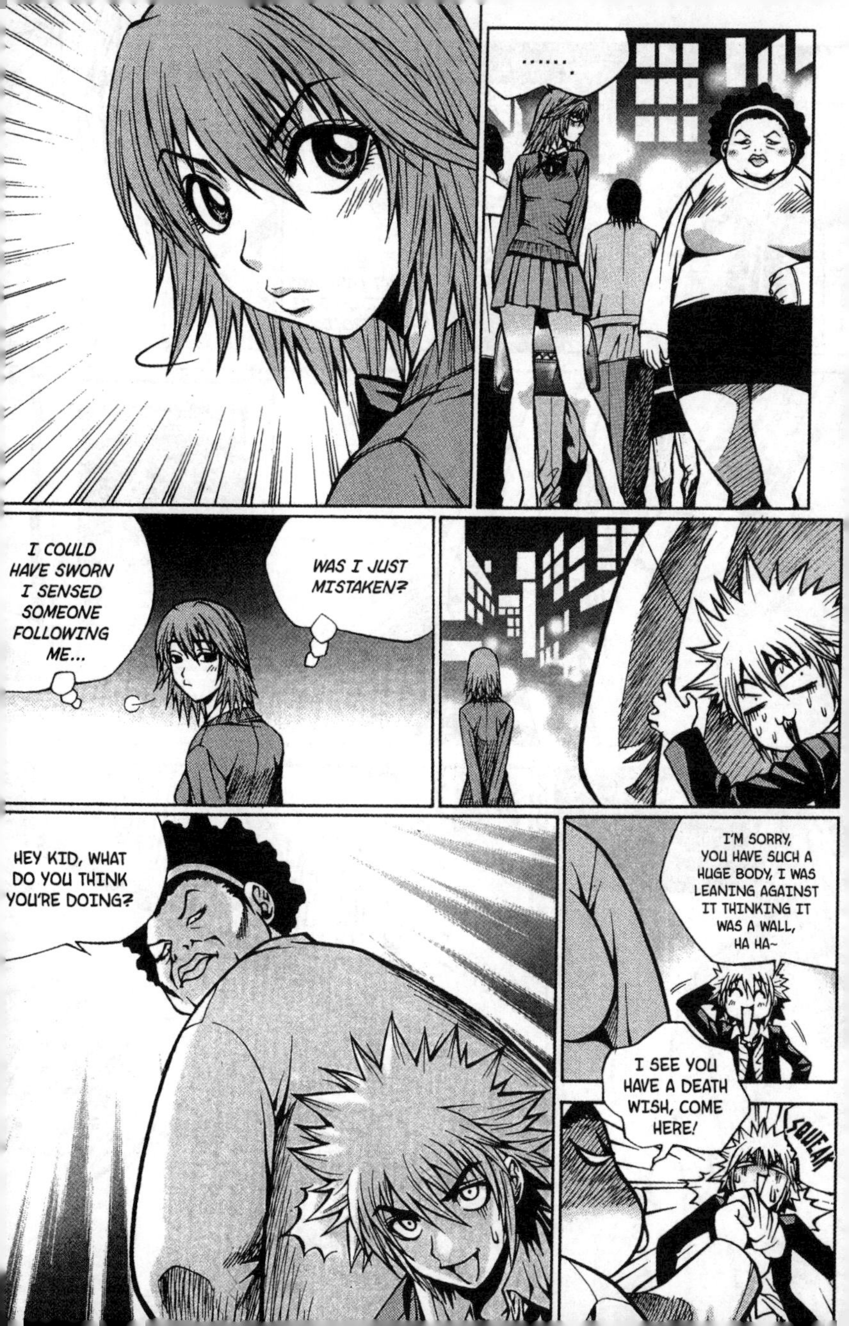
....
I COULD HAVE SWORN I SENSED SOMEONE FOLLOWING ME...
WAS I JUST MISTAKEN?
HEY KID, WHAT DO YOU THINK YOU'RE DOING?
I'M SORRY, YOU HAVE SUCH A HUGE BODY, I WAS LEANING AGAINST IT THINKING IT WAS A WALL, HA HA~
I SEE YOU HAVE A DEATH WISH, COME HERE!
SQUEAK

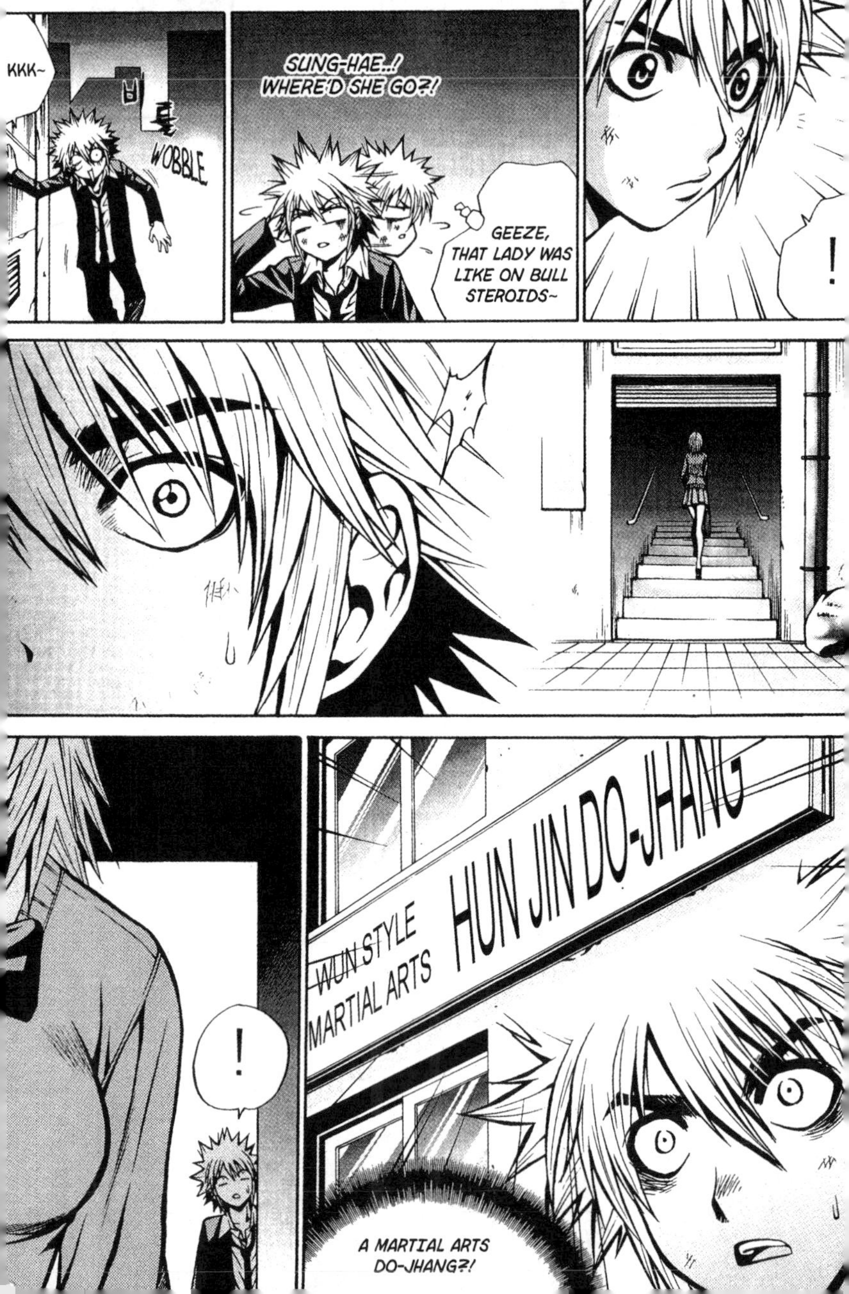
KKK~
WOBBLE
SUNG-HAE..! WHERE'D SHE GO?!
GEEZE, THAT LADY WAS LIKE ON BULL STEROIDS~
!
!
WUN STYLE MARTIAL ARTS
HUN JIN DO-JHANG
A MARTIAL ARTS DO-JHANG?!

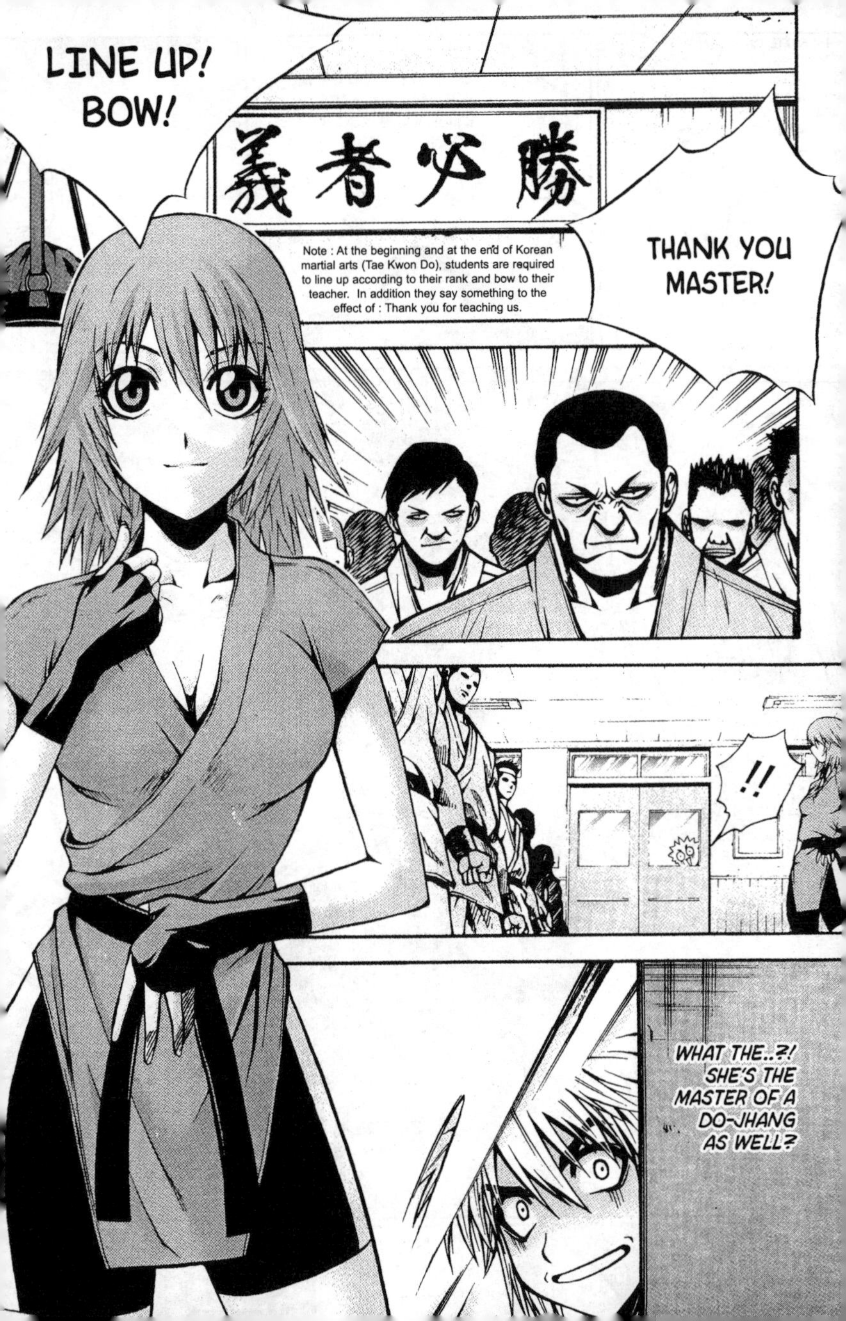
LINE UP! BOW!
義者必勝
Note : At the beginning and at the end of Korean martial arts (Tae Kwon Do), students are required to line up according to their rank and bow to their teacher. In addition they say something to the effect of : Thank you for teaching us.
THANK YOU MASTER!
!!
WHAT THE..?! SHE'S THE MASTER OF A DO-JHANG AS WELL?

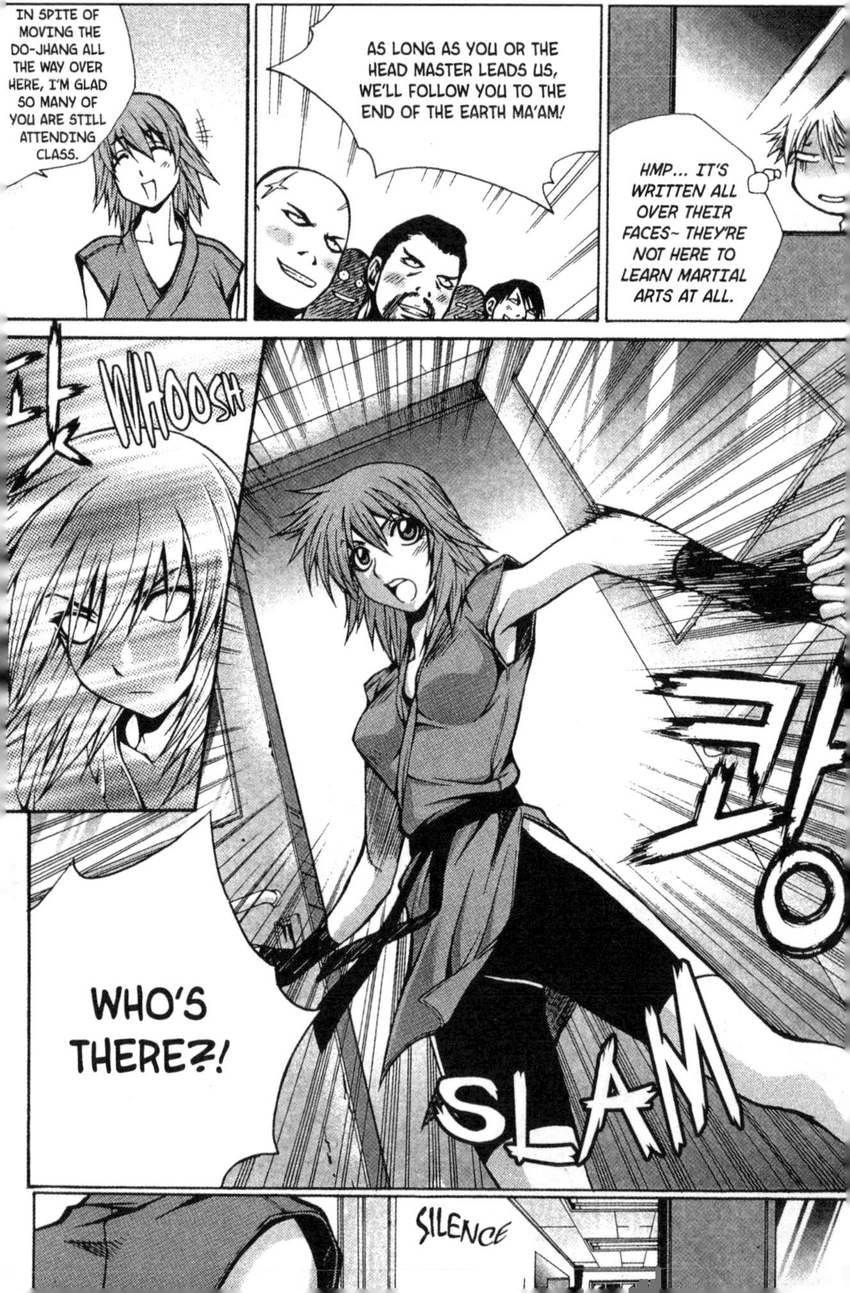
IN SPITE OF MOVING THE DO-JHANG ALL THE WAY OVER HERE, I'M GLAD SO MANY OF YOU ARE STILL ATTENDING CLASS.
AS LONG AS YOU OR THE HEAD MASTER LEADS US, WE'LL FOLLOW YOU TO THE END OF THE EARTH MA'AM!
HMP... IT'S WRITTEN ALL OVER THEIR FACES~ THEY'RE NOT HERE TO LEARN MARTIAL ARTS AT ALL.
WHOOSH
WHO'S THERE?!
SLAM
SILENCE

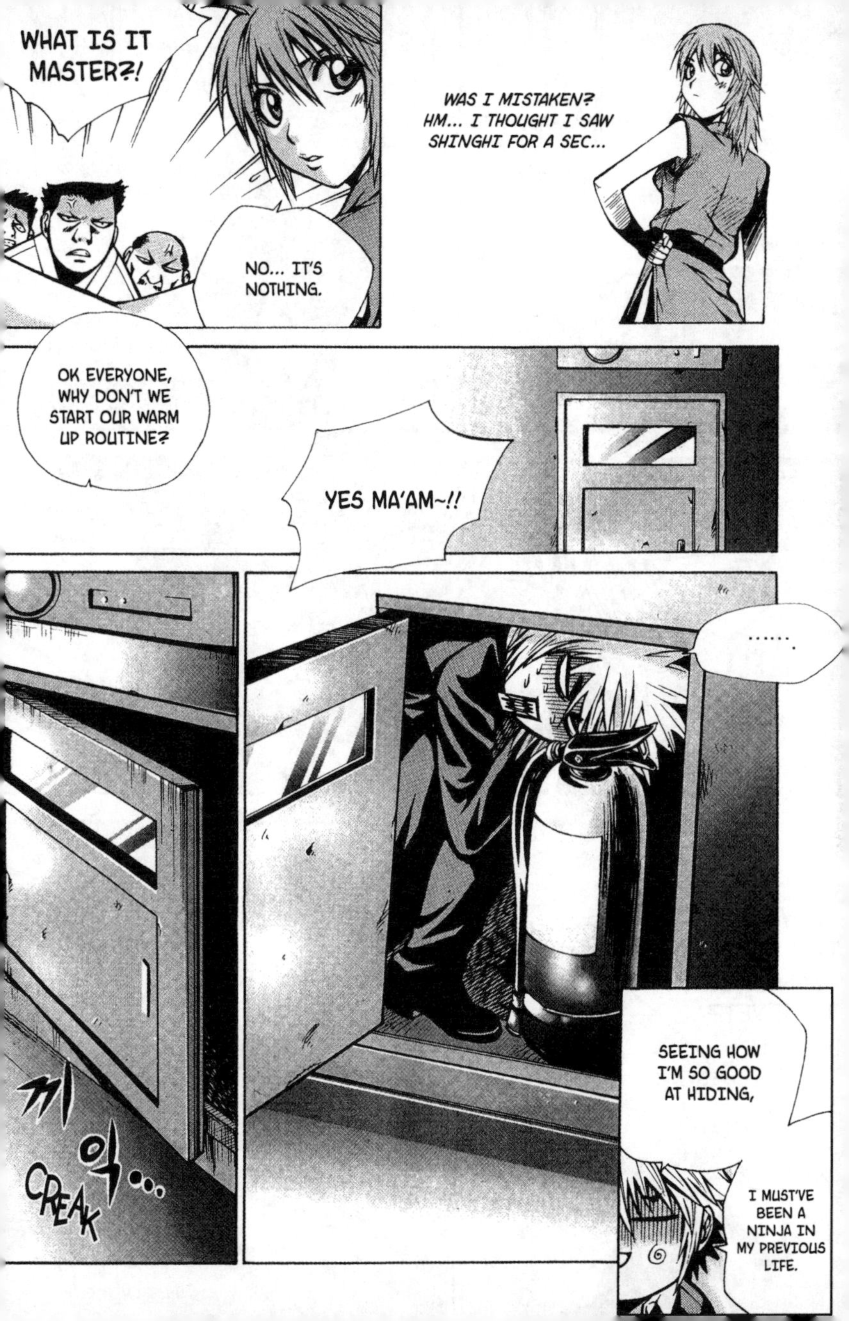
WHAT IS IT MASTER?!
NO... IT'S NOTHING.
WAS I MISTAKEN? HM... I THOUGHT I SAW SHINGHI FOR A SEC...
OK EVERYONE, WHY DON'T WE START OUR WARM UP ROUTINE?
YES MA'AM~!!
끼이익...
CREAK
....
SEEING HOW I'M SO GOOD AT HIDING,
I MUST'VE BEEN A NINJA IN MY PREVIOUS LIFE.

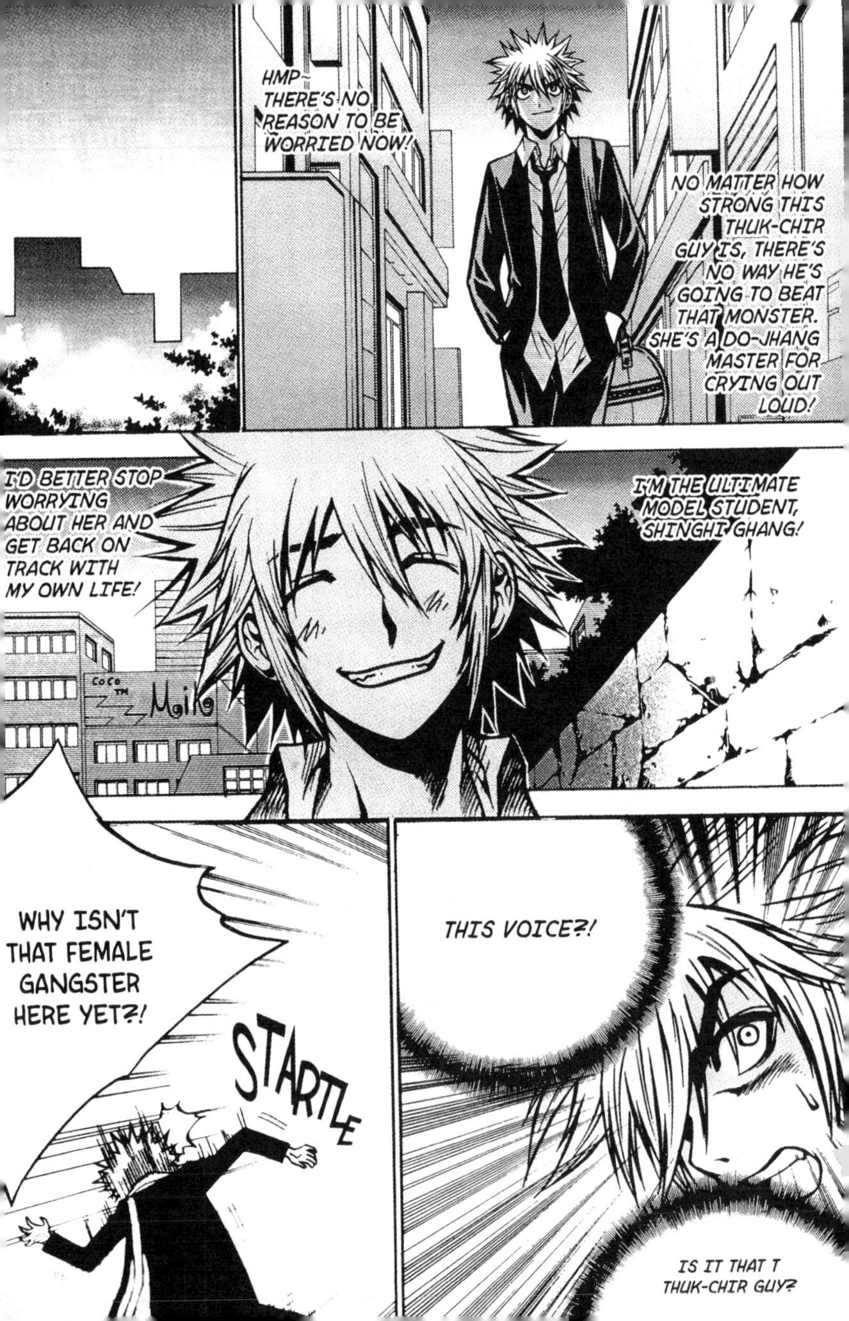
HMP~ THERE'S NO REASON TO BE WORRIED NOW!
NO MATTER HOW STRONG THIS THUK-CHIR GUY IS, THERE'S NO WAY HE'S GOING TO BEAT THAT MONSTER. SHE'S A DO-JHANG MASTER FOR CRYING OUT LOUD!
I'D BETTER STOP WORRYING ABOUT HER AND GET BACK ON TRACK WITH MY OWN LIFE!
I'M THE ULTIMATE MODEL STUDENT, SHINGHI GHANG!
COCO
Maik
WHY ISN'T THAT FEMALE GANGSTER HERE YET?!
STARTLE
THIS VOICE?!
IS IT THAT T THUK-CHIR GUY?

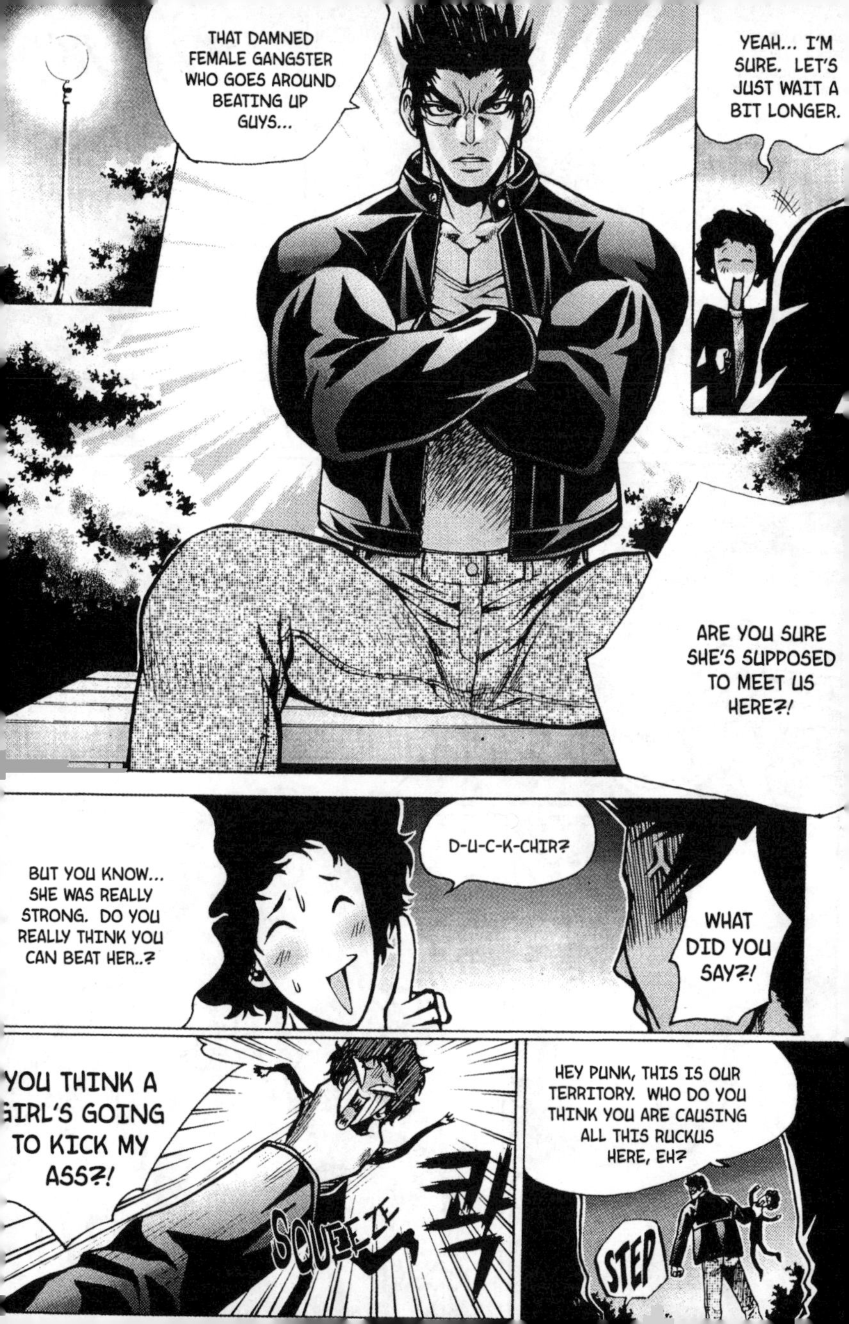
THAT DAMNED FEMALE GANGSTER WHO GOES AROUND BEATING UP GUYS...
ARE YOU SURE SHE'S SUPPOSED TO MEET US HERE?!
YEAH... I'M SURE. LET'S JUST WAIT A BIT LONGER.
BUT YOU KNOW... SHE WAS REALLY STRONG. DO YOU REALLY THINK YOU CAN BEAT HER..?
D-U-C-K-CHIR?
WHAT DID YOU SAY?!
YOU THINK A GIRL'S GOING TO KICK MY ASS?!
SQUEEZE
HEY PUNK, THIS IS OUR TERRITORY. WHO DO YOU THINK YOU ARE CAUSING ALL THIS RUCKUS HERE, EH?
STEP

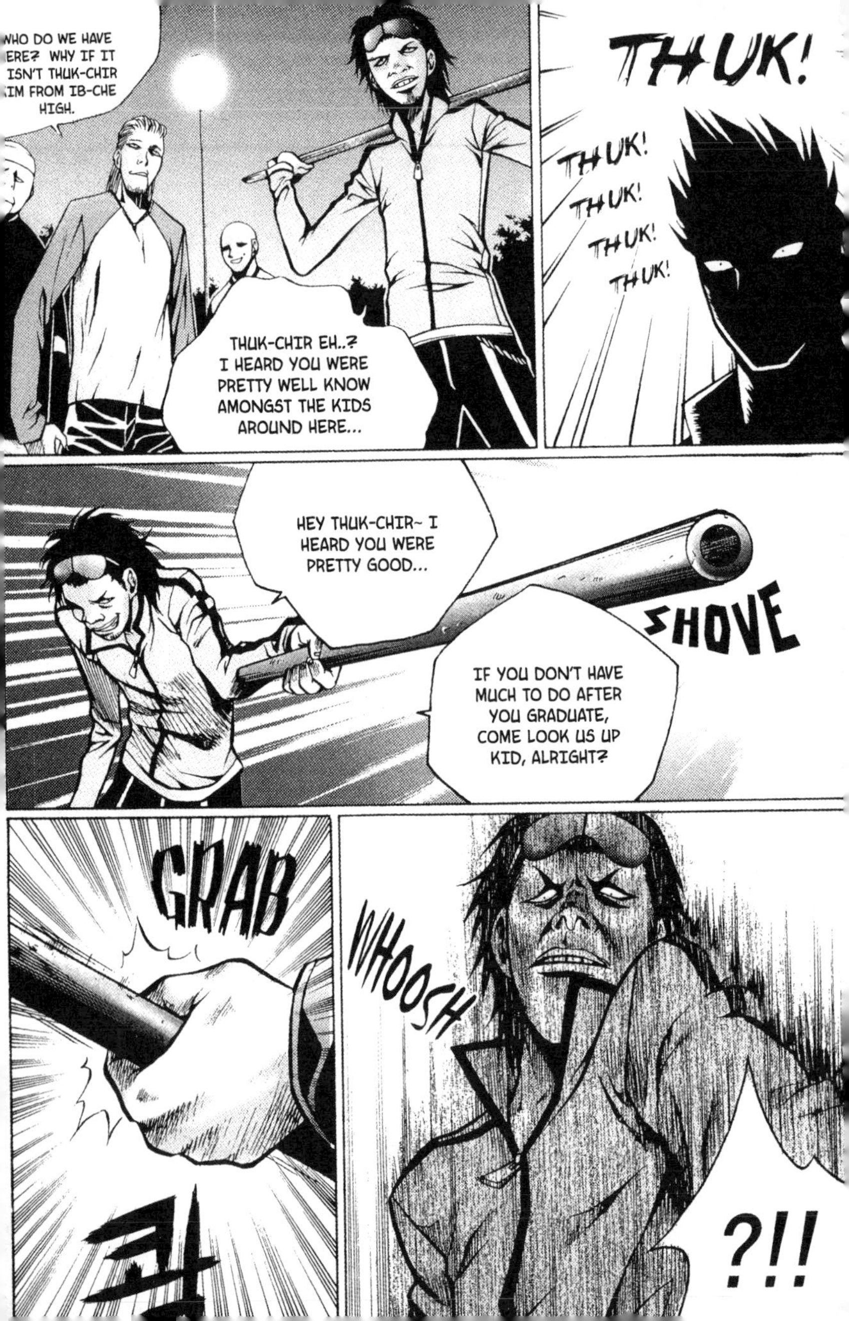
WHO DO WE HAVE ERE? WHY IF IT ISN'T THUK-CHIR IM FROM IB-CHE HIGH.
THUK-CHIR EH..? I HEARD YOU WERE PRETTY WELL KNOW AMONGST THE KIDS AROUND HERE...
THUK!
THUK!
THUK!
THUK!
THUK!
HEY THUK-CHIR~ I HEARD YOU WERE PRETTY GOOD...
SHOVE
IF YOU DON'T HAVE MUCH TO DO AFTER YOU GRADUATE, COME LOOK US UP KID, ALRIGHT?
GRAB
크
WHOOSH
?!!

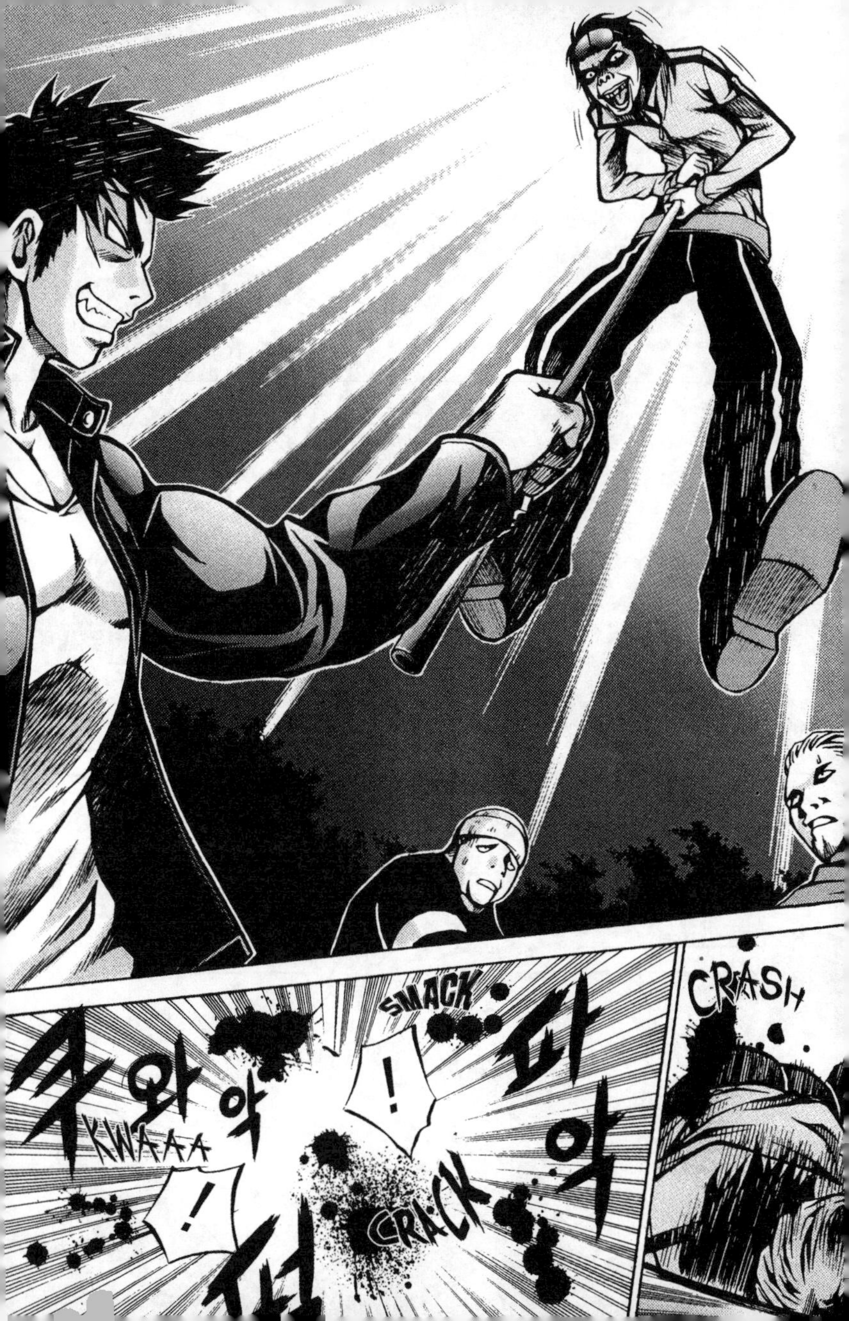
KWAAA
!
SMACK
!
CRACK
CRASH

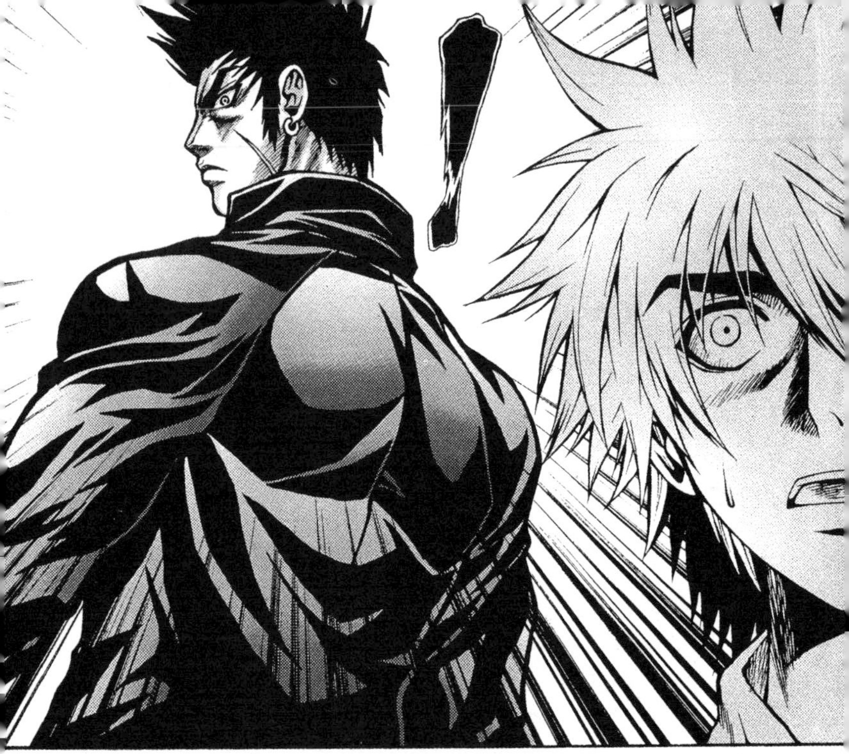

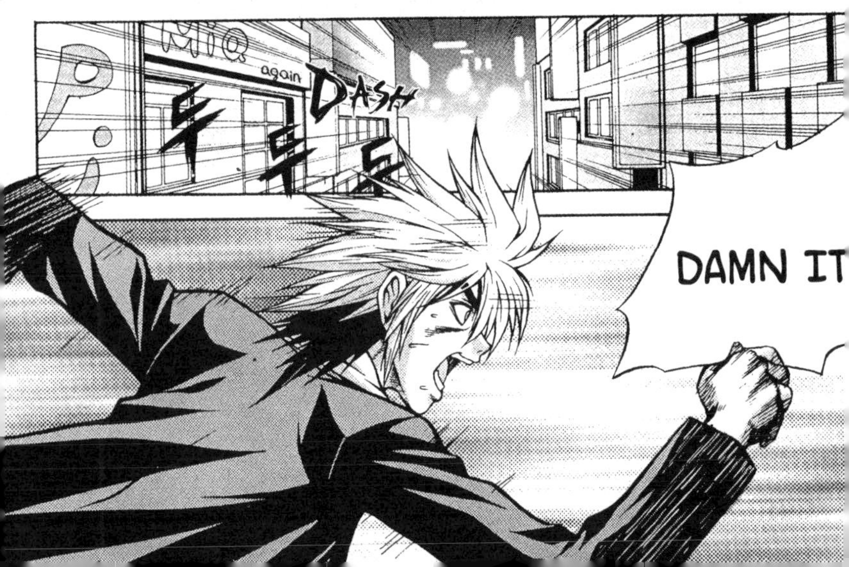
again
DASH
DAMN IT

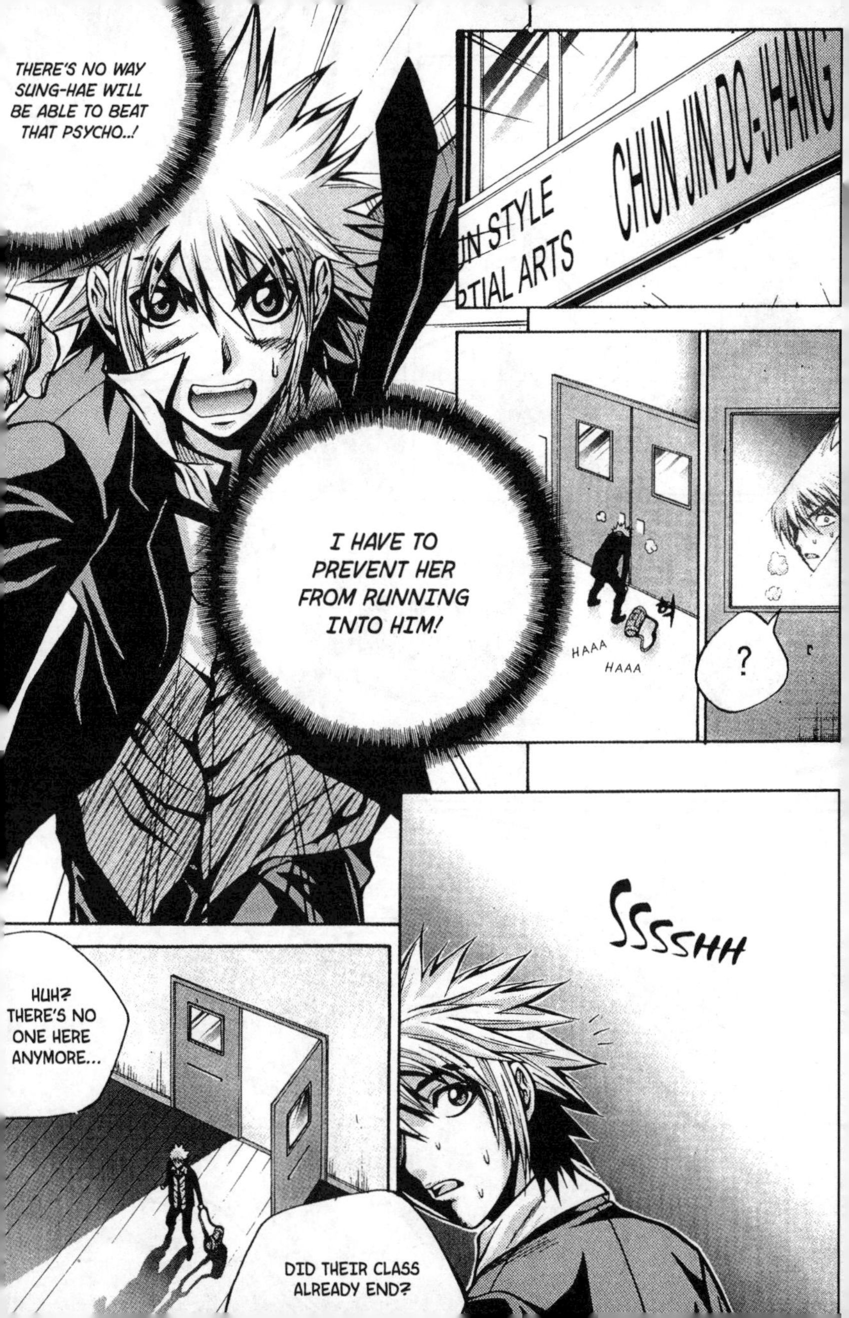
THERE'S NO WAY SUNG-HAE WILL BE ABLE TO BEAT THAT PSYCHO..!
I HAVE TO PREVENT HER FROM RUNNING INTO HIM!
CHUN JIN DO-JHANG
UN STYLE
TIAL ARTS
HAAA
HAAA
?
SSSSHH
HUH? THERE'S NO ONE HERE ANYMORE...
DID THEIR CLASS ALREADY END?

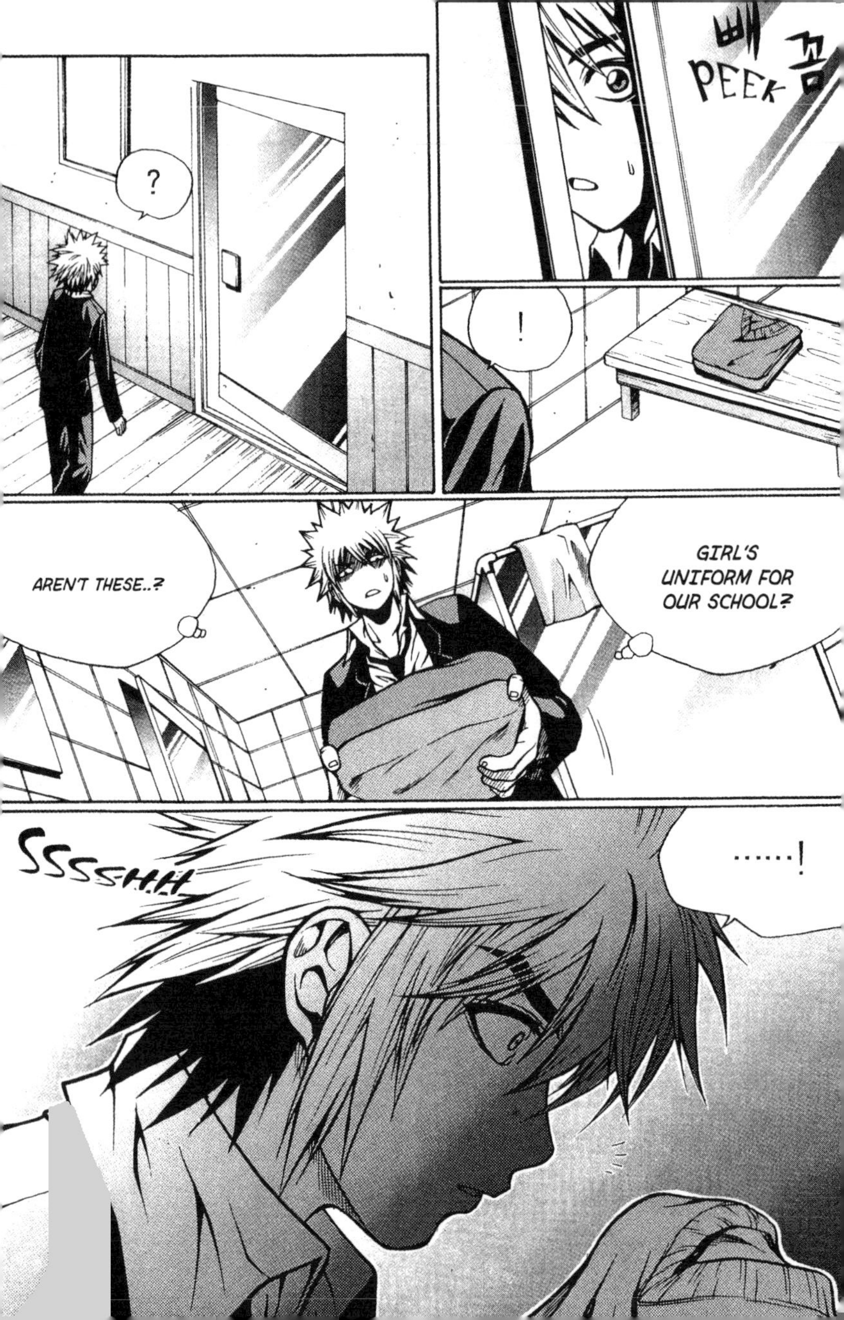
?
빼꼼
PEEK
!
AREN'T THESE..?
GIRL'S UNIFORM FOR OUR SCHOOL?
SSSSHH
......!

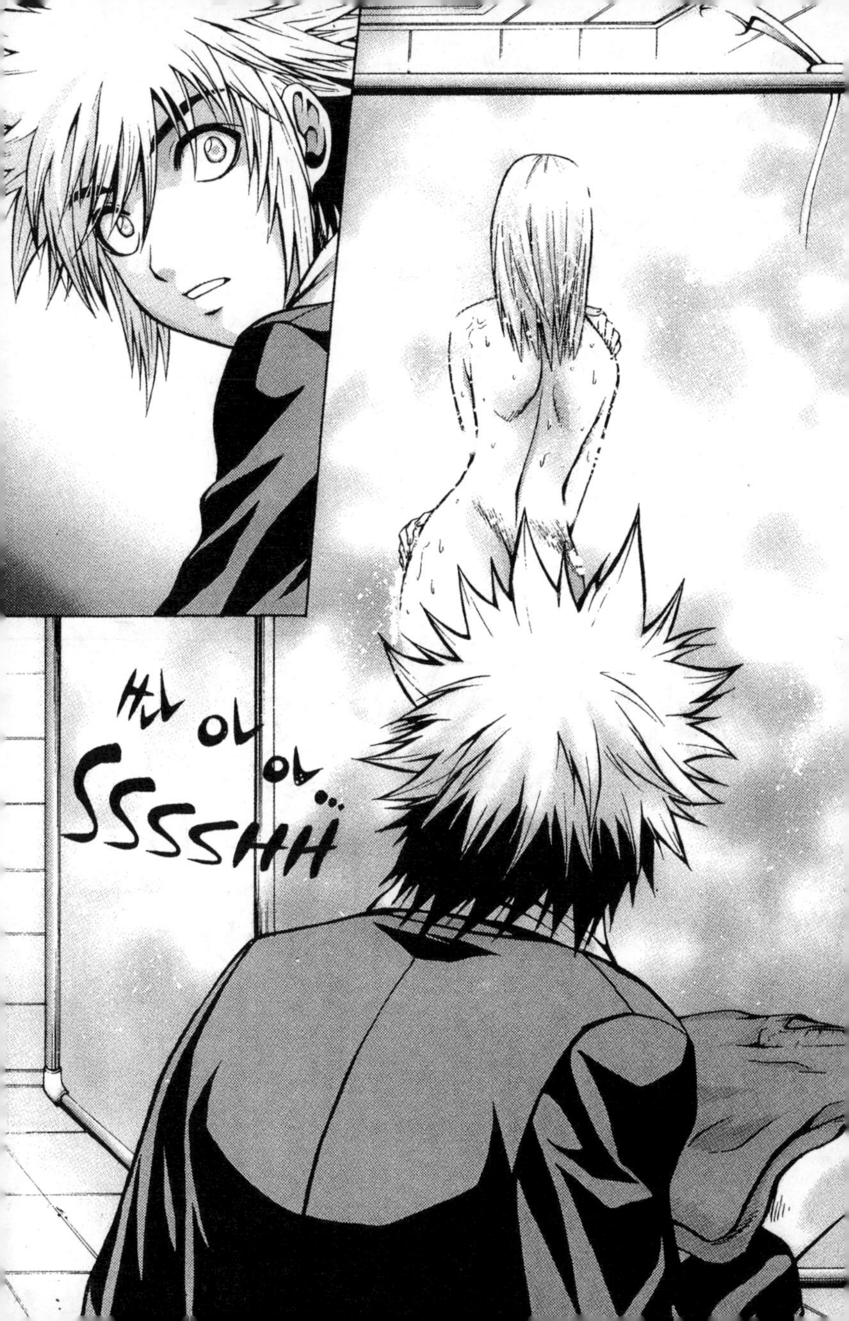
SSSSHH

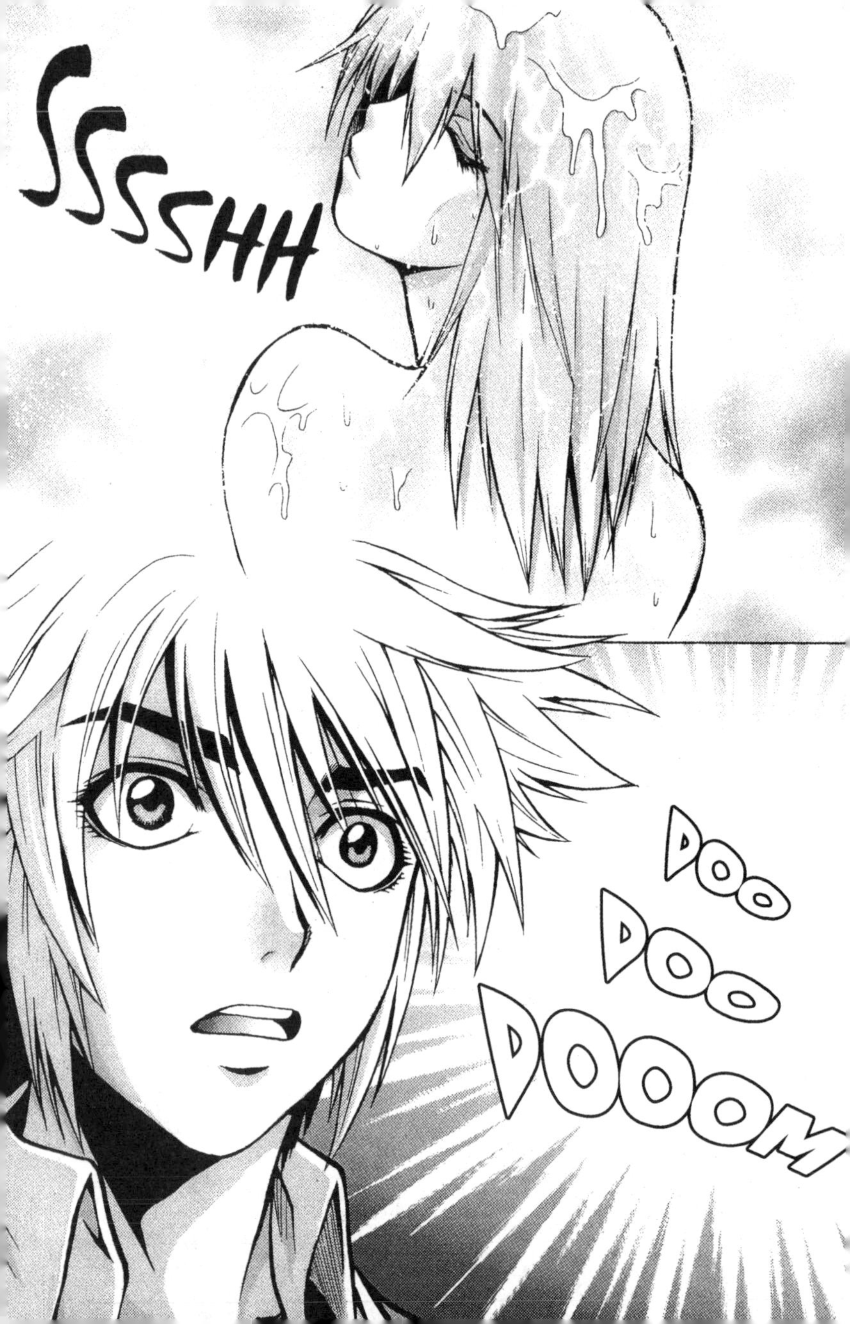
SSSSHH
DOO
DOO
DOOOOM

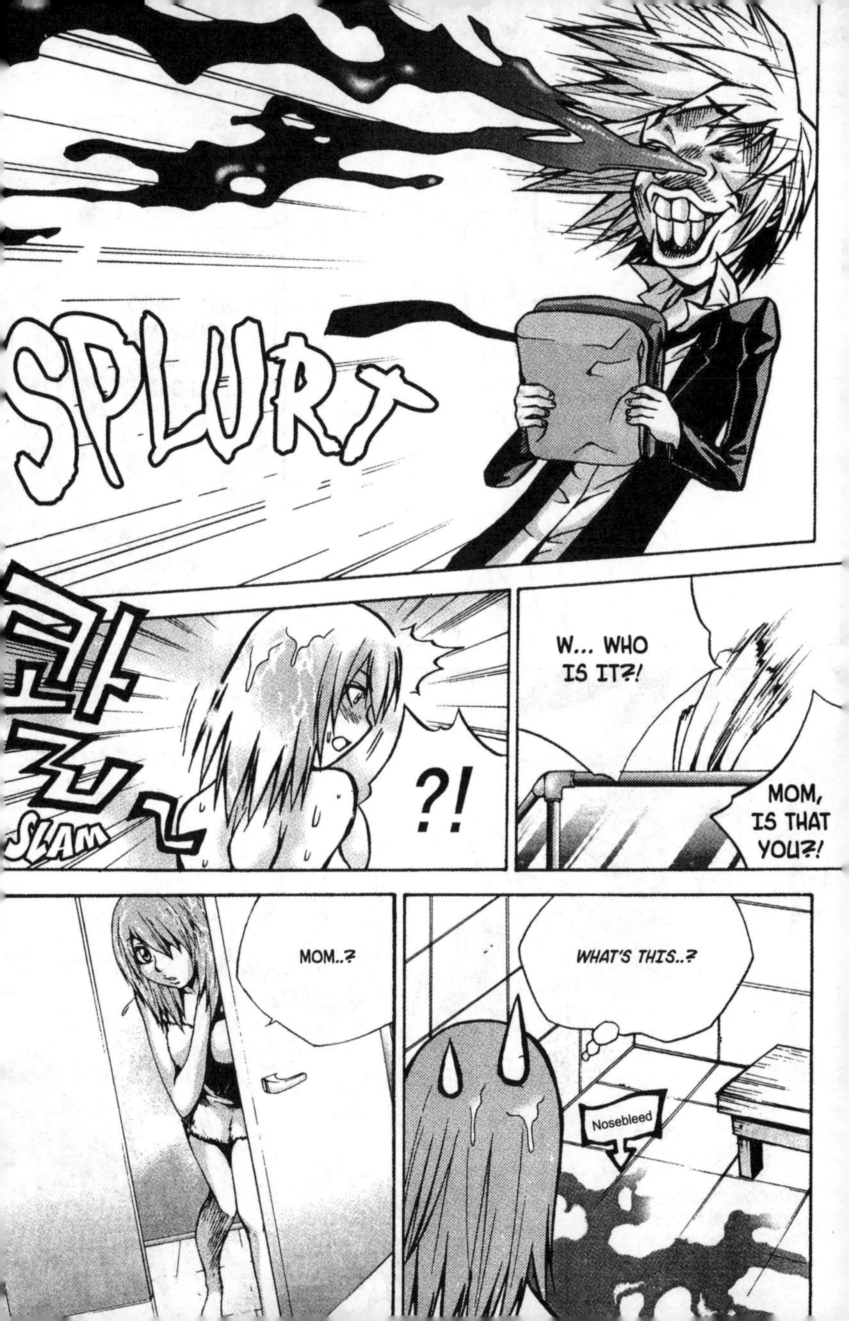
SPLURT
SLAM
?!
W... WHO IS IT?!
MOM, IS THAT YOU?!
MOM..?
WHAT'S THIS..?
Nosebleed

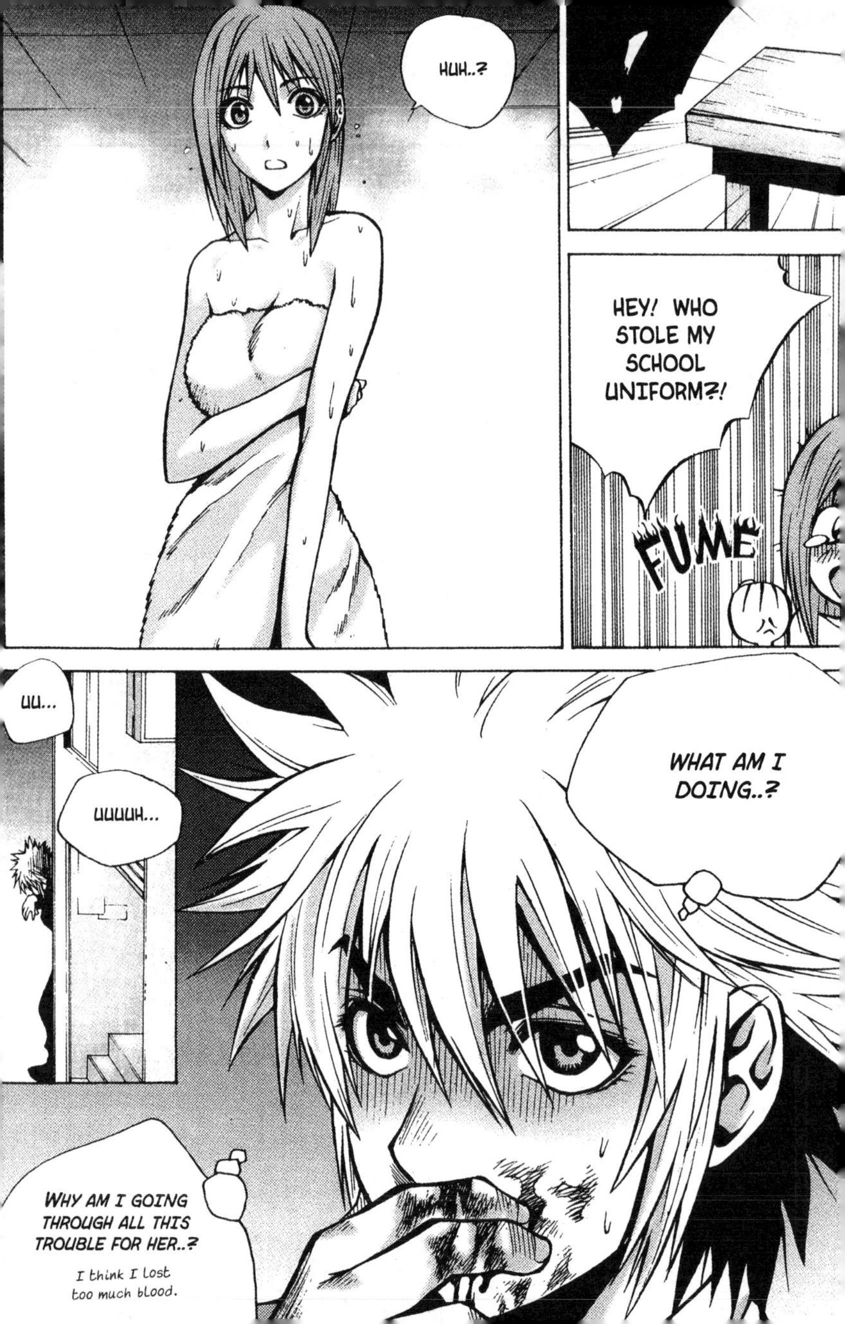
HUH..?
HEY! WHO STOLE MY SCHOOL UNIFORM?!
FUME
UU...
UUUUH...
WHAT AM I DOING..?
WHY AM I GOING THROUGH ALL THIS TROUBLE FOR HER..?
I think I lost too much blood.

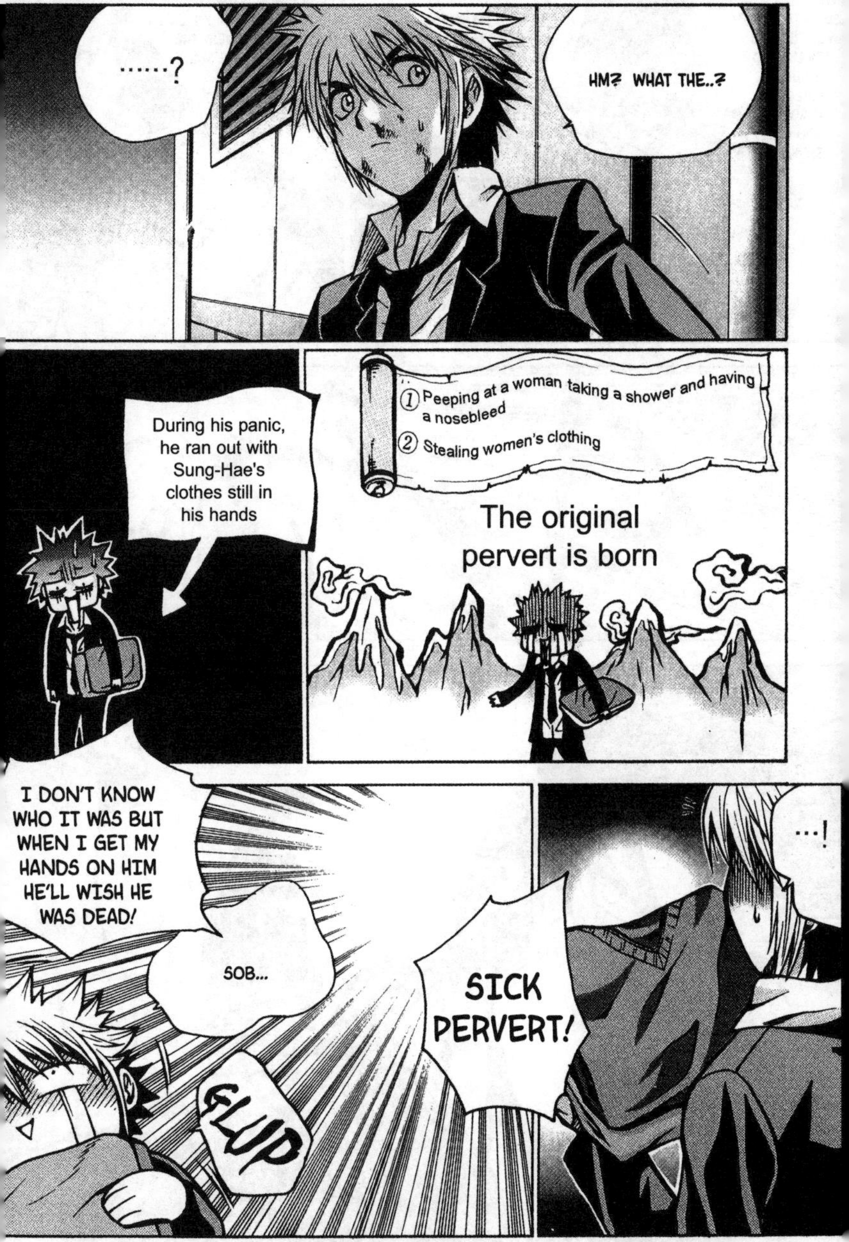
......?
HM? WHAT THE..?
During his panic, he ran out with Sung-Hae's clothes still in his hands
1 Peeping at a woman taking a shower and having a nosebleed
2 Stealing women's clothing
The original pervert is born
I DON'T KNOW WHO IT WAS BUT WHEN I GET MY HANDS ON HIM HE'LL WISH HE WAS DEAD!
SOB...
GLUP
SICK PERVERT!
...!

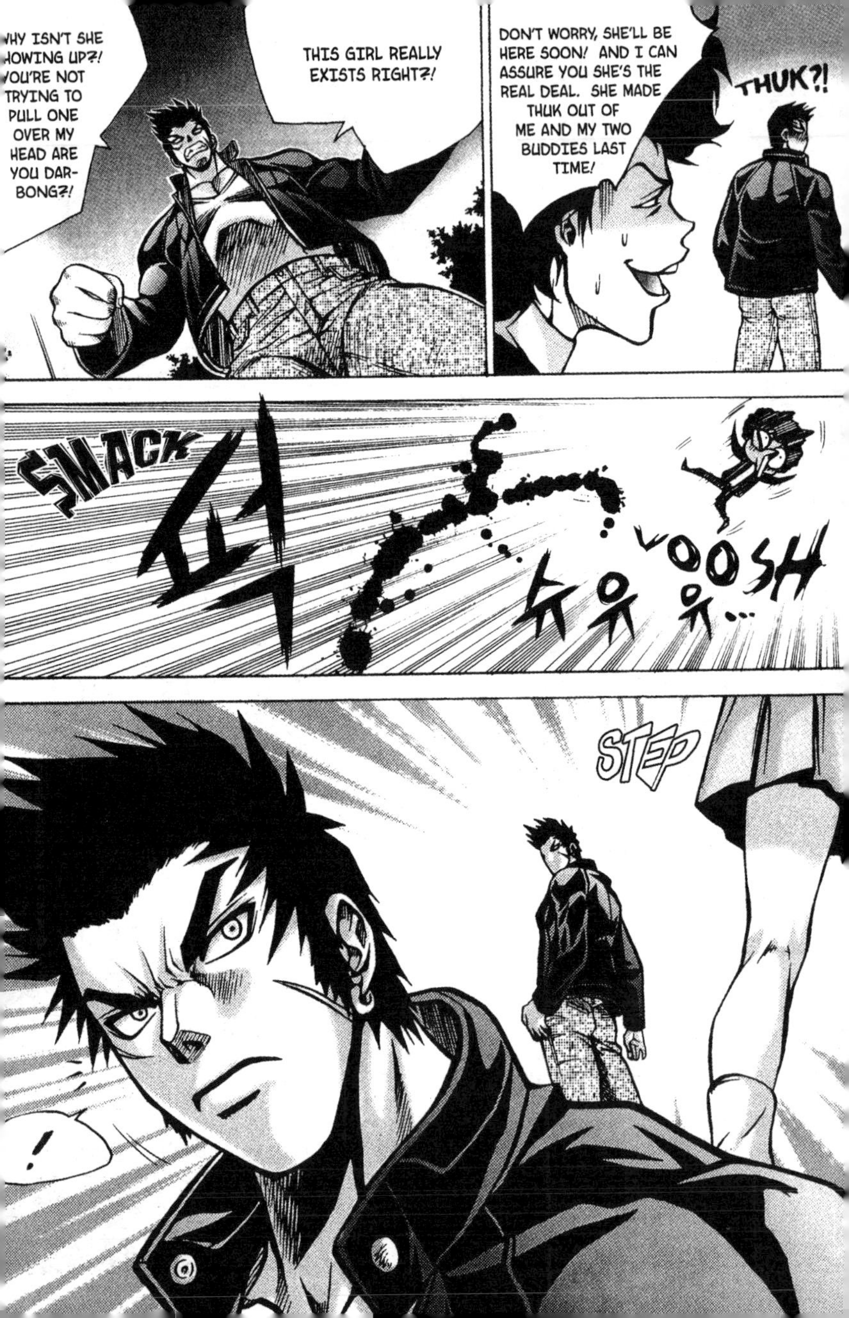

WHY ISN'T SHE HOWING UP?! OU'RE NOT TRYING TO PULL ONE OVER MY HEAD ARE YOU DAR-BONG?!
THIS GIRL REALLY EXISTS RIGHT?!
DON'T WORRY, SHE'LL BE HERE SOON! AND I CAN ASSURE YOU SHE'S THE REAL DEAL. SHE MADE THUK OUT OF ME AND MY TWO BUDDIES LAST TIME!
THUK?!
SMACK
퍽
WOOSH
STEP
!

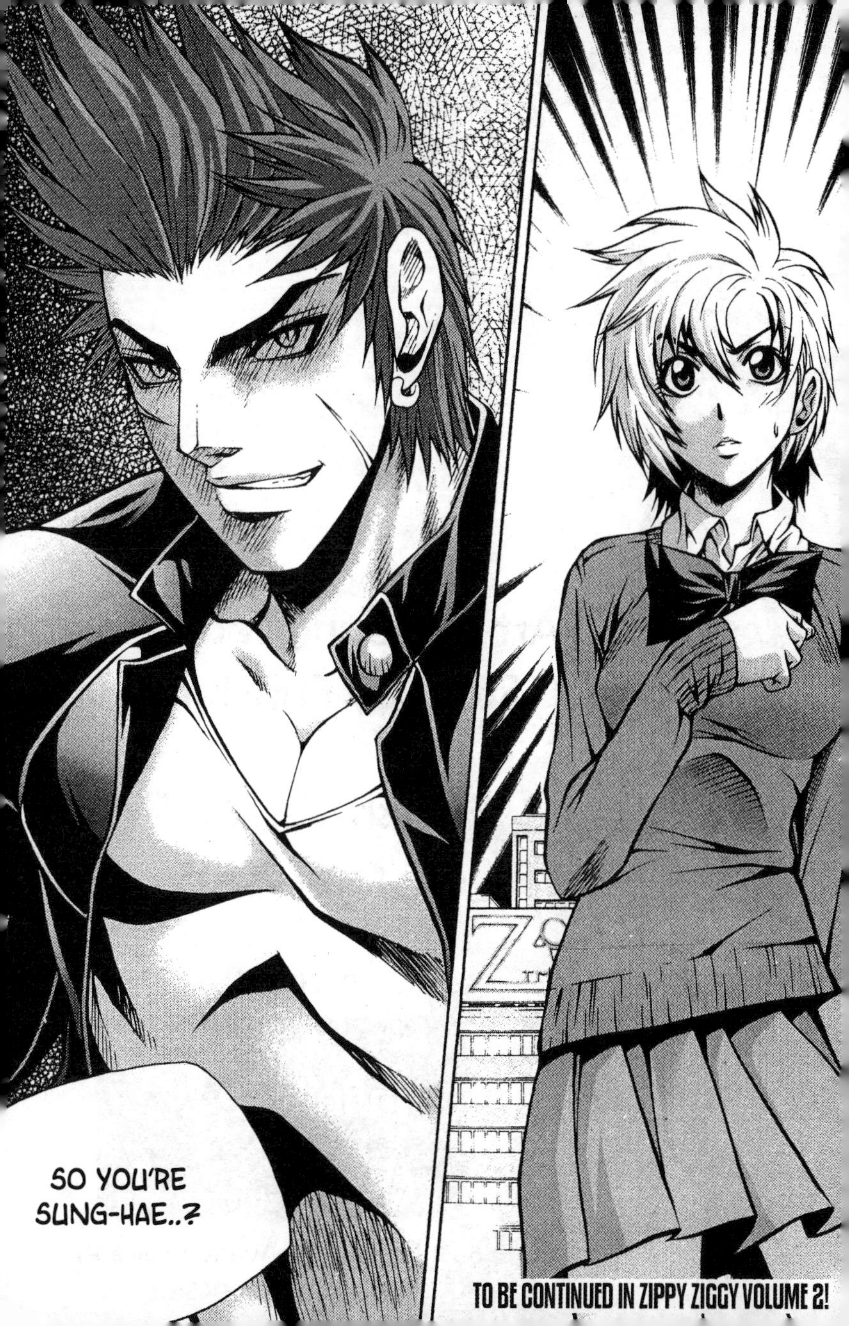
SO YOU'RE SUNG-HAE..?
Z
TO BE CONTINUED IN ZIPPY ZIGGY VOLUME 2!

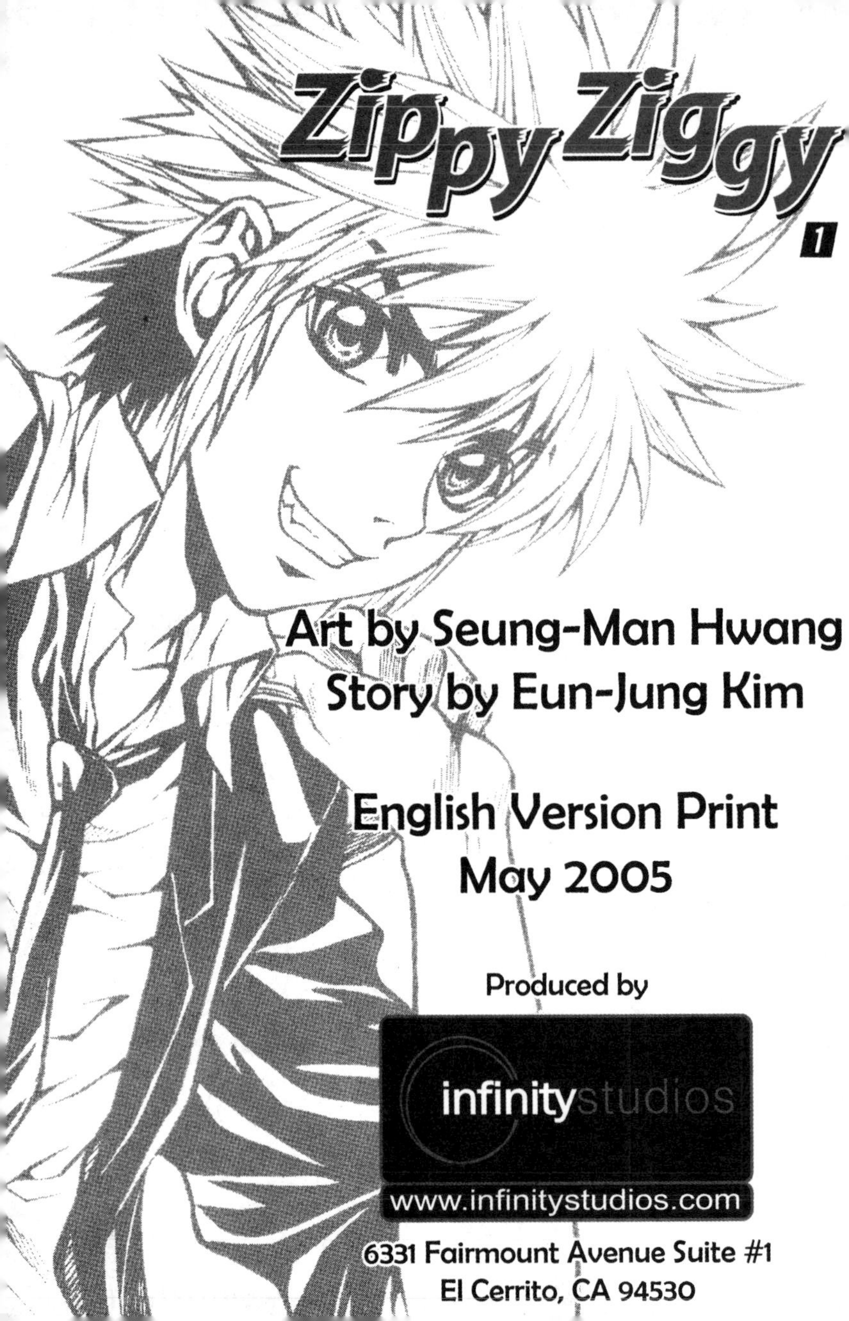

Zippy Ziggy

1

Art by Seung-Man Hwang
Story by Eun-Jung Kim

English Version Print
May 2005

Produced by

infinitystudios

www.infinitystudios.com

6331 Fairmount Avenue Suite #1
El Cerrito, CA 94530

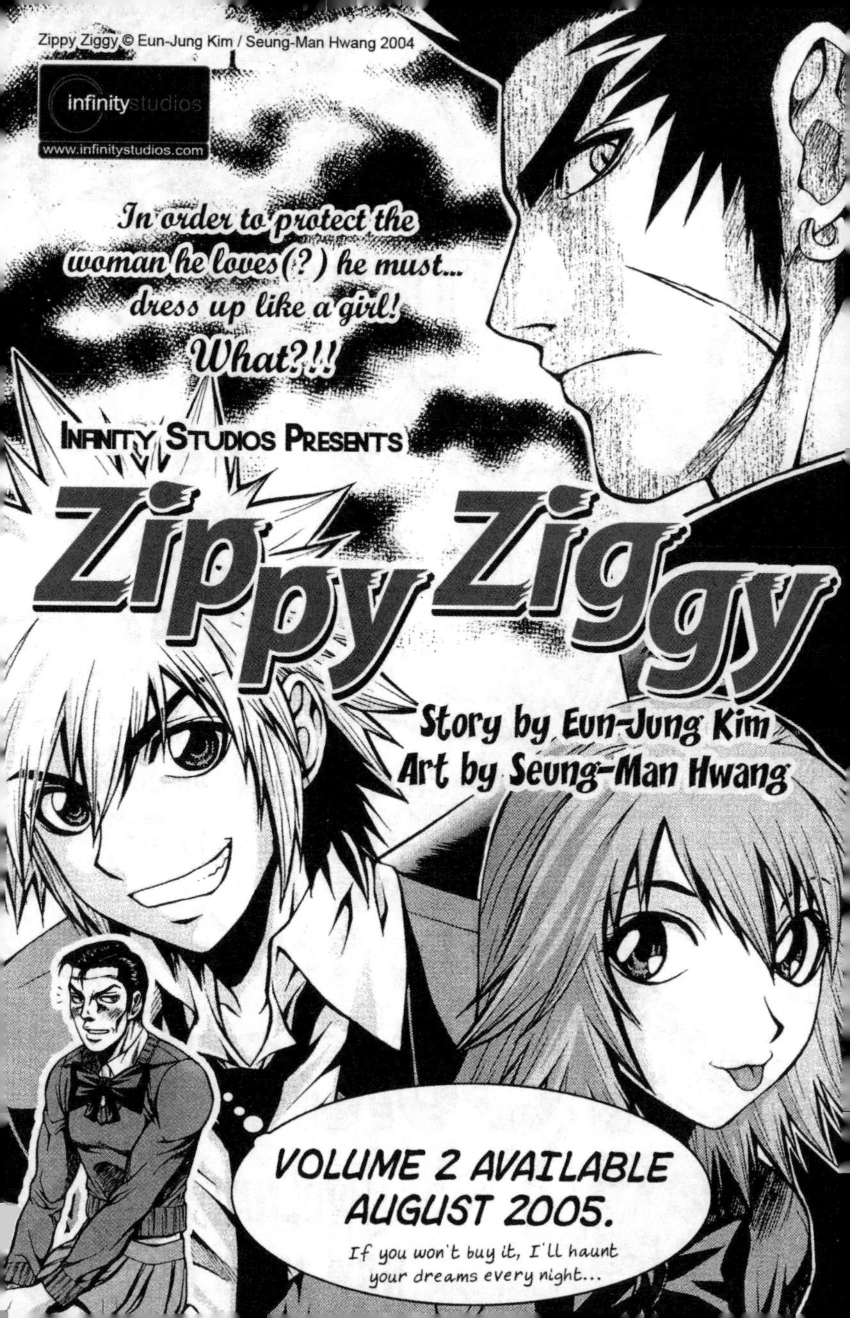
Zippy Ziggy © Eun-Jung Kim / Seung-Man Hwang 2004
infinitystudios
www.infinitystudios.com
In order to protect the woman he loves(?) he must... dress up like a girl! What?!!
INFINITY STUDIOS PRESENTS
Zippy Ziggy
Story by Eun-Jung Kim
Art by Seung-Man Hwang
VOLUME 2 AVAILABLE AUGUST 2005.
If you won't buy it, I'll haunt your dreams every night...

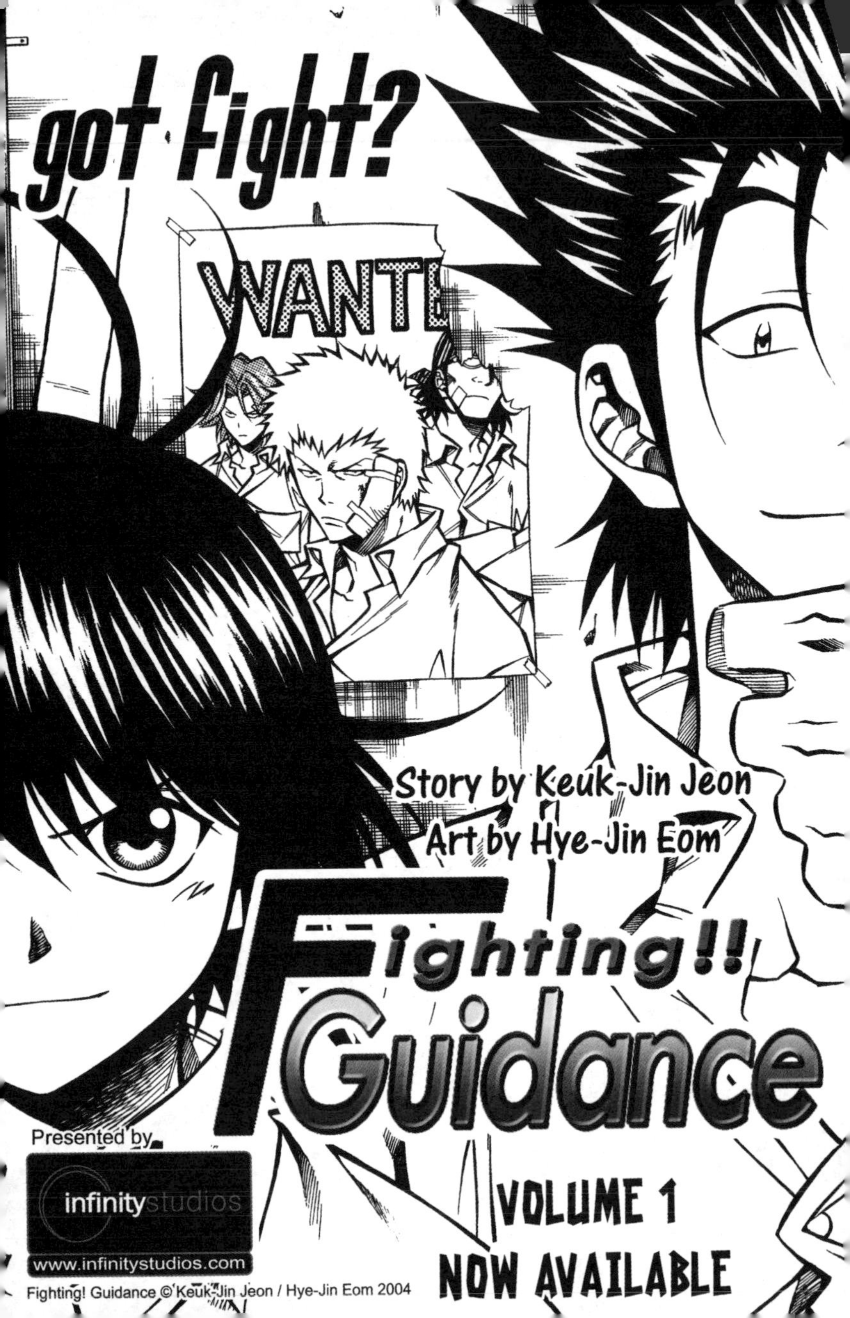
got fight?
WANTE
Story by Keuk-Jin Jeon
Art by Hye-Jin Eom
Fighting!! Guidance
Presented by
infinitystudios
www.infinitystudios.com
Fighting! Guidance © Keuk-Jin Jeon / Hye-Jin Eom 2004
VOLUME 1
NOW AVAILABLE

Infinity Studios Presents
Show=TAROU HARADA's

WE CAN SENSE DANGER COMING A MILE AWAY...

WE LEGIONS ALWAYS LOOK OUR BEST.

WE'RE ALWAYS RELIABLE, DEPENDABLE, AND NEVER BREAK DOWN.

KYAA!!

ALLOW ME TO INTRODUCE THE LATEST IN ANDROID TECHNOLOGY KNOWN AS 'LEGIONS'.

WE MUST PROTECT THE CITIZENS OF THIS FAIR CITY!

OK, JUST LET ME FINISH THIS BOX OF DONUTS FIRST...

SMACK

Volume 1 Now Available

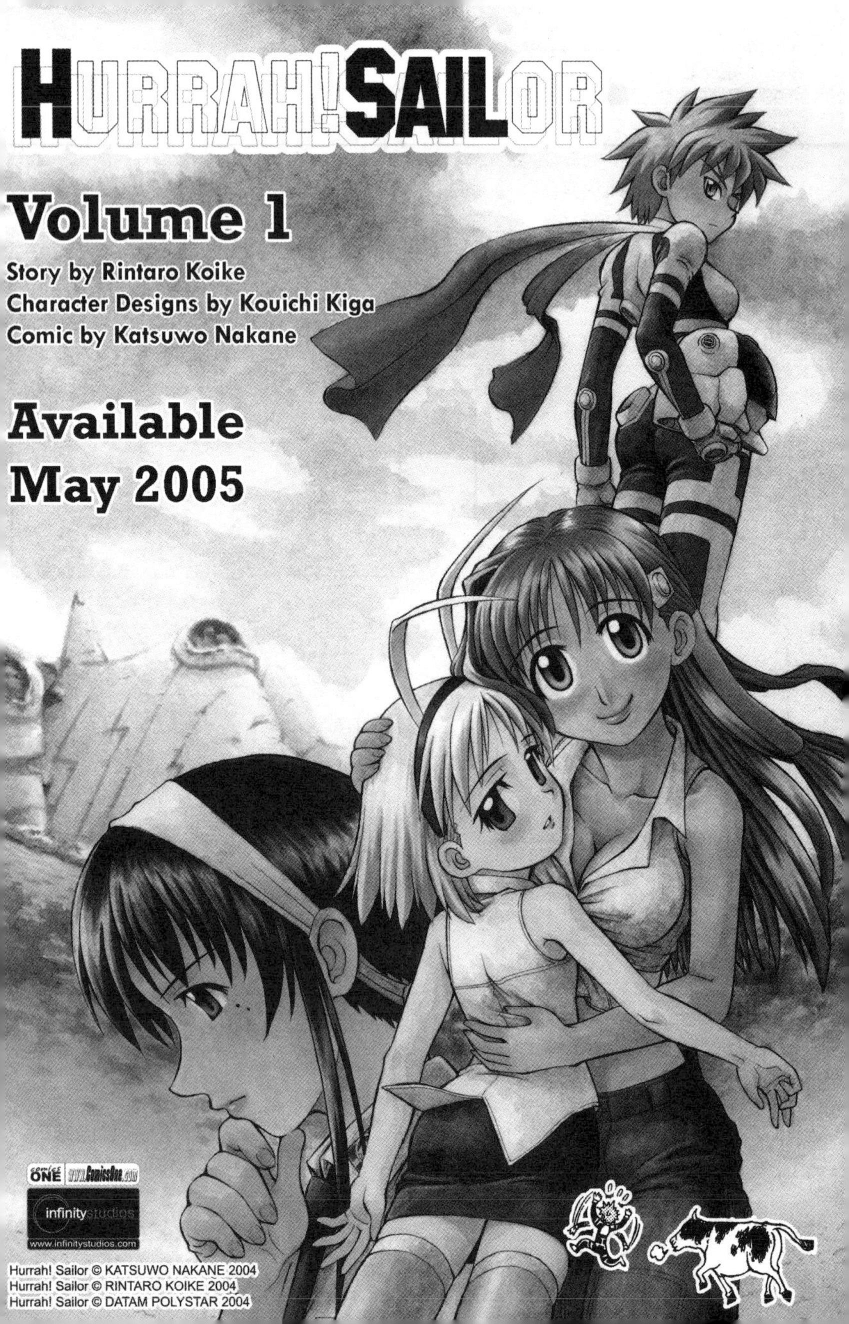
HURRAH! SAILOR
Volume 1
Story by Rintaro Koike
Character Designs by Kouichi Kiga
Comic by Katsuwo Nakane
Available
May 2005
comics ONE
www.ComicsOne.com
infinity studios
www.infinitystudios.com
Hurrah! Sailor © KATSUWO NAKANE 2004
Hurrah! Sailor © RINTARO KOIKE 2004
Hurrah! Sailor © DATAM POLYSTAR 2004

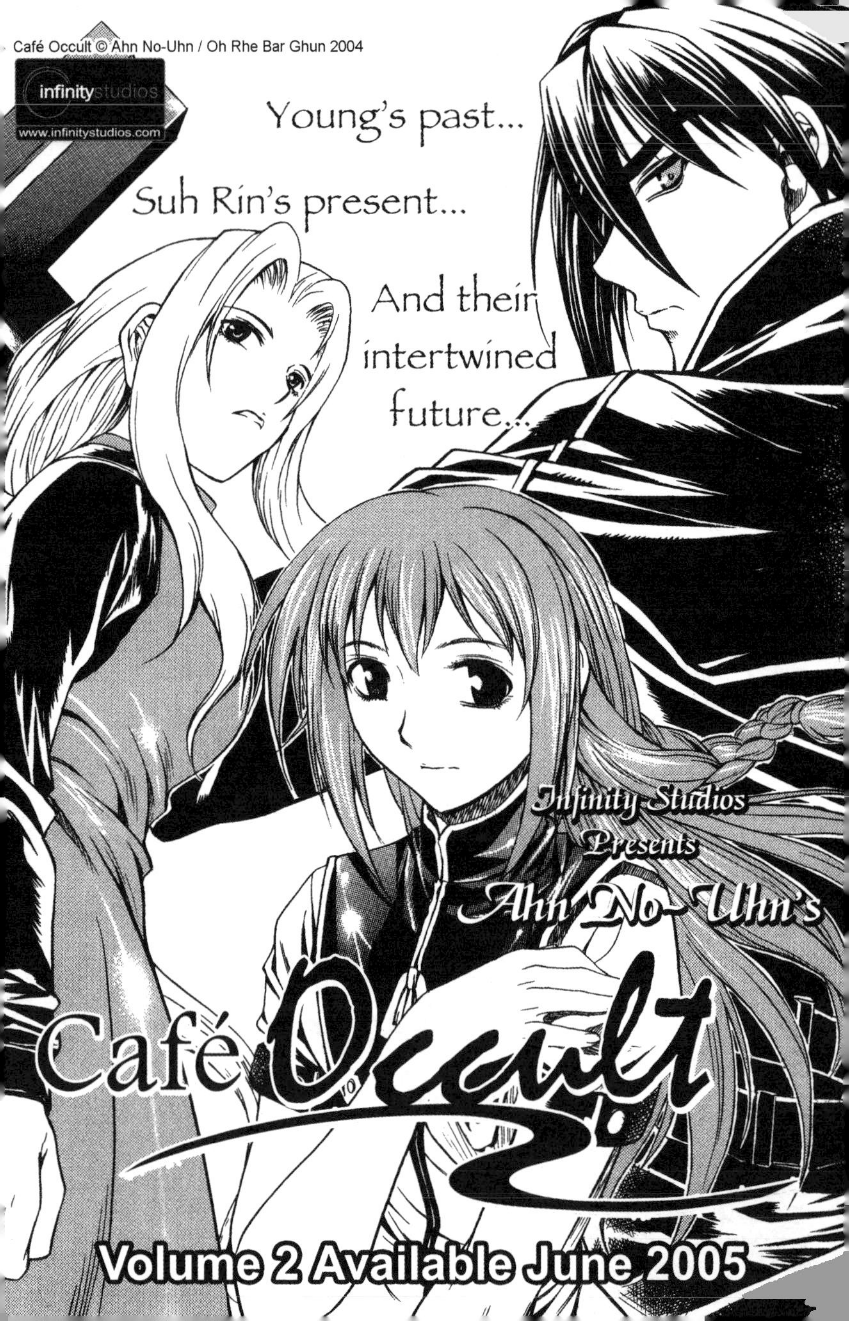

Café Occult © Ahn No-Uhn / Oh Rhe Bar Ghun 2004
infinitystudios
www.infinitystudios.com
Young's past...
Suh Rin's present...
And their intertwined future...
Infinity Studios Presents
Ahn No-Uhn's
Café Occult
Volume 2 Available June 2005

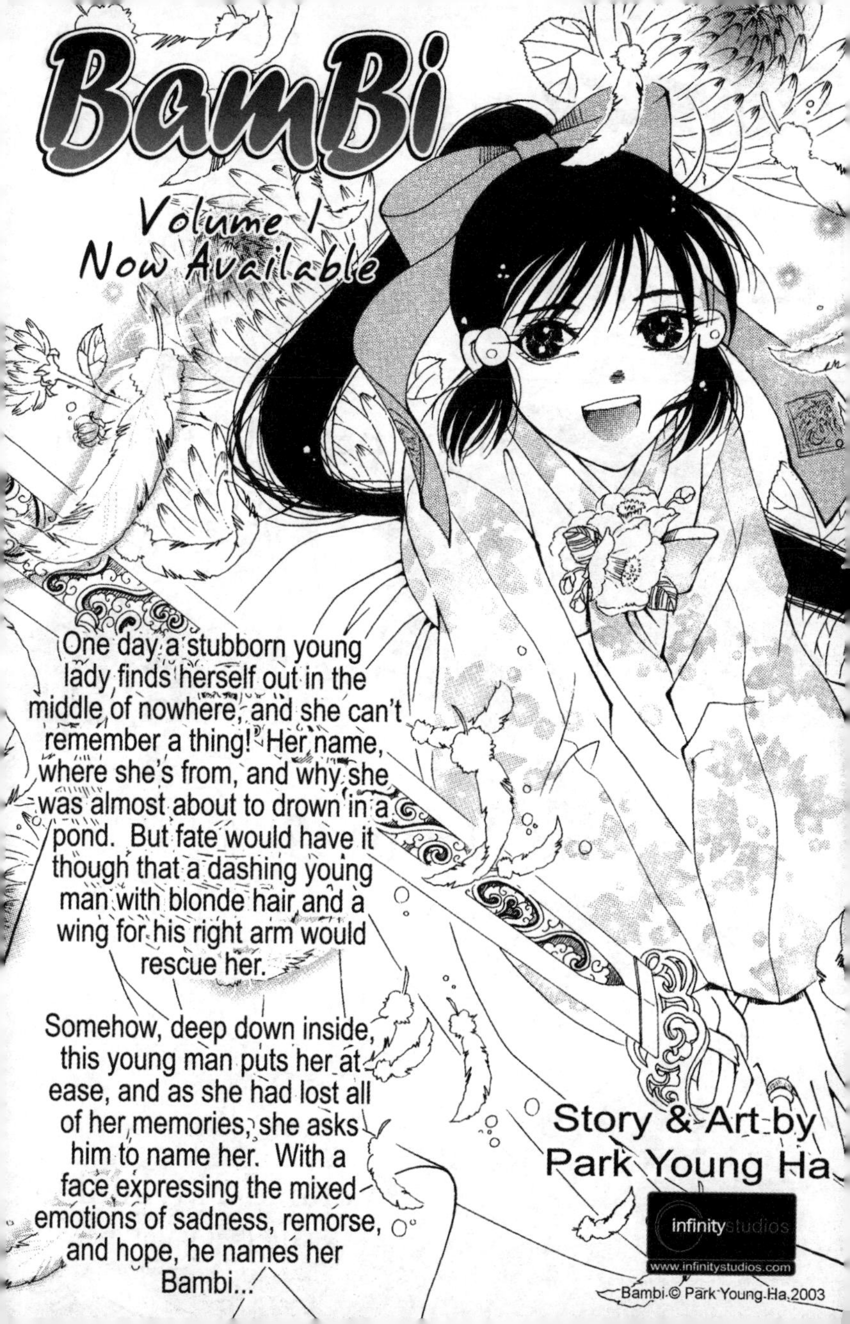
BamBi
Volume 1
Now Available
One day a stubborn young lady finds herself out in the middle of nowhere, and she can't remember a thing! Her name, where she's from, and why she was almost about to drown in a pond. But fate would have it though that a dashing young man with blonde hair and a wing for his right arm would rescue her.
Somehow, deep down inside, this young man puts her at ease, and as she had lost all of her memories, she asks him to name her. With a face expressing the mixed emotions of sadness, remorse, and hope, he names her Bambi...
Story & Art by
Park Young Ha
infinitystudios
www.infinitystudios.com
Bambi © Park Young Ha 2003

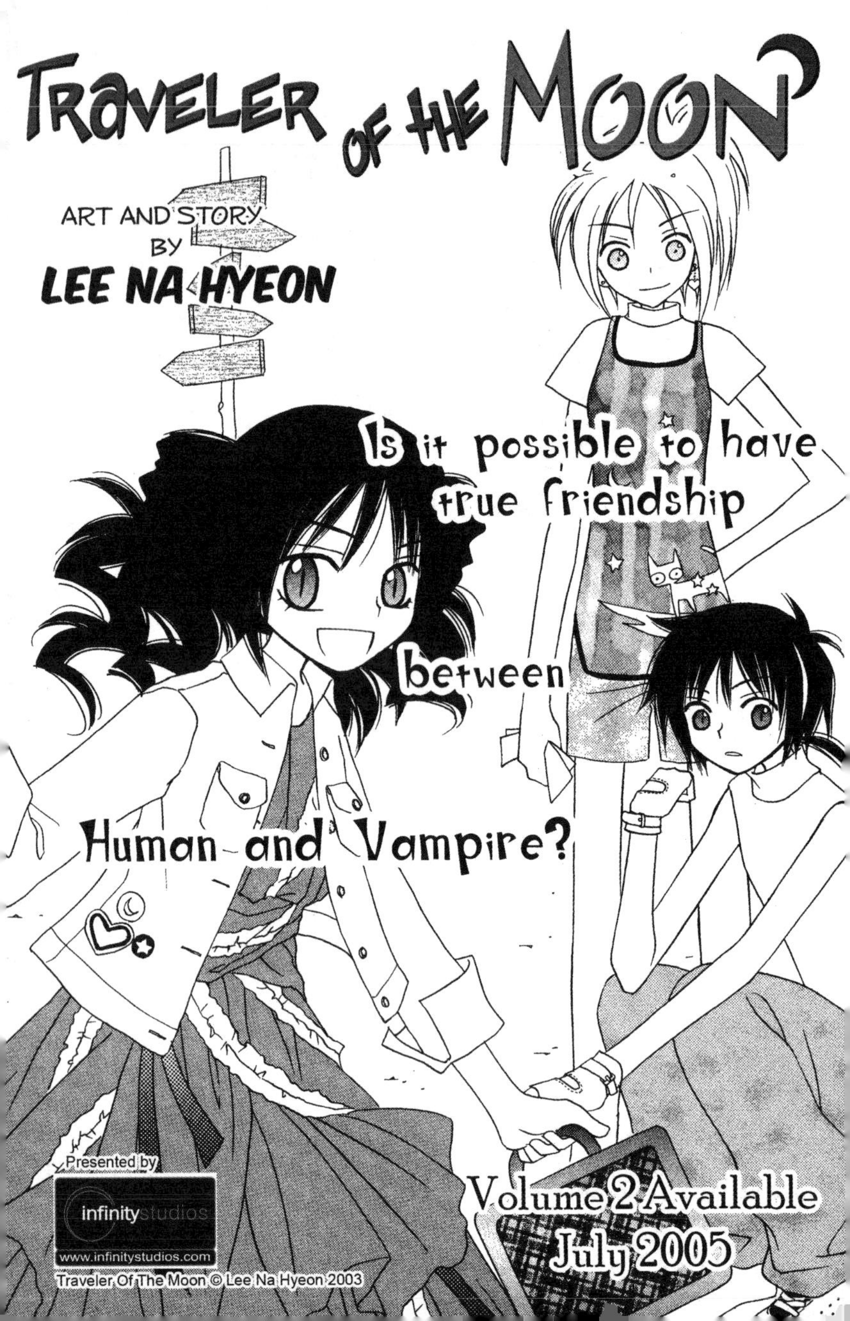

TRAVELER OF THE MOON
ART AND STORY BY
LEE NA HYEON
Is it possible to have true friendship
between
Human and Vampire?
Presented by
infinitystudios
www.infinitystudios.com
Traveler Of The Moon © Lee Na Hyeon 2003
Volume 2 Available
July 2005

The Missing White Dragon

Infinity Studios Presents

STORY COLLECTIONS
by
PARK YOUNG HA

Volume 1
Now Available

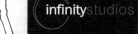

www.infinitystudios.com

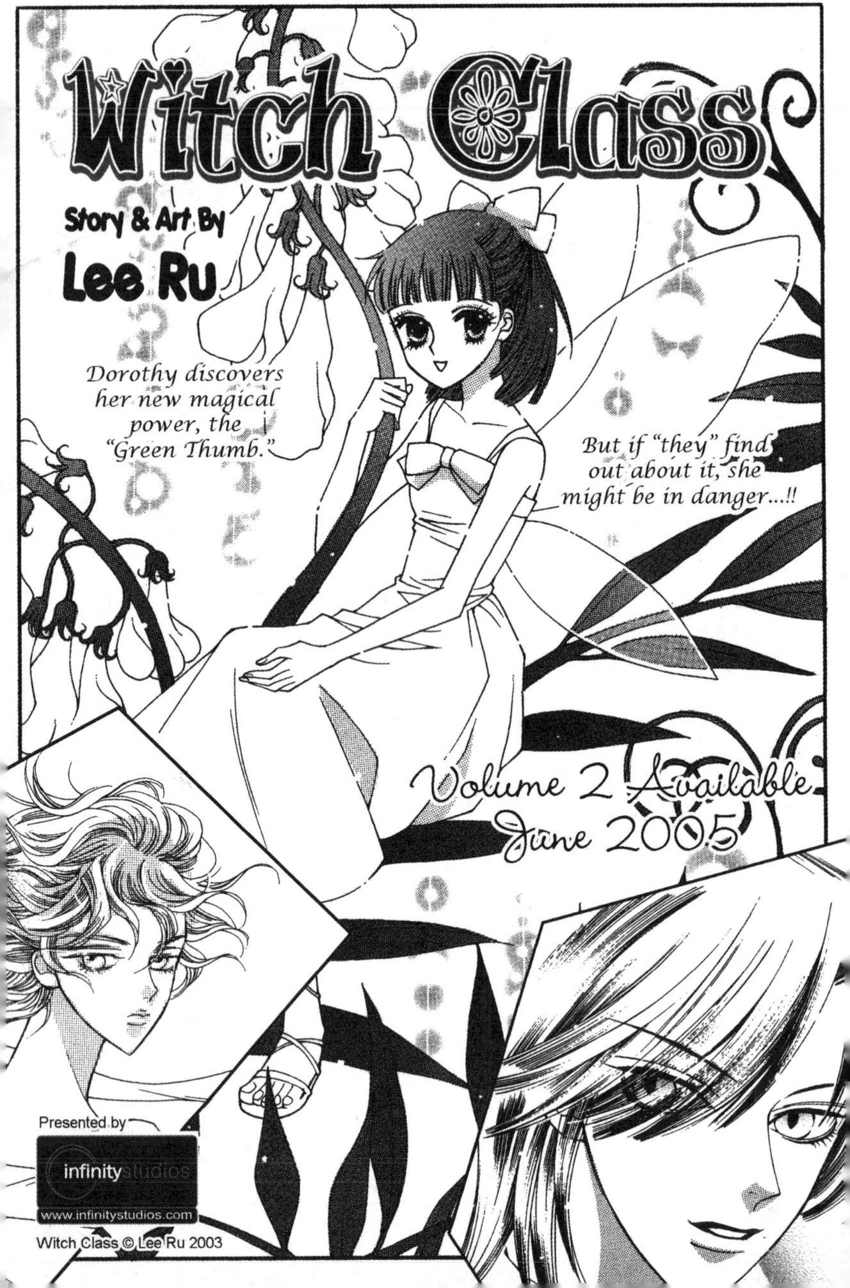

Witch Class
Story & Art By
Lee Ru
Dorothy discovers her new magical power, the "Green Thumb."
But if "they" find out about it, she might be in danger...!!
Volume 2 Available June 2005
Presented by
infinitystudios
www.infinitystudios.com
Witch Class © Lee Ru 2003

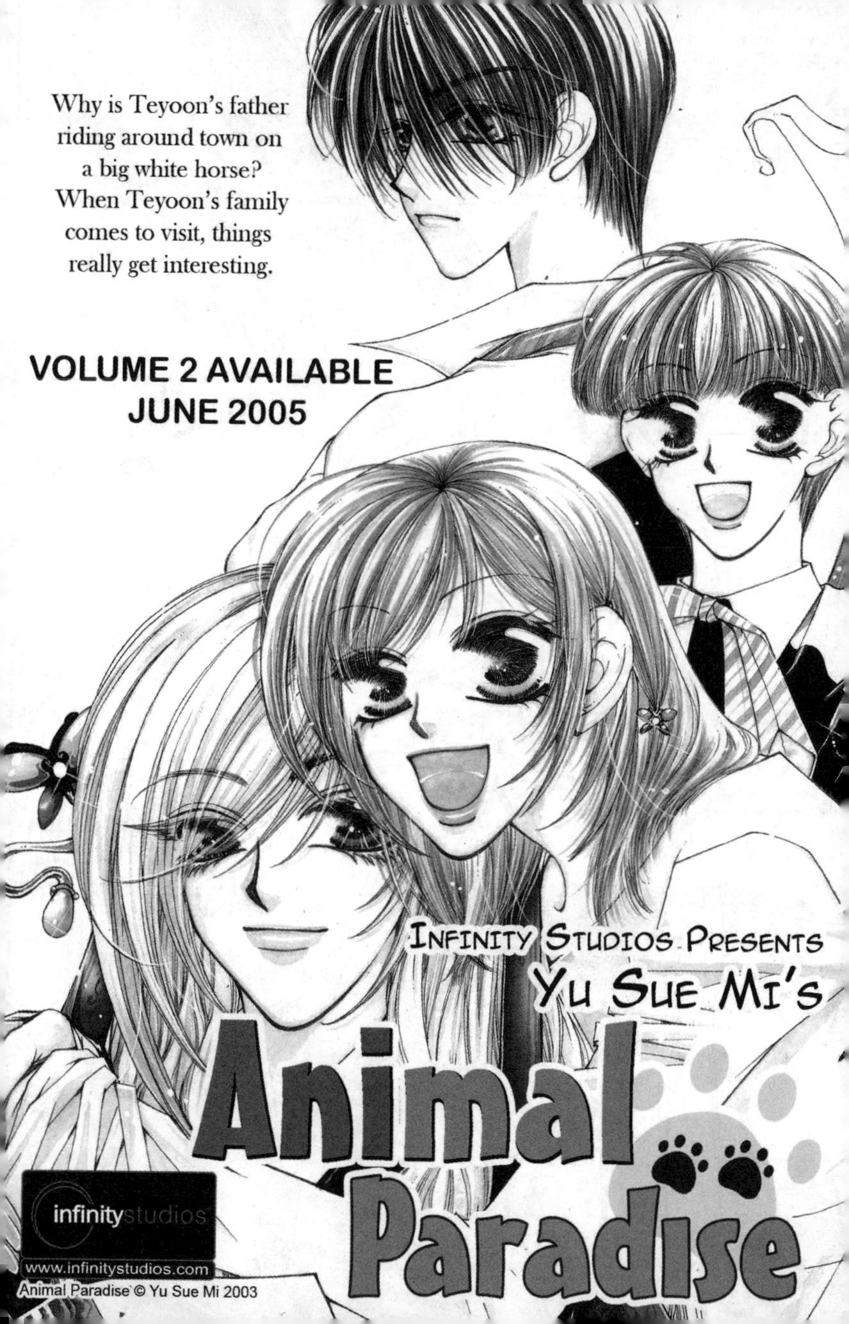

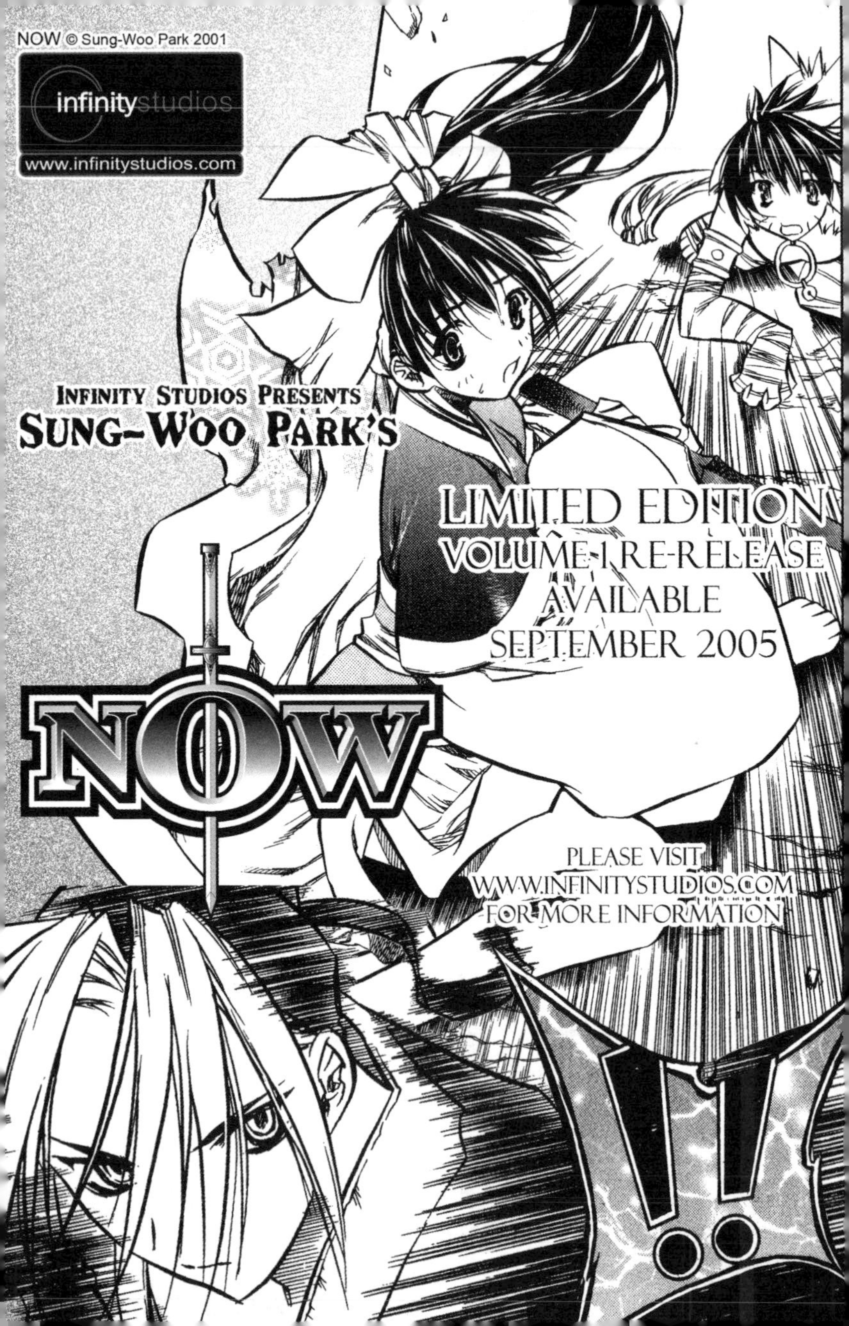
NOW © Sung-Woo Park 2001
infinitystudios
www.infinitystudios.com
Infinity Studios Presents
Sung-Woo Park's
NOW
LIMITED EDITION
VOLUME 1 RE-RELEASE
AVAILABLE
SEPTEMBER 2005
PLEASE VISIT
WWW.INFINITYSTUDIOS.COM
FOR MORE INFORMATION

Péigenz
Volume 6

Art by : Park Sung Woo
Story by : Oh Rhe Bar Ghun

"Trapped and injured, that's when Cathy must have seen me... She called for me with all her might, but I just couldn't hear her...

She must have felt betrayed when I didn't return to rescue her. I guess there's no way she could forgive me..."

Available September 2005